# MODERN CHINESE LEGAL REFORM

# MODERN CHINESE LEGAL REFORM

*New Perspectives*

Edited by

XIAOBING LI

and

QIANG FANG

UNIVERSITY PRESS OF KENTUCKY

Scholarly publisher for the Commonwealth,
serving Bellarmine University, Berea College, Centre College of Kentucky,
Eastern Kentucky University, The Filson Historical Society, Georgetown College,
Kentucky Historical Society, Kentucky State University, Morehead State
University, Murray State University, Northern Kentucky University, Transylvania
University, University of Kentucky, University of Louisville, and Western
Kentucky University.
All rights reserved.

*Editorial and Sales Offices:* The University Press of Kentucky
663 South Limestone Street, Lexington, Kentucky 40508-4008
www.kentuckypress.com

17  16  15  14  13      5  4  3  2  1

Library of Congress Cataloging-in-Publication Data

Li, Xiaobing, 1954- editor.
  Modern Chinese legal reform : new perspectives / Edited by Xiaobing Li and
Qiang Fang.
     pages cm.
  Includes bibliographical references and index.
  ISBN 978-0-8131-4120-6 (hardcover : alk. paper) —
  ISBN 978-0-8131-4121-3 (epub) — ISBN 978-0-8131-4122-0 (pdf)
  1. Rule of law—China. 2. Law reform—China. I. Fang, Qiang, 1968-   editor.
II. Title.
  KNQ2020.L459 2013
  340'.30951—dc23                                      2012045880

Manufactured in the United States of America.

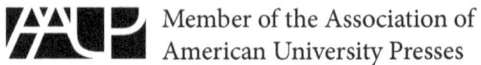 Member of the Association of
American University Presses

# Contents

**Part Three. Civil Liberties and Human Rights**

# Illustrations and Tables

**Figures**

**Maps**

**Tables**

# Abbreviations

| | |
|---|---|
| ACFTU | All-China Federation of Trade Unions |
| AFL | American Federation of Labor |
| AIDS | Acquired immunodeficiency syndrome |
| ALL | Administrative Litigation Law |
| ASEAN | Association of Southeast Asian Nations |
| BBC | British Broadcasting Corporation |
| CCP | Chinese Communist Party |
| C&R | Custody and Repatriation Law |
| CIO | Congress of Industrial Organizations (U.S.) |
| CL | Criminal Law |
| CPL | Criminal Procedure Law |
| CPPCC | Chinese People's Political Consultative Conference |
| *CYD* | *China Youth Daily* |
| EU | European Union |
| FCCC | Foreign Correspondents' Club of China |
| GAPP | General Administration for Press and Publications |
| GATT | General Agreement on Trade and Tariff |
| GMD | Guomindang |
| HIV | Human immunodeficiency virus |
| HPRS | Household Production Responsibility System |
| ILO | International Labor Organization |
| IPR | Intellectual property rights |
| KMT | Kuomintang (or Guomindang, Chinese Nationalist Party) |
| L&V | Letters and Visits |
| MOFTEC | Ministry of Foreign Trade and Economic Cooperation |
| NGO | Nongovernmental organization |
| NPC | National People's Congress (PRC) |
| OHCHR | Office of the High Commissioner for Human Rights (United Nations) |
| PAP | People's Armed Police |
| PBC | People's Bank of China |
| PLA | People's Liberation Army |

| | |
|---|---|
| PNTS | China's permanent normal trading status |
| PRC | People's Republic of China |
| RFA | Radio Free Asia |
| RMB | *Renminbi* (Chinese currency) |
| ROC | Republic of China |
| RTL | Reeducation through Labor |
| SARS | Severe Acute Respiratory Syndrome |
| SEZ | Special Economic Zones |
| SME | Small and medium enterprises |
| SPC | Supreme People's Court |
| STD | Sexually transmitted disease |
| TAR | Tibet Autonomous Region |
| UN | United Nations |
| VOA | Voice of America |
| WHO | World Health Organization |
| WTO | World Trade Organization |

# Note on Transliteration

The *hanyu pinyin* romanization system is applied to Chinese names of persons, places, and terms. The transliteration is also used for the titles of Chinese publications. Names of individuals are written in the Chinese way: surname first, such as Mao Zedong. Some popular names have traditional Wade-Giles spellings appearing in parentheses after the first use of the *hanyu pinyin*, such as Jiang Jieshi (Chiang Kai-shek), as do popular names of places like Guangzhou (Canton). The order is reversed for a very few places whose names are widely known, such as Tibet (Xizang) and Yangtze (Yangzi or Changjiang) River.

# Chronology

## 1949

**September 29:** The Chinese People's Political Consultative Conference (CPPCC) passes the Common Program as China's provisional constitution.

**October 1:** Mao Zedong proclaims the founding of the People's Republic of China (PRC) in Beijing. Mao becomes the chairman of the Central Military Commission of the Central Government. The First CPPCC Plenary Session creates the Supreme Court, and Shen Junru is named its president.

## 1950

The Marriage Law, Trade Union Law, and Agrarian Reform Law are promulgated.

**September:** China launches a mass movement to suppress counterrevolutionaries in rural areas; 1.27 million are incarcerated and 800,000 executed.

**October 19:** The PRC sends a large number of Chinese troops to the Korean War as a "volunteer force" to fight against UN forces.

## 1951

The government launches the Three Antis and Five Antis movements in the cities to support its War to Resist America and Aid Korea. The central government signs an agreement with the Tibetan government, Measures for the Liberation of Tibet, reorganizing Tibet as part of China and granting the region autonomous status.

**July 10:** Truce negotiations begin in Korea.

## 1952

Mao calls for a national movement to learn from the Soviet Union under the leadership of Joseph Stalin. The Three Antis and Five Antis campaigns continue against manufacturing, finance, and trading operations in the private sector, and they are viewed as the precursor to a looming deprivatization movement. China continues fighting the Korean War while negotiating for peace.

## 1953

The first Five-Year Plan (1953–1957) starts.

**January:** A committee, headed by Mao, is created by the twenty-first meeting of the central government to draft a constitution.

**February 11:** At its twenty-second meeting, the government passes the Electoral Law, which is published on March 1.

**July 27:** The armistice ending the Korean War is signed.

## 1954

**September 20:** The First National People's Congress (NPC) passes the constitution and elects Mao as the PRC's president, Zhu De as vice president, Zhou Enlai as premier, Liu Shaoqi as chairman of the NPC, and Dong Biwu as president of the Supreme Court. The First NPC Plenary Session creates the Ministry of Justice and promulgates the Court Organization Law and Procuratorial Law.

**December:** The NPC issues regulations on arrest, detention, and public security organizations.

## 1955

**June 1:** The Ministry of Internal Affairs publishes the Marriage Registration Law.

**July 1:** The State Council issues instructions to establish the Residential Registration System.

**July:** The Ministry of Public Security issues regulations on transportation, traffic, radio, telegrams, and electronic communication.

**July 30:** The Second NPC Plenary Session issues the Military Service Law.

## 1956

**May 8:** The NPC and CPPCC hold a joint conference and decide important legal issues, including a ban on public trials and criminals' loss of their political right to life.

**September 15–27:** The Eighth Chinese Communist Party (CCP) National Congress convenes and reelects Mao as chairman for its 6 million party members. Mao calls for the Blooming of the Hundred Flowers movement.

**October 10:** The State Council issues regulations on the police and law enforcement ranking system.

**1957**

Mao launches the Anti-Rights movement.

**August 3:** The NPC establishes the Reeducation through Labor (RTL) system to detain counterrevolutionaries without trial for one to twelve years, working as menial laborers on state-owned farms or in factories.

**October 22:** The NPC issues regulations on public security, management, and punishments.

**1958**

The second Five-Year Plan (1958–1962) begins.

**May 5–23:** The Second Plenum of the Eighth CCP Central Committee passes a new general line with the phrase "more, faster, better, and more economically sound" to build a socialist economy. As part of the general line, the Great Leap Forward movement begins.

**November 28–December 10:** The Sixth Plenum decides to launch the People's Commune movement as part of the general line.

**1959**

**March:** The State Council appoints the Panchen Lama to chair the Tibetan Preparatory Committee. People's Liberation Army (PLA) troops suppress the Tibetan rebellion. The Dalai Lama flees to India.

**April:** The Second NPC elects Liu Shaoqi as the PRC's president and Xie Juezai as Supreme Court president. The Ministry of Justice is closed, not to reopen until 1979.

**July 2–August 16:** The CCP Eighth Plenum accuses Peng Dehuai and some PLA generals of forming a "right opportunist clique" in the Party and the army.

**September 17:** Lin Biao replaces Peng as defense minister.

**1960**

The great Sino-Soviet polemic debate begins and lasts for three years. Mao criticizes the Soviet leader Khrushchev as a "revisionist" who had betrayed Communists throughout the world.

**August 13:** By this date the Soviet Union calls for all 12,000 Russian experts to leave China and terminates all Soviet economic and military aid.

## 1961

China experiences a serious economic depression known as the Three Hard Years, which is caused by "natural disasters." Serious shortages of food, fuel, and other daily needs claim millions of lives. The CCP calls for new efforts to overcome the economic difficulties by Party members, who total 17.3 million by June.

## 1962

**September 24–27:** The CCP holds its Tenth Plenum of the Eighth Central Committee and emphasizes class struggle.

**October 20:** The Sino-Indian War breaks out along the Tibetan border.

**November 22:** The Chinese government announces a cease-fire along the Chinese-Indian border and begins to pull Chinese troops out of Indian territories.

## 1963

**April 12–May 16:** President Liu visits Indonesia, Burma, Vietnam, and Cambodia.

**May:** Mao starts the socialist education movement, also known as the Four Cleanups, in rural areas.

**December:** Premier Zhou begins travels that will take him to fourteen countries in Africa by the end of January.

## 1964

**October 16:** China carries out its first nuclear bomb test.

**December 20:** The Third NPC opens, running through January 4. Liu is elected president and Zhou premier. Zhou calls for the Four Modernizations.

## 1965

**May 14:** China conducts its second nuclear bomb test.

**July:** China begins to send troops to Vietnam, along with the PLA's surface-to-air missile, antiaircraft artillery, combat engineering, and logistics units.

**September:** The Tibet Autonomous Region (TAR) is formally inaugurated.

## 1966

**May:** Mao launches the Great Proletarian Cultural Revolution, a nationwide political struggle accompanied by extensive purges. Students organize the Red Guards as the driving force for the movement. All schools and colleges are closed. The masses are urged to be guided by Mao's Thought instead of law.

**October:** President Liu, Vice Premier Deng Xiaoping, and many high-ranking government officials are publicly criticized and purged. Some of them are tortured and killed by the Red Guards.

## 1967

**January:** Mass organizations begin to overtake the power of the authorities in Shanghai; other cities follow. The legal system is attacked, and many existing government mechanisms are totally paralyzed. Armed clashes take place between different mass organizations when they try to take over local governments.

**July:** An armed clash occurs in Hubei, and more than 180,000 civilians and soldiers are killed or wounded. To prevent civil war, 2.8 million officers and soldiers of the PLA are deployed to restore order through military administrative committees.

## 1968

**October 13–31:** The Twelfth Plenum of the CCP Eighth Central Committee is held and officially purges President Liu and many leaders from the party, government, and the PLA. By the end of the year China has sent twenty-three divisions, totaling 320,000 troops, to Vietnam.

## 1969

**March:** The Sino-Soviet border conflicts begin at Zhenbao (Damansky) Island, Heilongjiang, and then continue in many places along the border in the Xinjiang Uyghur Autonomous Region.

**April 1–24:** The CCP holds the Ninth National Congress and recognizes Lin as Mao's successor.

**April 28:** The First Plenum of the CCP Ninth Central Committee reelects Mao as party chairman and elects Lin as the vice chairman.

**November 12:** President Liu dies after two years of detention.

## 1970

The Sino-Soviet border conflicts continue.

**April:** China launches its first satellite. Henry Kissinger and Le Duc Tho begin secret talks to end the Vietnam War. China withdraws its troops from Vietnam.

## 1971

**September 13:** Lin and his family are killed in a plane crash in Mongolia. Mao begins another top-down purge and shakeup in the military and appoints Ye Jianying as defense minister.

**October:** China is admitted to the United Nations.

## 1972

**February:** President Richard Nixon visits China, where he signs the joint Shanghai Communiqué agreeing that there is but one China and that Taiwan is a part of China.

## 1973

**August 24–28:** The CCP Tenth National Congress meets and reelects Mao as chairman. The United States and China announce their intention to establish liaison offices in each other's capitals.

## 1974

**October:** Mao suggests bringing Deng Xiaoping back from the purge as the first vice premier. After his return, Deng also serves as the vice chairman of the CCP Central Military Commission and chief of staff of the PLA.

## 1975

**January 13:** The Fourth NPC promulgates the second constitution. The new constitution minimizes or eliminates the courts and procurators; individual rights such as freedom of speech and the press have not been retained.

**December:** President Gerald Ford visits Beijing and agrees to terminate the U.S.–Taiwan mutual security treaty and withdraw U.S. military forces from the island.

## 1976

**January 8:** Zhou Enlai dies.

**July 28:** An earthquake measuring 7.8 on the Richter scale rocks Tangshan and becomes the largest earthquake of the twentieth century by death toll; 240,000–255,000 people are killed and 164,000 severely injured.

**September 9:** Mao Zedong dies at age eighty-two. Mao's death ends the Cultural Revolution, during which an estimated tens of millions of people were killed, injured, or otherwise persecuted or victimized.

**October:** Maoist leaders called the Gang of Four, led by Mao's widow, Jiang Qing, are arrested by Hua Guofeng.

**November:** The Criminal Code is issued; it contains twenty-two crimes, including rape and robbery, that are punishable by the death penalty.

**1977**

Official statistics show that more than 250 million people are living below the poverty line.

**July 16–21:** The Third Plenum of the CCP Tenth Central Committee supports Hua's leadership and the purge of the Gang of Four.

**August 12–18:** The CCP Eleventh National Congress meets and elects Hua as chairman and Ye, Deng, Li Xiannian, and Wang Dongxing as vice chairmen.

**1978**

**March 5:** The Fifth NPC promulgates the third constitution on March 5. The new constitution restores the courts and procurators, and it also reinstates some of the citizens' rights.

**Fall:** A new democracy movement, the "Democracy Walls," begins to take hold in several major cities.

**December 13:** Deng Xiaoping becomes the key leader and begins an unprecedented seismic reform and opening up to the world to modernize China after giving his historic speech, "Emancipate the Mind," at the Third Plenum of the Eleventh CCP Central Committee.

**1979**

**January 1:** China establishes diplomatic relations with the United States. Deng becomes the first PRC leader to visit America, holding talks with Jimmy Carter and signing the protocols.

**February 17:** China invades Vietnam with 200,000 PLA troops. The struggles to save "Democracy Walls" become the "Beijing Spring" movement, which is suppressed by the government.

**July 1–4:** The Fifth NPC announces the Criminal Law and Electoral Law of the NPC and the creation of local people's congresses. The Ministry of Justice reopens after twenty years. The Standing Committee of the NPC approves the State Council's supplementary regulations regarding the RTL system. The family planning policy known as the one-child policy begins.

## 1980

**February 12:** The Standing Committee of the NPC approves the Criminal Procedure Law and the Regulations on Academic Degrees.

**August 30–September 10:** The Third Plenary Session of the Fifth NPC passes the new Citizenship Law, Marriage Law, Joint Venture Income Tax Law, and Individual Income Tax Law.

**November 20–December 29:** The Supreme Court holds open trials of the Gang of Four. The State Council issues new regulations regarding the RTL system by combining forced-labor education and detention into a single practice that allows detention without trial of no longer than four years for minor offenses.

## 1981

The CCP Central Military Commission elects Deng as chairman. Hu Yaobang replaces Hua Guofeng as chairman of the CCP Central Committee. Both Hu and Zhao Ziyang are appointed vice chairmen of the Central Military Commission, the de facto center of power in China.

**December 13:** The Standing Committee of the NPC issues the Economic Contract Law.

## 1982

**August 23:** The NPC Standing Committee issues China's Marine Environment Protection Law and Trademark Law.

**September 1–October 1:** The CCP holds its Twelfth National Congress.

**December 4:** The Fifth Plenary Session of the Fifth NPC adopts the new constitution, which, together with some amendments incorporated during the 1990s, remains in place. It recognizes the people's liberties and institutionalizes those rights as a component of the judicial system. The constitution and the Law on the Organization of Courts provide the accused with the right to a proper defense.

## 1983

The People's Armed Police (PAP) is established. The Ministry of Foreign Affairs starts a spokesperson system, opening an information channel for only diplomatic and other important political occasions.

**1984**

**April:** President Ronald Reagan visits China and meets with Deng.

**May 31:** The New Regional Autonomy Law and Military Service Law are issued.

**October:** The Third Plenum of the Twelfth CCP Central Committee decides to reform the economic structure. Fourteen coastal cities and the island of Hainan are opened to foreign investment.

**1985**

President Li Xiannian visits Washington and signs a pact allowing the sale of nonmilitary technology to China. Vice President George H. W. Bush visits China. Deng Xiaoping is named *Time* magazine's Man of the Year for the second time.

**January 20:** The PRC Accounting Law is issued.

**June 18:** China's Grassland Law is issued.

**1986**

The courts handle 2 million cases this year. Authorities send 870,000 persons to the RTL system (detention without trial for up to four years) in forced labor camps each year in the 1980s.

**April 12:** The PRC's Law of Foreign Capital Enterprises and Compulsory Education Law are issued.

**June 12:** General Principles of the Civil Law of the PRC are published.

**1987**

China has only four law schools, twenty-five law departments in universities, and 26,000 lawyers across the country, and the government carries out at least two hundred death sentences every month. The accused are often denied a meaningful appeal and are executed on the day of their conviction.

**September 6:** The Law of the Prevention and Control of Atmospheric Pollution is issued.

**November 24:** The Organic Law of the Villagers' Committees is issued.

**1988**

**April:** The First Session of the Seventh NPC adopts two constitutional amendments on private property and protection of the ownership of private property. The constitution recognizes "private economy" as a "supplement to the socialist state economy." China ratifies the UN Convention against Torture and signs the International Covenant on Civil and Political Rights.

**April 13:** Laws on Industrial Enterprises Owned by the Whole People and on Chinese-Foreign Contractual Joint Ventures are issued.

**December 29:** The Standardization Law is issued.

## 1989

**May:** Hundreds of thousands of students and citizens hold demonstrations in Beijing, which later spread to 116 cities.

**May 6–16:** The students encamp at Tiananmen Square and begin a hunger strike.

**May 19:** The government establishes martial law and deploys twenty-two infantry divisions in the cities.

**June 3–4:** The PLA troops open fire at the students and citizens at Tiananmen Square; an estimated one thousand casualties ensue.

**October:** The government issues the Act on Marches and Demonstrations, limiting citizens' rights to assemble and demonstrate. The State Council issues the Registration of Social Organizations, which includes many restrictions on the freedom of association.

## 1990

**April:** President Yang Shangkun promulgates the Basic Law of the Hong Kong Special Administrative Region (SAR) adopted by the Seventh NPC. The law is scheduled to take effect on July 1, 1997.

**September 7:** The Copyright Law of the PRC is issued.

**December 28:** The Law on the Protection of Disabled Persons is issued.

## 1991

The State Council issues the Provisions on the Administration of Religious Activities within the territory of the PRC. After the Tiananmen Square incident, Jiang Zemin becomes the top leader as the chairman of both the Party Central Committee and Central Military Commission.

**April 9:** The Civil Procedure Law is issued.

**November 4:** The Law on the Protection of Minors is issued.

## 1992

The State Bureau of Religions of the State Council approves the succession of the Living Buddha of the Seventeenth Karmapa.

**May:** Falun Gong, one of the *qigong*-based exercise groups, is established.

**February 25:** The Law on the Territorial Sea and the Contiguous Zone is issued.

**November 7:** The Maritime Code is issued.

### 1993

**March:** The First Session of the Eighth NPC adds nine important amendments to the constitution, including some changes to the preamble. It allows the Household Production Responsibility System (HPRS) to replace the People's Collective Communes and the private management of state enterprises.

**October 31:** The Laws on the Protection of Consumer Rights and Interests and on Individual Income Tax are issued.

### 1994

**January:** The State Council promulgates the Regulations on the Administration of Sites for Religious Activities, placing severe restrictions on family churches and citizens' faith-based activities. The number of lawyers increases to 70,000, but the country has 3.85 million legal cases this year. The courts report hearing merely 3.6 million cases this year, leaving as many as 250,000 defendants without legal aid or a chance for appeal.

**May 12:** The Foreign Trade Law of the PRC is issued.

**December 29:** China's Prison Law is issued.

### 1995

Only 6 percent of Chinese judges have college degrees (not necessarily a law degree). The new Criminal Code increases from twenty-six to sixty the number of crimes punishable by death.

**February 28:** The People's Police Law is issued.

**October 25:** The Law on the Prevention and Control of Environmental Pollution by Solid Waste is issued.

### 1996

The State Council issues the State Administration for Religious Affairs. In the spring China fires missiles near Taiwan and conducts military exercise in the Taiwan Strait.

**May:** The NPC passes new legislation to reform criminal justice procedures and the legal profession. For the first time China recognizes that lawyers represent their clients, not the state, according to the Lawyer's Law.

**July 5:** The Law on Control of Guns is issued.

**October 29:** China's Civil Air Defense Law is published.

### 1997

**February 19:** Deng Xiaoping dies at the age of ninety-two.

**March 14:** The Law on National Defense is adopted, defining the mission of the PAP. The amendment of the Criminal Code increases from sixty to sixty-eight the number of crimes punishable by death.

**July 1:** Britain hands Hong Kong back to China.

**October 27:** China signs the International Covenant on Economic, Social, and Cultural Rights. The Standing Committee of the NPC amends the Criminal Law.

### 1998

**June:** President Clinton meets Jiang in Beijing to challenge China on human rights issues.

**October 5:** China signs the International Covenant on Civil and Political Rights. Statistics show that more than 42 million Chinese people are living below the poverty line. The government conducts an internal shakeup of the judiciary, which results in the punishment of over 4,200 judicial branch employees. China accounts for over 70 percent of criminals executed in the world each year.

**November 4:** The Organic Law of the Villagers' Committees is issued.

**December 29:** The Securities Law is published.

### 1999

**March:** The Second Session of the Ninth NPC adopts six constitutional amendments. The constitution for the first time redefines the socialist state economy as a socialist market economy. The Supreme Court issues its first five-year plan for legal reforms. The courts handle 6 million cases this year.

**July:** The authorities outlaw the Falun Gong movement and arrest 90,000 members. The PAP increases to 1 million troops.

**December 1:** Portugal returns Macao to China.

### 2000

The CCP Central Committee and the State Council issue a joint decision to enforce the one-child policy. Official records show 3,082 fatalities in coal mining. About 20 percent of Chinese judges have college degrees.

**March 15:** The Legislation Law is issued.

**December:** The courts report hearing 5.85 million cases this year, including 560,000 criminal, 4.37 million civil, and 870,000 administrative cases. Police arrest 635,000 of 720,000 suspects and file charges against 610,000 detainees. An estimated 2,000 practitioners die as a result of the official persecution of Falun Gong. The People's Armed Police comprises 1 million members.

## 2001

The Law on Population and Birth Planning is promulgated to provide a general framework and more details for provincial regulations and operations.

**May:** Hundreds of residents of Shangzhou, Shaanxi, are found to be infected with AIDS, a rate of 4 percent. As many as 100 million rural laborers are on the move and seeking work in cities.

**October:** President George W. Bush visits Shanghai.

**December 11:** China joins the WTO.

## 2002

The State Council revises the Regulations on Prohibiting the Use of Child Labor. Official records show annual fatalities of 3,790 in coal mining. The government promulgates the provisions on administrative cases to tighten law enforcement procedure. The courts report hearing 5.58 million cases this year.

**February:** President George W. Bush visits Beijing.

**November:** Severe Acute Respiratory Syndrome (SARS) breaks out in southern China.

## 2003

China has 31 provincial bureaus of public security; 356 metropolitan police departments; 2,972 county police headquarters; and 41,941 local police stations. The PAP has 31 armies, including 508 armed police regiments and 42 special regiments, such as helicopter, artillery, chemical, and tank regiments. The PAP also has 32 commanding office academies and 29 hospitals. Chinese police crack 2.3 million criminal cases.

**July 31:** There are 5,328 SARS cases and 349 fatalities.

**September:** The State Council revises the Publications Administration Regulations and Regulations Governing the Administration of Audio-visual Products.

**November:** The Supreme Court formulates twenty documents of judicial interpretation of criminal, civil, and administrative law enforcement and regulations on legal aid. The Ministry of Justice formulates and implements the Regulations on Reform through Education in Prisons, Law on Prisons, and Regulations on the Procedures for Applications by Prisons for Commutation and Parole.

**December:** The courts have investigated 635,000 criminal first-instance cases and 88,000 administrative lawsuits this year. Procuratorial organs appeal court judgments of 2,906 criminal cases that they deem incorrectly tried. There are 58,000 mass protests this year. Official records show 4,143 fatalities in coal mining.

## 2004

**March:** The Second Session of the Tenth NPC adopts and publishes fourteen amendments to the constitution. Among the most important amendments is the phrase added to Article 33: "The state respects and guarantees human rights." This marks the first time the constitution mentions human rights. The Law on National Regional Autonomy, General Principles of the Civil Law, the Education Law, and the Labor Law are adopted.

**April:** The State Council revises the Law on the Protection of Women's Rights and Interests. By this year the State Council has issued eight hundred administrative laws and regulations that account for more than 60 percent of all of those in China.

**September:** A researcher for the *New York Times* is detained by authorities.

**November:** The government launches a new detention campaign targeting writers, journalists, and political commentators.

**December:** There are 74,000 mass protests this year. The courts report hearing 5.54 million cases this year.

## 2005

Mass protests increase to 87,000 for the year. Authorities have thirty-two journalists in jail this year. For the first time, about 50 percent of Chinese judges have college degrees.

**March:** The Third Session of the Tenth NPC adopts new laws, including the Compulsory Education Law, Electoral Law of the People's Congress, Organic Law of the Villagers' Committees, and Advertisement Law. It amends the Law on the Protection of Women's Rights and Interests by including a ban on sexual harassment, human trafficking, and the sex trade, which remain significant problems.

**June:** The Ministry of Public Security estimates that 10,000 women and children are abducted and sold each year, and between 2 and 4 million women are involved in prostitution.

**August:** The government spends at least $800 million on an elaborate system of censorship, which is also known as the Great Firewall of China, to control its citizens online.

**December:** Official records show 6,000 miners died this year. China signs two key international human rights treaties that include articles against the death penalty. Even though the execution total declines, the country still tops the world in executions with a total of 3,400 this year.

## 2006

More than 80,000 incidents of social unrest and protest take place this year. China has 490,000 police, 150,000 detectives and investigators, and 1.5 million PAP. At least 930 cases of police torture take place. More than 300 police officers have been killed every year since 1993.

**November:** Official statistics show that more than 31 million people are living below the poverty line. About 30 percent of families suffer from domestic violence; 90 percent of the victims are women and children.

**December:** The courts report hearing 5.7 million cases and try 933,156 criminal cases. Only 30 percent of the defendants have a lawyer or legal counsel on their cases. The conviction rate for first- and second-instance criminal trials is more than 99.85 percent. About 0.15 percent, or 1,400 of nearly 1 million criminal cases, are found not guilty.

## 2007

China has more than 580,000 police, 150,000 detectives, and 250,000 traffic cops and special police, all of whom are under the control of the Ministry of Public Security. Authorities arrest 270 priests of the underground Christian churches this year. The official records show that 101,510 administrative lawsuits are filed against the government this year. The country has more than 150,000 licensed lawyers. A total of 1.8 million prisoners are in jail.

**January 1:** The government issues temporary regulations to give foreign correspondents the freedom to interview anyone who consents and expresses his or her own opinions before and during the Olympic games, until October 17, 2008.

**April:** After the Chinese Catholic bishop, Fu Tieshan, dies, the government rather than the pope (as is customary) appoints his successor.

**June:** Xinjiang authorities began to collect Muslims' passports in order to prevent them from making non-state-approved pilgrimages to Mecca. The NPC passes the Law of Laborer Contracts.

**August:** The CCP Central Committee establishes the Bureau of Internet Propaganda, and the State Council establishes the Bureau of the Internet to censor online activities. They issue the Regulations for the Management of Internet Publishing and bring online magazines, or webzines, under the same controls as print publications.

**September:** The Ministry of the Information Industry issues a new set of rules aimed at curbing the spread of interactive Internet sites. Authorities close 14,000 "illegal" websites.

**October:** British TV reporters are arrested while interviewing and filming. Authorities have twenty-nine journalists in jail this year. The FCCC reports 160 incidents of harassment of foreign journalists when they conduct interviews this year.

## 2008

151,000 party and government officials are disciplined this year. FCCC reports that 178 incidents of harassment of foreign journalists occurred when they conducted interviews this year.

**March 14:** Buddhist riots occur in Lhasa. Authorities arrest Tibetans arbitrarily, including monks and nuns. Official state media report the detentions of 4,434 persons.

**March 28:** The government confirms 28 civilians and one police officer dead and 325 civilians injured during the "3-14 Riots." According to the India-based Tibetan government-in-exile, more than 220 Tibetans were killed and 7,000 Tibetans were arrested.

**April 29:** The Lhasa Intermediate Court sentences thirty Tibetans to three years to life in prison for their participation in the 3-14 Riots.

**May 12:** An earthquake measuring 8.0 on the Richter scale rocks Wenchuan County, Sichuan. Official statistics show at least 69,000 killed, 374,000 injured, 18,000 still missing, and 4.8 million people homeless.

**August 8–24:** China hosts the Olympic Games in Beijing; 10,500 athletes participate in 302 events in 28 sports. The same month the Propaganda

Department of the CCP Central Committee issues a twenty-one-point directive outlining how the domestic media should handle certain stories during the Olympics.

**September:** The FCCC reports that local authorities continue to infringe on the freedom of foreign journalists to travel and conduct interviews. In Xinjiang police detain and beat two Japanese journalists attempting to cover the aftermath of a deadly attack on a PAP unit.

**October 17:** The government makes permanent rules granting foreign journalists greater freedoms by eliminating previous requirements that they seek permission from local officials before conducting interviews.

**October:** The NPC issues fifteen laws and legal decisions concerning national defense and the armed forces.

## 2009

The government sentences and executes four Tibetans in connection with their involvement with the "3-14 Tibetan Riots."

**July 5:** Tens of thousands of Uyghur demonstrators gather in the city center of Urumqi, Xinjiang, protesting the government's handling of the death of two Uyghur workers. After confrontations with police, the demonstration escalates into riots; 197 people die and 1,721 others are injured, according to the government reports.

**July 18:** The World Uyghur Congress reports 600 dead during the "7-5 Xinjiang Riots." An official confirms that more than 1,500 rioters have been arrested. The government cuts off almost all Internet access to the entire region of 19 million people in Xinjiang.

**November 14–17:** President Barack Obama visits China and explains the significance of civil liberties to Chinese students in Shanghai.

**December 29:** A British citizen, Akmal Shaikh, is executed by lethal injection by Chinese authorities after being convicted of drug smuggling in October.

**December:** Authorities sentence twenty-two Uyghurs to death for their participation in the "7-5 Xinjiang Riots."

## 2010

China calls for a campaign against "illegal text messages" and "unhealthy content." Cellular service companies automatically scan text messages for key words provided by the police. They must inform the police by forwarding "illegal and unhealthy content" for police evaluation.

**January:** Google announces that it will no longer cooperate with China's censorship laws.

**February 12:** The government lifts its online blackout of Xinjiang, which has been enforced since July 2009, just before the Chinese Lunar New Year.

**February 18:** President Obama meets the Dalai Lama in the White House.

**April 30:** The World Expo opens in Shanghai, the first time a Chinese city has held a World Expo.

**October 8:** The Chinese dissident Liu Xiaobo is awarded the 2010 Nobel Peace Prize, which draws a protest from the Chinese government.

## 2011

The Chinese government is facing increasingly combustible problems. On the one hand, the demonstrations and riots in the Middle East raise fears among top leaders that similar things will happen in China; on the other hand, official corruption, high housing prices, and economic woes are still fomenting anger among the masses. In addition, the struggle for power in the upcoming Party Congress (2012) is becoming more intense and fierce among different factions inside the Party.

**February 23:** Inspired by the recent demonstrations in North African states such as Tunisia and Egypt, a small group of Chinese call for a Jasmine Revolution in China. The demonstrations are quickly overwhelmed by police officers.

**April 28:** The National Bureau of Statistics of the PRC announces the sixth official census: China has 1,339,720,000 people, including 665,570,000 urban and 674,150,000 rural citizens.

**May 20–26:** Invited by President Hu Jintao, the North Korean leader Kim Jong-il pays an unofficial visit to Beijing, Jiangsu, Jilin, and Heilongjiang.

**June 15–18:** President Hu Jintao visits Russia for the fifth time since 2003.

**July 16:** President Obama meets the Dalai Lama at the White House.

**July 17:** Xi Jinping, vice president of the PRC and vice chairman of the CCP Central Military Commission, attends the sixtieth anniversary celebration of the Tibetan liberation.

**October 11–12:** Russian Prime Minister Putin visits China.

# Introduction

# Legal Reforms in Twentieth-Century China

*Xiaobing Li and Qiang Fang*

Few areas of research in China studies pose more difficulties than that of the Chinese legal system, primarily because of its unique position in Chinese society and relationship to the legitimacy of the nation's Communist authority. The Chinese Communist Party (CCP) is still the state's dominant political party and controls the executive, legislative, and judicial systems. Since 1978 the CCP's leaders have launched the reform movement, and China has experienced a tremendous wave of change. The shifting nature of the ongoing reform, however, is plagued by contradiction, uncertainty, and the clash of tradition and modernity.

The reform movement has produced three major problems confronting students of Chinese legal practice: continuing Party influence, frequent changes of laws, and a gap between the government's promise and the courtroom reality. That gap between the promise of legal reform and the reality of legal practice makes understanding Chinese law and order very difficult for Westerners. This book examines the country's legal system and major judicial problems; it also introduces and explores the history and practice of constitutional rights by identifying key issues in Chinese ideology, government, and society. Using an analytical approach through new perspectives, this volume identifies some of the contradictions and even confrontations in Chinese policy making, explains the dilemma Beijing faces, and provides a better understanding of China's economic change, political concerns, social transitions, and legal reforms.

Reform is never an easy task, especially in Chinese history. Many great reformers, such as Gongsun Yang (Shang Yang, 390–338 BCE), Wang Anshi (Wang An-shih, 1021–1086), and Zhang Juzheng (Chang Chu-cheng, 1525–1582), having devoted much of their energy and time to strengthening their states, were executed, demoted, or denounced posthumously.[1] At the end of the nineteenth century the Qing Empire (1644–1912), in deep crisis, experienced unprecedented challenges that were for the first time not from the "barbarians" but from "superior" powers, mostly in the form of Western states. If Qing's defeats by Western states such as Great Britain and France in both Opium Wars (1840–1842 and 1856–1860) failed to alarm the ruling elites, especially those advocates of the Self-Strengthening Movement,[2] about the necessity of a thorough political change, the unexpected defeat in war by its junior neighbor Japan in 1895 prompted a massive call for a fundamental change from reformers inside and outside the court.

Three years later Kang Youwei (K'ang Yu-wei, 1858–1927), a provincial degree holder and the driving force behind the 1898 reform, wrote to the young Emperor Guangxu (Kwang Hsu) (reigned 1875–1908) that a reform was urgent for the empire:

> The problem of [China] today is sticking to the old law and refusing to change. [China] is now situated in a world in which states compete with one other. If [the ruler] continues to do nothing, it will be like a person who wears a heavy coat in the summer or sits in a tall wagon moving into the water. There is no doubt that the person will be sick or drowned. . . . It is the natural principle that something new is strong, worn things are old; new things are fresh, worn things are rotten; new things are unobstructed, worn things are impassable. Once a law is too old, it must have many defects. Thus, no law can last over a hundred years without change.[3]

Emperor Guangxu, an admirer of the Meiji Reform (1868–1912), which made Japan a modern and powerful state in two decades, agreed with Kang and launched the 1898 Reform in an effort to transform China into a "rich and powerful country." Yet, because of strong opposition from conservative forces led by his aunt, Empress Dowager Cixi (Tz'u Hsi, 1835–1908), the reform was short-lived and lasted only 103 days. Kang Youwei, whose fate was not very different from those of previous reformers, barely escaped with his life and was forced into exile; his brother and five other reformers were executed.

# China Political Map

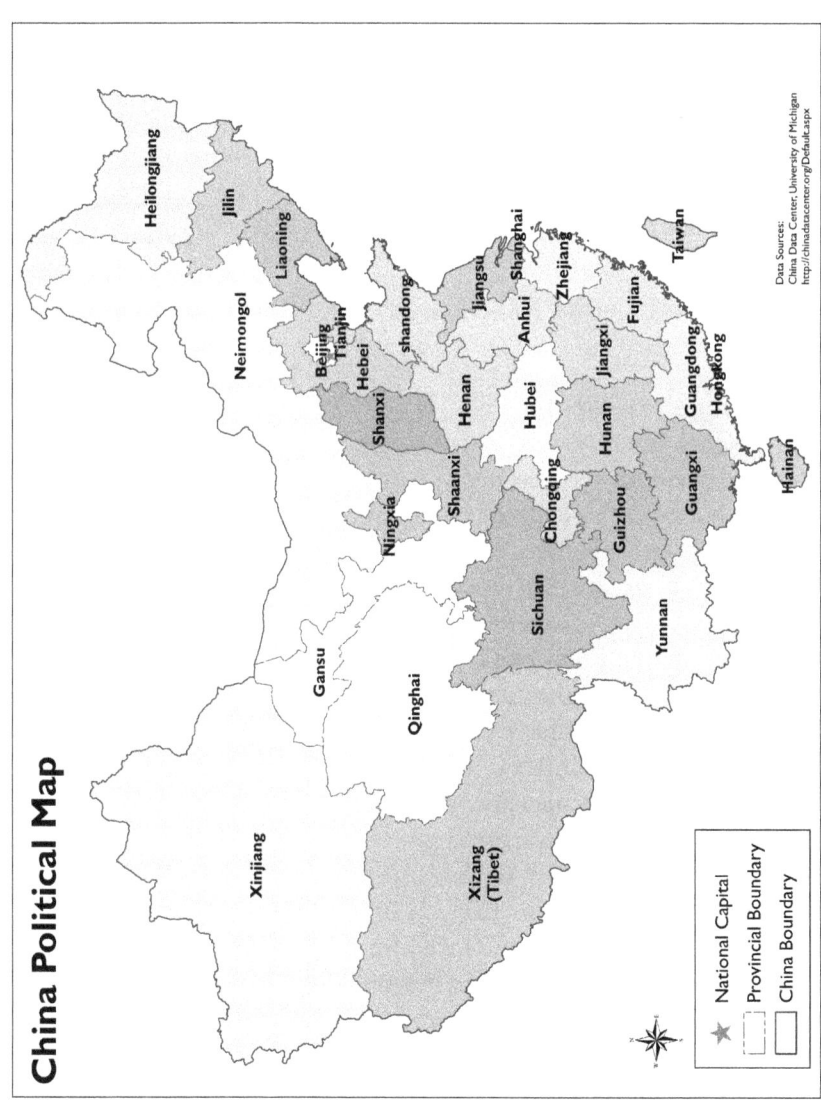

Data Sources:
China Data Center, University of Michigan
http://chinadatacenter.org/Default.aspx

National Capital
Provincial Boundary
China Boundary

(Map by Jing Duan)

The animosity toward and harsh treatment of the reformers quickly diminished, however. The same suppressors of the 1898 reform turned into the chief advocates of a far more drastic and thorough reform. The late Qing reform, whose most notable achievements were its legal reform, marked the beginning of the three major legal reforms in twentieth-century China: the late Qing and Republic of China (ROC), the early People's Republic of China (PRC), and the post-1978 legal reforms.

## The First Legal Reform: Response to the West (1901–1949)

It was not until 1901, after the Eight-Nation Alliance stormed Beijing and forced the Qing rulers to flee to western China, that Empress Dowager Cixi realized previous reforms had incorporated only the "skin and hair" of the West, but not its essence. She therefore urged a sweeping reform patterned after Western practices that was later known as the New Policies. The New Policies covered most aspects of the empire, and among its most remarkable goals was legal reform. As most scholars concur, this began in 1901, when Zhang Zhidong (Chang Chih-tung, 1837–1909), governor general of Hunan and Hubei, and Liu Kunyi, governor general of Jiangxi (Kiangsi), called for comprehensive legal reform, including the abolition of many corporal punishments.[4] Generally speaking, the late Qing legal reform made dramatic achievements in four areas: criminal law, civil law, administrative law, and the constitution.

After another proposal to end corporal punishments from the renowned jurists Shen Jiaben (1837–1910) and Wu Tingfang (Wu T'ing-fang, 1842–1922) in 1904, the late Qing reform moved the next year toward eliminating death by slicing (*lingchi*), exposure of the head (*xiaoshou*), and mutilation of the corpse (*lushi*), the three most atrocious punishments in the eyes of Westerners. Also in 1905 other corporal punishments such as flogging and whipping were replaced with fines, known as "a widespread Western practice."[5] In 1910 the late Qing formally promulgated the Criminal Law of the Great Qing Currently in Use (*Daqing xianxing xinglu*), which had been drafted by the leading Japanese specialist Okada Asataro and was modeled on the new Japanese criminal code. Unlike the Great Qing Code, which had five categories of punishment (whipping, flogging with bamboo canes, enslavement, exile, and death), the new criminal law's penalties were only death, imprisonment, and fines. The new criminal law, strongly influenced by the West, was more humane than the old one.

Another major step forward in the late Qing reform was the drafting of a civil law. In the Qing, the civil law was part of the Qing code, not separate. But the late Qing reformers distinguished the civil law from the criminal law. The late Qing hired Matsuoka Yoshimasa, a Japanese judge of the Tokyo Court of Appeals, to draft the civil law. Though the new civil law was never formally circulated in the late Qing, the first three books, "General Principles," "Obligations," and "Rights over Things," were presented to the ruler in October 1911, one month before the 1911 revolution.[6] Based on German and Japanese civil law, the Draft of the Great Qing Civil Law (*Daqing minlu caoan*) tended to advocate for individual property rights, while at the same time it retained the old laws regarding family members and inheritance to safeguard family harmony.[7]

To protect people's rights to defend themselves against government abuse, the late Qing worked out a plan to establish a Western-style administrative court. In 1909 the late Qing created the Draft of the Bureaucratic System of the Administrative Court (*Xingzheng caipanyuan guanzhi caoan*). The prologue to the draft, which resembled the 1890 Japanese administrative appeals law, stated that the purpose of an administrative court was to protect people from official violations and to "satisfy all the grievances under heaven." Article 1 of the draft noted that the court was responsible for all charges of official abuse. It also specified that "only appeals against ministries, governors, and governors general will be allowed to be addressed directly to the court," and "all other appeals should go to local governments."[8] Like the civil law, the draft was not enacted in the late Qing; rather, most of it became law in the early republic.

The last achievement in the late Qing was the constitution, drafted under tremendous internal and external pressures. The constitution of 1908 was closely modeled on the Imperial Constitution of Japan (1889); it included more terms upholding the emperor's divine power and subjects' duties rather than addressing subjects' legal rights and freedoms. A month before the fall of the dynasty, the late Qing in November 1911 rushed to enact the Nineteen Important Credenda (*Xianfa zhongda xintiao shijiutiao*), which constrained the emperor's power and expanded congress's power. As Zeng Xianyi, a law professor at China Renmin University, argues, the 1908 constitution was merely a promise of the Qing, whereas the credenda were virtually an interim constitution.[9]

Aside from the above four legal reforms, the late Qing also took steps to repudiate the discriminatory laws among Manchus, Mongols, and Hans, construct model prisons, legalize lawyers, and advocate for judicial independence.

In October 1911 the Republican Revolution led by Sun Zhongshan (Sun Yat-sen, 1866–1925) ended the Qing dynasty and established the Republic of China. The revolutionaries and some warlords joined forces, set up a provisional government in Nanjing, elected Sun as president, and inaugurated him on January 1, 1912. As the founding father of the ROC and the Chinese Nationalist Party (known as the Guomindang, GMD, or Kuomintang, KMT), Sun mobilized the people by his "Three Principles of the People": nationalism (both anti-Manchu and anti-imperialist), democracy (a constitution with people's rights), and people's livelihood (a classic term for social equality). These three principles resemble the famous phrase "government of the people, by the people, and for the people," coined by President Abraham Lincoln (1809–1865) at Gettysburg in 1863.

Before a formal constitution was drawn up, the ROC government endorsed a provisional constitution in early 1912, which was a far cry from its late Qing counterpart in terms of content and rhetoric. The provisional constitution stipulated that the sovereignty of the ROC belonged to all Chinese citizens and that all citizens were equal before the law regardless of nation, class, or creed. The essence of the constitution was preserved in most subsequent constitutions in the Republican period.

Apart from its constitution, the ROC retained most of the fruits of the late Qing legal reform.[10] To ensure that the late Qing laws suited republicanism, the ROC made certain important modifications, most of which, like those of the late Qing, reflected strong Western influence and pressure.[11] For instance, one of the crucial motives underlying the legal reform in the early ROC was the negation of the extraterritoriality first imposed by the United States in 1844 and later extended to other foreign states. For reformers in both the late Qing and early ROC, the terms of extraterritoriality were humiliating for the empire. Furthermore, many Republican ministers of justice, such as Wu Tingfang and Xu Shiying (1873–1964), were staunch believers in the rule of law and many other Western-style legal tenets.[12]

The Administrative Law was one of the few laws planned in the late Qing and enacted in the Republic, in 1914. The administrative court was directly responsible to the Republican president, which greatly enhanced its power and efficacy against high-ranking officials.[13]

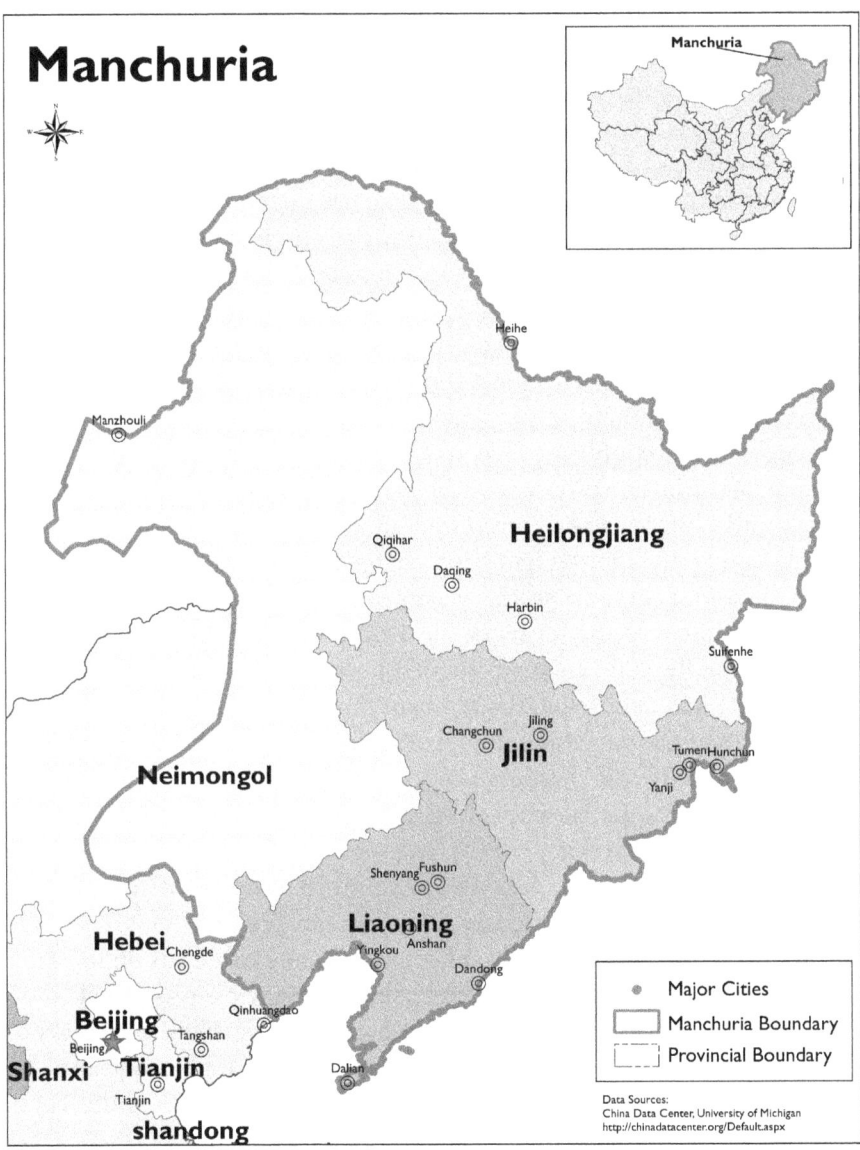

# Manchuria

Heihe

Manzhouli

Qiqihar

**Heilongjiang**

Daqing

Harbin

Suifenhe

Changchun    Jiling

**Jilin**

TumenHunchun

**Neimongol**

Yanji

Shenyang Fushun

**Liaoning**

Yingkou  Anshan

**Hebei** Chengde

Dandong

Qinhuangdao

**Beijing**

Tangshan

Beijing

**Shanxi** **Tianjin**

Dalian

Tianjin

**shandong**

● Major Cities

☐ Manchuria Boundary

⌐⌐⌐ Provincial Boundary

Data Sources:
China Data Center, University of Michigan
http://chinadatacenter.org/Default.aspx

Manchuria

(Map by Jing Duan)

The Draft of the Great Qing Civil Law in 1911 was not adopted by the early ROC. Yet many of its terms, influenced by the West (specifically Germany), had been frequently used by the Republican Supreme Court (*daliyuan*), with some revisions, before the Draft of the Civil Law of the Republic of China was finally enacted in 1926.[14] Compared to the civil code in the late Qing, the Republican law introduced more Western-style values, such as equality between males and females and individual rights. For example, the Republican Supreme Court ruled that without justification, parents had no right to determine the marriage partners of their adult children, a ruling that in fact deprived parents of this traditional power. Additionally, the Republican law increased women's social status by granting them some rights in divorce and inheritance.[15] Despite its merits, the Republican civil law continued to discriminate against women because of cultural concerns. For example, a husband could divorce his wife once she committed adultery, but a wife could divorce her husband only after he had been charged with illicit sexual activities. After the GMD came to power, it passed its own civil law in the 1930s, which kept most of the terms of the 1926 law. As Philip Huang argues, although the Republican law provided people with more rights in gender equality and debt relief, the law bent to custom by requiring children to take care of their aged parents. In the case of a widow, the Republican law paradoxically gave her less support than the Qing law had, because a widow could no longer appeal as she could have under the Qing law against forced remarriage.[16]

Like its civil law, the Republican criminal law, which had initially incorporated the terms of the late Qing criminal law, was revised in 1928 and 1935 by the GMD. The GMD law placed more emphasis on the individual perpetrator than the late Qing had. This principle was called "individualization of punishment." One significant modification in the law was that it made adultery punishable for men and women alike, unlike the previous laws.[17] This revision demonstrated GMD lawmakers' commitment to equal rights for women.

Other marked reforms in the ROC included increasing the number of courts and professional judges and improving the prison condition by making them a site of both transformation and rehabilitation.[18] The most notorious change or setback of the GMD legal reform was "partyizing" the judiciary,[19] which, as Xiaoqun Xu points out, considerably weakened the Republic's long efforts toward judicial independence.[20]

## The Second Legal Reform: A Triumphant PRC Rejects the Western Model (1950s)

From its founding in 1921, the Chinese Communist Party (CCP) espoused the Marxist theory of history and claimed that its ultimate goal was to eradicate the system of private property and gradually attain the goals of Communism. Taking advantage of the Soviets' assistance, responding to the invasion from Japan, and benefiting from the internal divisions in the GMD, the CCP eventually developed into a major political force supported by a powerful army. In 1949 the CCP successfully toppled the GMD on the mainland and founded the PRC. If the PRC was a relatively weak state at its inception, it soon emerged as a powerful country after it forced the United States to sign an armistice over Korea in 1953. A triumphant PRC, with its profound faith in Communism and solid popular support, strongly repudiated Western political and legal systems (exemplified by democracy and judicial independence) and conducted a comprehensive legal reform in 1952 that aimed to overhaul the existing GMD legal systems.

The idea of a legal reform was also in line with the Soviet leader Lenin's argument that a proletariat revolution should abolish the old laws, smash repressive institutions, and establish new legal systems.[21] Shortly after the PRC was established and particularly during the Three Antis and Five Antis movements, the CCP found that most "old" GMD lawyers and judges were unqualified or corrupt or had sheltered capitalists or former GMD officials.[22] For example, the CCP mouthpiece, *People's Daily,* published an article in September 1952 charging "dark [evil]" GMD lawyers with having allegedly extorted 500 million yuan from their clients since 1949 and assisted many unlawful capitalists in winning lawsuits or obtaining reductions in their punishments.[23]

As a result of the distrust of GMD judicial personnel, the CCP not only abolished almost all GMD codes, but also discharged GMD judges and lawyers. The CCP appointed politically reliable cadres, most of whom were veterans, workers, and farmers, to replace the GMD judges. When facing questions about the amateurship of these workers and farmers, the Party contended that the fundamental issue of adjudication was nothing but to make clear who should be the target of the proletariat dictatorship of democracy.[24] Because of their palpable class status, worker- and farmer-judges could deal with adjudication very well.[25] By criticizing many GMD judges for believing in judicial independence, the CCP stressed that law was an instrument only of the ruling class (the proletariat or the capitalist) that was used to secure its power. As Stanley Lubman remarks, the CCP at this time also attacked "legal procedures," which were denounced as reactionary. While rejecting Western judicial norms and eliminating the GMD legal systems, the CCP embraced Soviet models by adopting the procuratorial and lawyer systems. Law schools and university law departments were established, and some Soviet-style law offices were opened sporadically from 1955 to 1957.[26]

Despite scholarly criticism of judicial dysfunction, massive torture, and police abuse of power in the early PRC,[27] various sources showed that certain forms of proceedings, if not Western procedural justice, were adopted in the early PRC. For instance, in August 1950 a circular from the Party Center regarding legal procedures stipulated that all judicial adjudications should stress hard evidence and not oral confession and prohibited extracting confessions through compulsion.[28] In many cases, the Supreme Court justice Dong Biwu (Tung Pi-wu, 1886–1975) in the early 1950s admonished Party officials—however futilely—not to interfere in the judicial process.[29]

Among the few bright spots in the early PRC legal system was the new marriage law created in 1950 and put into effect in 1952. Although the new PRC marriage law was similar in both particulars and objectives to the 1931 GMD code, it had taken steps to improve women's status in marriage. For example, unlike the GMD stipulation that had demanded couples marry in "an open ceremony" with at least two witnesses, the PRC law refused to recognize any marriage that "had not been registered with the local 'people's government,'" which the law claimed would prevent bigamy, a so-called feudal custom.[30]

## THE THIRD LEGAL REFORM: "VOLUNTARY" REOPENING TO THE WEST (POST-1978)

In 1977 Deng Xiaoping (Deng Hsiao-ping, 1904–1997), a veteran CCP leader who had been attacked during the Cultural Revolution (1966–1976), staged his third comeback as the head of the CCP. Firmly in control of Beijing and having removed the Maoists, he made a historical speech, "Emancipate the Mind," at the Third Plenary Session of the Eleventh Party Central Committee in 1978—a declaration of unprecedented seismic reform and an opening up to the world, to bring about the Four Modernizations of

China.[31] Having moved the nation away from the radical revolution and political struggles led by Mao Zedong (Mao Tse-tung, 1893–1976), Deng, as the leader of the second generation of the CCP, began a new era of dramatic economic reconstruction, which resulted in one of the fastest economic growths in world history. In addition, to avoid another "lawless" Cultural Revolution, the new PRC leaders, as Kang Youwei had some eighty years before, felt the urgent need for comprehensive legal reform. Deng in 1983 stated that it was imperative that both democracy and the legal system be strengthened. He also noted that more laws had to be enacted to meet the requirements of the ongoing economic reform.[32] Unlike their counterparts in both the late Qing and the ROC who had conducted legal reforms largely because of Western pressures, the PRC reformers in the post-1978 era reformed the legal system largely through a voluntary openness to the Western model from the top.[33]

Three decades after the PRC kicked off its voluntary legal reform, the achievements are phenomenal. By 2003 the National People's Congress (NPC) alone had passed 430 laws or relevant legal statutes. The State Council and local people's congresses had endorsed or passed 900 and 9,000 laws, respectively.[34] Many important legal instruments, such as the constitution, the Civil Law, the Civil Procedural Law, the Criminal Law, and the Criminal Procedural Law, were enacted in this period, especially after 1990. In 1999 the establishment of the rule of law in China was written into the constitution. To prohibit officials from violating people's rights, the PRC restored the former GMD Administrative Procedural Law in 1989, in the form of the Administrative Litigation Law. Furthermore, many laws have been revised several times to conform to the changing socioeconomic situation. According to one statistic, about 69 percent of laws passed by the NPC have been revised at least once, and 19.7 percent have been revised twice.[35] The constitution that was passed in 1982 has undergone three revisions, in 1988, 1999, and 2004.

As the legal reform deepened, the number of judges and lawyers sharply increased. In 1979 there were only 58,000 judges, but that figure rose significantly to 250,000 in 1997. Lawyers who had not been seen since 1957 reemerged during the legal reform. The number of lawyers jumped from virtually zero in 1979 to 50,000 in 1992 and 200,000 in the early twenty-first century.[36] As Harold M. Tanner notes, lawyers see their role as defenders of criminal suspects strengthened.[37] In this period people have also greatly expanded their legal consciousness, the result of massive coverage of law-related topics by national and local public media. In contrast to their countrymen in the past, Chinese people in the reform period are more willing to use laws to solve disputes. For example, in 1990 Chinese courts dealt with a total of 2.91 million cases. Since then, lawsuits have increased dramatically. For instance, in 2006 the number of cases accepted by Chinese courts had almost quadrupled.[38] One of the biggest gains in the legal reform was the CCP's promise to construct the rule of law in China, which became part of the 1999 constitution.

Some scholars have praised the progress made in the current legal reform. For instance, Randall Peerenboom argues that the PRC, despite many of its problems, has attained a somewhat "thin" rule of law.[39] Gong Pixiang, a Chinese legal scholar and official, even hails the present-day legal reform as a "revolution" from a rule of man to the rule of law.[40] Other scholars would, however, while acknowledging the achievements of the legal reform, paint a grim picture and find many problems in the legal system that would be difficult to resolve without fundamental political reform.

One of the key problems in the current legal system is the Administrative Litigation Law, which was passed by the NPC in 1989 and is aimed at protecting people from official infringement. More than twenty years after its passage, however, the law is largely ineffective. Only about 11.7 percent to 21 percent of administrative litigation cases have been successful.[41] Plaintiffs who are commoners seeking to appeal to an administrative court will face several almost insurmountable obstacles: persuading the court to accept their cases, hiring lawyers, getting official defenders to show up in court, implementing the court's decisions, and dealing with possible revenge.[42] For instance, many judges are military veterans whose inadequate professional training often results in unlawful judgments. In addition, all PRC courts, like those in the GMD period, are controlled by the Party, and local governments undoubtedly undermine both judicial independence and law enforcement.[43]

The biggest problem in the Chinese legal system is that the CCP itself often violates the law. Since the founding of the PRC, the CCP has launched many political campaigns, including the 1989 crackdown on the Tiananmen Square demonstrations in which numerous people were attacked, tortured, and even killed. In the reform period, the Party prefers to "strike hard" at crimes in ways that often violate the rights of persons to due process.[44]

In hindsight, we can see that significant progress has been made in all three legal reform movements since the late Qing. In the late Qing the reformers introduced a Western-style civil law that was separate from the criminal law, the dominant code in the dynasties. In the early ROC an administrative court was established to protect commoners' rights from government violations. Though temporarily abolished, the administrative court functioned in both the ROC and the PRC. From the late Qing to the PRC, women have seen a steady increase in their legal rights and are no longer legally inferior to men. Cruel and repugnant as they were to Westerners, corporal punishments such as slicing and whipping were abolished in the late Qing and their prohibition has generally continued into the twenty-first century. Although often ignored, all the constitutions that have been enacted and continually revised since the late Qing have granted Chinese people basic political and legal rights.

Unfortunately, the ruling party has been largely above the law and often violated the law, a persistent problem beginning from the late Qing to the PRC; it remains a critical hurdle to ongoing Chinese legal reform. Even on the eve of the 1911 revolution, the late Qing ruling party insisted on the supremacy of the emperor and emphasized in its constitution his subjects' duties over their rights. Similarly, while the ROC constitutions made people the masters of the state, the warlords and the GMD repeatedly violated the laws. The GMD even politicized the judiciary and made it virtually a tool of the party, especially in dealing with political enemies such as the CCP. Jiang Jieshi (Chiang Kai-shek), the president of the GMD, gave personal orders to assassinate political opponents.[45] In the early PRC the judiciary lost what little independence it had and became one of the state apparatuses of the CCP. Since 1978, despite all the laws passed by central and local congresses, numerous rights violations, such as massive crackdowns on political dissidents (e.g., the imprisonment of China's 2010 Nobel Peace Prize–winner, Liu Xiaobo), untold tortures, and property seizures, have been meted out in the name of the CCP.

## PROMISE AND REALITY

In comparison to the first two legal reforms, the post-1978 legal reform has drawn much more attention from scholars around the world. Most research has been done either by Western or Chinese scholars on a single topic or by groups of Western and Chinese scholars on a number of issues.[46] This book will be the first one whose authors are exclusively West-based Chinese scholars. Educated in both China and the United States, these scholars have the advantage of understanding both Chinese and U.S. cultures and therefore are able to provide cross-cultural contributions. Unlike the writers of most other books on Chinese legal reform, the authors of this book come from a variety of disciplines, such as political science, history, law, and sociology. For that reason, this book is able to examine modern-day Chinese legal reform from different perspectives. Moreover, as legal reform proceeds further, many aspects of the Chinese legal system, having already been transformed to some degree, are still evolving. To keep up with the ever-changing reform, many essays in this book also offer the latest developments in Chinese legal reform.

The chapters in this volume fall under three general headings: an approach toward the rule of law, legal reform, and civil liberties and human rights. Those that cover the first topic examine the Chinese government's ongoing efforts to construct the rule of law and the obstacles China faces. The chapters focusing on the second topic seek to explore various aspects of the country's legal reform, such as the sociolegal system, labor and business law, the death penalty for economic crimes, and the problems of drugs and prostitution. Chapters on the last topic analyze the effect of legal reform on civil liberties and human rights in China.

The first topic provides a historic overview and a case study to show China's difficult transition from its lawless past to a promised rule of law. In the first essay Qiang Fang studies the role of the public media in China's efforts to attain the rule of law, a topic that has rarely been touched by scholars. Fang centers his research on the *China Youth Daily*, one of the most influential newspapers in China, which published a total of over 10,000 law-related reports from 1979 to 2006. Fang shows that the newspaper, in conformity with the CCP's goal of moving toward the rule of law, has made significant contributions as it undertook three consecutive strategies. From 1979 to 1985 the newspaper was largely a staunch mouthpiece for the Party's new legal policies; it also functioned as an elementary educator of law in hopes of instilling basic legal knowledge in its readers. Then, between 1986 and 1998, as the pace of the legal reform escalated, the newspaper issued many more law-related columns to spread legal knowledge. In the years after 1998, when most people had acquired basic knowledge of the law, the newspaper shifted to comments on the problems of the legal system and to suggestions for improvement. On the question of whether legal reform has weakened the CCP's control over the public media, Fang argues that it has not. His study clearly demonstrates that the newspaper had always been a loyal tool of the Party and acted closely in accord with the Party's policies.

The political scientist Yuchao Zhu seeks to examine China's current construction of the rule of law through the "deviation in law practice," or, in other words, the disparity between law and actual practice. In the case of the Custody and Repatriation Law, Zhu shows that, though the original notion of the law was not harmful and was largely compatible with the socioeconomic environment, three elements (broad coverage, powerful police, and intrusiveness and coerciveness) have changed the measure in practice. His second case, the Letters and Visits Regulations, is an extrajudicial mechanism designed to assist people in obtaining legal justice. The latest regulations, in 2005, however, "seem to strengthen functional control rather than to correct deviation," as local governments have sent their agents to intercept complainants in Beijing or provincial capitals. Zhu argues that China's efforts to build a rule-of-law order are problematic because of the serious deviation of the practice of law. He attributes the deviation to the internal problems of China's legal and political systems, such as judges' subordination to same-level officials and political restriction on the judiciary. Zhu concludes that China currently does not have the requisite qualities for the rule of law in spite of its noticeable progress in legal reform.

Like Yuchao Zhu, Xiaobing Li also looks at the gap between the promise of the Chinese constitution and its real enforcement, an important yardstick of the efficacy of the rule of law in China today. Under the rule of Jiang Zemin, Li argues, the Chinese government intended to proceed to the rule of law and "adopted some measures for respecting and safeguarding political and human rights." Li shows, however, that the real practice of the rule of law has encountered serious setbacks in protecting people's freedom of speech and religion, both of which were addressed in the constitution. Aside from legislative limitation of people's freedom of speech, such as that itemized in the Four Basic Fundamental Principles, many nonlegal restrictions enacted by government agencies or Party policies have also checked public criticisms, complaints, and suggestions. Although Li acknowledges that the CCP is more tolerant of officially recognized religions, the Chinese government continues to crack down harshly on any unofficial popular religious movements and activities. In his conclusion, Li argues that it is up to the Chinese government to continue legal reform to conform to international standards and ensure the success of "further political reform."

The second topic, legal reform, offers a specific assessment of several important aspects of legal reform. The different legal policies on economic and political sectors set by the Chinese government in the reform period have drawn the interest of Jieli Li. Li defines difference as a "'double-track' socio-legality," which means the Chinese government is pursuing a legal formalization in the areas of the economy and commerce, but an administrative control over politics and ideology. Despite repeated legal reforms, the judiciary is "far from being a primary agent of social control because of its limited functions." Li also notes a tug-of-war between the Chinese government and lawyers that often results in government disbarment of dissident lawyers. In particular, Li studies the new labor law, which allows workers to resolve labor disputes through arbitration, but which ends up having limited efficacy. The reason is, as Li argues, that the law exists largely in name and not in real practice. The policy of double-track socio-legality should be regarded as an attempt by the Chinese government to regain its organizational grip over grassroots society. The nature of the current double-track legality in China, in Li's view, will tend, however, toward the rule of law with Chinese characteristics, which suits single-party socialism.

Yunqiu Zhang's study centers on labor law, a telling topic during Chinese economic and legal reform. Zhang's chapter probes the development of the labor law in a context of globalization. Zhang first looks at globalization's challenges to China's labor system. Because of superfluous labor forces, foreign employers tend not to respect Chinese workers' rights as they do those of their own countries' workers. At the same time, the Chinese government tries to appease foreign investors. The result is mounting disputes between Chinese labor and foreign employers that have triggered reform in labor laws. Influenced by the international labor convention, the Chinese labor law grants workers numerous rights, including freedom in employment, limited working hours, paid vacations, and the like. However comprehensive the labor law is, Zhang finds that there are several crucial omissions that will compromise the efficacy of labor law reform. One problem is that China has yet to incorporate into its labor law the core labor standards of the International Labor Organization, such as freedom of association, lest doing so scare foreign employers away. In addition, the labor law fails to outlaw child labor and Reeducation through Labor (RTL; *laojiao*), a system of administrative detention for petty crimes.

The relationship between China's entry into the World Trade Organization (WTO) and its legal reform is close. In his chapter, Xiaoxiao Li studies the enormous efforts of the Chinese government to conform to the requirements of the WTO after China joined the WTO in late 2001. Li argues that the WTO "offers the best opportunity" for China's legal reform and approach toward the rule of law. During the past decade or so China, as a WTO member, has actively promoted judicial reform. Li summarizes the most significant features of this legal reform as one shifting from quantitative to qualitative and from a government-driven model to a market-dominated model. In its attempt to enter the WTO, China was forced to make some legal modifications. One example is China's move to promulgate, revise, or cancel more than 2,300 regulations or rules by the State Council and to make laws public in order to change its image of lacking transparency. Li also discusses China's efforts to fulfill its commitment to the WTO. In addition, China has taken step to reform the structure of the customs system, improve officers' basic legal awareness, and develop organizations to oversee foreign trade. Li concludes that China has done much to adapt itself to the requirements of the WTO, and he hopes that the Chinese government will further diminish its interference in trade.

The death penalty for economic crimes is rather new for China. As LiYing Li's chapter shows, only two of twenty-eight crimes were capital crimes under the 1979 Criminal Law. The addition of death penalties for economic crimes started in 1982, and the number has grown as China's reform deepens. The 1997 criminal code made crimes such as bribery, currency speculation, and tax fraud subject to the death penalty. Li discusses the debate over the recent increase in these penalties. Some legal scholars have argued against the practice, and the Supreme People's Court responded by overturning problematic death sentences imposed by local courts. Li finds, however, that the Chinese public remains overwhelmingly supportive of death penalties for economic crimes, especially those committed by corrupt officials. Although China will maintain the death penalty in the near future, Li argues, the Chinese government has made plans to reform the Criminal Law and balance severity with leniency. The new direction of China, Li predicts, will leave unresolved such dilemmas as the large number of executions and the lack of government transparency.

Bin Liang and Liqun Cao question the current policies of the Chinese government on drug abuse and prostitution, both of which have existed for millennia. Liang and Cao first discuss the history of drug abuse and prostitution from early periods to the founding of the Republic of China. They argue that both problems were eliminated "entirely" in the early years of the PRC. Yet after China launched its ambitious economic reform in the late 1970s, drug abuse and prostitution reemerged and increased sharply. To crack down on these social vices, the Chinese government has created numerous laws and regulations, such as the Criminal Law and Anti-Drug Law. Serious violators of the laws and regulations are subject to harsh punishments, including the death sentence. Liang and Cao argue, however, that those policies have failed to repress drug abuse and prostitution. Using Western models, especially those from the United States, both authors recommend that the Chinese government abandon its draconian policies on drug abuse and prostitution because the problems are a part of a normal society and cannot be eliminated. A viable choice for the Chinese government, as Liang and Cao write, is to provide "a more sensible policy to minimize their harmful effects and provide medical treatment to those who need it."

The third topic, "Civil Liberties and Human Rights," include two chapters that deal with the effects of freedom of the press and human rights. Yuchao Zhu's chapter in this section deals with legal reform and human rights in China. While acknowledging the efforts made by the Chinese government toward legal reform since the early 1980s, Zhu shows that crucial instruments, such as the constitution, criminal procedural laws, and administrative laws, have failed to protect human rights. For example, Zhu argues that the constitution lacks provisions "to guarantee political and civil rights, and there exist very few restrictions on the state's arbitrary power." Likewise, despite the passage of the criminal procedural law, China still focuses more on substantive rather than procedural justice. In addition, lawyers' power remains limited, and judicial independence is compromised by the "structures of the court system." Zhu finds two trends in China, however: bringing the state back in and reinforcing a new rule of law. Although China subordinates human rights to economic reform, legal reform has heightened people's consciousness of their rights, and Chinese society has taken steps through media groups and citizens' open petitions to press the state to move toward human rights protection. To better protect human rights, Zhu suggests the need for a change in the legal institution and the "prudent or even conservative treatment of the current legal system."

Freedom of the press is an important constitutional right and key to the rule of law. Xiaobing Li examines the Chinese government's control over the public media. For a long time the CCP has regarded the media as its mouthpiece. During the reform period the Party has promised to increase citizens' access to information. Although it is true that the public's access to information has improved, the Party has taken several measures —such as government censorship of sensitive stories—to maintain its strict control over the media. Those measures, as Li shows, effectively limit the freedom of the public media and keep the bulk of the media in the national propaganda system. In addition, Li's chapter deals with the Party's control over the Internet, whose skyrocketing growth has posed a major threat to the Party's dominion over information and its circulation. As it has done to control the printed media, the CCP has increased its censorship in cyberspace in three ways: adopting new guidelines and technologies; enhancing identification procedures, including online registration; and punishing violators harshly. Li ends his chapter with calls for the Chinese government to respect people's constitutional rights.

Ever since the end of the Cultural Revolution, the second generation of the CCP's leaders, led by Deng Xiaoping, has promised to reform China's legal system to avoid a repetition of the "lawless Cultural Revolution." To fulfill its promise, all levels of Chinese governments and congresses have instituted thousands of laws in the past three decades. If the sheer number of laws enacted is not enough to demonstrate the CCP's intention of a lawful administration, then surely the restoration of judges, lawyers, and legal education that had been repudiated in the Cultural Revolution and the reestablishment of the ROC administrative court—its aim to better protect people from official violations—can be viewed as additional proofs. The culmination of the CCP's promise to overhaul its legal system came in 1997 when President Jiang Zeming declared that China would construct the rule of law. That promise was even written into the 1999 constitution.

Despite all the efforts the Chinese government has made to realize its promises to attain the rule of law, there exists considerable disparity between these promises and the reality. There is no denying that no country in the world has a perfect rule of law, but the government-backed violations of laws that it has enacted pose the biggest threat to the promise. As many authors in this volume show, the CCP does not intend to scrap its one-party rule and has violated its constitutional promises of freedom of speech and religion; the labor law that is designed to safeguard labor rights has fundamental defects; the deviation in law practice vitiates the CCP's promise of the rule of law; and the existence of a double-track sociolegality will also be a major obstacle to China's achieving the rule of law.

Though the CCP has tried to develop the rule of law with Chinese characteristics, the effort will not bear any concrete fruits as long as the Party itself is above the law.

It is conspicuous that most of the problems in the Chinese legal system more or less have correlations with the political institutions. Chinese leaders since Deng Xiaoping have all realized the importance of political reform to China's march toward the rule of law. They therefore have repeatedly promised to conduct political reform. Yet that promise has progressed little, a verdict that became especially clear after the 1989 Tiananmen Square incident. Today, more than one hundred years after Kang Youwei called for reform to save China, the biggest impediment to China's construction of the rule of law remains in the CCP's refusal to reform the political system. Until substantive reform in China's political sector occurs, the rule of law will still be a dream that exists more in the government's promise than in reality.

## Notes

1. Gongsun Yang, also called Lord Shang, was a famous legalist who conducted sweeping reform in the state of Qin that helped pave the way for Qin's eventual unification of China in 221 BCE. Wang Anshi was a renowned writer and reformer in the early Song dynasty (960–1270) who tried to strengthen the state. His reform was from the outset under heavy attacks by conservatives and was largely unsuccessful. After a new emperor ascended the throne and his conservative opponents regained power, Wang was dismissed. Zhang Juzhen was the prime minister in the late Ming dynasty (1368–1644) whose economic reform greatly improved the financial situation of the country. Zhang, unlike the other two reformers, was more fortunate for having escaped punishment during his lifetime, but he was denounced posthumously and his family became the scapegoat of his reform policies.

2. The Self-Strengthening Movement was initiated by reform-minded officials such as Zeng Guofan and Li Hongzhang in the midst of their military campaigns against the Taiping Rebellion (1851–1864), the largest farmers' rebellion in human history, in which approximately 20 million people perished. The officials generally believed in the doctrine that "Chinese learning is an essence and Western learning is an application" and thus refused to touch the realm of political reform.

3. Tang Zhijun, ed., *Kang Youwei zhenglunji* (The Political Comments of Kang Youwei) (Beijing: China Books, 1981), 1:212.

4. M. J. Meijer, *The Introduction of Modern Criminal Law in China* (Batavia: De Unie, 1950), 127–136; Philip C. C. Huang, *Code, Custom, and Legal Practice in China: The Qing and the Republic Compared* (Stanford: Stanford University Press,

2001), 15; and Xiaoqun Xu, *Trial of Modernity: Judicial Reform in Early Twentieth-Century China, 1901–1937* (Stanford: Stanford University Press, 2008), 27.

5. Xu, *Trial of Modernity*, 33.

6. Huang, *Code, Custom, and Legal Practice in China*, 33.

7. Zhang Sheng, *Minguo chuqi minfa de jindaihua: Yi guoyoufa yu jishoufa de zhenghe wei zhongxin* (The Modernization of the Civil Law in the Early Republic: Centered on the Integration of the Native Law and the Foreign Law) (Beijing: China University of Political Science and Law Press, 2002), 24–35.

8. *Guangxüchao xinfaling* (New Laws during the Reign of Guangxü) (Shanghai: Commercial Printing Publishers, 1909), 115–116.

9. Zeng Xianyi, ed., *Zhongguo fazhishi* (The Legal History of China) (Beijing: Beijing University Press, 2002), 246.

10. Ibid., 303.

11. Xu, *Trial of Modernity*, 58; Huang, *Code, Custom, and Legal Practice in China*, 51–58, 146; Klaus Mühlhahn, *Criminal Justice in China: A History* (Cambridge: Harvard University Press, 2010), 67; Qiang Fang and Roger V. Des Forges, "Were Chinese Rulers above the Law? Toward a Theory of the Rule of Law in China from Early Times to 1949," *Stanford Journal of International Law* 44, no. 1 ( 2008): 101–146.

12. For Wu Tingfang see Han Xiutao, *Sifa duli yu jindai zhongguo* (Judicial Independence and Modern China) (Beijing: Tsinghua University Press, 2003), 158–159, and for Xu Shiying see *Zhengfu gongbao* (Government Gazette) (Taiwan: Wenhai Publishing House, 1971), 8:358.

13. Huang Yuansheng, "The First Administrative Court in the Early Republic: Editing and Preliminary Study on the Pingzhengyuan in the Early Republic," in *Ershi shiji zhongguo fazhi de huigu yu qianzhan* (Retrospect and Prospect of the Twentieth-Century Chinese Legal System), ed. Zhang Jinfan (Beijing: China University of Political Science and Law Press, 2002): 211–212.

14. Zhang S., *Minguo chuqi minfa de jindaihua*, 36, 160.

15. Ibid., 126.

16. Huang, *Code, Custom, and Legal Practice in China*, 150, 192.

17. Mühlhahn, *Criminal Justice in China*, 66.

18. For a complete study on Republican prison reform, see Frank Dikötter, *Crime, Punishment, and the Prison in Modern China, 1895–1949* (New York: Columbia University Press, 2002); also see Mühlhahn, *Criminal Justice in China*, 83.

19. "Partyizing" the judiciary refers to the judiciary's being tightly controlled by the GMD. For example, judges had to be GMD members or had to support GMD principles.

20. Xu, *Trial of Modernity*, 84–90.

21. Guangdong renmin chubanshe (Guangdong People's Press), ed., *Jianjue daji youpai de jingong* (Resolutely Resists Rightists' Attack) (Guangzhou: Guangdong People's Press, 1957), 75.

22. Gong Pixiang, *Dangqian zhongguo de falü geming* (The Current Legal Revolution in China) (Beijing: Law Press, 1999), 116.

23. Lin Cheng, "Yanli jinzhi heilushide bufa huodong" (Strictly Forbidding Dark Lawyers' Illegal Activities), *Renmin ribao* (People's Daily), September 14, 1952; also see Guangdong renmin chubanshe, *Jianjue daji youpai de jingong* (Resolutely Resists Rightists' Attack), 74.

24. The term *proletariat dictatorship or democracy* is based on Karl Marx's classic works *The Communist Manifesto* and *The Civil War in France;* it means that after the working class takes power, it should establish the proletariat dictatorship and punish its class enemies (capitalists).

25. Guangdong renmin chubanshe, *Jianjue daji youpai de jingong* (Resolutely Resists Rightists' Attack), 74–75.

26. Stanley B. Lubman, *Bird in a Cage: Legal Reform in China after Mao* (Stanford: Stanford University Press, 1999), 73–76; and Bin Liang, *The Changing Chinese Legal System: 1978–Present* (New York: Routledge, 2008), 19.

27. Lubman, *Bird in a Cage,* 77.

28. "Passing the Circular of the Preliminary Opinions regarding the Legal Process and Form of Trial," *Hubei zhengbao* (Hubei Political Gazette) 9 (August 15, 1950): 100.

29. Mühlhahn, *Criminal Justice in China,* 187.

30. Susan L. Glosser, *Chinese Visions of Family and State, 1915–1953* (Berkeley: University of California Press, 2003), 172.

31. Deng Xiaoping, "Emancipate the Mind, Seek Truth from Facts, and Unite as One in Looking to the Future," in *Selected Works of Deng Xiaoping* (Beijing: Foreign Languages Press, 1994), 2:150–163.

32. Deng, "Neither Democracy nor Legal System Can Be Weakened," in *Selected Works of Deng Xiaoping,* 2:189.

33. Pitman B. Potter, *The Chinese Legal System: Globalization and Local Legal Culture* (New York: Routledge, 2001), 4; and Lubman, *Bird in a Cage,* 149.

34. *Renmin ribao* (People's Daily [Overseas Edition]), January 3, 2003; for a more detailed account of the laws passed by the NPC, see Guoli Liu, "Political Culture and Legal Reform," *American Review of China Studies* 1 (Winter 2000): 1–25.

35. Li Lin, "Kaifang sanshinian zhongguo lifa zhuyao jinyan" (Main Experiences of China's Legislation in the Thirty-Year Open Policy), *Xuexi shibao* (Study Times), August 2008.

36. For the number of judges see Lubman, *Bird in a Cage,* 253; for lawyers see Weixing Chen and Yang Zhong, *Leadership in a Changing China* (London: Palgrave Macmillan, 2004), 72.

37. Harold M. Tanner, *Strike Hard: Anti-Crime Campaigns and Chinese Criminal Justice, 1979–1985* (Ithaca: Cornell University Press, 1999), 19.

38. "Guansi xunmeng pansheng, fayuan ruhe yingdui" (How Do Courts Deal with Rigorously Rising Litigations?), *Jiaxing ribao* (Jiaxing Daily), July 24, 2007.

39. Randall Peerenboom, *China's Long March toward Rule of Law* (Cambridge: Cambridge University Press, 2002), 5–7.

40. Gong, *Dangqian zhongguo de falü geming* (The Current Legal Revolution in China), 5.

41. *Zhongguo falü nianjian* (The Encyclopedia of Chinese Law) (Beijing: China Law Encyclopedia Press, 1998–2004), 1999:1023; 2001:1258; 2002:1240; 2003:1321; 2004:1055; figures from between 1990 and 1997 are in Lubman, *Bird in a Cage,* 208.

42. Kevin O'Brien and Lianjiang Li, "Suing the Local State: Administrative Litigation in Rural China," in *Engaging the Law in China: State, Society, and Possibilities for Justice,* ed. Neil J. Diamant, Stanley B. Lubman, and Kevin O'Brien (Stanford: Stanford University Press, 2005), 31–53; Keyuan Zou, *China's Legal Reform: Towards the Rule of Law* (Leiden: Martinus Nijhoff, 2006), 22.

43. Lubman, *Bird in a Cage,* 3, 252–253; He Weifang, *Yunsong zhengyide fangshi* (The Way of Distributing Justice) (Shanghai: Sanlian Publishers, 2003), 8–11, 66–68; Benjamin L. Liebman, "China's Courts: Restricted Reform," in *China's Legal System: New Developments, New Challenges,* ed. Donald C. Clarke (Cambridge: Cambridge University Press, 2008), 90–120, esp. 72–73.

44. Lubman, *Bird in a Cage,* 168.

45. Frederic Wakeman Jr., *Spymaster Dai Li and the Chinese Secret Service* (Berkeley: University of California Press, 2003), 173–180.

46. See, for example, Clarke, *China's Legal System,* Diamant, Lubman, and O'Brien, *Engaging the Law in China,* and Karen Turner, James V. Feinerman, R. Kent Guy, eds., *The Limits of the Rule of Law in China* (Seattle: University of Washington Press, 2000); Gong, *Dangqian zhongguo de falü geming* (The Current Legal Revolution in China); Liu Junhai, ed., *Zhongguo ziben shichang fazhi pinglun* (A Review of the Rule of Law of China's Capital Market) (Beijing: Law Press, 2008).

Part One

# From Lawlessness
# to the Rule of Law

1

# Chinese Media and the Rule of Law

*The Case of the* China Youth Daily, *1979–2006*

## Qiang Fang

Since the early days of the Chinese Communist Party (CCP), CCP leaders such as Mao Zedong have repeatedly stressed the importance of public media to serve the people. According to Julian Chang, Mao first perceived the importance of political propaganda in the 1920s.[1] In 1942 Mao evidently stated that literature and art should serve only four kinds of people: workers, farmers, soldiers, and the urban petite bourgeoisie.[2] One year before the CCP took over China, Mao further addressed the role of newspapers, which would "allow the Party's principles, guidelines, policies, working goals, and methods to be spread to the masses in the quickest and broadest way." Because of the importance of newspapers, Mao also said that it was crucial for the Party to make them appealing to the masses and to correctly publicize the principles and policies of the Party.[3] In 1957, with Mao's encouragement, major intellectual newspapers began lambasting the wrongs of the Party. But as some criticisms went beyond the tolerance of the leaders, Mao and his adherents launched the Anti-Rightist Movement. They accused the editors of those newspapers of being reactionaries and rightists and believed that they stood against the masses.[4] During the Cultural Revolution (1966–1976) public media remained a pivotal tool of the CCP and, as Merle Goldman and Lowell Dittmer have argued, were even used as a weapon in political warfare.[5]

Shortly after the end of the Cultural Revolution, however, a reform occurred in public media that became a part of China's open policy. Indeed, the recent reform of the media is not the first one in the history of the CCP. According to Leonard L. Chu, three media reforms were conducted in the 1940s and the 1950s.[6] Yet, in terms of width and depth, the latest reform dwarfs all previous ones. Because of its significance, scholars around the world have spilled much ink over the post-1976 media reform in China.

Some scholars study the Chinese public media as a whole, while others center their attention on specific and individual media in this period.[7] Despite different approaches, most scholars tend to agree that this reform and consumerism have brought certain freedoms to China's press.[8] After the 1989 crackdown on the democratic movement, however, the Chinese government briefly tightened its control over the media.[9] After Deng Xiaoping made his "southern tour" to support further reform in 1992, and especially after the CCP terminated its subsidy to the government media, Chinese public media have undergone even more profound reform.[10] For the question of whether the media reform has weakened or strengthened the CCP's control over propaganda, however, there has been a disagreement between two schools of scholars. Researchers such as Daniel Lynch, James F. Schotton, William A. Hachten, Leonard Chu, and Paul Siu-nam Lee argue that the media reform has resulted in the receding of CCP's ability to mold people's values and beliefs,[11] whereas scholars such as Zhongdang Pan, Ashley Esarey, Marie Brady, and David Shambaugh contend that the reform has actually buttressed the Party's control over propaganda.[12] Both schools, as Guoguang Wu comments, have "certainly contained partial truth" and have enriched our understanding of the development of the Chinese public media in this period.[13]

In this chapter I shall not try to deal with this question directly. Instead, I shall examine one area that most scholars of Chinese public media have yet to explore: the role of Chinese newspapers in the CCP's repeated promises of the rule of law.[14] To better fill that gap, I shall study the *China Youth Daily* (*Zhongguo qingnianbao;* hereinafter *CYD*), a national newspaper that is both influential and representative. The reasons for choosing it are numerous. First, the *CYD* is run by the Chinese Communist Party Youth League, making the paper's importance second only to that of the CCP's primary mouthpiece, the *People's Daily*. Second, the *CYD* is one of the most popular newspapers in China.[15] Third, because most readers of the *CYD* are

毛泽东思想万岁

The Cultural Revolution. (University of Michigan)

young people, who constitute the biggest proportion of the criminals, the legal reports of the newspaper are very important. Fourth, as we will see, the *CYD* has since the mid-1980s devoted much energy and space to covering law-related reports that help promote the CCP's efforts to construct a rule-of-law China. More important, the *CYD* has always been regarded as one of the boldest national dailies, owing to its harsh criticisms and exposure of lawbreaking officials.[16]

Some questions to be asked in this research are: What kind of role did the *CYD* play in tandem with the CCP in promoting the CCP's goal toward the rule of law? When did the *CYD* begin to focus on legal issues? What steps did the *CYD* take to promote the rule of law in China? How and why did the newspaper adapt to the ever-changing political and legal situations in this period? Was the newspaper merely a propaganda tool of the Party? How did the *CYD* balance its reports to serve both the Party and the general readers? To what extent did the *CYD* help promote the cause of the rule of law in a reformed China? What are the limitations of the *CYD*?

To answer those questions, I shall first entertain the CCP's call for the rule of law[17] in the aftermath of the Cultural Revolution. Then I shall analyze the three major shifts of the strategies of the *CYD* from 1979 to 2006. Finally, I shall examine the historical role of the *CYD* in the course of China's march to the rule of law as well as its limitations.

## CCP's Engagement with the Rule of Law

Shortly after the tumultuous Cultural Revolution officially ended in 1976, the new leaders, including Deng Xiaoping, who had been attacked during the Cultural Revolution, called for legal reform. At the Third Plenary Session of the CCP held in late 1978, Ye Jianying, the president of the National People's Congress (NPC), claimed that since the establishment of the PRC, China had never had a decent legal system, which was the main reason that the Gang of Four was able to destroy the socialist legal system and cause numerous deaths. Therefore, Ye noted that "all nations should have a legal system that must have stability, continuity, and immense authority."[18] In 1979 Deng Xiaoping admitted that China had too few laws and asserted that China should have hundreds of new laws. "Neither democracy nor legal system," Deng continued, "should be loosely grasped."[19]

Indeed, legal reform marked a momentous period in China's lawmaking after 1978.[20] China's new leaders restored the procuratorate in 1978, which had been terminated in 1975, and the Ministry of Judiciary in 1979. Also in 1979 both Beijing and Shanghai allowed the reestablishment of the Lawyer Association. In 1979 and 1986 the NPC passed the Criminal Law and the Civil Law. The most important law enacted in the 1980s was the 1982 constitution, which stated that no person or organization "has the privilege of surpassing the constitution and law."[21]

In the 1990s, especially after the Fourteenth Plenary of the CCP in 1992 proposed the establishment of the socialist market economy and Jiang Zemin's call for making China a state governed by the rule of law in 1996,[22] legal reform drastically sped up its pace. A key rationale underscoring the rule-of-law effort was that leaders such as Jiang and some scholars believed that the market economy should be a rule-of-law economy.[23] Consequently, both the NPC and local congresses enacted thousands of laws. In the NPC alone, more than two hundred laws were established between 1989 and 2002, almost three times as many as were enacted in the 1980s. Many important laws such as the Judge Law, the Procurator Law, and the Criminal Procedure Law were promulgated in the 1990s. As Stanley

B. Lubman aptly notes, "Virtually every element of Chinese law today was either revived or newly created in the course of two decades of extraordinary economic and social change."[24]

As the mouthpiece of the CCP, public media have played a significant role in fostering the rule of law in this period. Being one of the most renowned and influential newspapers in the nation, the *CYD* undoubtedly played a role that was commensurate with its political and social status. To examine the role of the *CYD* in China's construction of the rule of law, I have collected and recorded almost all law-related reports published by the *CYD* between 1979 and 2006. During those twenty-eight years, there were a remarkable number of reports: about 13,670.[25] All the law-related reports can roughly be classified in the following five categories,

1. Propaganda: *CYD* carried out the principles of the CCP's leaders and the central government by publishing leaders' speeches and governmental orders on law, laws newly passed by the NPC, and crucial editorials from the *People's Daily*.
2. Problems of law enforcement: *CYD* published stories about cases involving problems of the courts, judges, police, and other law enforcement agencies.
3. Crusader and protector: *CYD* acted as a crusader against official violations of people's legal rights and a protector of aggrieved persons.
4. Comments, letters, and debates: *CYD* published commentary and letters written mostly by its reporters and legal specialists regarding the nature and internal problems of the modern-day legal system. Debates on certain legal issues were printed.
5. Educator and deterrent: Partly to follow CCP leaders' calls for constructing the rule of law, and partly to help instill legal sense and knowledge in the populace, the *CYD* served as both an educator and a transmitter of legal knowledge by telling readers what was illegal and what was legal through specific reports or cases. In addition, reports of the punishments imposed on the culprits functioned as a deterrent to potential criminals.

If we simply read a year's worth of *CYD* reports with these five categories in mind, we may not find any significant pattern. But after I examined the *CYD* reports for twenty-eight years, three distinct periods, each of which contains different clear emphases, emerged: Propaganda and Elementary

Educator (1979–1985), Propaganda and Professional Educator (1986–1998), Critic and Advocator of the Rule of Law (1999–2006).

## Propaganda and Elementary Educator (1979–1985)

Although legal reform was ignited by the CCP in the late 1970s, it seems that the wave of reform did not reach the public media immediately. During the seven years from 1979 to 1985, there was only minuscule coverage of law-related news or cases in the *CYD*. As Table 1.1 shows, reports in the *CYD* corresponding to the five aforementioned categories averaged about twenty-two per year. Most of the reports, seventy-seven, came from the fifth category, educator and deterrent.

In this short period the *CYD* published a total of twenty-eight reports that fell into the category of Propaganda. On July 5, 1979, an editorial ran in the newspaper titled "Studying Law, Following Law, and Protecting Law," which conspicuously reflected the tone and principles of the Party. "The seven laws passed by the second meeting of the Fifth National People's Congress are a big issue in our people's life," the editorial said. "It is important to enhance the socialist democracy and perfect the socialist legal system." In particular, the editorial admonished youth that it is an honor to abide by law and a shame to violate it. Yet the editorial seemed unclear about the true meaning of the rule of law, because it further claimed that

**Table 1.1.** Legal reporting in *China Youth Daily*, 1979–1985 (number of stories)

|  | Propaganda | Problems of law enforcement | Crusader and protector | Comments, letters, and debates | Educator and deterrent | Total |
|---|---|---|---|---|---|---|
| 1979 | 4 | 0 | 6 | 3 | 7 | 20 |
| 1980[a] | 5 | 0 | 1 | 2 | 13 | 21 |
| 1981 | 4 | 1 | 0 | 2 | 12 | 19 |
| 1982 | 6 | 0 | 4 | 1 | 6 | 17 |
| 1983 | 5 | 2 | 3 | 6 | 15 | 31 |
| 1984 | 0 | 1 | 6 | 5 | 12 | 24 |
| 1985 | 4 | 0 | 7 | 3 | 12 | 26 |
| Total | 28 | 4 | 27 | 22 | 77 |  |
| Average | 4 | 1 | 4 | 3 | 11 |  |

[a] Issues from July to September 1980 are missing from the Shanghai Library.

following the law was tantamount to following the Party.[26] In that sense, the Party is law and vice versa. This is a distortion of the principle of the rule of law, which essentially means that no one is above the law and the law must be applied equally.[27]

As a tool of the Party, the *CYD* also published laws that had been passed or promulgated by the NPC or the State Council.[28] For instance, right after the new 1982 constitution was passed by the NPC, the *CYD* published the complete text.[29] This publication had two functions. On the one hand, it mirrored the Party's policy; on the other, it helped publicize the law among the populace, some of whom might use the law to defend their constitutional rights.

Aside from editorials and laws, the *CYD* also published decisions and documents of the CCP's leaders regarding law. On July 25, 1981, the newspaper reported a decision of the Central Political and Legal Commission (*zhengfawei*), which was in charge of the legal apparatus (courts, procuratorate, and police) in China, that it was necessary for law-enforcement organs to punish criminals swiftly and severely.[30] Another report in July 1985 covered an announcement made by the head of the Central Disciplinary Committee (*zhongjiwei*) that the statewide struggle against serious economic crimes in 1983 had attained notable success, and thousands of Party officials had been punished.[31]

Educating people about law and expanding their legal consciousness was one of the most vital goals of the Party and its mouthpieces in the reform era. In November 1978 the *People's Daily,* the primary tool of the Party, sharply denounced the Gang of Four for the destruction of law during the Cultural Revolution and called on the Party to instill legal concepts (*fazhi guannian*) in the country's youth.[32] In 1985 Deng Liqun, the head of the CCP Propaganda Department, reiterated in a legal propaganda meeting the idea that the Party should educate all countrymen about the law and let them "correctly use law and conscientiously follow law."[33]

In this period the most popular and effective way for the *CYD* to inculcate people was by launching a column named "Legal Mailbox" (*Falu xinxiang*), which regularly published and answered readers' questions regarding law. Most of the questions were elementary and simple. For example, in December 1979 the *CYD* published a letter from Cao Dihua, a Shanghai reader, asking how to differentiate "law violation" (*weifa*) from "crime" (*fanzui*). Two legal scholars from the China Academy of Social Science were invited to answer the question. They told Cao that only the violation of the criminal law was considered a crime, and all other law violations were "general law violations," not crimes.[34] On October 9, 1984, a reader asked the *CYD* whether it was against the marriage freedom (*hunyin ziyou*) to dissuade some youths from cohabiting. A specialist named Ding Zhong replied on behalf of the newspaper that cohabitation was illicit because the marriage law required young couples to register before the law could protect them. Ding called for the Party and the Youth League to persuade young people to register their marriages and noted that this requirement was not meddling in their marriage freedom.[35] However simple, these letters and replies were intended to help the general public acquire some basic legal concepts.

Another way for the *CYD* to educate people was by publishing crime stories that served as a deterrent or warning to potential lawbreakers. On June 6, 1981, the *CYD* reported a decision made by the Chengde Intermediate Court in Shandong that severely punished several criminals who had raped, detained, and injured some women, including a fifteen-year-old student. Undoubtedly, the harsh punishments (two death penalties and two life sentences) that appeared in this report could impose intense psychological intimidation on many potential lawbreakers.[36] On May 25, 1985, the *CYD* reported that over one hundred young soccer fans in Beijing had been detained by police after they had joined a disturbance following a loss by their favorite team. This report could be seen to comprise functions of both education and deterrence. It educates the culprits by explaining that their actions were illegal and also deters or warns other youths against being involved in similar mêlées in the future.[37]

There were a total of thirty-one reports involving problems of law enforcement and official violations of law. I will cite one case for each category. On February 19, 1982, seventy-one antismuggling-law enforcers in Haifeng, Guangdong, were punished for having illegally released smugglers and embezzled a large amount of confiscated goods.[38] On October 16, 1984, a case in the *CYD* showed that after Liu Longrong, a young woman in Neixiang, Henan, opened up a grocery store with her husband, the head of the Industrial and Commercial Bureau, Xu Wendou, often came in the store and harassed Liu. When Liu rejected his harassment, Xu deliberately made things difficult for Liu and almost forced Liu to close her store. Despite criticism from his superior, Xu reportedly continued to abuse his power.[39] By publishing those stories of officials' and law enforcers' wrongdoing, the *CYD* not only acted as the Party's tool in strengthening central control over local officials but also performed a role as a conscientious moral defender of the victims, which in part is in compliance with the CCP's claim as a populist party.

Like the cases in categories 1 and 3, the number of comments, letters, and debates related to law in this period was also very limited; there was an average of merely three reports annually. On June 21, 1980, an editorial commented on a recent case in which a son of the mayor of Changchun, Jilin, had been executed for having brutally raped many young women. Invoking the case of Gao Ya'nei, a notorious son of the grand marshal in the Northern Song dynasty (960–1127) who had ignored the law because of his powerful father, the editorial remarked that the era of the lawlessness (i.e., the Cultural Revolution) was over, and everyone in China would be punished by law if he or she violated the Criminal Law. On July 17, 1984, the *CYD* published a reader's letter that encouraged young farmers to study law. "Since the door of becoming rich is open," the reader argued, "many young farmers do not know how to protect their legal rights and thus have been manipulated by others." The reader called on certain propaganda and judicial organs to heed the situation and help young farmers learn the law.[40]

In the first period, 1979–1985, despite calls for legal reform from the top, the CCP seems to have paid more attention to economic reform than to legal reform. This inference can be made from the limited number of law-related reports published in the *CYD*. The *CYD* published few laws in this period simply because the NPC did not pass many laws and CCP leaders made few speeches on the law. Nonetheless, the *CYD* was aware of the importance of educating people about law and of publishing crime stories that might help avert future law violations. With commercialization in its infancy and Party Secretary Hu Yaobang demanding that 80 percent of newspapers' reports be on the Party's achievements, the *CYD* had little incentive to publish sensational legal cases—mostly involving officials' law violations—to attract readers and advertisements.[41]

## Propaganda and Professional Educator (1986–1998)

During the second period, 1986–1999, the CCP, with repeated calls from top CCP leaders such as Deng Xiaoping and Jiang Zemin, accelerated its move toward the rule of law. Even the 1989 crackdown on the democratic movement did not halt legal reform. In this period the NPC and the Party Center passed or promulgated more laws than had been enacted during any other period in Chinese history. The culmination of legal reform occurred in 1996, when President Jiang Zemin declared that China should establish the rule of law.

To comply with the CCP initiatives, the *CYD* developed various measures in promoting the rule of law, some of which proved quite popular and effective. As shown in Table 1.2, the newspaper in this period disproportionately placed its focus on the fifth category, educator and deterrent; there were an average of 296 reports of this nature in this period compared to just 11 in the earlier period. The most likely reason was that the *CYD* believed that the first step toward establishing the rule of law was to learn what was legal and illegal. To bolster its educator's role with regard to the law, the *CYD* created a number of columns, such as "Legal Society" (*Fazhi shehui*) and "Legal System and the Military" (*Fazhi junshi*), which focused specifically on law. Later, in the 1990s, as the scale and dimensions of the socioeconomic reforms deepened, new columns such as "Economic Information" (*Jingji lanxun*), "Weekly" (*Zhoukan*), "Life Special" (*Shenghuo tekan*), "Icepoint" (*bingdian*), and "Education Guide" (*jiaoyu daokan*) were initiated to cover the economy, education, and other aspects of society. Many of them also reported on legal cases and the news.

Being a major tool of the Party, the *CYD* in this period also contributed much space, especially on the front page, to newly passed laws, regulations, and CCP leaders' speeches on legal topics. Yet the *CYD* paid less attention to comments and debates on law; the annual increase in this category lagged far behind those of the first and fifth categories. As was true in the earlier period, reports on the problems of law enforcement and official lawbreakers were given the least treatment by the *CYD*.

At the beginning of 1986 the *CYD* inaugurated a column titled "The Legal Society," which heralded a new age for the newspaper's role in the ongoing legal reform. The column appeared every week and was devoted solely to legal reports and cases. Though there were pragmatic reasons behind the *CYD*'s move, such as intense media competition and a reduction in the Party's subsidies,[42] the column aimed mostly to broaden people's legal knowledge and intimidate potential lawbreakers.

On January 30, 1986, for example, in the column's initial appearance, the *CYD* published an article titled "They Don't Believe It Was a Theft." According to the article, four young men and women from Beijing who had been working in a private electronics factory in Shenzhen, the foremost special economic zone in China, for several years were ready to go

Table 1.2. Legal reporting in *China Youth Daily*, 1986–1998 (number of stories)

| | Propaganda | Problems of law enforcement | Crusader and protector | Comments, letters, and debates | Educator and deterrent | Total |
|---|---|---|---|---|---|---|
| 1986 | 15 | 0 | 5 | 8 | 139 | 167 |
| 1987 | 5 | 0 | 12 | 3 | 85 | 105 |
| 1988 | 7 | 4 | 17 | 11 | 89 | 128 |
| 1989 | 22 | 1 | 10 | 9 | 60 | 102 |
| 1990 | 24 | 0 | 2 | 10 | 82 | 118 |
| 1991 | 22 | 0 | 2 | 11 | 101 | 136 |
| 1992 | 16 | 0 | 3 | 5 | 123 | 147 |
| 1993 | 30 | 0 | 4 | 7 | 187 | 228 |
| 1994 | 64 | 2 | 10 | 14 | 319 | 409 |
| 1995 | 73 | 2 | 3 | 31 | 616 | 725 |
| 1996 | 62 | 0 | 7 | 5 | 771 | 845 |
| 1997[a] | 64 | 3 | 7 | 33 | 679 | 786 |
| 1998 | 49 | 5 | 7 | 22 | 603 | 686 |
| Total | 453 | 17 | 89 | 169 | 3,854 | |
| Average | 35 | 1 | 7 | 13 | 296 | |

[a] Issues from the month of October are missing from the Shanghai Library.

home. But they tried to "take" a few tape recorders, then a rare and precious product, from the factory with them to Beijing. They did not know their action was a theft because, as one of them said after they were tried by a court, " 'Taking' things from a capitalist should not be regarded as theft."[43] Obviously, this report intended to educate people, particularly young people, that "taking" things without permission or payment was a crime.

In another article, published in January 1995, the *CYD* reported that of a number of rape victims, from middle school students to young women, none had called the police. The report worried that the dearth of legal consciousness among young people could complicate relatively simple cases. The report thus called on responsible organs to educate the young regarding the law.[44]

In the first few years after 1986, the efforts of the *CYD* to impart legal consciousness were still centered on elementary and basic legal knowledge, mostly regarding violations of criminal law. As economic reform widened and people's legal consciousness increased, however, the newspaper gradually introduced more columns to cope with the increasingly complex socioeconomic situations and specific legal inquiries from its readers. As a result, the total number of legal reports jumped from about one hundred to several hundred after 1993. For instance, in October 1994 a reader named Lin Jun asked what the new law on the personal income tax meant and whether he should voluntarily pay that tax. Such a question had been irrelevant in the past because there had been no tax on personal income. For this specific and professional legal inquiry, the *CYD* responded that the new personal tax law had markedly stipulated all types of personal taxes. All earners of "personal income from salaries, wages, rewards for labor, bonuses, dividends, interest, and property rental," the *CYD* pointed out, "along with six other income types ascertained by the Ministry of Finance, should pay personal income tax." Also, the *CYD* indicated that an individual had to pay a tax only on the portion of his or her monthly income that was above 800 yuan ($120).[45]

On April 29, 1996, a company manager wrote to the *CYD* explaining that an employee had taken away the materials of some clients of the company after he resigned. When asked to return the materials, the employee argued that those clients belonged to him and he had the right to take their materials. The manager said that the missing materials caused a loss of 300,000 yuan ($45,000) to his company. He wondered whether the materials of clients were a commercial secret and whether the employee had any legal liability. The *CYD*'s answer confirmed that those client materials were a commercial secret as defined by the Anti–Unfair Competition Law: commercial secrets consist of both technological and managerial (*jingying*) materials. Hence, the *CYD* believed that the employee's activity was against the law and the manager should file a civil lawsuit against him.[46]

Besides inquiries about economic laws, the *CYD* also received and answered legal questions on other issues. In August 1994 a reader named Zheng Yunyan wrote the *CYD* a letter. According to Zheng, after a female farmer was knocked down by a motorcycle, she was sent to a local hospital. But two days later she was discharged by the hospital for unknown reasons and thereafter became paralyzed because of the lack of timely treatment. When the victim appealed to certain government officials, she was given only 1,000 yuan ($150). Zheng asked on behalf of the victim if she could lodge a lawsuit. Compared with issues raised in the 1980s, this question was more specific and "professional"—one that only a specialist could answer. A lawyer representing the *CYD* replied. "According to article 119 of the General Rules of the Civil Law [*minfa tongze*]," the lawyer noted, those responsible for "all injuries caused by impairing a citizen's body must pay the costs of medical treatment, reduced income due to delay of work [*wugong*], and living subsidies for paralyzed victims." The lawyer argued that because the victim's paralysis was caused by the motorcyclist, the motorcyclist had to be responsible for all compensation, and that the initial payment of 1,000 yuan was far less than the needs of the victim. The lawyer finally urged the victim and her relatives to appeal to the local court.[47]

The *CYD* sometimes encouraged readers to protect their rights through legal or other channels. In February 1997 an article titled "What to Do If [You] Can't Afford to Hire a Lawyer: Go to the Legal Aid Center" provided aggrieved people with a viable venue, the Legal Aid Center, to seek justice. According to the article, when tens of millions of poor Chinese encountered legal issues, it was almost impossible for them to hire lawyers. The article quoted an official of the Legal Aid Center Preparation Group of the Department of Justice as saying that the purpose of the Legal Aid Center was to ensure that all citizens, regardless of their social status, age, property ownership, and intelligence, could enjoy equal legal protection. Moreover, the Legal Aid Center was said to be an important extension of the effort to protect human rights.[48] Although the actual efficacy of the Legal Aid Center was dubious, it at least gave poor, desperate people some hope that their grievances would be redressed.

As was true in the first period (1979–1985), many cases reported by the *CYD* in this period had both educational and deterrent functions. For example, on April 1, 1991, the *CYD* reported that Wang Shuhua, an unemployed woman in Beijing, had illegally produced a fake medicine and sold it for profits. Wang was arrested in February 1990 and later sentenced to three years.[49] In another case, reported on August 18, 1994, a man from Henan province was sentenced to eight years because he had forged official documents, identification cards, and seals, including even military and judicial seals. Although the man made a profit totaling only 2,000 yuan ($300), his crimes were deemed serious by the court because they "adversely influence national governments' formal activities and images."[50]

Furthermore, in April 1997, when Yu Xiumei, a woman living in Chenguan, Henan, rushed to her natal home to see her sick mother, she forgot to tell her husband her whereabouts. When Yu came home the next day, her husband, Hu Dongpo quarreled with her and beat her for about half an hour. While Yu was staying in a local hospital for treatment afterward, Hu refused to apologize. Yu then sued her husband in court. The court ruled that Hu should apologize to Yu and pay 5,000 yuan (US$750) for the cost of Yu's care at the hospital. Hu later said that he now understood that it was unlawful to beat even his wife.[51] Similar functions could also be found in *CYD*'s reports of corrupt officials, though those reports were often meant more as deterrent than as education. In March 1988 the *CYD* reported that Liu Dazhao, the head of the Yexiang Court, Henan, had been detained for being involved in exorbitant gambling. Liu was subsequently stripped of his Party membership and lost his official position.[52]

Despite dwindling subsidies from the Party, the *CYD* remained a loyal propaganda tool in these years. This period also saw the CCP's legal reform reach a crescendo around 1996, when Chinese leaders formally announced the establishment of the rule of law. At the outset of this period, in January 1986, the *CYD* published an editorial that reflected the CCP's first five-year plan to enhance the public awareness about law (*puji falu guihua*). The editorial argued that disseminating legal knowledge was a mission proposed by the CCP and the State Council and was thus a major duty of all youth leagues. "To spread legal knowledge, [we] should educate all citizens, especially the young, to know, understand, and abide by the law," the editorial remarked. "[We] also want youths to know that they possess the most formidable weapon—law—in their fights with various illicit activities."[53]

The *CYD* continued to report top leaders' speeches, meetings, and orders regarding law. For example, on December 17, 1992, the *CYD* reported on President Jiang Zemin's talk at a national meeting on politics and law in which he addressed the significance of law in the establishment and running of China's socialist market economy. Jiang also noted that a major problem being faced by the government lay in law enforcement and the authority of the socialist legal system: "All levels of Party committees and governments must exemplarily enforce the constitution and the law, avoid and correct deeds such as using words to replace law, using power to press law, or interfering with the enforcement of law. Meanwhile, [the government] must take action to advocate and supervise courts' and procuratorates' exercising their power independently and enforcing the law impartially."[54] In March 1995 the *CYD* reported a talk given by Qiao Shi, the president of the NPC, pressing for China to speed up the pace and improve the quality of its legislation if China wanted to adapt itself to the development of the socialist market economy.[55] Like the *People's Daily*, the

*CYD* covered the whole report by Jiang that the CCP had clearly made the rule of law its basic principle in leading the country.[56]

Publishing new laws and regulations passed or promulgated by the NPC and the State Council was another mission of the *CYD*. There were far more laws and regulations created in this period than in the previous period. Although the *CYD* did not publish all the new laws and regulations, it published many of them in full. For instance, on April 15, 1991, the *CYD* reported the whole text of the latest Civil Procedural Law. On January 24, 1997, the newspaper published the full contents of a regulation of the Department of Central Propaganda regarding paid journalism (*youchang xinwen*) that strictly prohibited all public media and media workers from asking for any rewards for reports and from buying and selling book license numbers (*maimai shuhao*).[57]

Between 1986 and 1998 the average number of comments, debates, or letters on law published by the *CYD* was thirteen per year, which, unlike categories 1 and 5, was not considerably bigger than that in the first period. The comments, debates, and letters in this period, however, proved to be more sophisticated than those in the first period, when most comments or letters tended to stress the significance of law or to encourage people to learn basic laws. The *CYD* established columns such as "Youth Comments" (*Qingnian pinglun*) and "The Platform of Legal Debate" (*Falu bianluntai*) for professional comments and debates on law.

On November 28, 1992, the CYD published a comment titled "How Can Law Have Loopholes?" According to the piece, the head of a factory had been sentenced to fifteen years in prison for having been involved in prostitution and rape. But he was released by the government one year later because he was a highly capable manager and the factory could not prosper without him. "The nature of the case," the author wrote, "is no more than using power to replace law or using words to replace law." The commentator went on to argue that the legal loophole actually smashed the popular dictum of "equality before law."[58]

To dig out more loopholes in the legal system, the *CYD* introduced the column "The Platform of Legal Debate" in the early 1990s, which occasionally held debates on different topics among legal specialists and ordinary readers. For instance, on December 22 and 29, 1997, the *CYD* printed a debate on the issue of whether to adopt lethal injection or continue using the traditional method (shooting) in executions. Some readers believed that the traditional method of execution had an intimidating and therefore deterrent effect on potential criminals, particularly the most flagrant, but other specialists contended that lethal injection was more humane and that it also reflected the progress of human civilization.[59] Through the debate, readers of the *CYD* could come to a better understanding of the issue.

As they had in the first period, categories 2 and 3 continued to receive the least attention from the *CYD*. The average annual reports barely increased. Yet the *CYD* still unearthed many problems of law enforcement and official lawbreakers. In one case reported on December 1, 1997, Judge Zhao Huanchi of Minsheng Road Court in the Linwei district, Shanxi, issued a subpoena on November 4 to the manager of Weinan Food Service Company, requesting that the manager come to the court. On the next day, however, the company sent a letter to Zhao arguing that, according to a recent document of the Linwei district government, any court's subpoena first had to have permission from the district leaders. Thus, the company's letter noted, the manager would not come to the court as requested. This document, which surprised Zhao, was in fact against the Organic Law of the People's Court (*Fayuan zhuzhifa*). When asked, a district leader merely conceded that the document should be "perfected." The *CYD* report commented with sarcasm that it was not the document but some leaders' legal consciousnesses that needed to be perfected.[60]

In another case, the *CYD* disclosed a brazen case of law violation. In November 1997, when a female college graduate went to the Center of Exchange of Talent (*rencai jiaoliu zhongxin*) in Wulong county government, Chongqing, for a job interview, the head of the center, Luo Yongsheng, lured the student and raped her. After the student appealed to the county government, Luo admitted his crime. But the county Political and Judicial Commission, along with other judicial and police units, completely ignored the facts and later reached a consensus that Luo had actually had consensual sex with the student and had not raped her. Therefore, the county government rejected the police's request to prosecute Luo and simply dismissed Luo from all his official posts.[61] This case revealed that officials in Wulong could freely neglect the law and make their own decisions.

The period from 1986 to 1998 saw one of the fastest growing economies in Chinese history. As economic reform escalated, legal issues became more convoluted. The *CYD* responded to new challenges with law-related columns such as "Law and Society" and "Youth Comments," which included specialists' opinions. In addition, the CCP published more laws to deal with the ever-changing socioeconomic environment. Its loyal tool, the

*CYD,* served as the Party's mouthpiece publishing these new laws, regulations, and leaders' addresses and orders on law.

## CRITIC AND ADVOCATOR OF THE RULE OF LAW (1999–2006)

After President Jiang Zemin publicly stated that China would construct the rule of law in 1996, the CCP stepped up its efforts and made the rule of law a part of the 1999 constitution. As a CCP mouthpiece, the *CYD* adjusted its contents to suit the new Party direction. The newspaper developed columns such as "Youth Topics" (*Qingnian huati*), "Scholar's View" (*Xuezhe guandian*), "The Rule of Law and Society" (*Fazhi shehui*), and "The Legal Eye" (*Fayan*), which published comments and served as forums for legal specialists and the general public to critique the legal system, many of whom touched on the fundamental problems of the legal system as well as China's politics. As a result, the number of law-related comments ballooned dramatically in this period. In Table 1.3 we can see that the average yearly number of category 4 articles increased almost thirty times over the annual average in the second period (1986–1998), an increase far bigger than that of any of the other categories.

China joined the World Trade Organization (WTO) in 2002, which greatly expanded China's exports. Taking advantage of its membership in the WTO, China enjoyed almost another decade of economic boom.[62] The fast-growing economy, however, also triggered corruption among officials, who often benefited from violating the law or people's legal rights. Furthermore, pressed by the unprecedented, fierce competition among more than two thousand newspapers, the *CYD,* like other Party tools such as the *People's Daily* and the Xinhua News Agency, had no choice but to grasp for any revenues to survive.[63] Accordingly, to deal with the surge of officials' lawbreaking and also to attract both readers and advertisements, the *CYD,* as its Western counterparts have done for a century, covered more legal cases than it had before.[64] In many such cases, *CYD* journalists stood on moral ground and defended the rights of the commoner victims.

As Table 1.3 shows, the number of reports in categories 1, 2, and 3 also witnessed significant increases. Even so, the entire number in categories 2 and 3 was still minute in contrast with other categories.

The most striking feature in this period is, indeed, the extraordinary nearly thirty-fold increase in category 4 stories annually over the annual average in 1986–1998. To promote and perfect the rule of law, the *CYD*

| | | Problems of law enforcement | Crusader and protector | Comments, letters, and debates | Educator and deterrent | Total |
|---|---|---|---|---|---|---|
| | Propaganda | | | | | |
| 1999 | 138 | 16 | 19 | 112 | 583 | 868 |
| 2000 | 77 | 15 | 23 | 300 | 650 | 1,065 |
| 2001 | 84 | 13 | 6 | 375 | 769 | 1,247 |
| 2002 | 83 | 5 | 4 | 452 | 864 | 1,408 |
| 2003 | 61 | 8 | 8 | 361 | 684 | 1,122 |
| 2004 | 46 | 17 | 3 | 441 | 637 | 1,144 |
| 2005 | 31 | 10 | 3 | 387 | 639 | 1,070 |
| 2006 | 31 | 9 | 2 | 334 | 640 | 1,016 |
| Total | 551 | 93 | 68 | 2,762 | 5,466 | |
| Average | 69 | 12 | 8 | 345 | 683 | |

Table 1.3. Legal reporting in *China Youth Daily*, 1999–2006 (number of stories)

started several columns devoted to comments, letters, and debates on a wide variety of internal problems in the legal system, such as the rule of law itself, judicial problems, government violations of law, police abuse of power, loopholes in the law, and the like. Because of the large number of comments, some columns, such as "Youth Topics," were published almost every other day.

On May 29, 2000, Liu Wujun, a researcher at the Judicial Institute of the Judicial Ministry, argued in the "Scholar's View" column against the prevailing opinion that the rule of law was omnipotent. "Law can punish criminals but cannot cure marriage and family difficulties," Liu wrote, "In a word, law's functions are limited and relative. Any exaggeration of the rule-of-law functions is unacceptable and may even result in negative effects." Liu argued that people should be alarmed that overemphasis of the rule-of-law notion could engulf the autonomy of both market logic (*shichang luoji*) and the private sphere. "The most important aspect of the rule of law," Liu concluded, "is to respect legislative principles and judicial disposition."[65]

The internal problem of the judiciary was a magnet for commentary. For example, on July 1, 2002, the *CYD* published a comment on a legal case in Guangdong that had happened a week before. According to the writer, because the main shareholder of a company that had lost a case at a local court was the former head of the Guangdong Police Department, the Guangdong High Court, arguably under the influence of the shareholder and former official, "ordered" the local court to postpone the enforcement of the verdict. As a result, the winner of the lawsuit had to appeal to the Supreme Court and waited seven more years before justice finally came. The writer argued that the decision of the Guangdong High Court had violated the constitution and relevant laws, which explicitly stipulated that the upper courts could only supervise rather than lead the lower courts. Therefore, "no matter how complicated a case the judges are facing, they should not ask the upper courts for instructions."[66]

Another comment in the same year addressed the problematic coordination among police, the procuratorate, and the court. The comment brought a real case to light. When an execution was about to be carried out, an order from the Supreme Court suddenly came and stopped the execution. The author, the legal observer Tong Dahuan, argued that the problem in the case lay in the relations among the police, procuratorate, and the court. "To use a metaphor, the police is the cook, the procurator carries the food, and the court eats." Tong added, "In other words, whatever food the police cook, the procurator will carry, and the court will eat. It is the police, not the court, that decide the case." In that case, although the police did not have sufficient evidence against a suspect, the procurator still filed a public prosecution, which the judge would decide. The key to solving the problem, Tong wrote, "is to create a framework in which there exists an equal and balanced relationship between prosecutors and defenders. In that framework, judges will be neutral."[67]

Political meddling in court decisions, among other topics, has been and is still a critical problem in China's march toward the rule of law. In this period the *CYD* published many comments on this serious but ingrained issue. On October 8, 2001, the column "Icepoint Comment" (*bingdian shiping*) posted an article titled "'The Local Emperor' Gives Orders to the Gongjianfa [police, procuratorate, and court]." According to the article, before his arrest, Du Baoqian, the former Party secretary of Lushi, Henan, had been a typical "local emperor" who had made the Gongjianfa his "family servants" (*jiading*). The "family servants" would punish whoever petitioned the media or upper-level governments against Du. After a cadre exposed Du's illegal activities, Du ordered him imprisoned under the fabricated crime of "embezzling specific funds." When the local court decided that the cadre was innocent, Du rebuked the court and insisted on his order. "The existence of local emperors is not a surprise," the commentator argued; "what stuns me is that the judicial organs still have no legal consciousness after a dozen years of legal education. . . . The linchpin of the problem is that those judicial officials want only to protect their positions rather than to die for law."[68]

Three years later, in November 2004, a comment questioned an "Upright Promise" (*lianjie chengnuo*) in most governments that demanded leading cadres be the first in following law. The author's rationale was that abiding by the law is a duty of everyone and not just of the leading cadres. In other words, leading cadres' abiding by the law did not have any moral meaning. "In a rule-of-law society, following the law is the duty and obligation of every official. Why is any [person] to be the first [following the law]?" the writer asked.[69]

Police abuse of power was another major issue in the comments. In one example, the legal specialist Guo Songmin discussed a case in July 2006. After Cheng Bolin, the head of a health center in Renshou, Sichuan, filed a complaint with the provincial people's congress, the mail-and-visit office of the congress requested some leaders of Renshou to come to the congress for a talk. A group of Renshou county policemen broke through the barrier of the congressional guards, however, and forcefully took Cheng away. Guo argued that this case did not merely expose the police abuse of power but also showed that the police had actually tried to subordinate the highest organs of power to their will. "If they dare to break into the congress to seize the complainant today," Guo warned, "tomorrow they will capture the congressmen. . . . The termination of this road is that law completely loses its dignity." Guo finally offered two solutions: the monopoly of appointing cadres by the local top leader had to be halted, and the authority of law should be established.[70]

Some comments also focused on the insufficiency of the contemporary law. On July 14, 2006, the *CYD* published a comment by Wang Yijun, who raised concerns about the poverty, abuse, lack of education, and psychological trauma suffered by children whose parents were in custody. But, as Wang pointed out, there was not yet any law or regulation that could assist those children. Even though some warmhearted individuals or organizations had offered certain assistance, it was insufficient. The new measure of the Civil Department—Opinions Regarding Strengthening the Aid to Orphans—while promising, was limited to orphans. Wang concluded with an appeal for the state to fill the legal gap and help those innocent children.[71]

In this period there were a few legal debates reported by the *CYD*. In

April 2005 a debate over "covert law enforcement" (*anzhong zhifa*) by the traffic police appeared in the *CYD*. On the one side, the legal scholar Yang Tao argued that, despite the fact that the traffic police might create traps to obtain more fines, the key to eliminating this defect was for drivers to voluntarily follow the traffic regulations. As a supplement to the police, Yang argued, covert law enforcement is necessary. Contrary to Yang, Kang Jing, another specialist, asserted that it is wrong for traffic police to enforce the law secretly. "The legal ethics that 'everything is legal until it is against law' is an inalienable right for law-abiding citizens," Kang wrote, "but it means just the opposite to law enforcers, who hold that 'nothing is legal unless it is stipulated by law.'" Although the traffic police in many foreign cities practice covert law enforcement, they are invariably under checks and supervision. But in China the supervision of law enforcers is imperfect. Kang listed three preconditions for viable covert law enforcement—legitimate authorization, limited power of free adjudication, and broad complaint channels. Without them, covert law enforcement by traffic police would probably violate the law.[72]

With a total number of 5,466 for the years 1999–2006, the reports in the legal education and deterrence category remained the most popular. This was partly because of rising consumerism and the skyrocketing violations of the law by officials, both of which were byproducts of reform. Additionally, the *CYD*, assuming that most people, if not all, possessed sufficient basic legal consciousness after decades of legal education, tried to tell readers only what activities were unlawful, what the meanings of some laws were, and what the newly passed regulations and laws were.

For instance, in the spring of 2001, the brother of Gong Guangbin, an armed policeman in Hebei, went to a Shandong oil field to see his friends. But the guards there mistook him for a terrorist and beat him to death. When the guards realized that they had killed an innocent person, they offered Gong's father 1 million yuan ($150,000) to privately settle the case. Gong's father was inclined to accept the offer because of the huge amount of reparation. But after Gong heard about the case, he told his father and the guards that settling a case in private was illicit; he persuaded the guards to surrender themselves to the police. As a result, Gong's father got more than 100,000 yuan ($15,000) in compensation and the guards were punished according to the law. The writer of this case praised Gong and urged readers not to settle cases out of court.[73]

One year later the *CYD* published an article entitled "What Is the Constitution?" by Li Jian, a law professor at China Renmin (People's) University. Although most readers would have been familiar with the constitution, Li attempted to explore that document through its origin and historical development in the West. Li also stressed two important features of the constitution: the granting of citizens' rights and the restriction of government power. Li ended his article by lambasting some state organs, particularly county and township governments, for acting on their own will, which resulted in widespread violations of citizens' rights. "These phenomena [officials' violations of the law] seriously obstruct the formation of a constitutional order . . . and should be eradicated completely," Li wrote.[74]

The *CYD* usually reminded readers about certain new laws that they could use to protect their legal rights. In but one of these cases, the *CYD* on October 14, 2004, publicized a new regulation formulated by the Shanghai High Court that clarified in which cases citizens could apply for state compensation and how to do so. The new regulation made clear that, for example, the court should render compensation for: the false arrest of an innocent person in a criminal case, a loss caused by unlawful sequestration of property, or the injury or death of a citizen as a result of torture. The regulation also allowed citizens to appeal to the upper court for decisions on compensation. Undoubtedly, this report was a great help to citizens in their quest for state compensation after they had been wronged by law enforcers—although the state compensation system itself has many fundamental problems.[75]

As they had in the past, some educational cases also functioned as deterrents. Because of official pragmatism in the 1990s, cases involving official corruption sharply increased. To check rampant graft, the CCP and its mouthpieces exposed numerous corrupt officials. In one case, the *CYD* reported on August 11, 2000, that Zhang Xiufa, the former head of the Bureau of Hunan Post and Telecom, was being investigated for taking huge bribes. Zhang also lost his seat in the NPC.[76] In another report, in November 2003 four policemen in Hubei who had wrongly accused three virgins of prostitution and tortured them were sentenced to prison.[77]

In this period the *CYD* continued to be a faithful tool of the Party, publishing Party policies, newly passed laws, and leaders' repetitive speeches on justice and law. After 1999 the *CYD*, like all other mouthpieces, published numerous reports denouncing the Falun Gong, a religious organization that had been deemed a political threat by the Party. On March 24, 2004, the *CYD* reported President Hu Jintao's remarks delivered at a national lawyers' conference that the government should bolster the "thought work" of lawyers. Hu hoped that lawyers would enforce the law for the people and defend judicial justice. Similar speeches were also made by Supreme Court justices and the Legal System Office of the State Council (*Fazhiban*).[78]

In the first decade of the twenty-first century, the combination of drastic socioeconomic changes and China's die-hard one-party system further expanded the power of local governments and prompted more lawbreaking by officials or law-enforcement organs, many of them outrageous. Although the total number was far fewer than those of other categories, the *CYD*'s reports in category 3 and especially category 2 rose sharply in this period. In most cases the *CYD* journalists stood on moral ground and reproached those official lawbreakers.

On May 22, 2002, the *CYD* reported a case of urban relocation in Shanghai, a consequence of China's economic reform. According to the report, in 1998 one He Liming, who had inherited a beautiful three-floor house from his father, was told by the Luwan District Government that his house would have to be condemned and that the government was willing to pay him merely 150,000 yuan ($19,000 in 1998). He immediately rejected the offer and appealed to the court. But in February 1999 over one hundred people broke into He's house and, without any legitimate authorization, forced his family to move out. At the end of 2000 He was shocked to discover that his former house had been transformed into a luxury restaurant. He now realized that the Luwan District Government had actually confiscated his house and resold it to a Hong Kong businessman for a fortune. Yang Liangqing, the *CYD* reporter, argued that it was the Luwan District Government that had violated the law. "The market economy is after all a rule-of-law economy in which private rights prevail," Yang admonished. "If citizens' private property cannot be properly protected, or if citizens are afraid of claiming their private rights, the market economy will forfeit the mainstay on which it relies for its existence."[79]

In another case reported in May 2005, the Maoming Intermediate Court, in Guangdong, retracted in 1999 its 1998 ruling and declared that Wang Qing, a businessman who had been charged by the same court with engaging in speculative transactions, was innocent. In August 2000 Wang filed a court petition for state compensation. But the court denied any reparation for Wang's huge loss, which was due to the court's previous false judgment. Between 2002 and 2005 Wang complained to numerous local and central organs, including the Supreme Court, requesting state compensation. But in 2005 Wang got nothing except one hundred worn-out shoes, the result of years of unsuccessful complaints. Wang told *CYD* reporters that the State Compensation Law stipulated that state organs or staffs should make amends for their violations of people's personal and property rights. "The law is the same; why can victims use the law but the state organs cannot [follow the law]?" Wang asked.[80]

By reporting these cases and many police tortures, the *CYD* upheld its moral standard and stood on the side of the ordinary victims against official or judicial violations of the law.

In the early 2000s China was facing many novel challenges and opportunities. First of all, with the rule of law written into the constitution, the CCP ostensibly determined to move toward a rule-of-law state. Second, after China entered the WTO, its economy experienced another decade of boom. But what accompanied the fast-growing economy was unbridled official corruption and unlawful activities. Third, in the wake of decades of massive legal education, most Chinese had acquired at least a modicum of basic legal expertise. Moreover, the cancelation of Party subsidies forced newspapers, whether national or local, to engage in stiff competition with one another for profits and for survival. To meet this challenge, the *CYD* expanded its roles as Party tool, muckraker, and educator and promoter of deterrence by greatly augmenting the number of its reports. Even reports of judicial and official problems that had received little coverage in the earlier periods saw noticeable increase. The most important change in this period, of course, was the *CYD*'s immense emphasis on comments, letters, and debates that aimed to promote the rule of law in China.

## CONCLUSION

Many scholars have argued that the CCP's influence on public media has been diminishing since the outset of reform. In this chapter on the *CYD*'s role in China's legal reform, however, we have seen that the Party's control over public media (e.g., the *CYD*), as Shambaugh, Esarey, and Pan have argued, actually intensified between 1979 and 2006. Tables 1.1, 1.2, and 1.3 demonstrate that the *CYD*'s role as a major tool of the Party witnessed steady increases. In all three periods, especially in the second and third, during which the number of propaganda-related reports jumped phenomenally, the *CYD* was a dedicated servant of the CCP. The *CYD* not only disseminated important speeches and orders on legal reform and the rule of law made by CCP leaders, but also published many, if not most, of the latest regulations or laws promulgated by the central government or passed by the NPC. When the CCP tried to wipe out the potential threats to its power, such as the Falun Gong and many political dissidents, the *CYD* stood firmly on the Party side, its editorials accusing those enemies of violating Chinese law. Therefore, it is safe to say that in most of the reform period (1979–2006), the *CYD*, like most national newspapers, faithfully carried out the Party's policies regarding legal reform and the establishment of the rule of law.

This chapter has shown the increasing role of the *CYD* as a Party tool since 1979, but the evidence also clearly reveals that the *CYD* was more than just a tool of the Party and, similarly, that many *CYD* journalists were more than merely repeating the Party policies or pursuing paid journalism. Journalists' consciences and professional morality, intense competition among newspapers, and unchecked official corruption and lawbreaking activities within the Party combined to press the *CYD* to take systematic actions promoting the cause of the rule of law. The *CYD* reports on the legal system fell into five categories, and during each of the three periods I've discussed it strengthened the reports in one or more categories, a reflection of different socioeconomic and legal situations.

In the first period, when legal reform had just been embarked on and most readers had very limited legal consciousness, the *CYD* acted as a propaganda tool and an elementary educator about the law. After 1985, as the pace of legal reform stepped up as more laws were passed and, at the same time, most readers gained a basic legal education, the *CYD* became both a propaganda tool and a professional educator. The content of this legal education became more sophisticated and specific. Between 1999 and 2006, probably because most readers possessed basic legal knowledge after decades of education, the *CYD* shifted its focus to comments, letters, and debates on the nature and problems of the contemporary Chinese legal system. As a result, category 4 saw a number of reports annually that was nearly thirty times that in the previous period. In addition, because of fiercer competition and rampant official violations of the law, the *CYD* continued to make its educational and deterrent reports the biggest part of its legal coverage, in part to attract more readers and in part to expose official lawbreakers. If there is any progress in the rise of people's legal expertise and the rule of law in China today, we should not forget to give credit to the *CYD* and many other newspapers.[81]

However significant its contribution to the rule of law, the *CYD*, like other public media, has its own limitations in reformed China. For example, the *CYD* dared not raise questions about the lack of legality in the CCP's crackdown on the Falun Gong in 1999 and the arbitrary incarceration of the lawyer Zheng Enchong in 2003.[82] Even though the *CYD* uncovered and denounced many official lawbreakers, almost all those officials were from the township or county levels. There were very few, if any, reports on unlawful acts committed by provincial officials, let alone by high-ranking officials in the politburo or above.[83] Undoubtedly, as long as the *CYD* remains a tool of the Party, these two limitations of the newspaper cannot be resolved in the years to come.

## NOTES

1. Julian Chang, "The Mechanics of State Propaganda: The People's Republic of China and the Soviet Union in the 1950s," in *New Perspectives on State Socialism in China*, ed. Timothy Cheek and Tony Saich (New York: M. E. Sharpe, 1997), 79.

2. Mao Zedong, "Zai yan'an wenyi zuotanhui shangde jianghua" (Speeches at the Yan'an Forum on Literature and Art), in *Mao Zedong xuanji* (Selected Works of Mao Zedong) (Beijing: People's Press, 1991), 3:847–879.

3. Mao Zedong, "Duijinsui ribao bainjirenyuan detanhua" (A Talk with Editors of the *Jinsui Daily*), in *Mao Zedong xuanji*, 4:1213–1217.

4. Mao Zedong, "Guanyu zuzhi liliang zhunbei fanji youpai fenzi jingongde zhishi" (A Directive on Mustering Our Forces to Prepare for Repulsing the Rightists' Attack), in *Mao Zedong xuanji*, 5:431–433. Also see Hsiao Ching-Chang and Yang Mei-rong, "Don't Force US to Lie: The Case of the World Economic Herald," in *Voices of China: The Interplay of Politics and Journalism*, ed. Chin-chuan Lee (New York: Guilford Press, 1999), 111–121. For a general background of the Anti-Rightist Movement, see Maurice Meisner, *Mao's China and After: A History of the People's Republic* (New York: Free Press, 1990), 169–187; and Philip Short, *Mao: A Life* (New York: Owl Books, 1999), 464–471.

5. Merle Goldman, "The Role of the Press in Post-Mao Political Struggles," in *China's Media, Media's China*, ed. Chin-Chuan Lee (Boulder, Colo.: Westview Press, 1994), 39; and Lowell Dittmer, "The Politics of Publicity in Reform China," ibid., 98.

6. Leonard L. Chu, "Continuity and Change in China's Media Reform," *Journal of Communication* 44, no. 3 (Summer 1994): 4–21.

7. For studies on the whole public media, see Chu, "Continuity and Change in China's Media Reform"; Daniel C. Lynch, *After the Propaganda State: Media, Poli-*

tics, and "Thought Work" in Reformed China (Stanford: Stanford University Press, 1999); Chin-Chuan Lee, "Mass Media: Of China, about China," in Lee, Voices of China, 3–29; Chin-Chuan Lee, "Ambiguities and Contradictions: Issues in China's Changing Political Communications," in Lee, China's Media, Media's China, 3–22; James F. Scotton and William A. Hachten, introduction to New Media for a New China, ed. James F. Scotton and William A. Hachten (Hoboken, N.J.: Wiley-Blackwell, 2010), 1–10; Tsan-Kuo Chang, Jian Wang, and Chih-Hsien Chen, "News as Social Knowledge in China: The Changing Worldview of Chinese National Media," Journal of Communication 44, no. 3 (Summer 1994): 52–69; Paul Siu-nam Lee, "Mass Communication and National Development in China: Media Roles Reconsidered," Journal of Communication 44, no. 3 (Summer 1994): 22–37; for studies on specific and individual media see David Shambaugh, "China's Propaganda System: Institutions, Processes and Efficacy," China Journal, no. 57 (2007): 25–58; Anne-Marie Brady, "Guiding Hand: The Role of the CCP Central Propaganda Department in the Current Era," Westminster Papers in Communication and Culture 3, no. 1 (2006): 58–77; Lynn T. White III, "All the News: Structure and Politics in Shanghai's Reform Media," in Chin-Chuan Lee, Voices of China, 88–110; Hsiao and Yang, "Don't Force US to Lie"; Ashley Esarey, "Cornering the Market: State Strategies for Controlling China's Commercial Media," Asian Perspectives 29, no. 4 (2005): 37–83.

8. For example, Paul Siu-nam Lee, "Mass Communication and National Development in China"; Chu, "Continuity and Change in China's Media Reform"; Su Shaozhi, "Chinese Communist Ideology and Media Control," in Chin-Chuan Lee, China's Media, Media's China, 75–88; Chin-Chuan Lee, "Mass Media"; Esarey, "Cornering the Market," 43.

9. Dittmer, "The Politics of Publicity in Reform China," and Esarey, "Cornering the Market," 50.

10. Guo Ke, "Newspapers: Changing Roles," in Scotton and Hachten, New Media for a New China, 43–60.

11. See Lynch, After the Propaganda State; Scotton and Hatchen, New Media for a New China; Chu, "Continuity and Change in China's Media Reform"; Paul Siu-nam Lee, "Mass Communication and National Development in China."

12. See Zhongdang Pan, "Improvising Reform Activities: The Changing Reality of Journalistic Practice in China," in Power, Money, and Media: Communication Patterns and Bureaucratic Control in Cultural China, ed. Chin-Chuan Lee (Evanston, Ill.: Northwestern University Press, 2000), 68–111; Esarey, "Cornering the Market"; Brady, "Guiding Hand"; Shambaugh, "China's Propaganda System."

13. Guoguang Wu, "One Head, Many Mouths: Diversifying Press Structures in Reform China," in Chin-Chuan Lee, Power, Money, and Media, 45–67.

14. For example, Mechthild Exner, Mary Gallagher, and Daniela Stockmann focus on the media's role in legal dissemination and "shaping citizens' views and behavior toward the legal system," and Ben Liebman studies the role of the Chinese media in court decisions. See Mechthild Exner, "The Convergence of Ideol-

ogy and the Law: The Functions of the Legal Education Campaign in Building a Chinese Legal System," *Issues and Studies* 31, no. 8 (1995): 68–102; Daniela Stockmann and Mary E. Gallagher, "Remote Control: How the Media Sustain Authoritarian Rule in China," *Comparative Political Studies* 44, no. 4 (2011): 436–467, esp. 439; Benjamin L. Liebman, "Watchdog or Demagogue? The Media in the Chinese Legal System," *Columbia Law Review* 105, no. 1 (January 2005): 1–157.

15. A 1985 poll made by a Shanghai-based magazine, *Qingnian yidai* (Youth Generation), showed that *CYD* was the most popular paper among readers; the poll was reported by *CYD* on September 2, 1986. In 1994 a competition held by the China Journalists Association and the Beijing Worker Newspaper Collection Association named the *CYD* as second in the "Our Most-Loved One Hundred Nationwide Excellent Newspapers"; *CYD*, September 19, 1994. In 1999 college students in Shandong province called the *CYD* their favorite newspaper; *CYD*, January 21, 1999.

16. For example, Judy Polumbaum mentioned a case of northeast China forest fires in which the *CYD* exposed the negligence of some officials. See Judy Polumbaum, "Tribulations of China's Journalists," in Chin-Chuan Lee, *Voices of China*, 33–68.

17. Randall Peerenboom propounds two types of rule of law: thick and thin. He argues that rule of law has various forms that should not be lumped together under the term *rule of law*. In this chapter I nevertheless use the term *rule of law* as most legal scholars do today. See Randall Peerenboom, *China's Long March toward Rule of Law* (Cambridge: Cambridge University Press, 2002), 2–10.

18. Gong Pixiang, ed., *Dangdai zhongguo de falü geming* (The Current Chinese Legal Revolution) (Beijing: Law Press, 1999), 316.

19. Deng Xiaoping, *Deng Xiaoping xuanji* (Selected Works of Deng Xiaoping) (Beijing: People's Press, 1983), 189.

20. For a complete overview of China's legislations since 1978, see Guoli Liu, "Political Culture and Legal Reform," *American Review of China Studies* 1 (2000): 1–17; also see Ching Kwan Lee, *Against the Law: Labor Protests in China's Rustbelt and Sunbelt* (Berkeley: University of California Press, 2007), 18; Qiang Fang, "The Case of the Virgin Prostitute: Chinese Media and Legal Reform," *Stanford Journal of East Asian Affairs* 2 (2002): 26–27.

21. Despite the claim of the constitution, the Chinese Communist Party, including many of its top officials, is clearly above the law; *1982 Nian Zhongguo Xianfa* (The 1982 Chinese Constitution) (Beijing: People's Press, 1982), 14.

22. Jiang Zemin, *Jiang Zemin wenxuan* (Selected Works of Jiang Zemin) (Beijing: People's Press, 2006), 511.

23. For Jiang, see ibid.; for scholars, see Xia Yong, *Yifa zhiguo-guojia yu shehui* (Ruling the Country by Law-State and Society) (Beijing: Social Science Archival Press, 2004), 99. For a similar argument, see Stanley Lubman, *Bird in a Cage: Legal Reform in China after Mao* (Stanford: Stanford University Press, 1999), 123.

24. Lubman, *Bird in a Cage*, 102.

25. Because the number is so large, some omissions because of missing issues or counting mistakes were unavoidable. I would say that there is a margin of error ranging from 1 to 3 percent (137 to 520). Even so, 97 to 99 percent is still more than enough to support the credibility of the study.

26. "Xuexi falu zunshou falu weihu falu" (Studying Law, Following Law, and Protecting Law), *CYD*, July 5, 1979; for a similar report see "Fayang minzhu jiaqiang fazhi" (Promoting Democracy and Strengthening Law), *CYD*, January 13, 1979.

27. For a good description of the rule of law in China, see Peerenboom, *China's Long March toward Rule of Law;* also Qiang Fang and Roger V. Des Forges, "Were Chinese Rulers above the Law? Toward a Theory of the Rule of Law in China from Early Times to 1949 CE," *Stanford Journal of International Law* 44, no. 1 (2008): 101–146.

28. Zhongdang Pan argues that the higher the level of a newspaper, the closer the surveillance of the newspaper and the more it is subject to Party control. As the primary mouthpiece of the Communist Youth League, the *CYD* would be under close watch by the Party. See Pan, "Improvising Reform Activities," 77.

29. "Zhonghua renmin gongheguo xianfa" (The PRC Constitution), *CYD*, September 8, 1982.

30. "Zhongyang zhengfaweiyuanhui queding zhengdun chengshi zhi'an derenwu zhengce cuoshi" (The Central Political and Legal Commission Determines Measures to Rectify Urban Security), *CYD*, July 25, 1981.

31. "Daji yanzhong jingji fanzui douzheng chengji xianzhu" (The Strike against Serious Economic Crimes Attained Success), *CYD*, July 26, 1985.

32. For the history of the Chinese media's educational role, see Chang, "The Mechanics of State Propaganda, 83; "Puji falu zengqiang fazhi guannian" (Propagating Law and Strengthening Legal Consciousness), *Renmin ribao* (People's Daily), November 10, 1978.

33. Deng Liqun, "Falu yaowei renmin zhangwo" (Law Must Be Grasped by the People), *CYD*, June 21, 1985.

34. Li Yongji and Xiao Xianfu, "Weifayu fanzuibian" (Differences between Law Violation and Crime), *CYD*, December 29, 1979.

35. Duan Ming, "Zheshi ganshe hunyin ziyouma" (Is This against Marriage Freedom?) *CYD*, October 9, 1984.

36. "Yifa dongzhongcongkuai daji zhongda xianxing zuifan" (Striking Hard against Existing Serious Criminals under the Law), *CYD*, June 6, 1981.

37. Tan Li and Sun Jie, "Mangmu zuo fennu qiumi zhede zihui" (The Self-Contrition of Those Who Have Blindly Become "Angry Soccer Fans"), *CYD*, May 25, 1985.

38. "Zhifa fanfa guofa nanrong" (State Laws Cannot Tolerate the Violations of Law by Law Enforcers), *CYD*, February 20, 1982.

39. Ma Chengfa, "Gongshang suozhang lanchengwei fuqi xiaodian shoudiaonan" (The Head of the Commercial and Industrial Department Abused His Power, the Small Mom-and-Pop Store Was Harassed), *CYD*, October 16, 1984.

40. "Gao Ya'nei jue taobuchu renmin fawang" (Gao Ya'nei Can Never Flee the People's Legal Net), *CYD*, June 21, 1980; Zheng Xin, "Nongcun qingnian xuyao zhifa dongfa" (Rural Youth Need to Know and Understand the Law), *CYD*, July 17, 1984.

41. On Hu Yaobang, see Chin-Chuan Lee, *Voices of China*, 8.

42. For good arguments on the commercialization of the Chinese media in the 1980s and 1990s, see Jinglu Yu, "The Structure and Function of Chinese Television," in Chin-Chuan Lee, *Voices of China*, 101; Lynch, *After the Propaganda State*, 6; Esarey, "Cornering the Market," 55.

43. Zhou Baozhong, "Tamen renwei zhe busuantou" (They Don't Believe It Was a Theft), *CYD*, January 30, 1986.

44. Li Chunlin and Liu Cunxue, "Famang, kuaizouchu wuqu" (The Law-Ignorant Should Quickly Walk Out of the Wrong Region), *CYD*, January 21, 1995.

45. Lin Jun, "Geren suodeshui jiujing shuilaijiao" (Who Should Pay the Personal Income Tax), *CYD*, October 20, 1994.

46. Ren Chengyu and Fu Guoqun, "Zhexie ziliao shuyu shangye mimima" (Do These Materials Belong to Commercial Secrets?), *CYD*, April 29, 1996.

47. Zheng Yunyan, "Wohai nengbuneng shanggao" (Can I Still Appeal?), *CYD*, August 4, 1994.

48. Yan Hua, "Qingbuqi lushi dabuqi guansi zengmeban" (What to Do If [You] Can't Afford to Hire a Lawyer: Go to the Legal Aid Center), *CYD*, February 12, 1997.

49. Cheng Xi, "Fanmai jiayao guofa burong" (Selling Fake Medicine Will Not Be Tolerated by the State Law), *CYD*, April 1, 1991.

50. Ji Tianfu and Yu Xinnian, "Lu Yulin weizao gongwen zhengjian yinzhang beipanxing" (Lu Yulin Was Sentenced for Having Forged Official Documents, IDs, and Seals), *CYD*, August 18, 1994.

51. Li Chang and Lin Dong, "Zhangfu dashang qizi zhaopei buwu" (Husband Injured, Wife Must Also Pay Compensation), *CYD*, August 8, 1997.

52. Li Chengkui, "Shenwei zhengfa ganbu jingduoci judu, Liu Dazhao beikaichu dangji" (A Political and Legal Officer Involved in Many Gambles, Liu Dazhao Was Stripped of His Party Membership), *CYD*, March 16, 1988.

53. "Gongqingtuan yinggai weiwunian pufa jiaoyu douzheng" (The Communist Youth League Should Struggle with the Five-Year Enhancement of the Public's Awareness of the Law), *CYD*, January 9, 1986.

54. "Jiang Zeming tanjiaqiang zhengfa gongzuo" (Jiang Zeming Talked about Intensifying the Political and Legal Work), *CYD*, December 17, 1992.

55. "Qiao Shiza Shandong daibiaotuanshuo: Jianquan fazhi jiaqiang jiandu" (Qiao Shi Talked to the Shandong Delegation: Perfecting the Legal System and Strengthening Supervision), *CYD*, March 15, 1995.

56. "Jiang Zemin zai zhongguo gongchandang dishiwu ciquanguo daibiao dahui shangde baogao" (Jiang Zemin's Report at the 15th National Congress of the CCP), *CYD*, September 23, 1997; also see Jiang Zemin's talk at the National Politi-

cal and Legal Meeting in December 1997, "Jiada lidu tuijin yifa zhiguo" (Deepening the Rule of Law), *CYD,* December 26, 1997.

57. "Minshi susongfa" (The Civil Procedure Law), *CYD,* April 15, 1991; "Zhongxuanbudeng lianhe fachu guanyu jinzhi youchang xinwende ruogan guiding" (The Department of Central Propaganda and Other Organs Jointly Made Certain Regulations regarding Prohibiting Paid Journalism), *CYD,* January 24, 1997. Paid journalism occurred in the 1990s in the wake of the CCP's losing its control of the media. The problem became a serious one that besmirched the impartiality of journalists. For a good study on this issue see Pan, "Improvising Reform Activities," 85.

58. Xu Zhijie, "Falu qineng wangkai yimian" (How Can Law Have Loopholes?), *CYD,* November 28, 1992.

59. For the debates see "Falü luntan" (The Platform of Legal Debate), *CYD,* December 22 and 29, 1997.

60. "Yifa chuanhua faren daibiao jingyao qulingdao qianfa tongzhi" (Legally Summoning a Person Requires Permission from District Leaders), *CYD,* December 1, 1997.

61. "Wulongxian yiwen: quanda haishi fada" (A Doubt in Wulong County: Which One Is More Powerful, Law or Power?), *CYD,* August 6, 1998.

62. For the possible effects of joining the WTO on the Chinese economy, see Lubman, *Bird in a Cage,* 315.

63. For the number of newspapers see Esarey, "Cornering the Market," 48; for the Xinhua News Agency see James F. Scotton, "Xinhua: The Voice of the Party," in Scotton and Hachten, *New Media for a New China,* 115–127.

64. Polumbaum, "Tribulations of China's Journalists," 56.

65. Liu Wujun, "Fazhi bushi wanneng" (The Rule of Law Is Not Omnipotent), *CYD,* May 29, 2000.

66. Chen Jieren, "Shangxiaji fayuanshi shenme guanxi" (What Is the Relationship between Upper and Lower Courts?), *CYD,* July 1, 2002.

67. Tong Dahuan, "Qiangxia liuren xianxian sifa loudong" ("Holding the Execution" Reflects a Loophole of the Judiciary), *CYD,* July 22, 2002.

68. Lao Shi, "Tuhuangdi shihuan gongjianfa" ("The Local Emperor" Gives Orders to the Gongjianfa), *CYD,* October 8, 2001.

69. Huang Jianlin, "'Lingdao ganbu' daitou zunjin shoufa bufuhe fazhi jingshen" ("Leading Cadres Should Be First to Follow the Law" Does Not Fit the Rule-of-Law Spirit), *CYD,* November 4, 2004.

70. Guo Songmin, "Jingcha chuangsheng rendashi difang quanli sudahua debiaoxian" (The Police Breaking into the Provincial Congress Is the Embodiment of the "Sudanization" of Local Power), *CYD,* July 27, 2006.

71. Wang Yijun, "Teshu ruoshi qunti baohu zaoshou falu kongbai" (The Protection of Special Weak Groups Encounters a Legal Void), *CYD,* July 14, 2006.

72. Tang Tao and Kang Jing, "Jiaojing yingfou anzhong zhifa" (Should Traffic Police Enforce the Law Secretly?), *CYD,* April 14, 2005.

73. Gao Haibin, "Siliao bunengliao falu shuolesuan" ("Settling in Private" Cannot Settle, Only the Law Can Settle), *CYD*, November 10, 2001.

74. Li Jian, "Xianfa shishenme" (What Is the Constitution?), *CYD*, November 1, 2002.

75. "Cuopan bupei baixing kexiang shangji fayuan taoshuofa" (No Compensation for False Judgment, People Can Appeal to the Upper Court for Justice), *CYD*, October 14, 2004. On the problems of the state compensation system, see Fang, "The Case of the Virgin Prostitute."

76. "Yuanhunan youdian guanliju juzhang shexian ju'eshouhui" (Former Head of the Bureau of Hunan Post and Telecom Is Suspected of Taking Huge Bribes), *CYD*, August 11, 2000.

77. Wan Xingya and Xu Hatao, "Hebei chunu piaochang'an she'an jingcha beipan youqi tuxing" (Policemen Involved with Hebei Virgin Prostitutes Were Sentenced to Prison), *CYD*, November 21, 2003.

78. On the Falun Gong, see the *CYD*, July 23, 25, 1999, and January 1, 2004; on Hu's talk, see "Renzhen jianchi zhifa weimin qieshi weihu sifa gongzheng" (Meticulously Insist on Enforcing the Law for the People and Earnestly Defend Judicial Justice), *CYD*, March 24, 2004.

79. Yang Liangqing, "Shuiyouquan dongwode shikumen" (Who Has the Power to Move My Shikumen?), *CYD*, May 22, 2002.

80. For police torture in this period, see Qiang Fang, "The Case of the Virgin Prostitute." For the Wang Qing case, see Yang Dezhi, "Wunian paolan 100 shuanxie meinadao yifenqian guojia peichang" (Five Years with One Hundred Worn-out Shoes, Does Not Get One Penny of State Compensation), *CYD*, May 12, 2005.

81. Peerenboom argues that China has been building a thin rule of law in *China's Long March toward Rule of Law*, 6. On other newspapers see the *People's Daily*, *Gongren ribao* (Workers' Daily), and *Fazhi ribao* (Legal System Daily), which have since 2000 devoted much space to law-related reports and cases.

82. Zheng Enchong was a famous lawyer who had defended commoners' rights against governmental violations before 2003. Zheng had also reportedly accused top Shanghai officials of graft. The Shanghai High Court sentenced Zheng to three years in prison in late 2003, which was largely believed illegal. On Zheng's trial, see *CYD*, December 19, 2003.

83. Also see Polumbaum, "Tribulations of China's Journalists," 59; Zhou He, "Chinese Communist Party Press in a Tug-of-War: A Political-Economy Analysis of the *Shenzhen Special Zone Daily*," in Chin-Chuan Lee, *Power, Money, and Media*, 112–151.

# 2

# Deviation in Legal Practice

## Rule of Law with Chinese Characteristics

### Yuchao Zhu

One of the most important aspects of China's post-Mao transition is legal reform, and there are three main imperatives behind the proposed objectives. First is a political imperative: the post-Mao government began to understand the growing importance of various institutions for administration and rule making, realizing that the tradition of arbitrary, unpredictable, and highly secretive practices carries enormous costs. Thus, there is a growing need for procedural politics and more predictable results.[1] Second is an economic imperative: a new rule of law is essential for bringing basic efficiencies into the rapidly expanding Chinese economy. An economy based on competitive or quasi-competitive production requires commercial law, bankruptcy law, contract law, labor relations law, and so forth. This is a requirement of international investors and all those who participate in China's commercial activities.[2] Third is a social imperative: the development of the idea of citizenship and awareness of rights instigates demands in Chinese society for basic safeguards, such as legislative, adjudicative due process and general protection of rights. This is reflected mainly in the gradual establishment of the idea of *weiquan* (protection of rights) in Chinese society.[3]

Since the 1980s China's legal reform has been officially geared toward the rule of law.[4] Significant progress has been made in the areas of lawmaking and legal institution building;[5] however, severe deficiencies are still observed in legal practice. Some analysts argue that the central problem of China's legal reform is a gap between the law as written and the law as implemented in practice.[6] In fact, current legal practice often seriously deviates from its original purpose. This might be one of the most noticeable phenomena in the operation of China's legal system today.

In studies of legal reform questioning whether or to what extent China has established the "rule of law," conclusions vary.[7] For example, Randall Peerenboom suggests that China is actually building a "thin rule of law."[8] But Stanley Lubman contends that China does not have an authentic legal system because it lacks a unifying concept of law. This is a result of instrumentalist approaches and the fundamental reluctance of the Chinese Communist Party (CCP) to tolerate any significant diminution of its authority.[9] Other critics simply say that rather than make a legal regime to protect citizens' rights, the CCP continues to use the law as an instrument to hold unchecked power.[10] Chinese jurists also view legal reform from different perspectives. He Weifang advocates reform based on a Western rule-of-law model, with emphasis on essential elements such as judicial independence, transparency, procedural justice, and accessibility of the law.[11] But Zhu Suli prefers a Chinese-style rule of law that uses traditional normative methods, or "indigenous resources" (*bentu ziyuan*), in China's legal practice.[12] Overall, there is a consensus about building *fazhi* (the rule of law) in China, but there remain divergent views on what kind of rule of law to build and how to create such an order.[13] Some fundamental questions remain: Is the rule of law compatible with the current Chinese political system? How does legal reform cope with China's traditional norms? Or, put simply, is there a "Chinese-style rule of law"?

This chapter answers the above questions through an examination of the deviation phenomenon, particularly in the practice of China's administrative law. The reasons for focusing the discussion on administrative laws are as follows. First, administrative laws, regulations, and measures account for more than 60 percent of all laws in China. The State Council alone, as the main body that creates them, has issued more than eight hundred nationwide administrative laws and regulations since the early 1990s. Among the six thousand local laws and regulations, administrative ones account for more than half.[14] Second, the practice of administrative laws, regulations, and measures represents the most common legal and extralegal activities in China, and it also forms the central legal mechanism for managing state-society relations in general.[15] Third, since the lack of judicial independence is a traditional hallmark of China's legal system, a unique dimension of the present-day Chinese legal scene is "indistinctness of administrative and adjudicatory functions."[16] This makes administrative laws uniquely dominant in China's overall legal practice; in short, administrative lawmaking and practice are essential to China's political and legal system. Therefore, to fully comprehend China's legal reform and transitional legal order, one must pay special attention to the practice of administrative law.

This research analyzes two administrative laws or measures, one already abolished and the other still in operation: the Custody and Repatriation Law (C&R, *shourong qiansong fa*), and Letters and Visits (L&V; *xinfang*). The aim is to identify and explain the chasm between a law or measure's intention and its practice. It should be noted that deviation in practice often occurs as a result of interactions of various legal and nonlegal factors. This appears to be the main obstacle to establishing the rule of law in China and also indicates the complex and changing nature of China's state-society relationship. Through an analysis of the deviation problem, we can see how the following factors influence the specific outcomes of legal practice: the changing socioeconomic environment, the political structure and discretionary authority, the intervention of various interest holders, and the accepted legal norms. Though some may argue that deviation in legal practice is a phenomenon typically associated with anomie,[17] one may also consider that deviation means China's current legal system remains in a state of flux.

## DEVIATION IN TWO MEASURES OF ADMINISTRATIVE LAW

What is "deviation" in legal practice? It may seem common sense not to expect legal measures to be implemented entirely in accordance with the written text. Surely, "every political or legal act, irrespective of regime type, has both intended and unintended consequences."[18] There are often political, societal, or cultural elements that may interfere in the process of law application and may lead to results that differ from what was originally intended. In this sense, deviation in legal practice is a common phenomenon in any polity or legal system. In other words, though deviation is certainly not something intended from a lawmaking perspective, it occurs all the time. But in an established rule-of-law order, there should be only limited deviation; and if it does happen, either the managerial system adjusts itself or a discretionary authority corrects it. Thus, deviation issues can be examined to assess the levels of compliance, effectiveness, and consistency in a legal system. Deviation appears more common in transitional legal systems than in well-established Western ones, and China is a prime example of the former.[19] We can examine the C&R to see what could happen in the application of China's administrative law.

In 1982 the State Council established the Decision on the Measures to Detain and Repatriate People Who Illegally Stay in Cities, which officially created the C&R. The Ministries of Public Security and Civil Affairs decreed specific instructions on detailed implementation. In the original document, three types of people were identified for coverage: beggars, vagrants, and those "wandering in cities with no work or income." The practical criteria used to identify these people were *sanwu* (absence of three conditions): no valid legal documents, no permanent urban residential status, and no work or income. The targeted people were picked up and sent back to their homes at the government's expense. The policy's central purpose was to control migration from rural to urban areas on the basis of the *hukou* (household registration) system.[20] According to the original document, the measure's scope was limited, and the intention of the C&R was mostly for social management and assistance.

As an administrative measure, the C&R was part of the government's effort to manage the social consequences of economic reform. The C&R's original notion did not seem harmful, and it was largely compatible with the socioeconomic environment in the early 1980s.[21] The use of an administrative legal mechanism to control urban-rural segregation and to maintain social order in urban areas was a policy goal of the state at that time, and there was no significant criticism or resistance in the early days of its implementation. In the process of the measure's application in the 1990s, however, three elements emerged that changed this administrative measure in practice. First, because of dramatic urbanization and a huge transient population in China's coastal areas and urban centers, the C&R's policy coverage became so broad as to include migrant workers, who were not the original target but who might have insufficient legal documents while living and working in cities. Also, a transient population in urban centers brought more pressure on local authorities, such as increased social stratification, discontent, and crime. Second, as cities faced these pressures, the C&R was coercively imposed on the target people by administrators and police officers who had very few restrictions placed on them. Third, the assessment of a fee provided implementing officials and local agents with a financial incentive to carry out the measure for their own benefit.[22] Thus, the C&R expanded in an intrusive and coercive nature and, in so doing, lost its original social management and assistance function. One might say that almost all the conditions and incentives conducive to the rule of law were absent in the practice of C&R. In fact, there were incentives that ran counter to the fulfillment of its original purpose.

In practice, the C&R was becoming a coercive, intrusive, but also profitable administrative measure, similar to an unrestricted license to collect rents. There were serious legal and nonlegal problems regarding this; for instance, the responsible administrative agencies for enforcement often acted arbitrarily, without necessary judicial authority and supervision mechanisms, and were widely criticized as "loose cannons."[23] Though the C&R was not punishment for a crime, but, rather, an administrative detention measure, in many ways the severity of the treatment meted out to those singled out by the law was similar to that administrated to "normal" criminal suspects. This became a coercive measure to deprive citizens of their freedom without due process, even though this freedom is guaranteed in China's constitution.

To make the matter more intriguing, one responsible government agency, the Ministry of Civil Affairs, began to realize problems with the C&R in the late 1990s. It was concerned especially about this deviation and tried but failed to make corrections. The key reason for this failure was China's political hierarchy. In the case of C&R implementation, the central authorities were two key agencies: the Ministry of Public Security and the Ministry of Civil Affairs. As this administrative measure was intended to maintain urban social order and stability, the Central Political Legal Commission (*zhongyang zhengfawei*), a central institution in the government, became the guiding and monitoring bureau for the measure's overall implementation. In China's political structure, every level of government has a Political Legal Commission (*zhengfawei*) that coordinates all security and judicial organizations.[24] According to the government's internal structure, the Political Legal Commission's general secretary (*zhengfawei shuji*) was usually the vice director of the party or government. The commission members usually consisted of chief officials from the departments of Public Security, State Security, Civil Affairs, Justice, as well as the Auditor, People's Procurator, and People's Court. The political system empowered the commission to oversee political and legal affairs and to intervene if necessary. Moreover, between the two agencies responsible for the C&R,

the public security chief was usually vice chairman or a senior member of the Political Legal Commission, and the Civil Affairs chief was often only a junior member. Although the Political Legal Commission was capable of deciding policy implementation, it usually took advice from Public Security rather than from Civil Affairs. In fact, as early as the late 1990s, the Civil Affairs Ministry had already proposed abolition of the C&R and planned to replace it with a new measure designed for social assistance. But the Central Political Legal Commission rejected the proposed change.[25] Also, in most of China's coastal urban centers, where the C&R was particularly widely implemented, local authorities made social stability, investment, and economic growth their top priorities. Therefore, they were not interested in managing the C&R as a social assistance mechanism but preferred to use it as an effective method to control the transient population and maintain order. This lack of political interest from the responsible agencies in the measure's application prevented the Ministry of Civil Affairs from correcting the deviation. In point of fact, it was mainly the tragedy of Sun Zhigang in 2003 and the newly formulated State Council's prompt action that finally led to the end of this measure.[26]

The rise and fall of the C&R is not an isolated case. It reflects the likelihood of deviation in the practice of most of China's administrative laws and measures. Moreover, it indicates a continuing tension between China's lawmaking and its legal practice. This tension arises because of increasing incompatibilities between the original conditions under which laws are made and the different circumstances under which they are applied that result from a rapidly changing Chinese society. In this sense, deviation seems inevitable, but timely correction is difficult. Unfortunately, the withdrawal of this administrative law involved a discretionary authority's decision to end the deviation but not to reform the overall political structure that needs a systematic correction. In other words, the root cause of deviation remains.

Another Chinese-style administrative measure to pursue justice beyond the normal legal process is called *xinfang*, or Letters and Visits (L&V). It is an avenue for ordinary citizens who feel the formal justice system has failed them or who seek justice against a local government's violation of their rights and interests.[27] Historically, even during the old dynasty periods, there existed political and legal mechanisms to which common people could appeal to resolve their grievances; these often played an important role in governance.[28] Thus, the availability of the L&V system today is understandable. Technically, it is more of a supplementary administrative remedy for judicial justice,[29] somewhat like ombudsman investigations in the West.[30] More precisely, rather than presenting their cases through the formal judicial process, L&V petitioners write letters or go directly to a higher political or legal authority, normally the provincial or central government, to present their cases. For the government, this measure serves an important function in that it is a useful remedy for injustices as well as a method of monitoring and correcting any wrongdoings of local officials. This is a traditional, norm-based, but extrajudicial means to pursue justice in China. For a long time L&V played a notable role in channeling social discontent into a moderating forum.[31]

An important characteristic of L&V is that it is not formal judicial practice. Petitions are often made when the legal process fails or is incomplete.[32] Sometimes a judicial procedure is not pursued at all, either because the petitioners do not trust it or because they do not have the necessary knowledge and resources to use it. In this sense, L&V is a political avenue for social justice, and in recent years the number of L&V cases has increased dramatically. For example, from 1992 to 2004 there was a 10 percent annual increase in L&V cases; in 2004 the number reached its highest, 13.37 million cases of L&V filed with different levels of government all over China.[33] The astonishing rise in the number of petitions filed indicates serious perceived problems of social stratification, corruption, inequality, and injustice in Chinese society. It can also be directly linked, however, to the effects of abolishing the C&R measure in 2003, which reduced stringent controls over the transient population and made L&V activities easier. For many ordinary citizens, this might be the only available avenue by which to pursue justice. Yet one may argue that L&V is not a formal aspect of the rule of law but another standard Chinese-style political accountability method. Even so, it assists in achieving social justice or even in building a rule-of-law order, as it can lead to the imposition of standards and discipline in China's public administration.

One reason citizens prefer the L&V over the formal judicial process is largely a result of deviation in the application of China's Administrative Litigation Law (ALL).[34] With the introduction of the ALL, a new legal outlet by which citizens can sue the government for wrongdoings was created. The results, however, have been limited. A high number of cases are either dropped or withdrawn from the process, and of cases that go forward, a low percentage claim victory. Many ALL plaintiffs are persuaded to withdraw their cases by the manipulation of legal agents or government officials. Also, many citizens feel that the economic costs of ALL cases are too high and the legal process is too time-consuming. So they simply do not see it as a feasible option.[35]

Therefore, as the ALL cannot fully protect citizens' rights, the availability of other practices like L&V gives them an alternative way to seek justice. Compared to a formal judicial process like ALL, L&V has some advantages; for example, it has a lower operational cost, it offers the possibility of overcoming local bureaucracies' networking obstacles, and, especially important, it is consistent with China's traditional legal norm.[36] According to Chinese tradition, litigation is not a popular option when people have disputes with authorities or with each other. Hence, L&V as a special remedy can be supplementary or complementary to administrative litigation. But there is a dilemma with this kind of extrajudicial means to legal justice: emphasis on measures like L&V, which has no strict procedural requirements and monitoring mechanisms, means that formal legal institutions lose some of their legitimate functions or even relevance.[37] But if the government terminated this practice, people would be denied a crucial alternative channel for their pursuit of justice. Disappointment in, or distrust toward, the formal judicial system continues to make people choose informal, traditional legal mechanisms.

In the practice of L&V, however, there are problems as well, largely caused by local administrative management. On the one hand, petitioners are often referred by higher authorities to lower-level government agencies to resolve their cases. But administrative references, sometimes even judicial opinions, often do not have sufficient political weight.[38] Since even judges' rulings in Chinese court decisions have only a 68 percent compliance rate, administrative decisions carry little enforcement power, and the L&V resolution rate is ultimately low.[39] On the other hand, because no strict procedural requirement existed before 2005, many petitioners repeatedly took their cases to a higher level of government, even after administrative verdicts were given or legal settlements granted. So if petitioners are not satisfied with a particular result, they may continue to appeal, collectively or individually, to higher levels of government, which not only lengthens the process but also increases the L&V workload considerably. These two problems tend to make L&V less effective in fulfilling its original purpose.

As mentioned previously, L&V is consistent with the traditional practice of justice throughout the dynastic era. In Imperial China ordinary people often pursued justice through petition to the highest authority. In their minds, the higher the authority that heard their case, the more likely it was that their demand for justice would be fulfilled. One common practice, therefore, was the direct appeal to the "Palace Gate."[40] Political power hierarchy in Imperial China was the structural condition on which people's petitions were based, and often injustice was resolved because of intervention from the top.[41]

Today this pattern remains popular as well as functional. Though only about 0.2 percent of all L&V cases were settled in 2003, some of them were eventually resolved through extrajudicial intervention by high-ranking officials.[42] For example, one well-known case in 2004 involved a migrant worker's wife, Xiong Deming, who made a direct appeal to Premier Wen Jiabao regarding the issue of wages not paid to migrant workers. Wen made an investigative visit to her village, and it was primarily because of Premier Wen's direct intervention that the woman's grievance was immediately redressed. The State Council then decreed that every level of government has to deal with similar issues.[43] This direct intervention and "justice from above" helped vulnerable migrant workers, but the fact that this kind of injustice widely occurs in society indicates the failure of governmental labor protection laws and ineffective administrative supervision. Though Xiong's case may have been justly resolved, many other citizens are not as fortunate and must continue to use L&V to seek justice. In other words, though L&V cases can result in some "justice from above," there is no functional mechanism to guarantee success.[44]

Since various levels of government are facing pressure from an increased number of L&V cases, in early 2005 the State Council decreed a new guideline on how to manage such activities.[45] This new guideline is intended to regulate L&V more effectively by, for example, enforcing a thirty-day time frame for answering petitions and, particularly, forbidding sending a petitioner's case to the same government department or office that is accused. But the most notable part of this new measure is explicit control mechanisms: (1) a petitioner's demand is restricted to the immediate next level of government rather than being allowed to go directly to the provincial government or the central government in Beijing; (2) if this is a repeat petition, the authority may deny the demand for investigation; (3) petitioners must obey the law and not disturb the normal social order; otherwise, they will be punished accordingly; and (4) petitioners may make their demands collectively, but the representatives for a single case should number no more than five. These new guidelines have caused heated debates, as they impose more restrictions and also reduce the accessibility of the L&V. Thus, they seem to strengthen functional control rather than to correct deviation. Since the new measure was implemented, there have been no signs of improvement in terms of the original purpose of more accessible justice. One negative consequence is that various levels of local governments have sent their agents to Beijing or provincial capitals to prevent petitioners from visiting higher-level L&V reception offices. This is called *jiefang* (blocking visits), a practice that is becoming increasingly abusive to petitioners.[46] The deviation problem surrounding the L&V remains, which demonstrates that the government still sees practices like L&V as an instrument to manage society and to control the population. This may not represent progress toward rule of law, but the pertinent practice in L&V management is consistent with traditional instrumentalist views of law and policy within the government and normative views of pursuing justice within society at large. It is important to note the key implication based on L&V practice: as long as the normative expectations of a particular measure remain strong in society on the whole, the measure usually continues to function even if deviation is serious.

In sum, through the above examination of two administrative laws and their divergent applications, we can identify some contributing factors to deviation in general: hierarchical political power held by discretionary authorities, instrumentalist distortion of the law, bureaucratization, involvement of self-interested agents and social actors in the application of the law, and the influence of traditional legal norms. In the case of C&R, the deviation was so serious it finally destroyed the established normative foundation and brought an end to the law. In the case of L&V, however, continued deviation in practice does not subvert the political expectations and normative aspects of the measure and, therefore, it remains functional. As all these factors are more or less present in China's political and legal processes, it can be said that deviation is routine, widespread, and even largely accepted as part of China's legal practice today. Furthermore, deviation is more likely to occur in the practice of China's administrative law rather than in other legal areas owing to the close association between administrative legal practice and China's bureaucratic political structure. Since most Chinese laws are administrative laws, deviation in that area has significant political implications for China's efforts at building a rule-of-law legal order.

## IMPLICATIONS OF DEVIATION FOR LEGAL REFORM

As we have seen, deviation in China's application of its laws indicates that its effort to build a rule-of-law order remains problematic, and the result of its legal reform is still uncertain. It should also be noted, however, that the entrenched factors causing severe deviation do not function individually or separately. They often interact and, in combination, determine the resulting legal application. Many laws and policies function only partially or selectively, as "state agencies often work at cross-purposes" and citizens become "increasingly adept at engaging the state at multiple levels."[47] Thus, when state agencies have multiple purposes and citizens have multiple outlets through which to pursue their interests and goals, various forms of interaction occur in the engagement of legal and political processes. Because of the complexity of motivations, interests, and agents in legal practice, deviation may be manifested in different ways. The final result of the application of the law in each case is not necessarily predetermined. This is why an in-depth analysis of the relationship between the legal and political processes, as well as between law and society, is needed.

In the course of studying China's legal system, one discovers how the political power structure, particularly through discretionary and administrative authorities, determines the relationship and interaction of different actors in the system. For example, all legal and judicial institutions, such as People's Courts, People's Procurators, the Public Security Bureau, and L&V Offices, are subordinated to the same-level party or government. All levels of the People's Courts and People's Procurators rely on the same-level government for their budget. Personnel appointment, transfer, and promotion are decided by the local government and the local Party organizations, which are required to submit formal reports to the local People's Congress annually.[48] This is what Jean-Pierre Cabestan calls "court's lingering financial dependency on local government as well as the CCP's cadre system."[49] In other words, China's political hierarchy fundamentally limits judicial independence and its freedom of action.[50] Within this political system, the judiciary is structurally parallel to the State Council or administrative institutions, but its real political status is actually lower than the same-level administrative bodies.[51] The political restriction on the judiciary is systematic, and it gives the administrative branch of government greater legal power. Very often local administrative agencies carry their own interests into the execution of the law, which may or may not be consistent with the original intent of the law. Individual interests and concerns may become a priority, which causes widespread deviation and corruption in China's legal and policy processes. Nonetheless, given these conditions, expecting legal authorities and enforcement agencies to act completely according to the law and to perform independently with no outside intervention seems unrealistic in China.

On the other hand, China's legal practice is becoming more like an interest-bargaining game. Many stakeholders are involved, especially in civil and economic legal disputes. Many of those who participate in the legal process seek favors and support from a higher political power, rather than pursue fairness and justice according to the rules, regulations, and procedures of China's legal system. Under these conditions, even a just result may not be reached through legitimate legal means, but rather through intervention by politically powerful persons. In sum, China's legal regime in relation to matters of application of the law remains in a state of flux. The legal result, either just or unjust, is actually very much ad hoc: many informal rules remain part of the game, which reflects the increasingly interactive and complex relationship between law and society.

Wang Hengqin summarizes China's legal reform, pointing out at least four issues detrimental to building a rule-of-law order: localization of the judicial process, bureaucratization of the judicial process, the legal pyramid linked to China's political power hierarchy, and judicial corruption.[52] It is interesting to note that most of these problems are not new. These were present during the Guomindang (GMD, or Kuomintang, KMT; the Chinese Nationalist Party) era (1929–1949) as well.[53] History seems to be repeating itself under the CCP, and this is why some studies trace these problems back to China's traditional legal culture. Perry Keller asserts that "the most interesting parallel which exists between late imperial and contemporary sources of law in China lies in the dichotomy which exists between the formalistic and symbolic use of primary legislation and the flexible and pragmatic use of sub-statutory rules."[54] As René David and John Brierley once observed, the "Chinese codes and laws were traditionally only applied to the extent that they corresponded to the popular ideas of equity and propriety. When they conflicted with tradition, they were in fact ignored."[55] According to Zhu Suli's "cultural interpretation of law" analysis, at the grassroots level in judicial practice, traditional ethical norms and other social methods of resolving civil disputes are more influential and useful than judges making rulings in court on the basis of precise legal codes and documents. The L&V practice demonstrates that traditional norms continue to constitute the social foundation for law application.

Yet we know that any resulting deviation does not specifically lean one way or the other in a predetermined fashion. That is, though deviation may indicate the inferior capacity of government in law application, or the low degree of legal authority in China, or the failure of a formal legal process, deviation itself refers only to the resulting difference between the law in practice and the law in its original intent. In fact, deviation may lead to different results, depending on which agencies are involved, their preferred goals, and the environment in which they operate. According to the rule-of-law theory, it is logical that deviation should be significantly reduced when the rule of law is fully established. On the basis of the preceding analysis of the deviation problem in China's administrative law regime, however, we may expect continued deviation because it serves as an indicator of persistent tension between modern legal institution building and traditional legal norms, between the imposition of codified rules and China's self-contained legal order, and between positivist law influences and culture-specific characteristics in China's legal system. This persistent tension reveals the unique dynamics of China's legal regime and social transformation, and it also shows the frequent interactions between a more assertive society and a state that must constantly redefine its role in transition. In terms of reducing deviation, when deviation is linked to the political structure and mismanagement on the part of social agents, the discretionary authority might be able to eliminate the deviation by abolishing a law altogether, as happened with the C&R. But in the case of deviation linked to traditional norms, any real correction must be accompanied by overall social transformation, such as what seems to be happening to L&V.

One should not deny the achievements China has made since legal reform began in the 1980s. For example, China has built a comprehensive law regime, the legal profession is becoming institutionalized, citizens have an increased awareness of the law and of their rights, an expansion in legal education has taken place, and a discourse of legitimation in society as a whole has developed.[56] There are also some groundbreaking legal cases to advance the rule of law. The Qi Yuling case in 2003 was seen by many Chinese legal scholars as the first case on adjudication of a citizen's constitutional right, and it was finally sent to the Supreme People's Court.[57] The Sun Zhigang case started a formal demand for constitutional review.[58] But all this has been accomplished without changing the nature of China's political system, which represents the overall political environment for legal order. So the question remains: Can China's legal reform build a modern authoritarian legal system in which the ruling party (CCP) is above the law, while maintaining judicial fairness? In this regard, one certainly does not see judicial fairness as being compatible by nature with authoritarianism. But legal reform in China is not "all or nothing." In fact, it is still unfolding in an interactive process. As Pitman Potter once predicted, "The operation of law is subject to evolution and challenge by reference to external standards: once a principle of law is enunciated it becomes part of the public domain and open to uses that the regime may not be able to control."[59] When the state establishes and accepts new rules and regulations, it must largely act in accordance with them. Actually, according to Murray Tanner, "The shift away from policy-making by Party edict to increasing the 'rule of law' means the Party-State's rules for social behavior are clearer and more predictable and may even herald the beginning of a contractual state-society relationship."[60] In an effort to establish the rule of law, though perhaps only for instrumental reasons, the state also becomes subject to this new order. Within China's legal community and legislative bodies, more autonomous functions are demanded, and institutional assertiveness (like the NPC's) becomes compelling. What also emerges is the ideological power of law, which explains voluntary submission to law, as well as other institutions of social control.[61]

But one cannot expect China to achieve a Western standard of the rule of law and constitutionalism in the near future. As mentioned previously, the practice of the rule of law in China is very sensitive to its distinctive legal culture and traditional norms. It should be noted that China's legal institution building is beginning to show an "adaptive tendency" in terms of conforming to international standards.[62] Generally speaking, however, though direct legal transplantation from the Western system is often undertaken in developing countries,[63] results are not encouraging, as they range from "legal irritant"[64] to "legal impossibility."[65] China is no exception. Thus, in order to make China's legal reform successful, lawmakers and law enforcers will be required to work together to reconcile new reform measures and existing norms. According to my observation, administrative rule making and adjudication, as well as administration-imposed supervision, control, and correction of state officials, although very informal, represent a major part of China's new legal practice. But still, the deviations analyzed here in various areas of application reveal the serious problem and uncertainty of China's ongoing legal reform. Among its culture-specific judicial characteristics, which lack a positivist law-building tradition, self-controlled order is more important and more reliable than imposition of codified rules and modern legislation.[66] The current legal reform, if it is to succeed, must accommodate this established normative order, rather than abruptly abandon it. In this context, continued deviation in legal practice is to be expected.

## CONCLUSION

China's legal reform interacts with various social and cultural factors, parallels the process of its overall social and economic transition, and therefore should be conceived of as such. The outcome is far from certain, and it is likely that we will see what Peerenboom calls "a thin and informal rule of law legal order" with Chinese characteristics, but that deviation will continue to occur.[67] For legal reform to be viewed as progressive, the general principles of the rule of law must be accepted as normative in China's legal practice. In the operation of the legal system, the basic standards of justice, fairness, transparency, social consensus, and protection of legitimate rights should be increasingly strengthened. Until now, China has not had conditions adequate to support the rule of law, but its new legal system is becoming, though often awkwardly, a more institutionalized legal entity. Increasing numbers of people successfully defend their legitimate rights, but others still fail. Sometimes justice is achieved because of the right legislation or due process, but at other times bargaining and negotiation, good luck, or outside intervention is required. For pragmatic purposes of legal reform, therefore, the immediate goal might be to find ways to increase the possibilities for justice in practice. It is important to remember that common attitudes based on China's traditional legal culture will not change overnight, and that ordinary citizens are concerned more about achieving a just result than about the procedure and the institution behind it. They may tolerate deviations in the legal process, but they continue to pursue justice in various ways. For one thing, as multiple outlets for different interests are now open, new mechanisms may shape legal practice toward interaction rather than hierarchy, and toward a network paradigm rather than a pyramid paradigm. These changes will increase chances for justice.

The overall Chinese polity remains a one-party state that seems intrinsically incompatible with the rule of law. This political system is also in transition, however, as serious deviation indicates a temporary anomie. The development of different stakeholders, or new factions whose interests are divergent, makes unsustainable the old style of monolithic state control. The government's laws and policies must adjust to a new political, legal, and social environment. These complex social, political, and cultural factors largely determine deviation in China's legal application, and they might seem detrimental to the long-term goal of the rule of law. But, on the other hand, China's transitional political system continues to offer some extrajudicial or administrative avenues and informal means for ordinary citizens to participate in the legal process in order to protect their legitimate rights. Although sometimes acting reluctantly, the government is beginning to recognize the importance of a stable, fair, transparent, predictable, and multidimensional legal order.[68] Though the CCP continues to hold exclusive legislative, administrative, and judicial powers, it also has to allow more autonomy for each of the branches and levels of government. China certainly has a long way to go in terms of building a legal order of true rule of law instead of a traditional Chinese-style rule of law. It is expected that China's political transition will determine the success or failure of its legal reform, but it is also likely that progress in legal reform can promote more predictable, transparent, and institutional politics.

## NOTES

1. Murray Tanner, *The Politics of Lawmaking in Post-Mao China: Institutions, Processes, and Democratic Prospects* (New York: Oxford University Press, 1999), 11.

2. Daniel C. K. Chow, *The Legal System of the People's Republic of China in a Nutshell* (St. Paul: Thomson/West, 2003), 34; Randall Peerenboom, *China's Long March toward Rule of Law* (Cambridge: Cambridge University Press, 2002), 19–20; also see Stanley B. Lubman, "Looking for Law in China," *Columbia Journal of Asian Law* 20, no. 1 (2006): 1–92.

3. *Weiquan* (literally "protection of rights") denotes various forms of citizens' actions to protect their rights. It is becoming one of the most frequently used words in the Chinese media. *Weiquan* actions also represent major cases in administrative, civil, and economic legal disputes. For example, see Zheng Xianjun, *Ziyou de baozhang: Gongmin jiben quanli baozhang de jinzhan* (Protection of

Freedoms: Development of Protection of Citizens' Basic Rights) (Beijing: People's University Press, 2005).

4. China's 1999 amendment of its current constitution (1982) added the principle of rule of law, though only implicitly. On the discussion of China's view of the rule of law, see in particular Ronald Keith, *China's Struggle for the Rule of Law* (New York: St. Martin's Press, 1994); Zheng Yongnian, "From Rule by Law to Rule of Law? A Realistic View of China's Legal Development," *China Perspectives,* no. 25 (September–October 1999): 31–43; Yuanyuan Shen, "Conceptions and Receptions of Legality," in *The Limits of the Rule of Law in China,* ed. Karen G. Turner, James V. Feinerman, and R. Kent Guy (Seattle: University of Washington Press, 2000), 20–44; Peerenboom, *China's Long March toward Rule of Law;* Randall Peerenboom, "The Dynamics and Politics of Legal Reform in China," in *Law Reform in Developing and Transitional States,* ed. Tim Lindsey (New York: Routledge, 2007), 196–235; Zou Keyuan, *China's Legal Reform: Towards the Rule of Law* (Boston: Martinus Nijhoff, 2006).

5. Yuchao Zhu, "Legal Institution Building for the Rule of Law and Human Rights in China," *American Review of China Studies* 6, no. 1 (2005): 55–76.

6. Chow, *The Legal System,* 61–66; Peerenboom, "Dynamics and Politics of Legal Reform in China," 205.

7. For an overall review of China's legal reform, see the special issue of *China Quarterly,* no. 191 (2007), esp. Donald C. Clarke, "Introduction: The Chinese Legal System since 1995: Steady Development and Striking Continuities," 555–566.

8. Peerenboom, *China's Long March toward Rule of Law,* 6, and "Dynamics and Politics of Legal Reform in China," 205.

9. Stanley B. Lubman, *Bird in a Cage: Legal Reform in China after Mao* (Stanford: Stanford University Press, 1999), 317–318.

10. "Abusing Rights according to the Law," *China Rights Forum* (Winter 1999–2000), www.hrichina.org/what-we-do/research-and-publications/publication-list (accessed July 17, 2012).

11. He Weifang, *Yunsong zhengyi de fangshi* (Methods to Achieve Justice) (Guangzhou: Guangdong People's Press, 1999).

12. Zhu Suli, *Songfa xiaxiang* (Sending Law to the Countryside) (Beijing: Chinese University of Political Science and Law Press, 2000). It should be mentioned that both He Weifang and Zhu Suli are from the Faculty of Law at Beijing University. He Weifang is also the editor in chief of *Bijiao faxue* (Comparative Law), and Zhu Suli was the dean of the Faculty of Law, Peking University. Regarding Chinese jurists' opinions of China's legal reform, see Peerenboom, "Dynamics and Politics of Legal Reform in China."

13. It is worth noting that in Chinese *fazhi* has two different meanings (with the same pronunciation but different characters); one is "rule by law," the other is "rule of law." The former is very instrumental and was widely used as the guideline for China's legal reform. It was after 1996 that CCP leaders and state policy documents began to use *fazhi* (rule of law) to refer to the guiding principle

behind the building of China's legal system. Since then the discussion and debate about "rule of law" and "rule by law" among legal professionals and scholars has reached a consensus that confirms the principle of rule of law. On the debate about these two concepts of *fazhi* among the Chinese sources, Yu Xuede provides a good overview in "Fazhi haishi fazhi, zhimin haishi zhiquan: Guanyu yifazhiguo wenti taolun guandian zongshu" ("Rule by Law" or "Rule of Law," "Controlling People" or "Controlling Power": An Overview of the Discussion about the Question of "Rule of Law"), *Faxueyanjiu* (Jurisprudence Studies), no. 3 (1996); also see Li Buyun, "Yifazhiguo: Jianshe shehuizhuyi dazhi guojia" (The Rule of Law: To Build a Socialist Rule-of-Law Country), *Zhongguo renda xinwen* (NPC News), July 4, 2001; among English sources, see Shen, "Conceptions and Receptions of Legality," 24; Ronald Keith and Zhiqiu Lin, *Law and Justice in China's New Marketplace* (New York: Palgrave, 2001), 27–29.

14. On the importance of administrative law in China's legal system in general, see Jinfu Chen, *Chinese Law: Towards an Understanding of Chinese Law, Its Nature and Development* (London: Kluwer Law International, 1999), 133–139; Zuo Weimin and He Yongjun, "Zhengfa chuantong yu sifa lixing" (Political-Legal Tradition and Judicial Reasoning), *Sichuan daxue xuebao* (Journal of Sichuan University), no. 1 (2005): 107–118, www.wenhuacn.com/article.asp?classid=30&articleid=2109 (accessed May 2007).

15. Perry Keller, "Sources of Order in Chinese Law," *American Journal of Comparative Law* 42, no. 4 (1994): 738–743.

16. William P. Alford, "A Second Great Wall? China's Post-Cultural Revolution Project of Legal Construction," *Cultural Dynamics* 11, no. 2 (1999): 208–209.

17. For example, a sociologist at Tsinghua University, Sun Liping, in borrowing Durkheim's social theory to examine the current state-society relationship, describes China's social and legal order as "broken down" and experiencing "anomie." Sun Liping, *Zhuanxing yu duanlie* (Social Transformation and Social Breakdown) (Beijing: Tsinghua University Press, 2004); also see Chen Cheng, "Dangqian woguo shehui shifan de leixing fenxi" (Typological Analysis of Anomie in China), *Society*, no. 12 (2002): 20; Zhu Li, "Guanyu shehui jizhi shifan de tantao" (Exploration of Societal Anomie Mechanisms), *Sociology Studies*, no. 5 (2006): 111.

18. Neil J. Diamant, Stanley B. Lubman, and Kevin J. O'Brien, eds., *Engaging the Law in China: State, Society, and Possibilities for Justice* (Stanford: Stanford University Press, 2005), 13.

19. Lindsey, *Law Reform in Developing and Transitional States.*

20. The direct translation of *hukou* is "household registration." For a detailed description and analysis of the *hukou* system, see Tiejun Cheng and Mark Selden, "The Origins and Social Consequences of China's *Hukou* System," *China Quarterly*, no. 139 (1994): 644–668.

21. Xiao Han, "Jiannan bashe zhong de renshen ziyou—Shourong qiansong zhidu jianyao pingshu" (Personal Freedom in Difficult Times—A Simple Review

of the C&R), June 27, 2003, www.china-review.com/gao.asp?id=16271 (accessed July 17, 2012).

22. Yuchao Zhu, "Proclamation, Implementation, and Abolishment of China's Custody and Repatriation Law: An Institutionalist Analysis," *American Journal of Chinese Studies* 13, no. 2 (2006): 193–195.

23. Lubman calls this kind of practice "non-judicial sanction" as a part of the "criminal process." Lubman, *Bird in a Cage,* 169. Regarding various forms of administrative detention measures and their function in China's legal system, see Peerenboom, "Dynamics and Politics of Legal Reform in China," 214–218.

24. Wei Luo, *Chinese Law and Legal Research* (Buffalo, N.Y.: William S. Hein, 2005), 74–75.

25. Interview, Ministry of Civil Affairs, Beijing, April 7, 2006.

26. Sun Zhigang, a newly graduated college student who worked temporarily in Guangzhou, was detained by the police in accordance with the C&R and later beaten to death in Guangzhou's C&R facility in April 2003. This outrageous crime then became a major media story nationwide and finally led to the abolition of the C&R by the State Council on June 18, 2003. So Sun Zhigang became the last-known victim of this notorious administrative measure. For the story of the process to abolish the C&R, see Zhao Ling, "*Feizhi shourong qiansong banfa de juece licheng*" (The Process of Abolishing the C&R), *Nanfang zhoume* (Southern Weekend), June 26 2003, http://bbs.cnhan.com/simple/?t4503.html (accessed July 17, 2012); Zhu, "Proclamation, Implementation, and Abolishment."

27. Carl F. Minzner, "*Xinfang*—An Alternative to Chinese Formal Legal Institutions," *Stanford Journal of International Law,* no. 42 (2006): 103–179; Laura M. Luehrmann, "Facing Citizen Complaints in China, 1951–1996," *Asian Survey* 42, no. 5 (2003): 845–866.

28. For a historical analysis of China's complaint system, see Qiang Fang, "Hot Potatoes: Chinese Complaint Systems from Early Times to the Late Qing (1898)," *Journal of Asian Studies* 68, no. 4 (2009): 1105–1135.

29. It should be noted that L&V activities also occur within the judicial system. For example, China's Supreme Court has a major L&V reception center, and responses to L&V petitions through the court system take the form of "judicial opinions," which do have legal status. But overall, L&V is often viewed more as an administrative measure; see Zuo and He, "Zhengfa chuantong."

30. Xu Zhiyong et al., "Xianzheng shiye zhong de xinfang zhili" (L&V Management from the Perspective of Constitutionalism), *Gansu lilun xuekan* (Gansu Theoretical Journal), no. 3 (2005), www.cnki.com.cn/Article/CJFDTOTAL-GLXK200503005.htm (accessed July 17, 2012); Regarding ombudsmen in the West, see Donald C. Rowat, ed., *The Ombudsman: Citizen's Defender* (Toronto: University of Toronto Press, 1965). It should be noted that there are significant differences between China's complaint system and the Western ombudsman system. According to Rowat, the real ombudsman mechanism may not function properly

in a one-party state; see Donald C. Rowat, "Recent Developments in Ombuds-manship," *Canadian Public Administration* 10, no. 1 (1967): 36–37.

31. Minzner, "*Xingfang,*" 105–106.

32. For example, according to Hao Jing's investigation, among 632 cases of L&V in 2005, 401 tried the legal process, but 43 percent of their legal appeals were denied. See Hao Jing, "Xinfang zhidu buying qianghua qi quanli jiuji gong-neng" (We Should Not Strengthen the L&V's Judicial Remedy Function), *Guang-dong xingzheng xueyuan xuebao* (Journal of Guangdong Administrative College), no. 6 (2005): 41–44.

33. See Wang Xuejun, "Guanyu dangqian de xinfang xingshi he renwu" (About the Contemporary Situation and Task of L&V), http://wenku.baidu.com/view/59bfdc1fff00bed5b9f31d6c.html (accessed July 17, 2012).

34. Yin Xing, "Zuowei teshu xingzheng jiuji de xinfang jiuji" (L&V as a Special Remedy for Administrative Recourse), *Faxue yanjiu* (Jurisprudence Studies), no. 3 (2004): 58–71.

35. Mei Ying Gechlik (Veron Hung), "Judicial Reform in China: Lessons from Shanghai," *Carnegie Papers,* no. 58 (March 2005), www.carnegieendowment.org/publications/index.cfm?fa=view&id=16784 (accessed June 2006); Minxin Pei, "Citizens vs. Mandarins: Administrative Litigation in China," *China Quarterly,* no. 152 (1997): 832–862.

36. Fang, "Hot Potatoes," 1106.

37. Yu Jianrong, "Xinfang zhidu gaige yu xianzheng jianshe" (Systemic Reform of L&V and Construction of Constitutionalism), *Twenty-first Century,* no. 7 (2005), www.cuhk.edu.hk/ics/21c/supplem/essay/0504050.htm (accessed May 2007).

38. There are mainly two types of management methods for dealing with L&V cases: *zhuanban* (transfer or referral treatment) and *duban* (supervised treatment); the former requires responsible government agencies to report only the result, and this method is not very politically accountable; but the latter requires L&V offices to supervise low-level agencies' responses and report the results, which is more politically accountable. Which method officials assign to specific L&V cases also depends on the government's internal structure and bureaucratic hierarchy. For example, L&V officials usually cannot *duban* the cases at a higher level of govern-ment. This information comes from an interview I conducted in the Tianjin L&V Office on June 15, 2008.

39. Margaret Y. K. Woo, "Law and Discretion in Contemporary Chinese Courts," in Turner et al., *The Limits of the Rule of Law in China,* 163–195.

40. Fang, "Hot Potatoes," 1107–1108.

41. Minzner, "*Xingfang,*" 111–114.

42. Hao, "Xingfang zhidu."

43. See "Taoxin Chongqing funu xiongdeming xiang wen zongli shuoshi-hua yiyan chengming" (Chongqing Woman Xiong Deming Demanding Unpaid Wages Became Famous Because She Spoke to Premier Wen Frankly), *Jinghua*

*shibao* (Beijing Times), February 6, 2008, http://beijing.jinghua.cn/c/200803/06/n766032.shtml (accessed July 17, 2012).

44. Regarding case studies of the pursuit of "justice from above," see Kevin J. O'Brien and Lianjiang Li, *Rightful Resistance in Rural China* (Cambridge: Cambridge University Press, 2006); regarding the argument about resolving social justice issues locally, see Ethan Michelson, "Justice from Above or Below? Popular Strategies for Resolving Grievances in Rural China," *China Quarterly*, no. 193 (2008): 43–64.

45. Decree of the State Council of the People's Republic of China (No. 431) "Regulations on Letters and Visits," adopted at the Seventy-Sixth Executive Meeting of the State Council on January 5, 2005, and effective as of May 1, 2005.

46. Some local government agencies even hire security companies in Beijing to coercively detain and send L&V people back to their hometowns; this practice has become very abusive and seriously violates human rights. See, for example, Long Hua, "Anyuanding: Beijing jiefang heijianyu diaocha" (Anyuanding: An Investigative Report about a Beijing "Dark Prison" and Its Blocking L&V Activities), September 24, 2009, http://gcontent.oeeee.com/f/6c/f6c9dc70ecfd8f90/Blog/4a3/c0aee0.html (accessed July 17, 2012); also see Guo Yukuan, "Beifen de chaosheng zhilu" (Sad and Angry Road of Appeal—Investigation of L&V Petitioners and Thoughts about the Institutional-Cultural Roots of L&V), May 29, 2007, http://boxun.com/news/gb/yuanqing/2007/05/200705290006.shtml (accessed July 17, 2012).

47. Diament, Lubman, and O'Brien, *Engaging the Law in China*, 18.

48. Cheng Zhuru, *Sifa gaige yu zhengzhi fazhan* (Judicial Reform and China's Political Development) (Beijing: Chinese Social Science Press, 2001), 158; Randall Peerenboom, "A Government of Laws: Democracy, Rule of Law, and Administrative Law Reform in China," in *Debating Democracy in China: Rule of Law vs. Democratization,* ed. Suisheng Zhao (New York: M. E. Sharpe, 2006), 58–78.

49. Jean-Pierre Cabestan, "The Political and Practical Obstacles to the Reform of the Judiciary and the Establishment of a Rule of Law in China," *Journal of Chinese Political Science* 10, no. 1 (2005): 56.

50. Hung, "Judicial Reform in China," 13.

51. Cheng, *Sifa gaige,* 94.

52. Wang Hengqin, *Zhongguo sifa zhidu gaige yanjiu* (Research on the Reform of China's Judicial System) (Beijing: Knowledge Press, 2004).

53. Zhang Renshan, *Sifa fubai yu shehui shikong, 1928–1949* (Judicial Corruption and Losing Social Control) (Beijing: Social Science Archival Press, 2005).

54. Keller, "Sources of Order in Chinese Law," 715.

55. René David and John E. C. Brierley, *Major Legal Systems in the World Today,* 2nd ed. (London: Stevens & Son, 1978), 483.

56. On China's review of the development of the rule of law, the most comprehensive annual is *Fazhi lanpishu* (Blue Book of Rule of Law: The Development

of Rule of Law in China) (Beijing: Social Science Archival Press, 2003, 2004, and 2005).

57. The case of Qi Yuling involves a young woman (Qi) who took an examination to qualify her for further study. But the letter informing her of her success was intercepted by another woman with the collusion of her father, a locally powerful person. Qi discovered the fraud and sued, claiming among other things infringement of her right to her name and deprivation of her right to an education. The Higher-Level People's Court hearing the case asked the Supreme People's Court whether she could be awarded damages on the basis of this infringement of her constitutional right. The SPC answered yes. This was considered ground-breaking because it had long been a dogma of Chinese law that the constitution could not be cited by courts or used as a basis in their judgments. See http://lawprofessors.typepad.com/china_law_prof_blog/2009/01/supreme-peoples.html (accessed June 2012).

58. In the Sun Zhigang case, five famous Chinese legal scholars openly demanded that the NPC conduct a constitutional review of the C&R. Though in the end this formal constitutional review did not happen, the State Council organized a public inquiry session to hear their arguments and made the decision to abolish the C&R immediately. See "Wuwei faxuejia tiqing renda qidong tebie chengxu diaocha sunzhigang an" (Five Legal Scholars Demand People's Congress to Launch a Special Procedure to Review the Sun Zhigang Case), *Zhongguo qingnianbao* (China Youth Daily), May 28, 2003, www.china.com.cn/chinese/2003/May/337024.htm (accessed July 17, 2012).

59. Pitman B. Potter, "Riding the Tiger: Legitimacy and Legal Culture in Post-Mao China," *China Quarterly*, no. 138 (1994): 326.

60. Tanner, *The Politics of Lawmaking*, 8.

61. Edward J. Epstein, "Law and Legitimation in Post-Mao China," in *Domestic Law Reform in Post-Mao China*, ed. Pitman B. Potter (New York: M. E. Sharpe, 1994), 29.

62. Zhu, *Legal Institution*, 62–63.

63. Alan Watson, *Legal Transplants* (Athens: University of Georgia Press, 1993).

64. Gunther Teubner, "Legal Irritants: Good Faith in British Law or How Unifying Law Ends Up in New Divergences," *Modern Law Review* 61, no. 1 (1998): 11–32.

65. Pierre Legrand, "The Impossibility of 'Legal Transplants,'" *Maastricht Journal of European and Comparative Law* 4, no. 2 (1997): 111–124.

66. Werner Menski, *Comparative Law in a Global Context: The Legal Systems of Asia and Africa*, 2nd ed. (New York: Cambridge University Press, 2006), 522.

67. Peerenboom, *China's Long March*, 3–4.

68. Alford, "A Second Great Wall?" 209.

## FURTHER READING

Biddulph, Sarah. *Legal Reforms and Administrative Detention Power*. Cambridge: Cambridge University Press, 2007.

Clarke, Donald C. "Power and Politics in the Chinese Court System: The Enforcement of Civil Judgement." *Columbia Journal of Asian Law* 10, no. 1 (1996).

Fu, Zhengyuan. *Autocratic Tradition and Chinese Politics*. Cambridge: Cambridge University Press, 1993.

Keith, Ronald, and Zhiqiu Lin. *New Crime in China: Public Order and Human Rights*. New York: Palgrave, 2006.

Lü Peng. "Zhidu shi ruhe fengbi de" (How a System Is Closed), *Xuehai* (Journal of Studies), no. 1 (2006). http://guancha.gmw.cn/show.aspx?id=7930 (accessed May 2006).

O'Brien, Kevin J., and Lianjiang Li. "The Politics of Lodging Complaints in Rural China." *China Quarterly*, no. 143 (1995): 756–783.

Peerenboom, Randall. *China Modernizes: Threat to the West or Model for the Rest?* New York: Oxford University Press, 2007.

Potter, Pitman B. *The Chinese Legal System: Globalization and Local Legal Culture*. New York: Routledge, 2001.

# 3

# The Dragon's Tale

*China's Efforts toward the Rule of Law*

## Xiaobing Li

China's current constitution, which incorporated important amendments between 1978 and 2004, has finally addressed citizens' liberties and has institutionalized these rights as a component of the nation's judicial system that was created with the founding of the People's Republic of China (PRC) in 1949. Since the creation of the PRC, China has promulgated four state constitutions, in 1954, 1975, 1978, and 1982. The current constitution was adopted by the Fifth National People's Congress (NPC) on December 4, 1982, and it underwent important changes and revisions in 1988, 1993, 1999, and 2004. Even though some civil liberties and legal codes are provided by the constitution, many others have not been enacted. This chapter provides a historical overview of the PRC constitutional reform and identifies some contradictions in government policy making in the promotion of legal reforms.[1] It suggests that legal reform in China has failed to deliver on its promises and thus that there is a gap between the promise of reform and the reality of legal practice.

In the past sixty years the Chinese constitution has undergone periods of acceptance, rejection, and rewriting. In 1949, in preparation for the emergence of a new Communist state, the CCP leadership named the country the "People's Republic of China" in order to differentiate it from the old Nationalist state, the Republic of China (ROC), established in 1912. The PRC, however, did not empower its citizens or protect their civil rights and liberties. During its early years, the new China followed the Soviet model and limited people's rights by breaking with tradition and expanding state power through political campaigns and class struggle. After the first constitution was promulgated in 1954, it encountered challenges from radical political movements during the 1960s. After the Sino-Soviet split in the 1960s, the Chinese government failed to promote civil liberties and to protect individual rights. Until 1978, Chinese society was centered on a unitary party-state that maintained complete control of all social resources. The Chinese Communist Party Center utilized the government, including courts, law enforcement, and the legal system, to serve its Communist political agenda. The constitution of the three decades preceding 1978 was merely a history of the CCP's experiment in political establishment and institutional dominance, which created many obstacles to serious legal reforms at the end of the century.

## Deng's Reform and New Constitutions

In 1978, after his third return to the Party Center, Deng Xiaoping led the second generation of the CCP. He became focused on putting China on the road to prosperity by deprogramming Mao's system and convincing Chinese citizens, after ten years of turmoil and Cultural Revolution, that economic reconstruction should become their first priority. Deng defended a market economy by stating that it did not contradict socialism but was simply an economic tool to serve an ideological cause. In Deng's system, Marxism and Mao's Thought became the means to support reform rather than a goal to attain.

To start his reform movement, Deng urged the NPC to develop a new constitution. On March 5, 1978, at the Plenary Session of the Fifth NPC, the third PRC constitution was adopted. It doubled its articles from thirty to sixty and contained a new preamble. Two years after the downfall of the Maoists, such as the Gang of Four, the new constitution restored courts and procuratorates. It also reinstated some citizens' rights, such as the right to strike. For the first time, the new constitution declared that Taiwan is part of China and must be liberated by the PRC, thus finishing the immense task of reunifying the motherland. In 1979 the government added an amendment that dropped the liberation stance and opted rather for peaceful reunification.

Since the 1978 constitution was adopted just two years after the Cultural Revolution, it carried radical terms, such as "Revolutionary Commit-

Deng Xiaoping and Jimmy Carter at the arrival ceremony for the vice premier of China, January 1979. (National Archives)

tees." It required support for the leadership of the CCP, and participation in the socialist system remained a component of citizens' duties. The new constitution did not create legal norms, and noncompliance with the document's provisions became a common occurrence. For example, cadres and law enforcers still acted extralegally. More than 10,000 cases of violations of personal rights, especially illegal search and detention, extortion, and confession by torture were discovered and prosecuted by the procuratorates.[2] The 1978 constitution was replaced four years later during Deng Xiaoping's era of reform.

The market economy has dramatically changed the structure of Chinese society, especially in rural areas. After 1978 the concept of Mao's People's Communes weakened considerably. Deng was the first Communist leader to encourage people to strive for wealth. With his slogan "To be rich is glorious," he won the people's support, most prominently in rural areas.

Chinese peasants were determined to improve their living conditions, and they often succeeded, which led directly to the collapse of the entire commune system and the state's substantial retreat from rural society.[3]

Long-dissatisfied peasants began redistributing land to households on the condition that each would submit a certain portion of its output to the government. This practice immediately achieved great success because, once again, individual farmers gained complete control of their input and output. The practice was officially accepted nationwide after a short pioneering experiment in select areas and was soon promoted as the Household Production Responsibility System (HPRS) in 1979. The production contracting system gave peasants the right to control production, but potential redistribution of land prevented them from leaving their villages, which resulted in a decline in interest in serving in the military. The larger an agricultural family, the larger the piece of land it received, and parents sought to keep their sons on the farm to ensure success in the new competitive market. In the early 1980s, when a sizable portion of land was in able hands, some of the peasants in the southern provinces became relatively wealthy, achieving an annual income of approximately $3,000, compared to a national peasant average of $60.

Social stratification in China manifested itself as a new challenge to the government. After the late 1970s economic reforms improved the food supply to cities and abolished the food rationing (or quota) system for urban residents. Economic growth somewhat diminished the boundaries between different social statuses that had been clearly and rigidly marked in the past. The loosening of government control over people's mobility allowed farmers to take up occupations originally available only to urban residents. All these changes helped diversify the homogeneous group of farmers into different social groups and quickly boosted a considerable number of them into a higher-income stratum. The prominent social feature of the 1990s was the rapid accumulation of wealth.

Another striking feature of China's social change is the mobile or transient population. As the old apparatuses of migration control became less effective, rural people began moving spontaneously into urban areas without obtaining government approval. By the late 1990s, approximately 48 million individuals had successfully completed this transfer. In the first decade of the twenty-first century, as many as 110 million rural laborers were estimated to be on the move, seeking work in cities.

A market economy based on competitive production requires a stable rule of law in areas such as commerce, trade, contracts, labor relations, bankruptcy, and the like. A sound, reliable legal system is essential, not only for bringing basic efficiency to the Chinese economy, but as a requirement of international investors and those who participate in the country's other commercial activities. This economic imperative pressured the second generation of CCP leadership to engage in numerous legal reforms, including the revision of the 1978 constitution.

To prepare a new constitution, the Committee to Amend the Constitution was established on September 10, 1980, and it completed a draft version in February 1982. It was submitted to the NPC Standing Committee for national discussion, and on December 4, 1982, the Fifth Plenary Session of the Fifth NPC adopted the new document by secret ballot. The 1982 constitution was the longest document in PRC history: it included 138 articles. It was a mix of continuity and change to the previous versions. Many sections of the 1982 document were adapted directly from the 1978 constitution, though some new concepts and articles were added. For example, the 1982 constitution stated that class struggle was no longer the most important issue for the country and its citizens; it placed economic development and improvement of people's standard of living as the top priority. In addition, it affirmed the idea of legality and other related concepts, expressly stating that the Party had to operate within the scope of the constitution and the law. It did, however, stress that any exercise of rights or freedoms violating any of the Four Basic Principles[4]—to keep the country on the socialist road, to uphold the people's democratic dictatorship, to promote the leadership of the CCP, and to follow Marxism-Leninism and Mao's Thought—is unconstitutional and therefore unlawful.

The 1982 constitution has four chapters, including "The Fundamental Rights and Duties of Citizens." It contains a complete, detailed, and elaborate list of rights, none of which was set forth in the constitutions of 1954, 1975, or 1978. Some of the new provisions were specifically designed to avoid the civil and human rights violations of the Great Cultural Revolution of the 1960s. The chapter also lists several fundamental rights and duties of citizens that had been enacted after the constitution was ratified. After 1982 the legal system was revived in China, and many law schools reopened. More textbooks and legal magazines were being published, and lawyers once again began to practice. The courts handled more cases than at any other time in the past: more than 2.5 million were reported in 1986.[5] The Ministry of Justice was reestablished under the State Council. In public discourse, slogans such as "Rule the country by law" and "Rule the country according to law" have been increasingly used.

## Legal Reform under Jiang Zemin

Following Deng's retirement, the third generation of CCP leadership recognized that the authoritarian power structure and secretive policy making helped create the crisis of 1989, in which hundreds, if not thousands, of demonstrators were killed during the Tiananmen Square incident. Accordingly, in the 1990s the new government began to avoid arbitrary policy construction and unpredictable risk. The political and economic imperatives made it increasingly desirable for the new leader, Jiang Zemin, to develop more consistent procedural policies through legal reform. Inadequate laws and their selective enforcement had seriously undermined the market economy and stunted the state reform movement. In the mid-1990s cronyism was rampant, and corruption had been accepted as a necessary tool in loosening the machinery of the government. The new administration intended to cut off old-guard connections and get rid of past problems by normalizing the legal system and establishing new regulations. The new leaders saw the rule of law as the only mechanism that could provide an underlying structure on which the free market could take hold, thereby pushing China toward becoming a more modern state. Concurrently, the Chinese people became more aware of their rights as citizens. Much of Chinese society is increasingly demanding legislative and adjudicative due process and the general protection of their rights from the interference of the state. In 1997 Jiang Zemin, then chairman of the Party, called for the rule of law at the Fifteenth CCP National Congress. By the late 1990s China was on course to deepen its legal reform.

In 1999 the Supreme Court issued its first five-year plan for reforming the country's court system. It addressed problems such as competence, fairness, judicial training, and regularity in court procedures. The plan embraced some important reforms such as the creation of rules regarding the use of evidence, and separation of cases from adjudication and of adjudication from enforcement. During the 2000s the legal profession has become increasingly institutionalized, marked by an expansion in legal education and a growing awareness on the part of citizens of their rights under the law.

As a result of this reform, the legal system has been somewhat depoliticized. A discourse on the legitimization of the law has developed in society, primarily from the bottom up. The courts are slowly evolving from serving as political tools for the campaigns of the past to providing justice in individual cases. Many judges now wear robes, in contrast to the military uniforms previously worn, and they increasingly wish to have their courts separate from other branches of the Party-state. Court discussions and decisions have changed from enforcing Party policy to being neutral in order to resolve disputes fairly. The new requirements for the selection of judges reflect a change from a primary reliance on political backgrounds, focusing instead on members of the judiciary who have significant professional experience.

The changes in the courts signify the decentralization of the Party-state during the 1990s. During the political turmoil of the late 1980s, the judiciary had not been a challenge to Party authority, but it contributed to local stability and social order, which the Party Center desperately needed. The influx of the Internet and other communication technologies has made political control outside Party channels more difficult. This development, among others, has challenged the Party leadership, as the centralized government was supposed to solve the problems that accompanied a move toward capitalism. Instead of government's successfully addressing these issues, however, the situation has created new class divisions and a new set of problems, proving again that the cure can sometimes be far worse than the disease. The Party Center has a dilemma: either it accepts local control, or it risks losing control altogether, which makes the former a necessary transformation. But the Party Center lacks both the ability and inclination to monitor its local agents in a consistent manner across all sectors; this deficiency ensures that law enforcement remains distanced from the Party apparatus.

As a result of these legal reforms, courts have increasingly been used for rights-based litigation. In 1999 the courts handled 6 million cases, 5 million of them civil, more than double the number heard in 1986. In addition, more than 10 million letters were sent to courts, accompanied by a corresponding increase in visits.[6] The strengthened institution is also enjoying an increase in power as it enhances its supervisory function. Like the police, the courts answer to local government in most cases. Although they are not yet at the level of courts in Western countries, the increasing role of the judiciary is a significant development. In 2000, for the first time, over 20 percent of Chinese judges had college degrees, thus tripling the number in 1995, when only 6 percent had attained this educational level.

China has one of the largest law enforcement organizations in the world. According to official statistics from 2007, the PRC has more than 580,000 police and 150,000 detectives and investigators, all of whom are under the control of the Ministry of Public Security in Beijing. This ministry has a bureau of public security in each province and county, a metropolitan police department in each city, and precinct offices in each district. In 2003 this top-down centralized police system had 31 provincial bureaus of public security, 356 metropolitan police departments, 2,972 county police headquarters, and 41,941 local police stations. There are also more than 250,000 traffic officers, street patrollers, special police, and occasionally even antiriot units. Estimates of the total of China's law enforcement forces vary, but they are usually in the vicinity of 1 million and rising.

As part of legal reform, China strengthened the People's Armed Police (PAP) in the 1990s. This national organization was established in 1983 and consists of regular troops that are similar to a combination of National Guardsmen and SWAT (Special Weapons and Tactics) teams in the United States. In late 1996 the Chinese government transferred fourteen infantry divisions of People's Liberation Army (PLA) regular soldiers, a total of 150,000 men, to the PAP force. In 2000 the PAP comprised 1 million members.[7] The PRC Law on National Defense, adopted on March 14, 1997, describes the chain of command and defines the mission of the PAP. Article 22 reads, "Under the leadership and command of the State Council and the Central Military Commission, the Chinese People's Armed Police is charged by the state with the mission of safeguarding security and maintaining public order."[8] The duties performed by the PAP in the routine maintenance of internal security are considerably different from those of the police. In addition to guarding their own facilities, the branch's troopers perform standard public security missions, serving as guards at important bridges and government and party buildings, safeguarding foreign diplomatic areas, and ensuring protection of senior leaders. Additionally, they participate in street patrols and ceremonial duties and back up police forces.

The late 1990s and early 2000s were years of extraordinary changes in China's legal system. There was a high degree of continuity, however, from previous periods of rule and earlier constitutions, especially in the area of civil liberties and people's rights. China's problems and its excuses can be clearly seen in government documents published by the State Council, such as the "Progress in China's Human Rights Cause" (March 1997),

"Freedom of Religious Belief in China" (October 1997), "New Progress in Human Rights in the Tibet Autonomous Region" (February 1998), and "National Minorities Policy and Its Practice in China" (September 1999).[9] During this decade, the country faced new challenges as well as old problems, such as human rights violations, suppression of religions and political dissent, the abuse of prisoners, and women's rights. The PRC's conduct in these fields remains a top concern for the American government, which has pledged to support intensive efforts to promote freedom in all countries. The challenges facing China require serious political will and new resources. The Chinese government must interact with all its citizens and civil society groups in ongoing legal and political reforms.

## IMPROVING THE PEOPLE'S RIGHTS

The country has reached a crossroads in development that will continue and consume the next decade. Its low production costs and export-oriented economy reached their apogee in 2008, and the following year saw a substantial slowdown in the growth of the economy. To offset this reality, the government must deal with the social and political issues that have arisen in the past two decades, largely a result of rapid economic expansion, including labor relations, unemployment, inflation, social stratification, a damaged environment, corruption, and organized crime. China is in the midst of a momentous transition, and more and more of the nation's people are demanding greater government accountability. They reject the increasing human cost that has accompanied this "economic miracle." Many of them, including 700 million rural inhabitants, an estimated 150–200 million migrant workers, and more than 2 million former employees of state-owned enterprises, have lost jobs, homes, and access to basic health care and an affordable education for their children. The unemployment rate has increased to 9 percent in recent years. In most cases, however, the government continues to ignore these issues and to cover up problems by censoring public voices and media criticism as well as denying legal liability. The Chinese legal system has failed to protect freedom of speech and to provide judicial supervision. According to the annual reports released by the U.S. Department of State, the U.S. Congressional Executive Commission on China, Amnesty International, and Human Rights Watch, the condition of civil liberties in China continued its "deterioration in key aspects" in 2011.[10]

With a population of almost 1.4 billion people, China faces challenges that are enormous and complex and that require new efforts in legal and political reforms. Despite provisions in the Chinese constitution that claim to protect freedom of speech, association, privacy, and communication, a clear gap exists between law and reality. The government has little tolerance for criticism or calls for its greater transparency and accountability, and it ignores especially the need for a harmonious society and political stability during an economic recession. Beijing continues to restrict some of its citizens' fundamental rights, and it employs law enforcement and a legal system to suppress political dissent, nonregistered organizations, and so-called unauthorized activities. These government restrictions draw criticism from journalists, activists, and intellectuals, some of whom also organized demonstrations in China during the first decade of the twenty-first century. Their stories present a small window into the struggles endured by the Chinese people as they attempt to speak out and demand accountability and responsibility from those in power.

An examination of China's current system of civil rights protection should begin with an analysis of the constitution's relevant provisions. In the present constitution, promulgated in 1982, the second chapter, titled "The Fundamental Rights and Duties of Citizens," has a list of civil rights, including freedom of speech, freedom of the press, and freedom of assembly. Article 35 states, "Citizens of the People's Republic of China enjoy freedom of speech, of the press, of assembly, of association, of procession, and of demonstration."[11] Article 40 states, "Freedom and privacy of correspondence of citizens of the People's Republic of China are protected by law. No organization or individual may, on any ground, infringe on citizens' freedom and privacy of correspondence, except in cases where, to meet the needs of state security or of criminal investigation, public security or procuratorial organs are permitted to censor correspondence in accordance with the procedures prescribed by law."[12] In article 41 there are much more detailed and elaborate protections of the rights of citizens to criticize the government than in the corresponding parts of the previous constitutions. Obviously, some of the provisions in the present constitution are specifically designed to prevent the kinds of civil and human rights violations that took place during the Cultural Revolution and other political movements during Mao's era of 1950–1976.

Among other rights, the constitution pledges the citizens' right to equality before the law, political rights to participate in elections, and certain personal freedoms. Even though the constitution also promises various social and economic rights, the Chinese government always locates civil and human rights issues within the category of feeding the largest population in the world, which is China's fundamental human rights issue, differing from that in the West. The PRC government has been able to save the nation, whereas a liberal or democratic government might have failed, being too weak and ineffective to do so. Nonetheless, after 1982 Beijing continued to show improvements in its civil liberties and human rights legislations.

In April 1988 the First Session of the Seventh National People's Congress adopted two constitutional amendments regarding private property and protection of the ownership of private property. In March 1993 the First Session of the Eighth NPC made nine important changes in the form of amendments, including some changes in the preamble to the constitution. In March 1999 the Second Session of the Ninth NPC adopted and published six constitutional amendments. According to an official report in 2003, the Central Committee of the CCP proposed amendments to the constitution, including this assertion: "The state respects and guarantees human rights." On March 14, 2004, the Second Session of the Tenth National People's Congress adopted and published fourteen important amendments to the constitution. Within the most prominent amendment is this declaration added to article 33: "The state respects and guarantees human rights."[13] This marked the first time the Chinese constitution mentioned human rights, and, according to the government, it indicates that safeguarding these rights is no longer limited to Party and government policy, but is an ideal enshrined in the fabric of the nation and critical to the progress of the state.

Moreover, in 2003 the government revised Publications Administration Regulations and Regulations Governing the Administration of Audiovisual Products, which placed increased stipulations on the previously mentioned freedoms. The Publications Administration Regulations state that "citizens may, in accordance with these regulations, freely express in publications their opinions and expectations of state affairs, economic and cultural undertakings, and social affairs, and freely publish the results of their scientific research, literary or artistic creations, and other cultural pursuits."[14]

According to the official annual report, the Chinese government has promoted the press, providing favorable conditions for citizens to enjoy their freedoms. This new vigor on the part of the press has had a significant effect on the development of democracy in the country, especially as citizens can now, for the most part, talk about the government privately. The democratic development has begun at a local level for the peasants and villagers. Of the thirty-four provinces, autonomous regions, and centrally administered municipalities, twenty-eight have implemented the Organic Law of the Villagers' Committees, and thirty-one have organized village election committees. The average rate of participation in elections is 80 percent; the rate exceeds 90 percent in Guangdong, Hainan, Sichuan, and Hunan provinces. Although Western scholars do not yet believe China is a democratic society, most will agree that the freedom of speech for its citizens has dramatically improved. On some issues, however, individuals in the country are required not to violate the Four Basic Principles of the constitution, a requirement that in itself is a restriction on the freedom of speech.

China claims that it has given top priority to people's lives, health, and basic human rights. An official Human Rights Report published in March 2004 pointed out that the government has adopted an attitude of "holding itself accountable to the people, acting in their interests, and accepting their supervision." The government has furthermore formulated the following principles of governance: "Governing the country for the people, using the power for the people, sharing the feelings of the people, and working for the interests of the people."[15] To show its efforts, the Chinese government has adopted some measures for respecting and safeguarding political and human rights. In 2005 the Chinese government promised to release political prisoners who had been jailed since 1989, in order to curb worldwide criticism and to win support for its Olympic games bid. After the International Olympic Committee voted for Beijing to host the games, the Chinese government continued to demonstrate improvement in protecting political and human rights. In 2006, for example, China continued to allow local villagers to elect their village chiefs through a democratic and open election. More than 500 million villagers voted at 624,000 villages across the country. In 2007 the government issued new regulations to allow, for the first time, foreign media to film local events and to interview Chinese citizens, and in 2008, especially during the Olympic games, more effort was made by the Chinese government in this direction. Many China watchers and international rights groups, however, believe that the Chinese government has not done enough to improve civil liberties and human rights conditions.

## RIGHTS LIMIT AND POLITICAL CONTROL

The limits and problems of China's civil liberties protection can be identified in legislative, executive, and judicial procedures. The constitution stresses in its preamble that any expression of rights or freedoms is unlawful if it violates the Four Basic Principles. Moreover, a citizen's exercise of individual rights and freedoms cannot conflict with the state's interests and other citizens' rights. In the existing laws, the restrictions on freedom of speech primarily include three main parts. First, article 51 of the constitution stipulates, "Citizens of the People's Republic of China, in exercising their freedom and rights, may not infringe on the interests of the state, of society, or of the collective, or on the lawful freedoms and rights of other citizens."[16] Second, speeches may be judged according to the provisions of Criminal Law, such as crimes of antirevolutionary propaganda, insults, slander, and false witness. Third, similar restrictions on speech can be found in civil and administrative law. Thus, the Chinese government can easily restrict freedom of speech and the press wherever it wants to link them to the jeopardy of national, social, and collective interests.

In addition, following the constitutional restrictions on civil liberties, the Chinese government continues to issue more regulations to limit citizens' rights. As the executive branch, the State Council makes administrative rules and regulations to restrain freedom of speech and freedom of assembly. For example, after the Tiananmen Square incident in June 1989, the State Council on October 31, 1989, issued the Act on Marches and Demonstrations, which provides regulations that limit citizens' rights to assemble, march, and demonstrate. Before citizens organize an assembly, a march, or a demonstration, they must first apply for permission from the authorities (seventh clause). It also stipulates that under any of the following circumstances, the application will not be approved: if the assembly, march, or demonstration opposes the fundamental principles of the constitution; if national unity, sovereignty, or territorial integrity is threatened; if a national split is advocated; or if enough evidence is garnered to prove the planned assembly, march, or demonstration will directly endanger public security and seriously disturb social order (twelfth clause). In addition, the act also stipulates that "citizens cannot initiate, organize, or incite citizens of cities outside the organizers' home cities to participate in the assembly, march, or demonstration" (fifteenth clause). Furthermore, "those who work in government offices must not organize or participate in the assemblies, marches, or demonstrations that violate duties and responsibilities stipulated by laws or regulations for government offi-cials" (sixteenth clause). And finally, "the time for assemblies, marches, and demonstrations is limited to the period from 6:00 A.M. to 10:00 P.M." (twenty-fourth clause). Another example of restrictions on the freedom of speech is in the Act on Guarding State Secrets. This administrative act enumerates seventeen categories of state secrets (in effect including almost anything not publicly released).

It is important to note that the Chinese judicial procedure also allows the legislature and legal system to restrain freedom of speech and freedom of the press. The Chinese legal system is different from other civil law sys-tems. The PRC constitution does not systematically outline general princi-ples that all administrative regulations and rules must follow. Instead, each governmental branch is allowed to set up its own guidelines, whereas the principles of legislation are listed in the basic laws enacted by the NPC and its standing committee. The provincial governments also make their local civic laws. Local laws and regulations are issued by provincial, city, and county governments, even though all these ordinary laws are, in theory, incorporated with those at the national level.

The way in which civil liberties can be compromised by ordinary laws can be illustrated by examining those relating to the freedoms of speech, publication, and procession. The Criminal Law, for instance, was adopted by the NPC's Standing Committee in 1979; it was amended in 1997 because of an increase in crimes throughout the country.[17] This body of legal pro-visions provides the principal punishments, including criminal deten-tion, fixed-term imprisonment, life imprisonment, and the death penalty. Under some criticism, the Criminal Law has done away with the offender category of "counterrevolutionary." A change, however, was made to "state-overthrowing" offences, such as spreading antigovernment propaganda, or other acts that "endanger the People's Republic of China" or are "commit-ted to the goal of overthrowing the political power of the dictatorship of the proletariat and the socialist system."[18]

Additionally, because the legal provisions for freedom of speech are not complete, the liberties of citizens within legal limits are restricted. There are so-called nonlegal restrictions, which include those enacted by government agencies, leaders, moral judges, and party policy, none of which is legally binding. These limits are primarily imposed on public crit-icism, complaints, and suggestions. What is especially crucial is govern-ment control of the mass media, which ensures that voices critical of the state will not be heard, and authorities have organized powerful institutions and related networks charged with specific duties, such as monitoring speeches, to attain this goal. A censorship system has been adopted for news of great importance, which must be issued by appointed authoritative bodies, but not by private media outlets. Controversial political topics may be discussed individually, or in small groups, but if a speech that includes controversial material is made in public or disseminated to overseas audiences, those involved may be, and often are, punished.

The problems and restrictions mentioned in this chapter constitute the final barriers that citizens must break down in order to enjoy their freedoms of speech and assembly. The Foreign Affairs Committee of the British House of Commons concluded in its "2007 Human Rights Annual Report" that there was only "glacial progress" in China's effort to guarantee people's civil liberties and human rights. In 2007 eight U.S. congressmen proposed House Resolution 610 to the U.S. Congress, which demanded further improvement of civil and human rights conditions in China; otherwise, the United States would boycott the Beijing Olympic games. Formerly, the Chinese government would rebut Western criticism of its constraints on freedoms of speech and assembly; however, in recent years, Beijing has acknowledged that the country has significant problems in the area of political rights and civil liberties protection.[19] Nevertheless, the Chinese government also argues that these issues can be addressed through the current political system, insisting that it takes time, since any push for fundamental change brings the risk of instability and a breakdown of economic development. These barriers are the last remnants of the Communist system of repression and persecution, and the gradual and substantive expansion of liberties in these areas will undoubtedly pave the way for China's democratization. By keeping the state out of these areas of sociopolitical life, Chinese civil society will grow and flourish for the benefit of all, including the functionaries of the state. Thus, while encouraging the rule of law, these restrictions actually run counter to the principles embedded in the Chinese constitution. Without these liberties, the Chinese people will never reach their potential for creativity, happiness, and development.

## FAITH AND FREEDOM

In the past decade China has seen a surging number of people turning to religions such as Buddhism, Islam, Protestantism, Catholicism, and

Daoism (Taoism). As a result of rapid economic growth and sweeping social, ideological, and political changes, more and more Chinese people are searching for meaning and emotional stability in their lives. According to the official statistics in 2008, there were more than 250 million followers of various religious faiths in China. The Chinese government has become more tolerant of officially recognized churches, temples, and religious groups by pursuing a more flexible policy toward them. On the one hand, the traditional Chinese religions, without subscribing to a personalized God, brought considerable support to the government by giving supernatural sanction to the emperor or the ruling party. The ethical systems of these religions reinforced traditional values such as loyalty, hard work, obedience, and sacrifice as part of an institutional system to maintain the ethical-political order. On the other hand, however, as more Chinese people desire freedom to join religious groups, they demand a new order of equality, justice, and plenty. The ruling CCP and the government has begun to limit religious freedom by banning followers from participation in religious activities.

The ultimate test of building a "harmonious society" in the 2010s rests on how the Chinese government handles freedom of religion and human rights. At the beginning of the second decade of the twenty-first century, the Chinese government uses a dual policy to maintain political control. Beijing allows organized religious groups and manages their official activities. Concurrently, the Communist regime continues to crack down harshly on any unofficial religious movements and other activities that have a strong popular following, fearing that they might grow powerful enough to challenge Party authority. Though the post-1978 reform has significantly decentralized state power and provided common people with more freedom in fields such as job seeking and starting businesses, China still has a long way to go to achieve a balance of social harmony and freedom to worship.

In the constitution, freedom of religion is a basic right, guaranteed to all citizens. Article 36 stipulates, "Citizens of the People's Republic of China enjoy freedom of religious belief." There are five officially recognized religions: Daoism, Buddhism, Islam, nondenominational Christianity, and Catholicism. It goes on to say, "No state organ, public organization, or individual may compel citizens to believe in, or not to believe in, any religion: nor may they discriminate against citizens who believe in, or do not believe in, any religion." Additionally, "the State protects normal religious activities."[20] Although the constitution recognizes that worship is part of a citizen's personal life, it requires respect toward those who do not have a religious belief. Since the 70 million CCP members do not have a religious belief, the Chinese government emphasizes that those who have one must get along and cooperate politically with those who do not. The government also makes it clear that any religion in China should be adapted to its society, and the reality is that China is a socialist country. Thus, the government requires all religions in China to align their activities with socialist principles and governmental policies.

Under the constitution, the governmental branches have issued many codes and regulations on religious practices in China. For example, in 2004–2005, the regulations regarding religious affairs were published as China's Law on National Regional Autonomy, General Principles of the Civil Law, Education Law, Labor Law, Compulsory Education Law, Electoral Law of the People's Congress, Organic Law of the Villagers' Committees, and Advertisement Law. The government claims that these laws stipulate that all citizens, regardless of their religious beliefs, have political, economic, and religious rights. Beijing believes that all these legal protections of a citizen's right to freedom of religion are basically in accordance with the main content of international agreements and conventions such as the UN Charter, Universal Declaration of Human Rights, International Covenant on Civil and Political Rights, the UN Declaration on the Elimination of All Forms of Intolerance and Discrimination Based on Religion or Belief, and the Vienna Declaration and Action Program. Some of the rules, however, limit freedom of worship by restraining religious activities. For example, the State Council issued the Regulations on the Administration of Sites for Religious Activities and the Provisions on the Administration of Religious Activities of Aliens within the Territory of the PRC. These administrative laws put limitations on freedom of worship, and according to these regulations, no religious group shall violate any of these rules, and no foreigner may attend religious rituals in China without approval by a government at or above the county level.

Beijing instructs government and Party officials from the top down to provide close supervision of religious groups. Governments at all levels should have effective control of religious activities by carrying out the Party policies and reinforcing governmental laws. Under the PRC State Council, the Religious Affairs Bureau acts as the central government's enforcement and management agency of religious affairs. Under the Chinese People's

Political Consultative Conference (CPPCC), there is the "Democratic Religious Council" representing the major religious groups by receiving and housing their representatives in Beijing. In the meantime, the government has increased the number of its officials to oversee and supervise religious affairs across the country—there are more than 24,000 between the two governmental offices, the NPC and CPPCC.

To serve more than 250 million followers of various religions, there are more than 85,000 sites for religious activities, 300,000 clergy, and 3,000 religious organizations. In addition, there are seventy-four religious schools and colleges run by ecumenical organizations for the training of clerical personnel.[21] As the largest religion in the country, Buddhism has more than 80 million followers. There are a total of 13,000 Buddhist temples, including 3,000 Tibetan and 1,600 Pali structures.[22] They house approximately 200,000 Buddhist monks and nuns, including 120,000 lamas and more than 10,000 Bhiksu and senior monks. Daoism has an estimated 45 million followers and more than 1,500 temples and 25,000 priests and nuns. Islam has a total population of 35 million, and their 30,000 mosques are served by 40,000 imams and akhunds.[23]

China presently has 5 million Catholics, 4,000 clergy, and more than 4,600 churches and meetinghouses. Protestants total 20 million, including 18,000 clergy, 12,000 churches, and 25,000 meeting places. In an apparent attempt to contain the flood of new Christian converts, authorities in Beijing built two new churches in the capital, the first when the Communist Party came to power in 1949, and the second in 1998. The Beijing Municipal Administration spent $4.8 million for the construction of these facilities, each of which accommodates approximately one thousand congregants.[24] The city's Religious Affairs Office stated that the city government will continue to endorse the officially recognized Beijing Municipal Christian Association.

Among the traditional religions, Buddhism, Islam, and Daoism not only are popular but also represent the different ways of life formed by minority groups in China. At present, fifty-five minorities in the country comprise a total of 76 million people, approximately 7.2 percent of the country's population; the majority group is the Han Chinese people, constituting 92 percent of the total population. Among the large minorities are the Mongolian, Hui, Tibetan, Uyghur (or Uighur), Miao, and Yi. Tibetan Buddhists and Muslims have formed large minorities among other religious groups, and with a total population of 3 million, the Tibetan Bud-

Shigatse monks at Tashilhunpo Monastery, Tibet. (Photograph by Peter Morgan)

dhists consist of Tibetan, Mongol, Lhoba, and Naxi ethnic minority groups living in Tibet. All these minority groups practice Buddhism and live in Tibet (Xizang), one of China's five autonomous regions set aside for ethnic minorities. According to official reports, there are more than 1,700 Buddhist temples in Tibet, and about 46,000 Buddhist monks and nuns live in these temples. Tibet also has other religious groups, including Muslims, Catholics, and Daoists. The Chinese government has been involved in some of the major religious activities to show its "support" of these religions. This involvement, however, has resulted in tension or even conflicts between government and religious groups, especially the Tibetan Buddhists. For example, in 1992 such tension resulted between Tibetan Buddhists and the State Bureau of Religions of the State Council in Beijing, which was directly involved with the transmission lineage system of the reincarnation of the great lama of the Tibetan Buddhists. The State Bureau of Religions approved the succession of the Living Buddha of the Seventeenth Karmapa, and for the first time the Communist government was involved in choosing the spiritual leader of the Tibetan Buddhists, who plays an important role in sustaining and developing Buddhist doctrines.[25]

With a total population of 35 million, Islam has ten minority groups among its adherents, including the Hui and Uyghur in Xinjiang. Xinjiang is a border region in northwest China and the hinterland of the Eurasian continent; it consists of approximately 550,000 square miles, or one-sixth of the total Chinese territory. Its population is over 20 million, including 12 million people from forty-seven different minorities, such as Uyghur, Kazak, Hui, Mongolian, Kirgiz, Tajik, Uzbek, and Tatar. It is one of China's five autonomous regions set aside for ethnic minorities. Historically, in Xinjiang the dominance of a particular religious group has changed over time, but the coexistence of multiple faiths has always been necessary. The region is primarily composed of Muslims, Buddhists (including Tibetan Buddhists), Protestants, Catholics, and Daoists. Most believers follow a faith along ethnic lines; for example, the Uyghur, Kazak, and Hui people practice the religious teachings of Islam. Xinjiang contains more than 24,000 venues for religious activities, of which 23,753 are mosques. At the provincial level, there are thirteen Islamic and three Buddhist movements, as well as one Three-Self Patriotic Movement Committee of the Protestant Churches. At the county level, the region hosts sixty-five Islamic associations, two Buddhist associations, and two Three-Self Patriotic Movement Committees.[26]

## Government Interference

Though the constitution protects the freedom of religious belief, the government has placed numerous restrictions on this liberty. Policies demand that religious groups maintain the unity of Chinese people and protect the security of their country. In other words, the church and temple should not divide the people or separate them from the majority of the citizenry, and their activities should not undermine national security. Additionally, "no one may make use of religion to engage in activities that disrupt public order, impair the health of citizens, or interfere with the educational system of the state."[27] Therefore, religious activity must conform to the regulations, interests, and safety of the state. In that regard, such activities should serve and protect national interests, and not endanger or harm national unity. The government also uses the rationale of protecting the freedom of those who do not believe in religion, stating that this is a more complete and comprehensive protection of citizens' basic rights. The ruling Party has its own political considerations, since the CCP is still an atheistic party and must protect its own political base. CCP members have not been allowed to practice any religion and are required to commit themselves to the atheistic revolutionary cause. They must actively advocate science and dialectical materialism to combat the stated "absurdity" of theism. Some Party members privately violate this rule, since doing so openly may limit their political careers and their professional development.

The government maintains control of religious practices through a registration process and through national organizations. All theistic groups must be registered with the authorities, and all religious publications, personnel appointments, and seminary programs must go through continuing official review and approval processes. A church or temple can conduct only government-approved worship and activities.[28] Oversight is handled by top-down national organizations, and among the five officially recognized religions are the Buddhist Association of China, Daoist Association of China, Islamic Association of China, Chinese Patriotic Catholic Association, Chinese Catholic Bishop's College, Three-Self Patriotic Movement Committee of the Protestant Churches of China, and the China Christian Council. All local groups must incorporate themselves into these national institutions. Additionally, teachings in these associations are monitored and sometimes modified by the government, which also scrutinizes membership, financial records, and employees. The national organizations working as a governmental agency can deny any application for regional programs or local activities. Any activity, publication, or appointment that fails to be registered or to get approved may be subject to criminal prosecution, fines, or closure.

The government maintains further control through leadership choices. The Chinese authorities, for example, have the power to ensure that no new Living Buddha can be identified. After the Panchen Lama died in 1989, the search began in Tibet to locate a soul boy as the reincarnation of the Panchen Lama and as a new Living Buddha for Tibetan Buddhism. The Dalai Lama followed Tibetan Buddhist tradition and completed the search in May 1995. The spiritual leader of Tibetan Buddhism announced that the search had identified the eleventh reincarnation of the Panchen Lama. The Chinese government rejected the recommendation by the Dalai Lama, who was in the United States at the time.

The Dalai Lama has been in exile since 1959, when he was accused by the Central Government of organizing, by force, a separatist movement in Tibet. Chinese troops suppressed the Tibetan Buddhist rebellion in March 1959, and the Dalai Lama escaped into India. For the past fifty years and more, the Dalai Lama and his government-in-exile have been campaigning for freedom of religion in China. They criticize China's violation of human rights and demand the independence of Tibet, and in 1989 the Dalai Lama received the Nobel Peace Prize. Having denounced the Dalai Lama's interference and sabotage in 1995, the Chinese government decided to become involved in the reincarnation of the Tenth Panchen Lama. Beijing adopted a method of lottery drawing to identify the reincarnated baby boy in Tibet. The new method effectively defended the supreme authority of the Central Government rather than the continuity of the Tibetan tradition. On November 29, 1995, a six-year-old boy was chosen at the lot drawing in Tibet as the Eleventh Panchen. The government of the Tibet Autonomous Region reported its selection to the State Council for approval. Since this incident in Tibet, the government has issued the State Administration for Religious Affairs, which includes fourteen regulations designed to limit the influence of the Dalai Lama. Most notably, it declared that after September 1, 2007, no "Living Buddha [may be reincarnated] without government approval."[29]

This type of control over religious groups is not limited to Buddhism. When the Catholic bishop in Beijing, Fu Tieshan, died in 2007, his successor was not appointed by the pope, as is customary, as the government does not allow foreign involvement in Chinese religious activities without official approval. Article 36 of the constitution stipulates that religious organizations and affairs must be free from "interference by foreign forces." That means no church in China should be under any foreign control or influence, and additional regulations issued by the government prohibit foreign religious groups and individuals from organizing subgroups, setting up offices, establishing schools for religious purposes, or opening places for activities. Foreign churches cannot appoint clerks, promote their religion, or conduct their activities in China. In 1998 the government barred the outspoken Catholic Hong Kong bishop Joseph Zen from traveling to mainland China following a speech he gave in the Vatican attacking the Communist country's lack of religious freedom. He repeated his demands that Beijing release detained underground Catholic bishops and provide religious freedom to all to worship outside state-backed "patriotic" organizations. In April 2005, after Pope John Paul II died in the Vatican, China permitted officially sponsored prayers for the deceased but refused to send an envoy to his funeral; however, in Beijing alone, nearly 10,000 Catholics attended Masses held in five major Catholic churches. Officially sanctioned ceremonies were also held in Shanghai, Tianjin, and other major cities. Many religious activists have asserted that the CCP is unlikely ever to allow direct ties between Chinese Catholics and the Vatican, which poses bureaucratic problems.[30] In the Catholic Church, priests and, especially, higher officials must take orders from the Vatican, which directly contradicts demands placed on Chinese clergy, who are required to take orders from the Party.

As long as the government maintains its dual policy, the Chinese people's struggle for religious freedom will continue into the second decade of the twenty-first century. After more than thirty years of economic reform and opening up to the outside world, many Chinese have improved their standard of living and have moved into the middle class. A large number of less fortunate individuals, however, particularly the less well educated, unemployed, urban poor, and much of the rural population, have experienced great injustice as the gap between rich and poor continues to grow. Many are looking for answers not from the government but from the spiritual world. This is a time when they truly need new guidance and must continue their search for faith. The government faces a difficult dilemma; it can either provide new opportunities to decrease economic problems, or allow more freedom of religious belief. There is another way for authorities to ease the tension and maintain harmony between the government and religious groups. The Freedom House, an international human rights organization, has suggested that the Chinese government open channels, such as town meetings and public hearings, that allow Catholics, Protestants, Buddhists, Muslims, and other believers to express their concerns and to provide suggestions.[31]

The decade 1999–2009 was one of extraordinary importance for the Chinese legal system. It experienced both continuity and changes, and a similar resilience can be predicted for the decade 2010–2020. Changes in the legal system are very significant because they are signs of monumental changes for civil liberties and democracy within the political system. To continue these changes, as some international rights organizations suggest, the Chinese government must continue to encourage growth and change in the legal system "to conform to international standards." The Chinese government should "allow the petition and court systems to play a larger role in combating corruption at local levels, while providing free rein to the media, NGOs [nongovernmental organizations], and citizens to expose cases of corruption."[32] Adequate protection from officials must be ensured for petitioners, litigants, and whistle-blowers. The authorities must ensure the success of further political reform in China.

## NOTES

1. Some of the historical background is from Xiaobing Li, *Civil Liberties in China* (Santa Barbara, Calif.: ABC-CLIO, 2010).

2. S. C. Leng and H. Chiu, *Criminal Justice in Post-Mao China* (Albany: State University of New York Press, 1985), 78, 89.

3. Merle Goldman and Roderick MacFarquhar, "Dynamic Economy, Declining Party-State," in *The Paradox of China's Post-Mao Reforms*, ed. Goldman and MacFarquhar (Cambridge: Harvard University Press, 1999), 8.

4. Standing Committee of the National People's Congress, Constitution of the People's Republic of China, 13.

5. Xiao Yang, "Zuigao renmin fayuan gongzuo baogao, 2007" (Supreme Court Work Report, 2007), March 14, 2007, www.chinacourt.org/public/detail .php?id=239089.

6. Ministry of Justice, *Zhongguo falu nianjian, 1994–2005* (China Law Yearbook, 1994–2005) (Beijing: Law Press, 2006).

7. Headquarters of the People's Armed Police (PAP), *The People's Armed Police (PAP) News* (Beijing: PAP Publishing, 1997–2000).

8. Xinhua News Agency, "Law of the People's Republic of China on National Defense," adopted at the Fifth Session of the Eighth National People's Congress on March 14, 1997, in Foreign Broadcast Information Service (FBIS)-CHI-97-255.

9. All the mentioned documents can be found in Information Office, PRC State Council, comp., *White Papers of the Chinese Government, 1996–1999* (Beijing: Foreign Languages Press, 2000).

10. Bureau of Democracy, Human Rights and Labor, U.S. State Department, "Country Reports on Human Rights Practices for 2011: China," www.state.gov/j/ drl/rls/hrrpt/humanrightsreport/index.htm#wrapper.

11. Standing Committee of the National People's Congress, *Zhonghua renmin gongheguo xianfa* (The Constitution of the People's Republic of China) (Beijing: People's Press, 2004), 37.

12. Ibid., 39.

13. Standing Committee of the National People's Congress, "Zhonghua renmin gongheguo xianfa xiuzheng'an" (Amendments to the Constitution of the People's Republic of China), in Constitution of the People's Republic of China, 122.

14. Information Office of the PRC State Council, comp., "Progress in China's Human Rights Cause in 2003," in Information Office of the PRC State Council, comp., *Zhongguo zhengfu baipishu* (White Papers of the Chinese Government) (Beijing: Foreign Languages Press, 2005), 4:410.

15. Ibid, 400.

16. Standing Committee of the National People's Congress, Constitution of the People's Republic of China, 43.

17. Xiaobing Li, "Social-Economic Transition and Cultural Reconstruction in China," in *Social Transition in China*, ed. Jie Zhang and Xiaobing Li (Lanham, Md.: University of America Press, 1998), 10–11.

18. Articles 90 and 102 of the Criminal Law.

19. Luo Haocai, "Actively Propelling the Development and Creation of the Theory and Practice of Chinese Human Rights," *People's Daily*, September 2, 2011, www.npopss-cn.gov.cn/GB/219470/15576305.html.

20. Standing Committee of the National People's Congress, Constitution of the People's Republic of China, 37.

21. See http://chinatesol.com/Religion_1/Religious_Freedom/religious_freedom.htoml.

22. Pali is one of the Buddhist sects in China, known as Theravada Buddhism, which has access to the earliest Buddhist scriptures. Pali was one of the ancient languages in Sri Lanka when it was used to record the Buddha's teaching in the first century BCE. Pali also means "text" or "original quotations" and thus differs from later comments or interpretation in Buddhist Sanskrit that are popular among many other Buddhist sects. Today Pali is in Tibet, Sri Lanka, Myanmar (Burma), and Thailand, which are Theravada Buddhist nations. For more details, see Steven Collins, *A Pali Grammar for Students* (New York: Silkworm Press, 2006); David Kalupahana, *Nagarjuna: The Philosophy of the Middle Way* (Albany: State University of New York Press, 1986); and W. E. Soothill and L. Hodous, *A Dictionary of Chinese Buddhist Terms: With Sanskrit and English Equivalents and a Sanskrit-Pali Index* (London: Paul, Trench, Trubner & Co., 1937).

23. Information Office of the PRC State Council, comp., "Freedom of Religious Belief in China" (October 1997), in Information Office of the PRC State Council, comp., *Zhongguo zhengfu baipishu*, 2:241.

24. Radio Free Asia, "Chinese Christian Dies in Police Custody, Others Detained," www.rfa.org/englilsh/news/politics.

25. Information Office of the PRC State Council, comp., "Regional Ethnic Autonomy in Tibet" (May 2004), in Information Office of the PRC State Council, comp., *Zhongguo zhengfu baipishu*, 4:529–530.

26. Information Office of the PRC State Council, comp., "History and Development of Xinjiang" (May 2003), in Information Office of the PRC State Council, comp., *Zhongguo zhengfu baipishu*, 4:278–279.

27. Standing Committee of the National People's Congress, Constitution of the People's Republic of China, 159.

28. See "Freedom of Religion" under "China: Events of 2007," www.hrw.org/legacy/englishwr2k8/docs/2008/01/31/china17604.htm.

29. "China Tells Living Buddhas to Obtain Permission before They Reincarnate," www.takungpao.com/news/-Hong Kong.

30. Radio Free Asia, "Faith without Freedom," April 8, 2005, www.rfa.org/english/vietnam/asia_pope-20050408.html.

31. See www.freedomhouse.org.

32. Sophie Richardson, "Challenges for a 'Responsible Power,'" in Human Rights Watch, *World Report 2008* (New York: Human Rights Watch, 2009), 33–34.

# Part Two

# Legal Reform

# 4

# In Transformation toward Socio-Legality with Chinese Characteristics

*A Critical View*

*Jieli Li*

Socio-legality is fundamentally the institutional arrangement of a social control system that may take the shape of formal legalism, informal legalism, or a combination of both for conflict mediation and resolution. Though informal legalism (or what Max Weber calls traditional authority) is generally predominant in premodern or preindustrial societies, formal legalism (or what Weber refers to as rational-legal authority) prevails in modernized or industrialized countries. It is thus in a long-run socio-legal process that informal legalism tends to give way to formal legalism, and the rule of law comes to take center stage in modern societies. The process of defining the rule of law, however, becomes an issue when it is applied to socio-legalities in non-Western countries. A case in point is China.

China, having produced an economic miracle through its own developmental model and thereby stunned the world, is likewise embarking on its own defined path toward a modern "rational-legal authority" while deviating from the Western model through the use of an institutional form. By all accounts, China is no longer a country dominated by the "rule-by-man" socio-legality of the Mao era (1949–1976), but a debate now rages over whether China is turning toward "the rule of law" or "the rule by law"; the concerns regard where legal reform is headed and what effect this reform will exert on the future Chinese socio-legal control system.

To address these issues, we are faced with a critical question: What constitutes the core structure of China's socio-legal system? And, further, have there been any radical changes in the core of such a system throughout the past decade? In socio-legal studies, law represents the technical apparatus for the exercise of state power on the one hand and the construction of political ideology on the other.[1] Chinese history of post-1949 legal developments indicates that the core structure of China's socio-legality is characterized by its parallel growth of both governmental administrative action and the ruling party's organizational control over society. So far, reforms have hardly altered the core of such dual leadership management at the major sectors of society. Building on this foundation is a new trend of socio-legal development; as of 1978, China opened up and started economic reform. This new socio-legality, though still in its developing stages, is manifest in what I define as a "double-track" legality, a hybrid nature of a social control system: while economic and commercial sectors are opened up and subjected to Western-style formalization and codification so that they can be compatible with the world's capitalist system, political and ideological sectors are kept away from legal formalization and regulated mainly through Party policy to ensure the legitimacy of the ruling party and its practice of social coercion.[2] All evidence indicates that such double-track legality in China has continued to this day.

## CONCEPTUAL AMBIGUITY OF "RULE OF LAW" AND "RULE BY LAW"

When going over the history of China's socio-legal development, we come across the two often-used Chinese literary terms *renzhi* and *fazhi*. It seems that though *renzhi* is commonly referred to as "rule by man" in English, we find it difficult to offer a proper English term for *fazhi* and *fazhihua*. Does *fazhi* refer to "rule of law" or "rule by law"? By extension, does *fazhihua* refer to "formalization" or "legalization"? We often see ambiguous descriptions such as "China is transforming to some form of the rule of law" or "some kind of form between the rule of law and the rule by law." So much literature discusses China's socio-legality, yet so little of it tries to distinguish among the conceptual differences of the various terms. The result of this disparity is that when Western scholars and Chinese scholars discuss China's socio-legal reforms, they are actually talking about different ideas even though they use the same term, *fazhi*. When Chinese scholars write about *fazhi*, they usually consider it as formalism or, simply, as a process of codification that can promote administrative efficiency in social control—a major move away from the pre-1978 mode of "rule-by-man" legality. Therefore, *fazhihua* advocates nothing more than *yifa zhiguo* (in compliance with law to achieve administrative efficiency). For Western scholars, legal formalism must meet pluralistic demands from society, not only in the need for administrative efficiency but also as a guard against manipulation by the state and ruling elites. For Western scholars, the legal codification procedure alone is not sufficient to attain justice, democracy, and human rights, as it must be accompanied by independent legislative and juridical organs. Thus, a distinction between "rule of law" and "rule by law" lies in a comparison between the goals and internal dynamics of different facilities of legal order.

James V. Feinerman makes a distinction between the latter two concepts, pointing out that in the rule of law, law is, "as . . . understood in the West," an embodiment of an independent judiciary and civil liberties, but "in 'the rule by law,' law exists not to limit state power . . . but to serve as a mechanism for state power—which can also be exercised by other available means, such as party discipline or leadership fiat." China's existing socio-legality, then, should be defined as "rule by law."[3] Randall Peerenboom makes another distinction between the two notions, as he attempts to define "the rule of law" as a legal system that can separate itself from the state and, in doing so, "impose meaningful restraints on the state and individual members of the ruling class." He defines "rule by law" as a legal system whereby law is merely an instrument of the state as well as the ruling class.[4] Many socio-legal scholars, however, especially those from the camp of the conflict school of thought, would argue that in a strict sense no socio-legality, even in Western countries, can hold its absolute position of institutional neutrality, being exempt from serving as a tool of social control for the state as well as the ruling class.[5]

So far, legal scholars are still struggling with this conceptual ambiguity while addressing the legal reforms that are currently taking place in China. This conceptual ambiguity leads to two unsatisfying research results: scholars are too quick to jump to a conclusion or too vague in addressing the complex realities of China's existing socio-legal infrastructure. For example, Peerenboom suggests that China's legality be defined as a state-centered socialist rule of law that combines a partially market-based economy with a nondemocratic political system.[6] This definition seems confusing, even in contrast with the aforementioned distinction Peerenboom makes between "rule of law" and "rule by law"—which he considers in his other work published in the same year, where the state-centered model is defined as "rule by law," not "rule of law."[7] For most Chinese socio-legal scholars, there is virtually no conceptual difference between "rule of law" and "rule by law," as Chinese legal tradition centers around *fa* (law), and *zhi* (rule) follows "*fa*" in the word *fazhi*.[8] Thus, the Chinese term *fazhi* can refer to "legal system" or "rule of law" or "rule by law." Those scholars with such understanding of the nature of law tend to refuse to accept the Western definitional distinction between "rule of law" and "rule by law."

This paper suggests that we should move beyond this endless fine-tuning process of conceptual definition because China is determined to proceed with its own developmental model through a series of legal reforms toward formalization or codification, notwithstanding how Westerners define it. Mounting evidence demonstrates that China is working on its own hybrid model of socio-legality that bears some elements of the Western model but contains, for the most part, its own distinctive institutional characteristics as a double-track system. Thus, the attempt to fit China into the category "rule of law" or "rule by law" becomes inherently less meaningful. In actuality, at least in the case of China, it does not really matter if we use "rule of law" or "rule by law" to describe a Chinese version of *fazhi*. I suggest that we consider China's ongoing legal reforms in a broader context of discerning the whole process from a macrostructural perspective. After all, from the sociological vantage point, law is only one of the social institutions for social control; it interacts with other institutions such as polity, religion, family, and education. With this context in mind, we may discover a different angle from which to perceive China's socio-legality as a unique institutional arrangement, differing from Western-based socio-legalities that are commonly aligned with liberal democracies.

My contention is based on three institutional factors. First, law as an institutional concept is instrumental by nature, which means that it serves only as a purposive tool for social cohesion regardless of the ideological nature of its political system. Thus, any socio-legality can be considered a combined function of law and the state (from the Weberian viewpoint) as well as a weapon used by the ruling class to resolve social conflict (from the

Marxian viewpoint). Second, post-1949 socio-legality in China is unique in the sense that it is marked by the single ruling party's tight organizational control over grassroots society, which actually departs from China's traditional past. And third, evidence indicates that Chinese leadership has never intended to abandon the core structure of its post-1949 socio-legality through its legal reform, but the reform itself, at its current stage, is actually facilitating the revitalization as well as reorganization of the party's controlling power base in order to ensure that its organizational domination is in parallel development with increasingly formalized legislative and judiciary bodies demanded by economic market expansion and globalization.

## The Dualistic Nature of China's Socio-Legality: A Review of Post-1949 Development

China's socio-legality as constructed after 1949 significantly changed the traditional pattern of its past in terms of its overall institutional arrangements. The difference lies in the power of the Party-state to intervene in mediation and adjudication. Before 1949 such governmental organizational control had never reached below the county level in traditional China, so most civil disputes in grassroots communities had been resolved through the mediation of gentry elites such as clan leaders or respected elders who played a dominating role in arbitration.[9] This traditional pattern of socio-legality is depicted by Philip Huang as "semiformal governance" or "centralized minimalism," in which an active and autonomous community participated in resolving local conflicts under an overarching centralized political system.[10] But after the Chinese Communist Party (CCP) regime took over national power in 1949, it initiated an organizational penetration deep into the once untouchable grassroots society, causing the Party's branches or organizational cells to become an indispensable part of mediation and arbitration. Therefore, if we consider how grassroots dispute resolution in pre-1949 China relied largely on the local community's self-administration, we must conclude that this traditional social control structure has been altered and replaced by a new control mechanism characterized by dual leadership at all levels of administrative organizations where the Party's local branch remains influential and dominant.

The period 1949–1976 witnessed a gradual change within the grassroots community, as it moved from administrative independence to organizational dependency in terms of its authority in managing local affairs.

In Stanley Lubman's consideration of the institutionalized Chinese Communist Party mediation and arbitration arrangements, he points out how it was through the branching out of the organization that the Party's authority over the mediation process was developed across the grassroots society.[11] The core of this transformation involved the establishment of a dual-leadership structure through the ruling party's organizational infiltration into local administration while sharing the power of governance. In a broader historical context, this institutional transformation toward dual leadership in management was part of the ongoing nationwide socialist reform movement aimed at building up People's Collective Communes in the vast countryside while making private enterprises in the urban regions partially state-owned or, later, fully state-owned.

The Party's absolute rule over all segments of society was completed during the Cultural Revolution period of the mid-1960s through the mid-1970s. With the death of Mao, which brought Deng Xiaoping back to central power, China entered a new era in 1978, reopening its door to the outside world; this was followed by unprecedented and radical market-oriented economic reforms that would dramatically alter the economic and social landscapes of the whole country. Since then, China has steadily formalized its socio-legality by promulgating more laws and decrees. For example, for the period of 1991–1995 alone (when the Chinese economy started prospering), the Chinese National People's Congress—a legislative organ—enacted more than 280 laws covering both civil and criminal arenas, and the state council of the central government issued over 700 administrative decrees. During the same period, provincial governments put into effect more than 4,000 local administrative decrees.[12]

Indeed, the reforms substantially undermined the institutional foundation of dual leadership management in socio-legality that had been constructed in the earlier period. From the mid-1980s through the 1990s, the reform policy, which was intended to free up the market, ended up undercutting the administrative role of the Communist Party branches in urban work units as well as in rural villages. This period witnessed a national campaign of "separating Party from administrative management" (*dangzheng fenkai*), initiated by the central government in an attempt to streamline bureaucracy and improve the efficiency of the administration. An unintended consequence for such reform became manifest, however, as the Party's grassroots organizations fell into disarray and dysfunction. Chinese leadership learned a hard lesson from the weakened power base in grassroots society, as the central government soon found itself seriously challenged by Falun Gong—an organized quasi-religious movement arising from the bottom of society.

Falun Gong emerged in 1992 and quickly grew into a powerful mass organization. Before it was banned in 1999 by the Chinese government, Falun Gong claimed to have 70 million members and to have set up thousands of well-coordinated exercise stations across the country. On several occasions it openly defied government authority by staging public protests and hunger strikes. The "Falun Gong phenomenon" alarmed the Party leadership, as it realized that its once formidable controlling base in grassroots society had been falling apart, generating a power vacuum that enabled Falun Gong to grow strong. The movement's growth led the ruling party to make a systematic effort to regain its grassroots organizational control. In fact, the Chinese ruling party's effort to reclaim its lost or weakened control has been part of the nationwide *fazhihua* (legalization) and *minzhuhua* (democratization) campaigns for more than the past ten years.

The real intent of both the *fazhihua* and *minzhuhua* reforms initiated by the Chinese government in recent years is to seek the so-called glocal (a combined global and local) approach to a socio-legality in order to meet increased challenges from the outside world. In this process, the double-track model was designed to deal with the challenge. One distinctive development of the "economic-commercial track of legality" is that legal culture and judicial behavior have become more consistent with international norms and practice—that is, Westernized in terms of how disputes are mediated and resolved through due process in the courts.[13] Yet on the political track of legality, the judicial procedures of mediation and arbitration have still been very "Chinese" in the sense that the legitimacy and vital interest of Party rule cannot be challenged or undermined. For example, in mediating and resolving conflict, the ruling party is now working closely with its affiliates, such as the workers' union, youth league, and women's association. The role of these Party-sponsored organizations should by no means be underestimated, as these seemingly non-Party-affiliated units are in fact the close associates of the central Party authorities, forming a highly organized collectivity that supports the Party's domination over society at large.[14]

For China's ruling elites, the bottom-line goals of any legal reforms they have initiated are to ensure that "formalization" only facilitates the Party's continued rule over society and that its legitimacy is not shattered and, in similar vein, to ascertain that "democratization" is guided in such a way as not to collide with the Party's domination as the paramount authority. I want to clarify that I am not arguing that China is reverting to its old tradition of monolithic Party control, as in the Mao era; rather, I contend that legal formalism, as long as it operates within the double-track mode of legality, will carry little weight in constraining the power of the ruling party. After all, the history of socio-legal evolution has revealed a pattern of power politics and justice in which formal laws are simply a matter of procedure; they can always be bent to serve the needs of the state or even "immoral ends" in the name of national interest if they are not supported by the democratic infrastructure of checks and balances.[15]

## Transforming toward a Socio-Legality with Chinese Characteristics

No strong evidence indicates that China's massive campaign to reform its legal system over the past decade or more was intended to dismantle the existing socio-legal control mechanism established under single-party rule. Instead, we see only the comeback of the Party's organizational control over society through different institutional channels. It is worth noting that in recent years the campaign of "strengthening" the party's grassroots organizations has been in parallel development with that of *fazhihua*. The Party-led workers' union, which is officially called the All-China Federation of Trade Unions (ACFTU) has succeeded in getting its cells set up in more than 80 percent of the newly established enterprises, and most of them are private companies. In some more highly developed coastal regions, the rate of unionization in private enterprises is as high as 90 percent. For example, by 2000, ACFTU was able to get assistance from local governments to set up its cells in three thousand enterprises, and it recruited about eighty thousand workers.[16] Considerable evidence, the result of economic reforms, confirms the Party's persistent membership drive into newly established social and economic organizations. For example, the Central Party Committee claimed that by the end of 2007 its membership in private enterprises (also known as "new economic organizations") and nongovernment associations (also known as "new societies") reached as many as 4 million, and many privately owned companies are now having the Party's branch offices set up as integral parts of their administrations.[17]

Evidence also points to a persistent Party-sponsored organizational infiltration into foreign-owned enterprises in China. According to China's two official English-language newspapers, *China Daily* (January 5, 2007) and *Shanghai Daily* (September 17, 2008), by 2007 ACFTU had successfully infiltrated about 70 percent of foreign enterprises, and Walmart became the most recent one to sign a pact with the union. It is therefore reasonable to assume that with the workers' union moving in, the Chinese government has gained an effective organizational niche of social control in those foreign multinational corporations on Chinese territory. On the other hand, in dealing with rising labor disputes as a result of the recent economic slowdown, the Chinese government relies on its organized control network through the direct involvement of the labor union, the women's association, and the youth league, which are structurally integrated in factories and businesses to work out mediation and arbitration on their own. The courts merely play second fiddle in labor dispute resolution, which indicates that despite repeated legalization reforms, the judicial institution in China is far from being a primary agent of social control because of its limited functions in the authority of arbitration. Moreover, in many recent localized land dispute cases, the Party branch (*dangzhibu*) still played an important role in mediation and arbitration, as the Party members in the neighborhood were often among the first to be summoned to participate as quasi officials in dispute mediation. By large measure, the local Party branch—in most cases, a village head is also the Party branch head—is reasserting itself in exercising a powerful influence, even though these two administrative organs should function separately in village affairs.

In another new effort to regain firm control of grassroots communities in rural regions, the personnel and organizational department of the Chinese central government launched a new five-year program called Constructing a New Countryside (2008–2012). Part of this program was to select and hire politically qualified new college graduates and dispatch them to rural communities across the country to serve at least two- or three-year terms as officials on various administrative committees that assist with local affairs. As an incentive, those whose performances are satisfactorily evaluated at the end of their terms are eligible to be elevated to a permanent position in a government office; alternatively, they can receive preferential treatment if they want to go back to school for advanced studies.[18] The campaign has proven very successful, as it has so far attracted about 200,000 college graduates to answer the call to serve as so-called *cunguan* (village officials) below county levels across thirty-one provinces. In the year 2010 alone, 36,000 college graduates were appointed to the *cunguan* position. New data indicate that of all those appointed *cunguan,* 74 percent are Communist Party members, and 24.1 percent are working directly in one of two leading village bodies: the village council or the Party's village branch office, also known as *Cun liang wei hui.* Additionally, 12.3 percent take leadership positions and become either village heads or Party branch office heads.[19]

Instead of considering this new "sent-down" campaign as one that, as some scholars have argued, employs governmental strategies to reduce the pressures on the job market that have resulted from the economic slowdown, I perceive this campaign to be another component of the ruling party's calculated move to regain its weakened control of the grassroots communities, working organizationally through market-oriented economic reforms. By sending down college graduates to be involved in the daily operations of a village council, the central Party authorities have inserted one more organizational cell into the control mechanism, to either improve or reinforce its grip over grassroots society. Indeed, as one survey indicates, the "sent-down" officials have become deeply integrated into village youth league activities, which makes them another source of community control that balances the power of some locally based political forces.[20]

Another battleground in the ongoing construction of double-track socio-legality is the tug-of-war between the government and the growing power of lawyers. As of the mid-1990s, with China's economic reform deepening, private law firms were reinstated in China. This privatization of law firms, however, hasn't changed much of the nature of the established socio-legality, as these firms are under close surveillance by the justice department, and, more important, the All-China Bar Association, like other professional associations, is government-controlled. In recent years, however, it has become apparent that Chinese private law firms are trying to step out of the shadow of government control and play a more assertive role in conflict resolution, especially in areas considered politically sensitive. One obvious change is that lawyers, as a newly rising political force, have gained prominence in seeking independence and challenging the authorities by representing disadvantaged social groups and rights activists. Among 190,000 lawyers, a group of "activist lawyers" is becoming very responsive in rights defense: they are involved in sensitive cases such as police brutality, ethnic minority discrimination, persecution of political dissidents, and forced eviction of people from their land and houses.

Though the growth of independent lawyers is a clear sign of an emerging civil society, the tolerance for such a trend seems to be limited; for example, punishment has been tactically meted out in an attempt to restrict "uncharted" development. According to a report by Dick Thornburgh in the *New York Times* (July 29, 2009), the justice department in Beijing canceled the licenses of fifty-three lawyers for allegedly failing to apply for reregistration. A close examination, however, discloses that it was no coincidence that all the disbarred lawyers were in some way involved in sensitive cases challenging the central and local authorities, such as the contaminated milk scandal and the shoddy construction of schools that collapsed in the 2008 earthquake. The bar association can turn into a handy government tool to intimidate and penalize those dissident lawyers; moreover, disbarment makes lawyers more vulnerable to job loss as well as to retaliation from the government. By most accounts, the continued reforms intended to raise the quality of the judiciary are very much restricted in the realm of jurisprudence, and one finds no clear sign of the Chinese central government's being willing to abandon its double-track legality of social control and its intolerance of any move to undermine or deviate from the Party-led administrative control of socio-legal institutions.

## LIMITS OF SOCIO-LEGALITY WITH CHINESE CHARACTERISTICS

There exists a structurally inherent problem with China's double-track socio-legality: whereas the legalization drive requires the increased role of the courts in mediation and arbitration, the Party-state's organizational control mechanism constantly adjusts itself to the change while still adhering to its sole aim to ensure the legitimacy and domination of the ruling party, particularly in the political and ideological sectors. Because of such institutional arrangements, friction and constraints stemming from incompatibility become inevitable, and evidence indicates that lawmaking and law enforcing contradict each other in actual implementation and have become problematic. For example, to protect workers' well-being, China's national People's Congress recently promulgated a labor law that stipulates a series of formal arbitration procedures designed to resolve labor-management disputes. Though more workers have indeed turned to labor-arbitration committees for assistance, however, only a small number of grievance cases have been processed. Legal provisions for workers' minimum wages, health care, and vacation benefits are clearly stated, but most of the labor-intensive industries are, nonetheless, rarely in compliance with these provisions. As a result, rather than reducing workers' discontents, the enactment of the labor law has achieved little, instead intensifying labor-management disputes as both sides have raised expectations in negotiations.

Such defiance is based on the growing awareness that the government simply has no real leverage over those labor-intensive factories, mines, and construction companies because of its fear of losing its tax revenues; on the other hand, most companies don't believe that the court is capable of enforcing the law and settling disputes. Neither enterprises nor individuals have much confidence in resorting to formal law.[21] In Aaron Halegua's 2008 study of labor dispute cases among China's migrant workers, he points out how China's economic reforms opened up an enormous labor market for the rural population in urban regions. The number of migrant workers in China is now estimated at 150 million. While living at the bottom of society, those migrant workers are considered a socially disadvantaged group that needs more legal protection, especially in their disputes with employers about unpaid wages. Research data, however, reveal that those migrant workers have found no satisfaction or little benefit by taking their disputes to the formal legal system, even when they win their cases: "All too often, even after prevailing in arbitration and two court trials, workers are left with just a slip of paper and no actual money. For instance, after a construction company failed to implement a court judgment to pay wages owed to a group of migrant workers for six months, in an act of desperation the workers stood on the street attempting to sell their court award of 6.53 million Yuan for 5.5 million Yuan."[22] This is not an isolated incident, and it occurred because of a long-standing institutional barrier to getting arbitral awards and court judgments effectively enforced.[23]

This situation illustrates a typical phenomenon characterizing the structural constraints of double-track legality: though conflicts are resolved mostly through mediated deals with government offices, with or without legal provisions, laws continue to exist largely in name and not much in actual practice. To make matters more frustrating, workers' strikes in China are often organized by disgruntled workers themselves in their search for justice rather than by labor unions, which often side with the government and factory management. Perhaps that fact is one of the reasons workers' strikes are more likely to turn violent, and it may also help explain a perplexing phenomenon in recent years: as more laws are promulgated, more social riots mount. Though formal laws lack a supportive infrastructure for enforcement, and though labor unions fail to mediate effectively in behalf of workers' interests, such institutional constraints limit the possibilities for mediation and conflict resolution, and violence thus is very likely to occur as the last resort.[24]

Indeed, recent years have witnessed growing social tension and conflict resulting from greater social inequality as well as increased disputes between the state and individuals over residential property, land use, and other issues. Some scholars attribute the mounting tension to the overloaded court system's inability to handle an increasing number of disputant cases, and they find it imperative to revitalize community mediation to serve as a supplementary institution that can share the burden.[25] I hold a different opinion on the issue. As I discussed earlier, rising social tensions have little to do with a short supply of formal judicial assistance because the courts are, to a large extent, incapable of handling sensitive cases or performing their job in a well-coordinated way. Moreover, people are unwilling to go to the courts because they don't trust the judicial system. In their research on Beijing *Hutong* residents, Haini Guo and Bradley Klein observed that the reason that people were reluctant to follow the formal legal channels to resolve disputes was not because doing so was too costly, but because they viewed the legal institutions as "fundamentally unpredictable and untrustworthy."[26] This popular perception hasn't changed much in recent years. In a *New York Times* report on Chinese courts, the constitutional scholar He Weifang was quoted as saying that "the public may be skeptical about judicial independence, given the quality of judges and judgments"; fundamentally it is a matter of accountability, and "you can only have accountability if you have independence. Otherwise, it is never clear who made a decision."[27]

Yongshun Cai and Songcai Yang reveal through their research that for litigants, the resort to either petitions or lawsuits against state authorities to resolve disputes has generally been ineffective or unsuccessful, and therefore many people choose not to go to court; they don't believe that judicial adjudication would give them justice.[28] According to another survey recently conducted in four Chinese cities, as many as 75 percent of litigants reported that they found it difficult to use lawsuits in conflict resolution.[29] Such institutional restriction on litigation has caused social tensions to escalate to such an extent that rural mass riots have increased in recent years, a phenomenon that has jeopardized social stability. It is worth noting that many riots were triggered by trivial disputes and could have been prevented if people had had confidence in court mediation and adjudication.

An important question, then, is why people lack confidence in jurisprudence. J. Yu points out two reasons: (1) they distrust the overall political system because of the corruption and incompetence of government officials, and (2) they have a strong disdain for corrupt judges and don't believe they can deliver justice and equity.[30] It seems to me, however, that Yu's explanation is quite superficial, as it fails to dig out the main culprit behind the growing grievances in China. I would argue that the root cause for this lack of public confidence lies in the unavoidable structural friction between the "rule of Party" and the "rule of law" in a double-track sociolegality, as they are the two institutional forces that clash with each other while running on the same course. Such friction is not obvious, however, in the commercial and economic sectors, where most cases are contract-related and the court's rulings are generally technical and fully codified to be compatible with the legal norms of the international community. Yet in the political sector or in areas where cases are deemed politically sensitive, the laws become less effective in arbitration, as the Party-dominated administrative power can always dictate an outcome or overrule judgments if they are considered to be a threat or harmful to the interest of the elite class or, more important, to the legitimacy of Party rule. The question regarding judicial independence is raised through the concern with the exclusive power of the Party's Organizational Department (*zuzhibu*) over judicial selection, appointments, and promotions. Undoubtedly, the appointments of superior and intermediate judges are determined by candidates' records of political correctness that are in line with the criteria of the Party's Organizational Department. This institutional arrangement promotes people's skepticism about judicial independence and justice that is free of ideological bias.

There is another case of institutional friction in the double-track sociolegality in which the roles of governmental administrative organs and of judicial organs in mediating and resolving conflict are blurred to such a great extent that they tend to negate each other. For example, one arm of governmental control dedicated to handling social grievances and disputes is the offices of Letters and Visits (*xinfangban*), where, instead of going to court, ordinary citizens can directly channel their complaints to the rel-

evant departments of central government. This governmental role of arbitration and adjudication, however, often overlaps and sometimes conflicts
with the role of judicial organs, which results in court-ruled cases that can
still be challenged by the offices of Letters and Visits. Also, the court may not
honor the adjudication made by the state office in charge. Such ambiguity
and even confusion of the institutional role leads to one popular concern:
"Who is the final arbiter of law?" And further, "Who serves whom—does
government serve the law or does law serve the government?" Many social
riots have erupted because of such institutional role confusion, a situation
that in turn creates hurdles for the quick delivery of justice and provides a
loophole for bribery and corruption.

## CONCLUSION

When pointing out the limits of China's double-track socio-legality, we
naturally wonder whether such a social control system will be able to survive. With the increased tension of social unrest characterized by what
Kevin O'Brien calls "rightful resistance," we tend to wonder if this is a sign
of ineffective control by the ruling elites, as it indicates the decline of the
Party's control over grassroots society despite its continued efforts.[31] Some
scholars see the looming crisis in the Chinese Party-state and argue that its
ongoing legal reforms will eventually wither the single-party rule, which
would result in a robust civil society's emergence in China. This opinion is
reflected in the research of Peerenboom, who argues that China's ongoing
legal reform toward the rule of law will undermine the ruling party's domination. I think Peerenboom correctly points out that China is in transition
to the rule of law, as this rule of law is compatible with a single-party socialism even though it is "not a liberal democratic version of rule of law."[32]
While I disagree with Peerenboom's first contention, I nonetheless agree
with his second one.

My analysis points to a different path for socio-legal development in
China. I see legal reform oriented toward the rule of law and carrying with
it Chinese characteristics in which the Party's organizational grip over
grassroots society has been revitalized by taking on a new organizational
structure that I define as double-track legality. Clear evidence supports the
argument that this new social control system is well on its way to being able
to adapt itself to a new social environment shaped by the ever-increasing
influences of economic globalization. As a matter of fact, the double-track

nature of the social control system has actually proved itself to be efficient and effective in controlling information flow on the Internet. The recent case of China versus Google exemplifies how the Chinese government is capable of managing the flow of information in favor of its political needs rather than succumbing to outside pressure. China not only has a platform as technologically advanced as those in Western countries to support its own search engine, such as Baidu.com, without relying on Google.com; China also has a unique social control infrastructure that makes it possible for the government to take on Google's challenge without disrupting its own economic or social order.

No apparent sign indicates that the ruling Communist Party is willing to give up its dual leadership in administrative management in the major state apparatuses such as the courts, police, and military. Nor does any clear sign indicate that the past decade or more of legal reform has caused the Party to loosen its organizational grip over society, where its legitimacy would then be weakened. On the contrary, since 1999 we have observed a persistent effort of Chinese leadership to search for a new mode of Party organizational control to suit the changing circumstances. China's recent debate on "the Chongqing Model" is illustrative of this search, as one recommended aspect of the Chongqing Model is the resilience and reenergizing of the Party's grassroots rule through the vigorous campaign of "Singing Red and Beating Black" (*changhong dahei*), which broadly implies "Reviving the Good Tradition of the Chinese Communist Party and Taking Back Grassroots Society."[33]

China is currently in a stage of learning by trial and error through continued legal reform (*fazhihua*), following Deng Xiaoping's legacy of "wading across the river by feeling for stepping stones." China's remarkable success in the pursuit of its own economic development has further convinced its leadership that the country will be able to find its own rule of law, which differs from the "Western consensus," while still being suited to its own political, economic, and cultural systems. All evidence indicates that the ruling Communist Party leadership is unwilling to embrace any radical legal reform that might prove detrimental to its authority and legitimacy. Instead, a great effort has been made in China to ensure the parallel development of a double-dimensional "legal space": one track aims to "globalize" its economic and commercial sectors, and the other track seeks to "localize" its political and ideological sectors. This "glocal" trend features China's current transformation toward the hybrid model of a social control system as becoming adaptable to the rapidly evolving social and economic environment brought about by the forces of globalization.

## NOTES

1. Weber's thesis on legality is embedded in his theory of rational-legal authority as well as his theory of legitimacy. See Roger Cotterrell, "Legality and Political Legitimacy in the Sociology of Max Weber," in *Legality, Ideology and the State,* ed. David Sugarman (New York: Academic Press, 1983), 69–94.

2. The concept of "double-track" legality was fully discussed in my earlier work on China's legal reform as of 1978, "The Structural Strains of China's Socio-Legal System: A Transition to Formal Legalism?" *International Journal of the Sociology of Law* 24 (1996): 41–59. In a more recent article I also discussed the development of double-track socio-legality in China's current campaign to revitalize the community role in mediation and arbitration as a supplement to formal legal channels (such as the courts) in dispute resolution. See Jieli Li, "An Institutional Transformation of Grassroots Mediation in Conflict Resolution: Where Is China Headed?" *Sociological Focus* 42, no. 3 (2009): 246–253.

3. J. V. Feinerman, "The Rule of Law . . . with Chinese Socialist Characteristics," *Current History: A Journal of Contemporary World Affairs* 96, no. 611 (1997): 278–281.

4. A more detailed discussion about the conceptual distinction between "rule of law" and "rule by law" can be found in Randall Peerenboom, *China's Long March toward Rule of Law* (Cambridge: Cambridge University Press, 2002), 8.

5. In the sociology of law, scholars of the conflict school of thought tend to view law as an arena as well as an instrument of class conflict in society. See Austin Turk, "Law as a Weapon in Social Conflict," *Social Problems* 23 (February 1996): 276–291. Also see Donald Black and Maureen Mileski, eds., *Social Organization of Law* (New York: Seminar Press, 1973).

6. See another version of the definitional distinction regarding the nature of rule of law in Randall Peerenboom, "Let One Hundred Flowers Bloom, One Hundred Schools Contend: Debating Rule of Law in China," *Michigan Journal of International Law* 23 (2002): 475–476.

7. There is a section devoted to the conceptual difference between "rule of law" and "rule by law" in Randall Peerenboom, *China's Long March toward Rule of Law,* 8.

8. Chinese scholars have a different perception about the nature of law, as they tend to go along with traditional Chinese legal culture in their belief that "law" is nothing but codified "order" for social cohesion. See Lin Li, "China's Thirty-Year Legal Construction: Review and Prospects," in *Rule of Law in China, 1978–2008,* ed. Chinese Academy of Social Sciences Legal Studies Institute (Beijing: Social Sciences Academic Press, 2008), 1–45.

9. The role of the Chinese gentry class in civil justice, including grassroots mediation and arbitration of disputes and conflicts, is fully discussed in Zhongli Zhang, *The Chinese Gentry: Studies on Their Role in Nineteenth-Century Chinese Society* (Seattle: University of Washington Press, 1955); Tongzu Qu, *Law and Society in Traditional China* (Paris: Mouton, 1961); Tongzu Qu, *Local Government in China under the Ch'ing* (Cambridge: Harvard University Press, 1962); Melissa Ann Macauley, *Social Power and Legal Culture: Litigation Masters in Late Imperial China* (Stanford: Stanford University Press, 1998); Phillip C. C. Huang, *Civil Justice in China* (Stanford: Stanford University Press, 1996).

10. For a more detailed discussion about informal mechanisms of civil justice in traditional Chinese societies, see Phillip C. C. Huang, "Centralized Minimalism: Semiformal Governance by Quasi Officials and Dispute Resolution in China," *Modern China* 34, no. 1 (2008): 9–35.

11. Lubman was among a few scholars who gave an insightful analysis of the unique organizational power of the Chinese Communist Party regime and how it reached deep into grassroots society. See Stanley Lubman, "Mao and Mediation: Politics and Dispute Resolution in Communist China," *California Law Review* 55, no. 5 (1967): 1284–1359.

12. Data were selected from Lin Li, "An Overview of China's Thirty-Year Legal Construction," in Chinese Academy of Social Sciences Legal Studies Institute, *Rule of Law in China, 1978–2008,* 15–16.

13. The effects of globalization on Chinese legal culture are discussed in Pitman B. Potter, *The Chinese Legal System: Globalization and Local Legal Culture* (New York: Routledge, 2001).

14. See a detailed discussion of the "double-identity" nature of Chinese workers' unions in F. Chen, "Between State and Labor: The Conflict of Chinese Trade Unions' Double Identity in Market Reform," *China Quarterly* 176 (December 2003): 1006–1028.

15. Some historical cases are illustrated to support this view in Karen G. Turner, James V. Feinerman, and R. Kent Guy, eds., *The Limits of the Rule of Law in China* (Seattle: University of Washington Press, 2000).

16. Data are from Wei Zhao, *China's Union Work in Private Enterprises* (Beijing: Chinese Economic Publishing House, 1999).

17. Data are from T. Liu, "The Role of the Chinese Communist Party in New Economic Organizations and New Societies," *Kaifang zazhi* (Journal of Openness) 10, no. 14 (2008): 4–8.

18. Data are from www.chinanews.com.cn/edu/zcdt/news/2009/05-04/1674296.shtml.

19. Data are from news report about *cunguan* in *People's Daily,* Overseas Edition, December 27, 2010, 1.

20. Data are from www.dxscglt.com/.

21. See a general discussion about such popular distrust or lack of confidence in formal legal channels in Aaron Halegua, "Getting Paid: Processing the Labor

Disputes of China's Migrant Workers," *Berkeley Journal of International Law* 26, no. 1 (2008): 254–322.

22. Ibid., 270.

23. Donald C. Clarke, "Power and Politics in the Chinese Court System: The Enforcement of Civil Judgments" *Columbia Journal of Asian Law* 10, no. 1 (1996): 52.

24. A report concerning the high-profile case of labor disputes and violence resulting from failed mediation can be found in "Arbitration Needed: What Lies behind the Gruesome Death of a Manager at Tonghua Iron and Steel?" *Economist,* Online Edition, July 30, 2009, www.economist.com/node/14140302.

25. Xiaohua Di and Y. Wu, "The Developing Trend of the People's Mediation in China," *Sociological Focus* 42, no. 3 (2009): 228–245.

26. Haini Guo and Bradley Klein, "Bargaining in the Shadow of the Community: Neighborly Dispute Resolution in Beijing Hutongs," *Ohio State Journal on Dispute Resolution* 20, no. 3 (2005): 827.

27. Jim Yardley, "A Judge Tests China's Courts, Making History," *New York Times,* November 28, 2005.

28. Some relevant cases are illustrated in Yongshun Cai and Songcai Yang, "State Power and Unbalanced Legal Development in China," *Journal of Contemporary China* 14, no. 42 (2005): 114–134.

29. Data are from Yongshun Cai, "Social Conflicts and Modes of Action in China," *China Journal* 59 (January 2008): 89–109.

30. J. Yu, "Emerging Trends in Violent Riots," *China Security* 4, no. 3 (2008): 75–81.

31. Kevin J. O'Brien, "Rightful Resistance," *World Politics* 49, no. 1 (1996): 31–55; O'Brien, *Rightful Resistance in Rural China* (Cambridge: Cambridge University Press, 2006).

32. Peerenboom, *China's Long March toward Rule of Law,* 10–11.

33. The "Chongqing Model," which has become very popular but also controversial in contemporary China, can be characterized as trying to reenergize the CCP and eliminate such social vices as mafia-like secret societies, misgovernment, and official corruption.

# 5

# Labor Law Reforms

## *China's Response to Challenges of Globalization*

### *Yunqiu Zhang*

During the post-Mao reform years, China carried out vigorous labor law reforms, as witnessed by the promulgation of numerous laws and regulations on labor issues. What were the dynamics behind these labor law reforms? This chapter is an attempt to answer this question by focusing on the influence of globalization, which is understood in two senses—economic and legal. It argues that in economic globalization, China was increasingly integrated into the world economic system, which compelled China to reform its traditional labor system and follow, or adjust to, internationally accepted rules or conventions in conducting economic activities, including labor management. In other words, economic globalization created the need for labor law reforms in China. Globalization also had a legal dimension: legal ideas or practices of different nations were disseminated globally and interacted with or were influenced by one another. In this legal globalization, China was apparently the recipient or borrower of foreign (Western and other Asian nations') legal ideas, including those about labor legislation. These foreign practices were introduced into China through various channels and exerted a significant influence on Chinese authorities and legal professions, inspiring them to build a new labor-directed legal system.

This paper is divided into three parts. The first part reviews the challenges globalization posed for China's traditional labor system. The second examines how the Chinese responded to these challenges by focusing on

China's labor law reform practices. The last deals with the limitations and prospects of China's labor law reform.

## Challenges of Globalization for China's Labor System

Since the early 1980s, when China formally adopted the open policy as a component part of its economic reform, China has been increasingly integrated into the world economic system and has become an important player in economic globalization. The presence of large numbers of foreign businesses in China and the country's steady involvement in international trade is proof of this fact.[1] Economic globalization posed significant challenges for many of China's orthodox or socialist institutions or practices, including the socialist labor system, and compelled China to change them in accordance with internationally recognized principles. Economic globalization challenged China's labor system in three ways. First, foreign businesses introduced China to a new and typical capitalist labor relationship, which needed to be handled with new mechanisms or rules. Furthermore, China's trading partners, especially the Western nations, increasingly linked international trade and labor standards, and they pressured China to raise its labor standards. In addition, international organizations such as the International Labor Organization (ILO) kept close watch over China's (and other countries') labor conditions and persistently urged it to follow the labor standards set by the ILO.

### Foreign Investments and the Emergence of New Labor Relations

The post-Mao reform era witnessed China becoming one of the most attractive destinations for foreign investments. As of the end of 1997, the total registered foreign-related enterprises in China amounted to 304,821. And 145,000 of these enterprises were in full operation.[2] Foreign enterprises introduced China to a typical wage-labor relationship unknown to Chinese workers under the socialist system of the Mao years and absent from Chinese state-owned enterprises in most of the post-Mao reform era. Compared with those in its socialist counterparts, the relationship in foreign-related enterprises had two salient characteristics. The first was the sharp division between labor and management (or employer) as two distinct entities, both attempting to maximize their own interests—wages and profits, respectively. (In socialist labor relations, the division between labor and management was blurred by the intrusion of the state.) Second, the formation of labor relations in foreign-related enterprises was based on the working of market mechanisms or the principle of supply and demand; employers enjoyed the right to hire or dismiss workers, and workers possessed the right to choose their employers. (Under socialism the allocation of labor was realized by the state through administrative means.) The labor relationship in foreign-related enterprises in post-Mao China can be understood as a contract between workers and employers and bears a strong resemblance to its counterpart in modern Western (capitalist) countries.

On the other hand, the labor relationship in foreign-related enterprises in China differed significantly from those in modern Western countries. In the Chinese context, the labor relationship was marked by the overwhelming power of foreign employers over Chinese workers and the precariousness of the workers' interests. The employers' advantages were derived not simply from their ownership of properties, but also from China's unique circumstances: the abundance of surplus labor, the appeasing attitude of Chinese officials (particularly at the local level) toward foreign investors, and the lack of labor legislation or effective enforcement of labor legislation, particularly in the 1980s and early 1990s.[3]

The market-oriented economic reforms in the post-Mao years brought about large numbers of surplus laborers and massive unemployment in both urban and rural areas. In cities, as state-owned enterprises were increasingly restructured (or rationalized and privatized), millions of workers were laid off. One source indicated that laid-off workers numbered 8,147,998 at the end of 1996.[4] In the countryside, as households became basic units of production, which greatly increased agricultural productivity, and arable land shrank, many rural laborers found themselves redundant. The number of redundant rural laborers in 1991 was estimated to be 150,000,000.[5] Hence arose the situation in which the supply of labor far and persistently exceeded the demand. The existence and availability of large numbers of laborers benefited foreign employers, allowing them room to maneuver in dealing with or controlling their Chinese employees, especially in holding down wages and enforcing labor discipline. Employers could easily find replacements for undesirable workers.

In the 1980s foreign employers' power in the workplace remained almost unchecked by the Chinese state. As local Chinese bureaucrats vied vigorously with one another to attract foreign investments, thereby promoting local economies and improving their own performance records, they were prone to appease foreign employers and show more favor to them than to workers. Obsessed with creating and preserving a favorable investment environment, local officials tried to forestall any labor unrest that would irritate foreign investors. To speed up the introduction of foreign investment projects, local bureaucrats stressed simplification of registration procedures and eschewed bargaining with prospective investors by lowering standards for sanitation and safety in workplaces. More often than not, they ignored foreign employers' misconduct.[6] The appeasing attitude on the part of local officials served to reinforce the power position of foreign employers over workers and even to encourage employers' belligerency in dealing with workers.

In short, foreign employers enjoyed a unique power position in their relations with Chinese workers. Some of them were ready to take advantage of this position to maximize their own economic benefits. In so doing, they often infringed on labor's interests and rights, which turned out to be the direct and major source of labor disputes in foreign enterprises. Violations of workers' interests included arbitrary extension of work hours, random deduction of wages, neglect of workers' welfare, poor working conditions, failure to sign or the abuse of labor contracts, and personal insults. These violations gave rise to increasing cases of labor disputes and labor unrest, which often involved stoppages, strikes, and petitions to state authorities and distribution of handbills or posters by workers to voice their grievances. In the city of Qingdao, cases of labor dispute that were handled directly by city- and district-level arbitration agencies alone numbered 750 in 1994, increased to 1,251 in 1995, and further increased to 1,426 in 1996. Approximately 80 percent of these disputes occurred in foreign-related enterprises. The number would have been much larger if cases of labor disputes settled by lower-level agencies, such as township- and enterprise-level mediation committees, had been included. Union leaders at the three levels (city, district, and enterprise), workers in foreign-related enterprises, and scholars of labor studies in Qingdao all acknowledged that the labor-management relationship in foreign enterprises had been fraught with tension.[7]

Some union leaders confided that the labor relations in these enterprises were so bad that they would feel embarrassed to disclose the circumstances to the outside world. Workers, however, had no misgivings in expressing their grievances.[8] In Guangdong province in 1995, there were 3,042 "collective visits to government agencies" (*jiti shangsu*) and stoppages, each involving at least thirty workers; and hundreds more occurred in 1996. Between 75 and 80 percent of these stoppages happened in foreign-related enterprises.[9]

The labor-capital conflict in foreign-related enterprises posed a serious challenge to the Chinese state, for the conflict threatened to disrupt the normal operation of foreign businesses, which were a main source of state revenue. If unchecked, the disruptions would spill over to other types of enterprises, including state-owned businesses, and cause widespread social instability, which would—in turn—undermine the state's legitimacy. In any case, the state's interests were at stake. It thus became imperative for the Chinese state to intervene to ensure harmony and stability in the relations between Chinese labor and foreign capital. Yet the Chinese state deemed it unwise to intervene directly by administrative means, as it had in the pre-reform years. After all, it was facing a different business world, one that involved foreigners. Within foreign-related enterprises, there was no established presence of state power. Any direct intrusion into the economic world by the Chinese state would arouse the suspicions of foreign investors, who had been used to operating businesses in the environment of a free market economy. In the meantime, the Chinese state became committed to building a market economy and refrained from direct interference with the management of enterprises, including those that were foreign-related. Therefore, it was necessary for the Chinese state to tackle the issue of labor-capital conflict in foreign-related enterprises by new means, the most important of which was labor laws or regulations.

### Pressure from Trading Partners and the International Labor Organization

As China became an increasingly influential trading nation, it came under even more pressure from its major Western trading partners, mainly the United States, to improve its human rights record, including labor conditions. Since the mid-1980s, the United States government had persistently advocated linking trade issues and labor standards, insisting that core labor standards (as set by the International Labor Organization) be adopted universally by all nations, developed and developing. These core labor standards, essentially based on conditions of developed nations and referring to workers' rights as human rights, included: (1) freedom of association; (2) freedom to bargain collectively; (3) freedom from forced or compulsory labor; (4) minimum age of employment; and (5) minimum standards of work. In the past decade or so, the U.S. government has issued annual reports on other countries' human rights situations, especially targeting and criticizing developing countries for their alleged violations of human rights. As a major trading partner of the United States, China also was subject to U.S. criticisms, perhaps more than other countries. Before the mid-1990s, the United States took labor issues into consideration in annually reviewing China's permanent normal trading status (PNTS). During the U.S.–China negotiations over China's accession into the World Trade Organization (WTO), the leading U.S. labor organization, the AFL-CIO, urged the U.S. representatives not to reach any agreement over China's WTO membership.[10] Furthermore, it requested revocation of China's PNTS on the ground that China failed to respect human (or workers') rights.[11] Although the Chinese government took pains to dismiss the American accusations and strongly defended its human rights record in its annual report of China's human rights, it could not afford to totally ignore these accusations and therefore took measures to improve workers' conditions in order to preserve its normal trade relations with the United States.[12] Strengthening labor legislation was one such measure adopted by China.

In the process of globalization, China also came under the scrutiny of the International Labor Organization (ILO). China was one of the founding states of the ILO and served as a permanent governing body member of the government group. Before 1971 China had been represented by the Taiwan regime in the ILO. The year 1971 witnessed the restoration of China's legitimate seat in the ILO. In 1983 China sent, for the first time, a delegation to the Sixty-ninth ILO Conference, thus formally resuming its activities in the ILO. Since then, China regularly has attended ILO-related gatherings and has become actively involved in its legislative and technical activities. In January 1985 the ILO set up its China-ILO Beijing Bureau, staffed with ILO officials, which has since significantly facilitated dialogue and cooperation between China and the ILO.[13] Using the ILO's unique tripartite structure, the Beijing bureau works in close collaboration with the government, the workers' unions, and the employers' organizations to promote decent work for all.

The concept of decent work is built on four strategic pillars: the promotion of fundamental principles and rights at work; employment, enter-

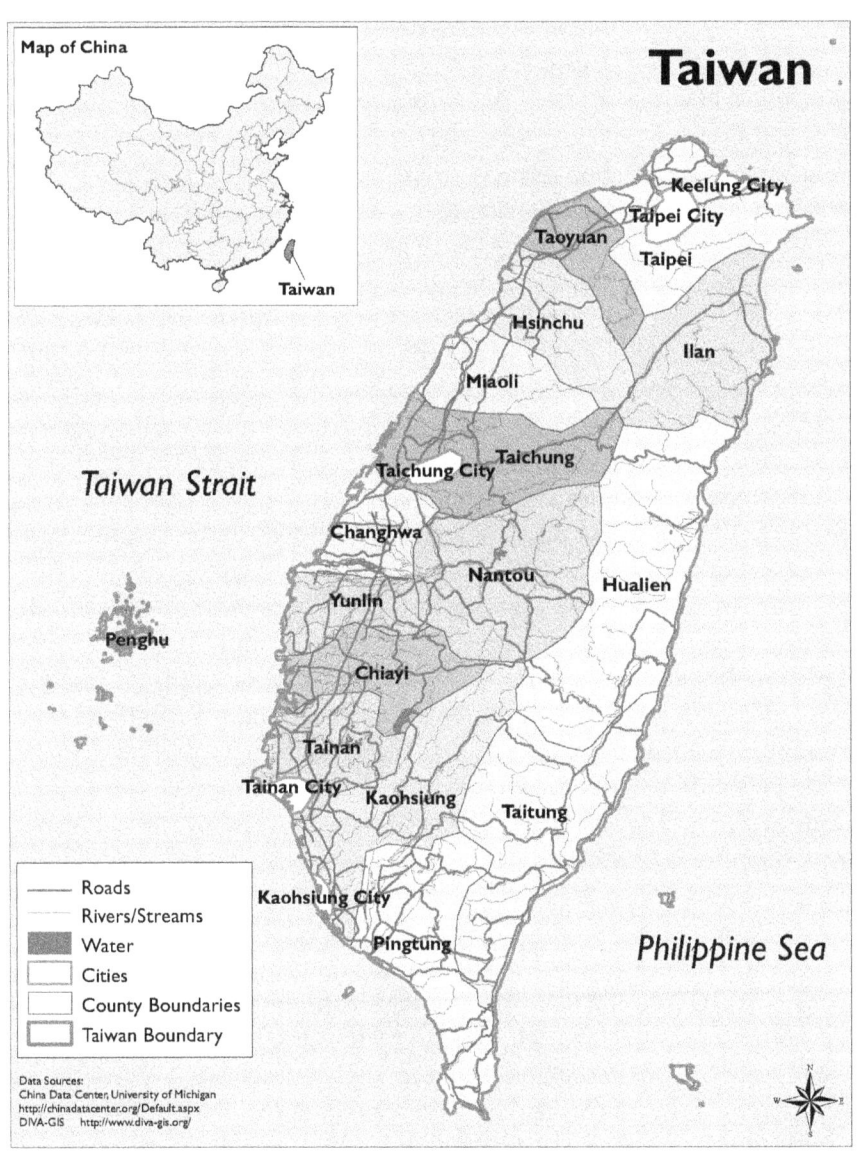

(Map by Jing Duan)

prise creation, and human resource development; social protection; and social dialogue. The Decent Work Agenda supports a move toward an integrated development strategy that links rights at work and social dialogue with employment policies and social protection. ILO officials and experts frequently conduct labor-related activities in China, such as offering seminars and training courses, assisting the Chinese in setting up vocational training centers, and organizing field trips and exchanges of personnel. The ILO has been known as the most vocal international champion of labor rights. Doubtless, its presence in China put the country's labor conditions under international scrutiny. If just for the sake of creating a good international image for itself, the Chinese government had to demonstrate its concern for workers' interests and rights in China, in one way or another. As of March 2, 2009, the Chinese government had ratified 25 of more than 170 International Labor Conventions passed by the ILO, 22 of which were in effect. These conventions would serve as indispensable references for China's labor law reforms.

Thus, economic globalization (foreign investment in particular) and the accompanying international pressure and scrutiny (especially from the United States and the ILO) created the need in China to establish new labor rules or laws congruent with internationally recognized labor principles. One strategy the Chinese adopted to meet this need was to vigorously conduct labor law reforms, and in doing so, they comprehensively reviewed foreign labor legislative practices and borrowed heavily from them.[14]

## LABOR LAW REFORMS

Before delving into the issue of labor legislation in the reform years since the late 1970s, it may be useful first to review briefly the labor legislation situation in the pre-reform era between 1949 and the late 1970s. This era can be divided into two periods, 1956 serving as the line of demarcation. During the first period (1949–1956), the Chinese regime attached enormous importance to labor legislation and proclaimed various labor laws and regulations, which covered a wide range of labor issues, such as labor contracts, wages, work hours and vacation, safety and sanitation, protection of female workers, labor insurance, trade unions, and settlement of labor disputes. Among these laws and regulations were the Trade Union Law of the PRC (1950), Provisional Measures on Handling Labor-Capital

Relations (1949), Provisional Measures on Signing Collective Agreements between Labor and Capital in Private Industrial and Commercial Enterprises (1949), Regulations concerning Procedures for Settling Labor Disputes (1949), and Regulations on the Organization and Functions of Urban Labor Dispute Arbitration Committees (1950).[15] The regime's interest in labor legislation was, to a large extent, shaped by the realities of the contemporary business world, whose main characteristic was the existence of large numbers of privately owned enterprises. Within these enterprises, labor and capital constituted two distinct interest groups and frequently became involved in disputes with one another. Keenly concerned with consolidating its power by restoring the urban economy, the Chinese Communist regime was anxious to maintain a stable industrial labor relationship. While claiming to be the representative of the working class, the regime had to accommodate itself to private businesspeople (particularly the so-called national bourgeoisie) whose managerial expertise was indispensable for operating modern enterprises. In the meantime, the bourgeoisie's suspicion of the new regime was strong. Such realities compelled the regime to handle labor relations with great caution—by labor legislation rather than by administrative power.

A turning point in the history of labor legislation came in 1956 with the establishment of the socialist command economic system, which remained intact until the late 1970s. Under this system, the previous labor-capital relationship was replaced by the labor-state relationship. The state owned and managed all major industrial and commercial enterprises and regarded all workers as its employees, which resulted in what Andrew Walder identifies as workers' "organized dependency" on the state.[16] Within these enterprises, egalitarianism prevailed and effectively precluded social differentiation among workers. Accordingly, labor disputes no longer constituted a major problem. Party ideologies and orders came to function as ultimate criteria for the handling of labor issues. Under such circumstances, labor legislation was no longer considered necessary and was neglected. Legislative bodies on labor issues either ceased to function or were dissolved, and many labor regulations were declared invalid.[17]

The situation began to change in favor of labor legislation in the late 1970s, when market-oriented economic reform was initiated. State-owned enterprises gradually became independent economic entities under the doctrine of separation of enterprise and government. Within these enterprises a relatively clear division emerged between labor and management as distinct interest groups, and labor disputes became inevitable.[18] More important was the emergence and flourishing of private and foreign-related businesses, which were basically outside state authority and within which a typical wage-labor system prevailed and labor disputes occurred much more frequently and intensely.

All these businesses combined to convince the Chinese regime of the necessity of labor legislation and prompted it to take action in this field. Up to 1994, more than 160 labor laws and regulations were promulgated and put into effect by the national authorities, and there were still others that were enacted by local authorities. Some of them were particularly concerned with labor relations in foreign enterprises. The first national-level labor rule that specifically concerned foreign enterprises was Regulations concerning Labor Management in Chinese–Foreign Equity Joint Ventures of the PRC (1980), promulgated by the State Council. Rules of this type also included Measures on Implementation of the Regulations concerning Labor Management in Chinese–Foreign Equity Joint Ventures of the PRC (1984); Regulations concerning the Autonomous Power over Employment and Wages, Insurances, and Benefits of Employees in Foreign-Related Enterprises (1986); and the Circular on Improving and Strengthening the Work on Labor Issues in Foreign-Related Enterprises (1993). All these rules were made by the Ministry of Labor Affairs and the Ministry of Personnel. Another rule was Regulations concerning Labor Management in Foreign-Related Enterprises (1994), enacted by the Ministry of Labor Affairs and the Ministry of Foreign Trade and Economic Cooperation. Similar national-level rules also were scattered in such legal documents as the Law on Chinese–Foreign Equity Joint Ventures of the PRC (1979); the Law on Foreign-Owned Enterprises of the PRC (1986); and the Law on Chinese–Foreign Contractual Joint Ventures of the PRC (1988), which were passed by the National People's Congress.

Legislation particularly directed at labor relations in foreign enterprises also was enacted at the local level (provincial and municipal). In this regard, the Special Economic Zones (SEZs) and other coastal open cities were in the vanguard in comparison with interior regions. Established in the 1980s, the five SEZs—Shenzhen, Shantou, Zhuhai, Xiamen (designated as SEZs in 1980), and Hainan (designated as a SEZ in 1988)—were the first Chinese territories opened to foreign investments and to the development of an export-oriented economy. Hence, these were the first regions in China to become involved in economic globalization. The majority of the enterprises were foreign-related: equity joint ventures (*hezi qiye*), con-tractual joint ventures (*hezuo qiye*), and wholly foreign-owned enterprises (*duzi qiye*). It was in these regions that a capitalist-style labor relation-ship made its first appearance. This explains why these SEZs also took the lead in pursuing labor legislation that would suit the needs of a globalized economy. Between 1981 and 1997 the authorities of the SEZs promulgated seventy-four local-level (*difang xing*) laws and regulations (*fagui*), nine-teen of which were made by local People's Congresses, and the rest by local governments. These laws and regulations can be put into two categories, general (or comprehensive) and special. A general labor law was a regula-tion that covered a variety of labor issues. A special labor law or regulation was devoted to one specific labor issue, such as employment, labor con-tracts, collective labor contracts, supervision, labor disputes, wages, safety and sanitation, workers' social security, or health insurance. In drafting these laws and regulations, local legislative authorities (policy makers) in the SEZs were inspired and drew heavily on international conventions or internationally accepted principles (as practiced by countries or regions with mature market economies) such as freedom and equality in employ-ment (freedom of job seekers and employers to choose each other); social-ization (*shehuihua*) of labor security (pensions and insurance covering health, industrial injuries, unemployment, and childbirth);[19] socialization of occupational training; labor dispute settlement mechanisms involving mediation, arbitration, and court trial; and labor market (or labor allo-cation) based on the supply and demand in the market. A more specific example of an SEZ's compliance with international labor conventions was the Shenzhen Special Economic Zone Regulations on Wage Default by Enterprises (1996), which was based on Hong Kong's legislation on wage defaults in bankrupt enterprises.[20]

Local labor legislation also proceeded in earnest in other open-coast urban centers after the late 1980s. For instance, the Qingdao city govern-ment and the city's People's Congress, respectively, promulgated Provisional Regulations on Labor Management in Foreign-Related Enterprises in Qing-dao (1988) and Regulations on Labor Management in Foreign-Related Enterprises in Qingdao (1993). The Shandong Provincial People's Congress passed Regulations on Labor Management in Foreign-Related Enterprises in Shandong (1994) and Regulations on Trade Unions in Foreign-Related Enterprises in Shandong (1996).[21] These regulations addressed all major aspects of labor relationships in foreign-related enterprises. While aimed at protecting the "lawful" interests of both labor and capital, they put over-whelming emphasis on labor's rights and interests.

For example, Regulations on Labor Management in Foreign-Related Enterprises in Qingdao (1993) consists of twelve chapters: (1) general pro-visions; (2) recruitment of workers; (3) labor contracts; (4) wages; (5) work hours and vacation; (6) social insurance and benefits; (7) labor training; (8) labor safety and sanitation; (9) labor disputes; (10) labor supervision; (11) legal responsibilities; and (12) additional notes. They can be divided into three groups in terms of their points of emphasis. Group 1 includes chap-ters 1 and 12, which outline the goals and principles of the regulation, as well as the scope of its application. Group 2 includes chapters 2, 3, 9, and 10, which are neutral and constrain both labor and capital. Chapters 3 and 9 are particularly important for the purpose of this study. The former stipu-lates that employers and workers must sign labor contracts, which should set forth the rights and obligations of the two sides, in accordance with the principles of "voluntarism and equality, and of negotiation and mutual agreement" (*ziyuan pingdeng, xieshang yizhi*). It also sets conditions for the suspension of labor contracts. Chapter 9 is about procedures for set-tling labor disputes through enterprise-based mediation committees, or district- or city-level arbitration committees or courts.

Group 3, including chapters 4, 5, 6, 7, 8, and 11, is the main body of the regulation and deals almost exclusively with employers' obligations and workers' interests. Chapter 4 provides wage standards: average wages should be 120 percent of those in state enterprises of the same industry; minimum wages should not be lower than those in state enterprises; wage rates should be raised every year in proportion to growth in production; and payment of wages should not be defaulted. Chapter 5 stipulates that daily and weekly work hours should not exceed eight and forty-eight; over-time should not exceed two hours daily, six hours weekly, and 120 hours annually;[22] payment for working overtime and on holidays should be 50 and 100 percent higher than normal wages, respectively; and breaks (forty-five minutes during an eight-hour workday) and nursing time for women workers (twice daily, thirty minutes each) should be allowed. Chapter 6 requires foreign enterprises to pay a certain portion of fees for workers' pensions, unemployment insurance, and medical care, as well as housing subsidies. According to chapter 7, employers should provide workers with vocational and technical training. Chapter 8 obliges management to take efficient measures to improve working conditions and strengthen labor protection and guarantee labor safety. Chapter 11 outlines legal penalties (mainly fines) that would be imposed on employers should they fail to fulfill their obligations.[23]

In addition to these labor rules, which relate particularly to foreign enterprises, a series of general laws and regulations was passed by the national authorities in the early 1990s and applied to all enterprises in China, both state-owned and foreign-related. The two most important of these were Regulations on Handling Labor Disputes in Enterprises within the PRC (1993) and the Labor Law of the PRC (1994), promulgated by the State Council and the National People's Congress, respectively. The former focused specifically on the two main kinds of agencies for settling labor disputes, namely, the enterprise mediation committee and the city or district (county) arbitration committee. It also focused on those agencies' composition and functions, as well as their working procedures. What seems important is that labor was given a greater say than capital in the labor dispute–solving process. In both types of agencies, which were tripartite (representatives from labor, trade unions, and capital formed the enterprise mediation committee; representatives from government, trade unions, and general economic administrative organs formed the arbitration committee), trade union representatives were integral and, in the case of enterprise mediation committees, served as directors. In addition to being represented by trade unions, workers were given a direct voice in the enterprise mediation committee.[24]

The Labor Law is China's most comprehensive national-level legislation on labor relations. In addition to all the main points covered in other labor regulations, the Labor Law contains new provisions, particularly concerning women's interests. Chapter 7, "Special Protection for Female and Non-Adult [between sixteen and eighteen years old] Employees," stipulates that women should not be asked to work high above the ground, in low temperatures, or in cold water or to do jobs of high labor intensity (above grade 3) while menstruating; women seven months or more pregnant should not be asked to work overtime and during night shifts; and their maternity leave should be at least ninety days. Like all other labor regulations, the Labor Law stresses workers' rights and interests and employers' obligations.[25] The rationale for such legislative orientation is that labor is too weak and vulnerable vis-à-vis capital and hence needs more protection. Within a year or so of the Labor Law's passage, a set of more specific national-level labor regulations was promulgated as its supplements, and all were applicable to foreign-related enterprises. Among them were Regulations on Minimum Wages; Regulations on Employees' Work Hours; the Labor Contracts Law; the Social Insurance Law; the Unemployment Insurance Law; the Safe Production Law; Regulations on Employees' Injuries during Work in Enterprises; and Regulations on Labor Supervision.[26]

The drafting of the national-level Labor Law, like that of local legislation in the SEZs, was influenced by international labor conventions and by labor legislation in those countries with mature market economic systems. In preparing the Labor Law, the Chinese referred to and translated into Chinese major conventions passed by the International Labor Organization and the labor laws of over fifty countries and regions, including the United States, Canada, Chile, Germany, France, Spain, Japan, the Philippines, Singapore, Taiwan, Hong Kong, Macau, and Saudi Arabia, and compiled them into four book-length volumes.[27] It is not surprising that China's Labor Law contains many stipulations compatible with the labor laws of these countries. The Labor Law, for example, stipulates that a labor contract must be signed by the employer and the employee on the principle of voluntarism and equality and that it can be terminated by either side.

Apparently, this stipulation legalized freedom in employment, a major market principle long practiced worldwide; it provided for the signing of collective contracts and negotiations between the trade union (as the workers' representative) and the employer over such matters as wages, work hours, vacations, safety and sanitation, insurance, and benefits. It also stipulated that a system of minimum wages be set up by local governments and that eight-hour workdays and forty-four-hour workweeks be practiced. (In 1995 the State Council further shortened the workweek to forty hours.) Finally, it set, as mentioned above, some basic standards for the protection of women and minor workers. All these stipulations reflected, to some extent, international influence on China's labor legislation.

Foreign enterprises in China were thus subjected to two sets of labor legislation, one related particularly to labor-capital relations in these enterprises and the other generally concerned with both Chinese and foreign enterprises. This dual labor legislation on foreign enterprises reflected the overriding concern of the Chinese regime over labor-capital conflicts in these enterprises, and it was the regime's response to an increase in labor disputes in them. Strained labor relations in foreign enterprises created enormous pressure on the Chinese regime and forced it to seek the help of labor legislation. Passing labor laws and regulations was one thing, however, but effectively implementing them was another; this proved to be more challenging. A major obstacle to implementation lay in workers' lack of "legal consciousness" (*falu yishi*) or "consciousness of the rule of law" (*fazhi guannian*).

Many workers were unaware of the passing and existence of labor laws and regulations, let alone utilizing them to protect their own interests. Coupled with such ignorance on labor's side was the unfamiliarity with or contempt for Chinese labor laws on the part of many domestic and foreign employers (such as those from Hong Kong, Taiwan, and South Korea), which resulted in frequent breaches of labor laws by foreign enterprises. To tackle these problems and ensure that labor legislation would not remain dead letters, the Chinese regime adopted a variety of measures, including promotion of legal education among workers and expansion of the labor supervisory system (*laodong jiancha zhidu*). Legal education was aimed at "awakening" workers to their rights and obligations as stipulated in labor legislation and enhancing their willingness and ability to resort to laws for self-protection.

In cities such as Qingdao and Nanjing, city- and district-level unions often organized legal study or discussion sessions among workers and provided legal advice to them.[28] Workers with relatively sound legal knowledge were encouraged to form volunteer legal consultation groups whose duty was to assist their fellow workers. These groups sometimes represented workers in proceedings against employers.[29] Though legal education was primarily intended to equip workers with the legal weapons for self-protection, it also had the effect of reminding workers of their obligations to abide by labor laws and refrain from any illegal activities.

If the legal education campaign focused on acquainting workers with labor legislation, the labor supervisory system was designed to check and redress breaches of labor legislation by employers. In Qingdao this system was initially put into practice on a trial basis in 1993, and it has expanded vigorously since 1995. Under the labor supervisory system, local authorities set up agencies composed of full- and part-time personnel known as labor supervisors; they are dispatched regularly to enterprises to check whether labor laws and regulations are followed by employers, and they can impose sanctions (such as fines) on law-violating employers, demanding that employers redress violations within a certain period. Sometimes labor supervisors check an enterprise after receiving letters of accusation from workers. It seems that foreign employers have been the primary targets of the labor supervisory system. In Qingdao in 1996, for example, 90 percent of foreign-related enterprises, and 80 percent of Chinese private businesses, were subjected to checking by labor supervisors, whereas only 30 percent of state- and collective-owned enterprises were checked.[30]

## LIMITATIONS AND PROSPECTS OF CHINA'S LABOR LAW REFORM

The preceding pages suggest that the Chinese authorities, local and central, made remarkable efforts to accommodate internationally accepted labor standards and principles in carrying out labor law reforms. In adjusting to these principles, they proved highly cautious and selective rather than hasty and indiscriminate, especially in conducting national-level labor legislation. Generally, it took them a long time to draft and pass each labor law or regulation. For instance, the central government spent fifteen years (1979–1994) producing the Labor Law, the nation's first such legislation. They hesitated partly because of the regime's uncertainty about whether China ought to accept and practice foreign (or, more accurately, capitalist) labor legislative principles. Only with the deepening of market-oriented economic reforms and increasing economic globalization, did the Chinese regime gradually come to realize the necessity and feasibility of doing so.

As it happened, Chinese authorities seemed interested only in those foreign labor standards that they felt fit China's concrete socioeconomic conditions—standards concerning specific or technical labor problems such as wages, work hours, labor contracts, vacations, job training, employment, and labor protection. As for the fundamental labor rights or "core labor standards" (which were set and advocated by the ILO and other international organizations), the Chinese authorities (legislators) proved unprepared to incorporate them in China's labor laws. Among these fundamental labor rights were freedom of association, the right to bargain collectively, freedom from forced or compulsory labor, nondiscrimination in employment, minimum age of employment, and minimum standards of work.[31]

These rights were either absent from or diluted in China's labor laws and regulations. For example, the Labor Law provided for the formation of trade unions, but not free and independent trade unions. According to this law, the formation of trade unions needed approval from higher-level unions, and ultimately from the official national-level All-China Federation of Trade Unions. Without independent trade unions, workers hardly could engage in meaningful collective "bargaining" (which was referred to as collective "negotiation" in Chinese labor regulations) with employers. The Chinese preferred "negotiation" because it sounded less confrontational than "bargaining." Chinese labor laws also failed to confirm workers' rights to stage strikes, which could be a potentially effective bargaining chip for workers in dealing with their employers. The Labor Law stipulated only that workers "may or can" rather than "have the right to" sign collective contracts with employers, which might mean dispensability of collective contracts. Although it outlaws discrimination in employment that is based on race, ethnicity, gender, or religion, the Labor Law ignores discrimination on the basis of social origins (for example, a rural background or rural household). Also absent from Chinese labor laws are stipulations on the abolition of forced labor and child labor. This partly explains why forced labor was prevalent in China, as embodied by the systems of reform through labor (*laogai*), Reeducation through Labor (*laojiao*), and child labor. All these problems with China's labor laws and regulations indicate that China's efforts to embrace internationally accepted labor standards or principles were far from adequate.

These problems, however, do not necessarily suggest a bleak prospect for China's labor law reforms, or for its accommodation to international labor conventions, especially those fundamental labor rights or core labor standards. Many Chinese policy researchers and scholars already have stressed the irreversibility of economic globalization, the accompanying legal globalization, and the necessity for China's further compliance (or convergence) with international rules. For example, some of them have already advocated that Chinese workers' right to strike and to organize free trade unions should be legalized, the rigid household registration system (which excludes peasant workers from many urban occupations) should be dismantled, and the system of reform and education through labor should be abolished.[32]

## CONCLUSION

Economic globalization, as embodied by the presence of foreign enterprises, changed the landscape of Chinese industrial relations by introducing into China a new wage-labor relationship. This relationship was characterized by tensions and conflicts between labor and management.

Keenly concerned with maintaining stability of production in foreign enterprises, the Chinese state deemed it imperative to intervene to help improve labor-capital relations in them. Yet the state became aware that the traditional way of handling labor issues by direct Party-state intervention was not applicable to foreign enterprises.[33] Foreign employers would not accept such intervention in the first place, and any abrupt intrusion of state power into foreign enterprises would undermine foreign investors' confidence in doing business in China and thus jeopardize China's economy.

China's integration into the world economic system also exposed China to mounting pressures from its major trading partners (and the ILO) to comply with internationally recognized labor standards. Under such circumstances, the Chinese state was compelled to establish and use new institutions that were compatible with international conventions and acceptable to foreign employers. One of the new institutions the Chinese resorted to was labor rules (laws or regulations). In short, economic globalization spurred the Chinese regime to pursue labor legislation. In carrying out labor law reforms, the Chinese authorities reviewed and borrowed foreign experiences and incorporated many internationally accepted principles into China's labor laws.

It should be clarified that the process of labor legislation in post-Mao China was, by and large, indigenous. It originated from the Chinese regime's need to build a market economy, under which the state-owned enterprises were to be transformed into independent economic entities and the government was to relinquish its direct management of these enterprises. Changes in this direction started in the late 1970s and early 1980s. With the receding of state power, enterprises gained more autonomy in their operations. In the meantime, labor relations in these enterprises underwent a transition from a labor-state relationship to a contract between labor and management, both acting as relatively independent entities. In other words, the labor relationship gradually became "marketized" and took on more traits of the management-labor relationship as it prevails under the capitalist system. These changes meant that it was no longer desirable or possible for the state to wield its power directly over labor issues within an enterprise and required that new mechanisms be designed for coping with such issues.

The new mechanisms that would be in agreement with the regime's general orientation of building a market economy could be none other than labor laws. Here lies the fundamental rationale for the state efforts to promote labor law reforms and labor legislation. These remarks by no means contradict the arguments made in this study about the critical influence of economic and legal globalization on the process of labor law reforms in China. My point is that this process sprang from the very logic of China's economic reforms, specifically from changes in labor relations within state-owned enterprises. Yet it was greatly accelerated, or given new impetus, by the presence of foreign enterprises and international pressures. The strained relationship between foreign employers and Chinese workers gave rise to a sense of urgency among Chinese policy makers to quicken their steps in formulating labor laws. This study has placed considerable emphasis on the efforts of the Chinese state in developing new labor laws. Indeed, the state was indispensable in this regard. Undoubtedly, labor legislation should be within the jurisdiction of the state, as it is in any other country, and China desperately needed such legislation during the period under discussion.

## NOTES

1. H. Guan and L. Zhao, "A Labor Law Reform," *Peace and Conflict Studies* 16, no. 2 (1995): 52.

2. *Zhongguo jingji nianjian 1998* (Almanac of China's Economy, 1998) (Beijing: Chinese Economic Publishing House, 1998), 340.

3. Guan and Zhao, "A Labor Law Reform," 53.

4. *Zhongguo laodong tongji nianjian 1997* (China Labor Statistical Yearbook, 1997) (Beijing: Chinese Statistical Press, 1997), 406.

5. N. Chen, ed., *Zhongguo laowu shichang de zuzhi yu guanli* (The Formation and Administration of Labor Markets in China) (Beijing: Economic Management Press, 1993), 303.

6. Zeng X., Tian J., and Ding G., "Guanyu bufen sanzi qiye yuangong quanyi qingkuang de diaocha zhisan" (The Third Report on the Situation of Employees' Rights and Interests in Some Foreign-Related Enterprises), *Gongren ribao* (Workers' Daily), November 11, 1993.

7. Guan and Zhao, "A Labor Law Reform," 54.

8. Interviews of unnamed sources by the author, Qingdao, summer 1997.

9. *Dubao cankao* (News References) 10 (1997): 17–19.

10. Guan and Zhao, "A Labor Law Reform," 55.

11. Liu J., ed., *WTO yu zhongguo falu gaigai* (WTO and Reforms of the Chinese Legal System) (Beijing: Xiyuan Publishing House, 2001), 451–452.

12. For the annual reports of Chinese human rights record, see http://news .xinhuanet.com/ziliao/2003-01/20/content_697520.htm.

13. Liu W., ed., *WTO yu zhongguo laodong falu zhidu de chongtu* (Conflict

between the WTO and China's Labor Legal System) (Beijing: Chinese City Press, 2001), 141–147.

14. Guan and Zhao, "A Labor Law Reform," 56.

15. Yuan S., ed., *Laodong fa quanshu* (A Complete Book of Labor Laws) (Beijing: Cosmic Press, 1994), 109–110.

16. Andrew G. Walder, *Communist Neo-Traditionalism: Work and Authority in Chinese Industry* (Berkeley: University of California Press, 1986); Walder, "Organized Dependency and Cultures of Authority in Chinese Industry," *Journal of Asian Studies* 43, no. 1 (1983): 51–76.

17. Yuan, *Laodong fa quanshu,* 110.

18. Guan and Zhao, "A Labor Law Reform," 57.

19. Ibid., 58.

20. J. Xia, ed., *Zhongguo laodong fa ruogan zhongyao lilun yu zhengce wenti yanjiu* (Studies on Various Important Theories and Policies regarding Chinese Labor Laws) (Beijing: Chinese Labor and Social Security Press, 2000), 163–199.

21. *Qingdao shi difangxing fagui guizhang huibian* (Compilation of Local Laws and Regulations in Qingdao, 1987–1988) (Qingdao: Qingdao City Government, 1989), 88–96; *Zhonghua renmin gongheguo difangxing fagui huibian* (Compilation of Local Laws and Regulations of the PRC, 1992–1994) (Beijing: Chinese Law Press, 1995), 1162–1167, 1118–1122; and *Dazhong ribao* (Populace's Daily), May 13, 1996.

22. Guan and Zhao, "A Labor Law Reform," 59.

23. *Qingdao shi difangxing fagui guizhang huibian,* 88–96.

24. *Zhonghua renmin gongheguo falu quanshu* (A Complete Book of Statutes of the PRC) (Changchun: Jilin People's Press, 1993), 690–693.

25. Yuan, *Laodong fa quanshu,* 309.

26. *Zhongguo laodong nianjian* (Chinese Labor Yearbook, 1995–1996) (Beijing: Chinese Yearbook Press, 1997), 155.

27. Yuan, *Laodong fa quanshu,* 13; Guan and Zhao, "A Labor Law Reform," 1047–1840.

28. Guan and Zhao, "A Labor Law Reform," 61.

29. Author interviews, 1977; *Gongren ribao* (Workers' Daily), August 22, 1995.

30. Author interviews, 1997.

31. Guan and Zhao, "A Labor Law Reform," 62.

32. Liu J., *WTO yu zhongguo falu gaigai,* 467–491.

33. Guan and Zhao, "A Labor Law Reform," 63.

## FURTHER READING

*Zhonghua renmin gongheguo laodong fa shiwu quanshu* (Complete Practical Book on Labor Laws of the PRC). Beijing: Economic Times Press, 1994.

# 6

# Adaptation to WTO Standards

## Changes and Adjustments to Business Laws and Regulations

### Xiaoxiao Li

On November 10, 2001, in Doha, Qatar, the Fourth Ministerial Conference of the World Trade Organization (WTO) adopted the decision on China's accession to the WTO. As of December 11, 2001, China officially became the 143rd member of the WTO, which marked the fact that China's "opening-to-outside world" policy had entered a new era. This chapter reviews the legal and regulatory preparations that were made as the Chinese government proceeded. Many disputes over weighted sacrifices have been compared to the benefits to China's economy, especially the effects on Chinese economic development. The question arose whether joining the WTO would halt or harm China's open-door policy and put state-owned enterprises in danger before they were ready and strong enough to compete in the world market.[1] For example, joining the WTO would mean deeper integration into globalization, and, as a result, this integration would closely relate to the Chinese legal system's change and evolution.[2] The changes and adjustments of Chinese business laws and regulations need to progress further to fully meet the requirements of being a WTO member.

Some people say that China continues to remain a major risk for investors. The one-country, two-system (socialism and capitalism) balance is a delicate one to maintain, and foreign businesses are often caught in the middle.[3] For instance, U.S. law firms operating in Shanghai had to halt their affairs until the government granted them new licenses. German and Japanese banks have found that collecting payments on loans from the government can be extremely difficult. In addition, some securities firms have learned that Chinese clients occasionally refuse to pay for trades that turn out to be losers, and government protection is limited for such actions.[4]

The collapse of the former Soviet Union and Eastern European socialist countries has given further proof of the drawbacks and potential danger of the planned economic system. Most Westerners think that the only way to change the status quo is to integrate China more tightly into the global community.[5] The process of engaging China more deeply with world affairs and of allowing China to play a more responsible role remains a question, however. Analysis shows that China's joining the WTO offers the best opportunity to reach this goal of integration. China's legal and regulatory practices and its increasing economic and political role in world affairs during this ten-year period support this point.

Joining the WTO gives a great deal of new meaning to the processes of China's rule of law, especially in its effect on Chinese legislation. The WTO puts the law first; the WTO provides a forum for negotiating agreements aimed at reducing obstacles to international trade and ensures a level playing field for all, thus contributing to economic growth and development.[6] The WTO also provides a legal and institutional framework for the implementation and monitoring of these agreements, as well as for settling disputes arising from their interpretation and application.[7] China's legislation must combine its domestic laws with the WTO rules and international practices. If the 1980s were the years during which China began to enter the legislative fast-track to catch up with modern, democratic societies, then in the early twenty-first century the initial formation of the legal system with Chinese characteristics has clearly revealed that China has entered a legislative period of actively promoting judicial reform. This reform is meant to protect achievements derived from its miraculous economic development and to generate more energy when a glimpse of political reform begins to slightly show signs of emerging. The most significant sign marking this period is the shift from the quantitative model to the qualitative model; from the government-pushed model to a market-dominant model; from the closed-door model to the open-door learning model.[8]

The WTO's influence on China's legislation was first reflected in the Chinese Trade Law. According to WTO principle, the regulations on foreign trade call for the abandonment of the quantitative restrictions on commodity imports, the uniform monitoring of both imports and exports, the use of tariffs as a major mechanism to manage imports, showing the transparency and predictability of trade law, and the opening of foreign trade rights to all eligible entities.[9] Beginning in 1987, China initiated its step-by-step reforms that were based on the General Agreement on Trade and Tariff (GATT) requirements in the areas of foreign trade policy, foreign trade systems, the customs tariff system, the commodity inspection approach, the foreign exchange control, and the price mechanism for imported and exported products.[10] When China published its first Foreign Trade Law in 1994, its contents were clearly consistent with WTO anti-dumping, anti-subsidy, and trade protection rules. This law enabled the GATT and the WTO free trade system to be operational in China. These types of changes were also made at the early stages to other laws and regulations, such as the Foreign Investment Law, which was revised in March 2001, the Maritime Commerce Law, first enacted in 1993, and the Anti-Dumping and Anti-Subsidy Rules, both issued in 1997.[11]

On the WTO platform, Chinese society started to reevaluate legislative quality and efficiency, focusing on the amendment and perfection of legislation, and learning from foreign legislative experiences.[12] The current body of trade agreements relating to the WTO consists of sixteen different multilateral agreements, to which all WTO members are parties, and two other multilateral agreements, to which only some WTO members are parties. The basic principle of WTO law is that China, as a member of this economic entity, must carefully follow international standards in its legislation. The important background of China's legislative history cannot be disregarded in this post-legislative time.[13]

More specifically, the WTO's major activities relating to China's trade and business legal reform are (1) negotiating the reduction or elimination of obstacles to trade, such as import tariffs and other barriers, and agreeing on rules governing the conduct of international trade; (2) administering and monitoring the application of the WTO's agreed-on rules for trade in goods and services and trade-related intellectual property rights; (3) monitoring and reviewing the trade policies of WTO members, as well as ensuring transparency of regional and bilateral trade agreements; (4) settling disputes among WTO members regarding the interpretation and application of the agreements.[14]

Above all, as a member of the WTO, China must, beyond its own willingness to do so, make clear adjustments and changes in order to fulfill its commitments to global trading partners. History reveals the true story concerning China's accession process: a long fifteen years followed the negotiations from 1986, when China formally applied to resume the GATT contracting party status, until November 11, 2001, when China was finally accepted as a member of the WTO, during which two of the most important bilateral negotiations played a decisive role in China's accession.[15] On November 10, 1999, the final round of Sino–U.S. negotiations for China's acceptance in the WTO started in Beijing. We witnessed the delegations of two parties being flown across the Pacific, where the leaders of the two countries met on different occasions to bargain over the issues.[16] According to the official documents of the Clinton administration, the major obstacle to China's entry was that the rule of law—which is the infrastructure that enables enterprises to flourish in any economy—was underdeveloped in China.

WTO membership, in the greatest sense, represents adherence to a set of accepted international rules. These rules include the development and publication of laws and regulations, consistency in decision making, recourse to law enforcement and judicial proceedings, and curbs on the arbitrary exercise of bureaucratic discretion. These concepts, in turn, rest on universal values and ideals, including transparency, public and enforceable commitments, and openness to the outside world.[17] Thus, accession to the WTO accelerated the trend toward development of the rule of law within China.[18] Only when China was able to satisfy such requirements was the country formally accepted; we will see, later in this chapter, precisely what China accomplished to reach an agreement with the United States.

In a similar negotiation between China and the European Union (EU), the EU raised concerns that were resolved before any agreement was reached. On March 28, 2000, China and the EU started bilateral negotiations on China's accession to the WTO. Less than two months later, on May 19, 2000, China and the EU reached an agreement on China's accession.

Before further analysis, I will provide a simple illustration of how China's legal system functions, examining it through its framework. Chinese laws and regulations can be divided into several levels. The first level is the fundamental law of the state constitution, which has the strongest effect and which was created by the National People's Congress (NPC). The second level is the laws enacted by the NPC and its Standing Committee, including civil laws, criminal laws, and administrative laws. The third level, which is also the most confusing one, includes the administrative rules and regulations that are made by the State Council, including decisions, orders, regulations, and the like. The reason for many outsiders' confusion about this level of legal and regulatory rules is that the rules have the force of law; most of the time, the administrative rules even exceed the power of laws, functioning as the symbol of government in daily economic operations.[19] The fourth level is the rules and regulations that are formulated and promulgated by the different departments of the State Council, including regulations, methods, and so on.

In accordance with the central government legal body, and issued in a similar manner, the local provincial legislative regulations and local provincial government regulations are formulated and promulgated by the National People's Congress and its Standing Committee, as well as the people's government in each province, autonomous region, and municipality. The application of law follows the principle that all laws and regulations must be consistent with the constitution: one regulation must not conflict with a law in the next-higher level. As soon as China was recognized as a member of the WTO on November 10, 2001, Shi Guangsheng, minister of Foreign Trade and Economics, clearly stated that China would abide by WTO rules and honor its commitments. Under WTO rules, China would undertake a series of WTO obligations, one of which was to fulfill "the principle of transparency."[20]

From this perspective, we are at a point where we can see the initial steps by the Chinese government to undertake the series of WTO obligations. China has long been considered by the international community to be a country of little transparency, and, in fact, this problem continues to exist.[21] In arranging the order of the applicable law in accordance with China legislative level, then, the enacted laws by the NPC and its Standing Committee should be at the first level, followed by the administrative rules of the State Council and its ministries and commissions, and then by local regulations. The explanatory statements by the government officials should not have a legal effect. China's past practice, however, often did not follow this order; China habitually went beyond the publicly announced laws and regulations to develop a number of "internal decisions" or "official documents," which became more important than the laws. Furthermore, some officials' speeches were more effective than the regulations. The existence of this so-called black box situation was inconsistent with WTO rules. For example, item number 17 in "Rules on Guangdong Special Economic Zone

(SEZ)" encouraged the enterprises operating in the economic zone to use Chinese-made equipment, raw materials, and other goods; favorable prices were set for export products and payments were to be in foreign currency.[22] Another, similar example is item number 57 in "Rules on Chinese Foreign Joint Venture Companies," which stated that the equipment, raw materials, and office supplies needed by a joint venture company should be procured in Chinese domestic markets. Chinese administration and legislation was faced with the mandate to clear, amend, or even abandon all rules and regulations inconsistent with WTO rules and to establish a new mechanism for administrative and legislative rules. Consequentially, in October 2001, the State Council announced the Decision to Stop Enactment of Administrative and Legislative Rules Issued before 2000," and it reviewed a total of 756 such administrative and legislative rules and regulations. During this process, the State Council abandoned 71 rules, invalidated 80 rules, and clarified and reconfirmed that 70 rules were abandoned.[23]

By the end of 2006, when attending a government policy forum in Hong Kong, the former vice minister of Foreign Trade and Economics, Long Yongtu, explained China's efforts on the implementation of the principle of transparency, which could be summarized by considering that (1) after China's commitment to membership in the WTO, the implementation of foreign trade activities follows only published laws and regulations—all other measures and any internal documents or provisions are unenforceable; (2) to ensure the transparency of laws and regulations, an official journal will be designated to publish all aspects of Chinese foreign trade and economic laws and regulations, which any WTO members, businesses, and individuals will have access to; (3) before the introduction of any foreign trade laws, except those involving national security, such as exchange rate changes and other important measures, there will be a waiting period during which enterprises and related parties can review various aspects, which will ensure that the enactment of the rules is in accordance with market economic principles; and (4) a corporate advisory and complaints mechanism will be established, and the central government is obligated to reply in no more than forty-five days.

At the end of 2006 the NPC and its Standing Committee had endorsed and passed six newly revised laws, three related to foreign investment and three related to intellectual property rights. The State Council and its relevant departments had also canceled or modified more than 2,300 rules and regulations. Following that, the State Council publicly announced a list of 221 repealed administrative regulations. For example, the State Council reevaluated trade-related regulations many times before the end of 1999 and found more than 40 laws and regulations that had to be revised, 12 regulations that conflicted with China's commitment to accession to the WTO and that thus had to be canceled, and more than 2,300 regulations or rules enacted by different departments in the State Council that needed to be changed or canceled before China joined the WTO.[24]

The requirements for transparency involved not only the legislative branch and the administrative bodies but also the judiciary. For laws and regulations to be amended or repealed, judicial interpretations had to be amended accordingly or repealed. These judicial interpretations had to be published in the media in a timely manner; in addition, details of the reform of the judicial system, including hearing and sentencing reform, had to be available to the public. At present, the People's Court is witnessing ongoing institutional reforms; the courts will establish the system to ensure the separation of the filing from the trial, the separation of the trial from the execution, and the separation of implementation from oversight. Many foreign companies have experienced the quasi transparency and even nontransparency of China's judicial system. The German Chamber of Commerce noted that, on the basis of German companies' experiences there, China has not done enough to amend its laws, which has resulted in a lack of policy transparency and a lack of protection of intellectual property as well. In response to this criticism, Zhou Jidong, the deputy director of the Legal Office of the Beijing Municipal Government, asserted that there is no transparency problem where many policies and interpretations by the legislative and judicial staffs are concerned. Su Chi, the deputy president of Beijing Intermediate People's Court, feels confident that China has fulfilled its commitment to the WTO and its members to judicial transparency, unified enactment, and judicial review procedures, a commitment that has been perceived by many WTO members. For example, in the early 1990s the Beijing Intermediate People's Court held its first public trial, attracting worldwide attention. At the onset of 1999 the Beijing Intermediate People's Court led the movement to make all judicial documents public, and now any citizen can consult the relevant court decision documents with his or her personal identification card in the court library.[25]

On the one hand, Chinese government at this initial stage cleared and canceled the regulations that were in conflict with WTO principles, established and amended relevant regulations and laws, changed the counter-vailing regulations into the Anti-Dumping Law according to existing WTO regulations, and intensified its efforts to enact and implement legal regu-lations following WTO requirements that those regulations would main-tain their authoritative power. On the other hand, the Chinese government was urged to establish a new foreign trade system to accord with common international practices and with the domestic and international economic situation. All these efforts reflect the fact that the Chinese government was committed to accepting the WTO's dispute-settlement and trade review mechanisms and to reforming the Chinese judicial system.

China's joining the WTO clearly demonstrated the benefits of such decision making, as there is obvious evidence from different angles of Chi-nese society. First, as soon as China joined the WTO, the volume of foreign trade started to grow at a fast pace. Between 2002 and 2004 the average growth rate reached 36.4 percent. Trade volume reached $1.43 trillion in 2005, up from $474 billion in 2000; exports increased threefold from $249 billion in 2000 to $762 billion in 2005. China's total trade volume was the third largest in the world, as it truly became a global trading power.[26]

Second, China's efforts to implement WTO standards have been appar-ent to all. In the first five years alone, China revised more than 2,000 legis-lative terms and regulations and eliminated more than 800. Foreign trade is now completely deregulated and open to all economic enterprises, which was the first and most important step in China's fulfillment of its WTO

**Table 6.1.** China Tariff Rates (percent) 2001–2009

| Year | Tariff average | Industrial average | Agricultural average |
|------|----------------|--------------------|----------------------|
| 2000 | 15.6 | 14.7 | 21.3 |
| 2001 | 14.0 | 13.0 | 19.9 |
| 2002 | 12.7 | 11.7 | 18.5 |
| 2003 | 11.5 | 10.6 | 17.4 |
| 2004 | 10.4 | 9.5 | 15.6 |
| 2005 | 9.9 | 9.0 | 15.3 |
| 2006 | 9.8 | N/A | N/A |
| 2007 | 9.8 | N/A | N/A |
| 2008 | 9.8 | 8.9 | 15.2 |
| 2009 | 9.8 | 8.9 | 15.2 |

commitments. For example, according to the Law on Foreign Trade that was passed at the Eighth Session of the Tenth People's National Congress, the Ministry of Commerce announced its Guidelines for Foreign Trade Operator Registration in June 2004 and enacted them in July 2004.[27]

Third, we have seen a significant reduction in tariffs. By the end of 2004 the total average Chinese tariff decreased to 10.4 percent from 42.7 percent in 1992. Tariff reduction was even greater for some major industrial products. Because of China's commitment as a WTO member, the average tariff rate continued to decrease to 10.1 percent in 2005 and 10 percent in 2008. Tariff rate reductions from 2001 to 2005 are listed in Table 6.1.

Last but not least, we have the legal establishment of the China Customs System. China Customs has already developed its legal framework, the Customs Law of the PRC being at its core; it has been accompanied by the Regulations on Import and Export Tariffs of the PRC, Regulations of the PRC on Origin of Import and Export Goods, Implementing Regulations of the PRC on Customs Administrative Penalties, other administrative laws, and customs standard operating rules.

China Customs seeks to improve officers' basic legal awareness. At the same time, however, it aims to promote compliance through strict enforcement and customs formalities, which include impartial, transparent, stable, and simplified procedures that promote enforcement efficiency.

China Customs attaches great importance to and is strengthening its protection of intellectual property rights (IPR) through legislation and process management, having gradually set up a working mechanism featuring unified coordination, high efficiency, and well-targeted measures. These include a series of special operations to fight infringements on imports and exports, effectively standardizing and rectifying entry and exit processes and safeguarding fair competition, which have won recognition and wide praise from different sectors at home and abroad.

In 2004 China Customs implemented the Administrative Licensing Law and achieved the goals of promoting officers' enforcement awareness, collating project files, improving supporting measures, and ensuring a stable transition. Customs enforcement has been optimized by the promulgation of a series of laws and regulations, such as Implementing Regulations of the PRC on Customs Administrative Penalties, Regulations of the PRC on the Origin of Import and Export Goods, and the like. To clarify my argument that China has made great strides in following WTO rules and international practices, I will discuss some changes in major economic policies and regulations.

The first major change is apparent through the enactment of anti-dumping rules. The Anti-Dumping Regulation of the PRC was passed by the forty-sixth executive meeting of the State Council in October 2001. It regards the importing of products that have been dumped into China's market, causing material injury or threat of material injury to existing domestic industry, or the material setback of the establishment of a domestic industry. The investigation and determination of dumping was led by the Ministry of Foreign Trade and Economic Cooperation (MOFTEC). The ministry starts an investigation when it receives applications from domestic companies, which automatically triggers a protective mechanism. Investigation and determination of damages are accomplished by the State Economic and Trade Commission. An investigation of the agricultural industry was led jointly by the State Economic and Trade Commission and the Ministry of Agriculture.

The second major change is apparent in the promulgation of the Countervailing Regulations of the PRC, passed by the forty-sixth executive meeting of the State Council in October 2001. If imported products are subsidized and have caused material injury or threat of material injury to an existing domestic industry or a material setback to the establishment of a domestic industry, the investigation and countervailing measures will be undertaken in accordance with the provisions of this ordinance. The investigation and determination of subsidies is accomplished through the MOFTEC; the investigation and determination of damages is accomplished through the State Economic and Trade Commission. If the case involves an agricultural products injury investigation, such an investigation is made through the State Economic and Trade Commission and the Ministry of Agriculture.

The third major change to economic policy and regulation is the promulgation of the Safeguard Measures Ordinance of the PRC, passed by the forty-sixth executive meeting of the State Council in October 2001. If an increase in the number of imported products causes direct, serious damage to domestic manufacturers producing similar or competing products, and if it produces or threatens serious injury to a domestic industry, an investigation is undertaken in accordance with the regulations, and safeguarding measures are carried out.

The fourth important change regards the enactment of the Regulations on Foreign Financial Institutions Management, passed by the fiftieth executive meeting of the State Council in December 2001. The regulations state that foreign financial institutions conducting business in Chinese currency must meet conditions regarding their operation in China: a financial institution must have operated for more than three years within Chinese territory at the time of its application and have had profits from its operation for two consecutive years, and it must meet other prudential requirements set by the People's Bank of China (PBC). Foreign financial institutions' lending rates and commission rates will be determined by the foreign financial institutions in accordance with the relevant provisions of the PBC. Foreign financial institutions must accept the PBC's and its branches' supervision and inspection according to law and regularly submit accurate relevant documents and written reports; they may not refuse this supervision or conceal information.

The fifth important change regards the cumulative revisions in the Import and Export Regulations. To regulate the import and export of goods and services, maintain order among imports and exports, and stimulate the healthy development of foreign trade, the Import and Export Regulations were passed by the forty-sixth executive meeting of the State Council in October 2001. All those who import goods for sale in the domestic market or export goods for sale outside China must abide by this ordinance. The Chinese government encourages free import and export of goods and assures trade on the basis of quality and order.

Additional important changes are those that have been expounded through the Technology Import and Export Regulations. To regulate the import and export of technology and stimulate national economic and social development, the Technology Import and Export Regulations were passed by the forty-sixth executive meeting of the State Council in October 2001. The Regulations on Technology Import Contracts of 1985 and the Guidelines on Technology Import Contracts of 1987 were abandoned at that time. All these laws and their amendments offer clear guidelines for all companies' business operations. Furthermore, they lead the way toward establishing a reliable market platform and a trustworthy business environment for all companies around the world.

As for the issue of greatest concern to foreign insurance companies, China announced the enactment of the Regulations for Foreign Insurance Companies' Operations, passed by the forty-sixth executive meeting of the State Council in October 2001. The goal of this legislation was to adopt an open-door policy and an economic development program, as well as to strengthen the oversight of foreign insurance companies' operations and to improve the health of the insurance industry in China.

In the past thirty years of economic reform, through the process of allowing investment and business and financial operations by foreign companies of all kinds, China has confronted numerous problems that have arisen from the flight of capital and problematic transferring of company wealth.[28] Consequently, to alleviate the negative effect of such problems on China's economic stability, China announced the enactment of the Regulations on Closure of Financial Institutions, passed by the forty-seventh executive meeting of the State Council in November 2001. The regulations seek to provide oversight of financial activities and to maintain financial order, as well as to protect national and public interests.

Throughout the 1980s and 1990s China's economy was dominated by tens of thousands of state-owned enterprises, big and small. The government interfered with the daily operations of these organizations. At the same time, the government discriminated against privately owned small and medium enterprises (SME), paying no attention to their legal rights and wishes. Many different government agencies established countless rules and regulations to limit the activities of these companies, which in turn gave incentives to the private sector to limit investment and caused the pace of economic development to slow, generating serious problems for the economy as a whole. As a result, China published the SME Promotion Law, the first of its kind in China, passed by the twenty-eighth session of the Ninth NPC Standing Committee on June 29, 2002; it went into effect on January 1, 2003. The SME Promotion Law stipulates that no organization or individual will harm small and medium enterprises' assets or their legal incomes and profits. The nation-state is in the position to protect all legal rights of small and medium enterprises, including participation in fair competition and fair trade, and the government will not discriminate and impose unfair trading terms on small and medium enterprises.

One common business practice in China is apparent through the government-issued guidelines for foreign direct investment. Every year these guidelines are updated on the basis of economic situations in China and China's need for certain technological products. In accordance with WTO rules, China also made significant changes to the Guidelines for Foreign Direct Investment, which state that the relevant departments of the State Council must, in a timely manner, review and revise the Guidelines for Foreign Direct Investment in accordance with the Regulations on the Direction of Foreign Direct Investment. After having been approved by the State

Council, the Guidelines for Foreign Direct Investment were published by the National Development and Reform Commission, the National Economic and Trade Commission, and the Ministry of Foreign Trade and Economics on March 11, 2002. The previous guidelines of December 31, 1997, were abandoned at that time.

Having discussed the changes to certain business rules and regulations in conformity with China's WTO commitment, I now want to draw a simple picture of the administrative organization that oversees foreign trade in China. The Ministry of Commerce is the integral part of the State Council, in charge of both domestic and foreign trade and of international economic cooperation. The main mandate of this administration is to formulate development strategies, guidelines, and policies for domestic and foreign trade and international economic cooperation; draft laws and regulations governing domestic and foreign trade, economic cooperation, and foreign investment; and devise rules and regulations for implementation.

The WTO Affairs Department studies and puts forward proposals for harmonizing domestic legislation on trade and economic affairs, while bringing Chinese economic and trade laws into conformity with multilateral and bilateral treaties and agreements. This department also formulates development plans for domestic trade, studies and puts forth proposals on reforming the commercial distribution system, develops and fosters urban and rural markets, and promotes the restructuring of the commercial distribution sector and the improvement of such modern distribution modalities as chain store operations, modern logistics, and e-commerce. The department also researches and formulates policies for regulating market operations and distribution order, breaking up market monopolies and regional blockages in order to set up and improve an integrated, open, competitive, and orderly market system.

Also, an administrative body, the Department of Fair Trade Practice, monitors and analyzes market activities and commodity supply and demand, organizing the adjustment of the market supply of principal consumer goods and the regulation of the distribution of the major means of production. This department studies and works out measures for the regulation of import and export commodities and compiles a catalogue thereof, organizing the implementation of import and export quota plans and deciding on quota quantities and issuing licenses. It also drafts and implements import and export commodity quota tendering policies, formulates and executes policies concerning trade in technology, as well as policies that encourage the export of technology. This department also presses for the establishment of a foreign trade standardization system; it supervises technology import, equipment import, export of domestic technologies subject to state export restrictions, and reexport of imported technologies, in addition to issuing export licenses pertaining to nuclear nonproliferation. The Department of Fair Trade Practice also studies, produces, and implements multilateral and bilateral trade and economic cooperation policies, while being responsible for multilateral and bilateral negotiations on trade and economic issues, coordinating domestic positions in negotiating with foreign parties, and signing the relevant documents and monitoring their implementation. Through the process of these latter responsibilities, it establishes multilateral and bilateral intergovernmental liaison mechanisms for economic and trade affairs and organizes the related work, handling major issues in country-specific economic and trade relationships as well as regulating trade and economic activities with countries lacking a diplomatic relationship with China.

In line with its mandate, and in order to handle the relationship with the World Trade Organization on behalf of the Chinese government, the Department of Fair Trade Practice must undertake such responsibilities within the framework of the WTO as multilateral and bilateral negotiations, trade policy reviews, dispute settlements, and notifications and inquiries. It must steer the work of the commercial branches of China's Permanent Mission to the WTO, the UN, and other relevant international organizations, as well as to Chinese embassies in foreign countries. It must keep in touch with the representative offices of multilateral and international economic and trade organizations in China and the commercial functions of foreign diplomatic missions in China while organizing and coordinating the work pertaining to issues related to fair trade for import and export. Also, it must institute a fair-trade early-warning mechanism for imports and exports and organize industry injury investigations.

Furthermore, the department must comprise certain entities to guide and coordinate domestic efforts in responding to specific investigations and other issues of concern. It must give general guidance to nationwide efforts in foreign investment through analyzing China's foreign investment developments and regularly submitting information concerning those developments and the corresponding proposals to the State Council. It must draw up and enforce foreign investment policies and reform schemes and participate in the formulation of mid-term and long-term planning and development strategies for foreign investment utilization. It must examine and approve, according to relevant laws, the establishment of and changes thereafter to foreign-invested enterprises where foreign input exceeds the state's fixed amount, or enterprises engaging in restricted business areas or in businesses subject to quotas and license administration. It must verify the contracts and statutes of large-scale projects with foreign investment and their major subsequent changes particularly stipulated in relevant legislation. It must supervise the enforcement of laws, regulations, contracts, and statutes regarding foreign-invested enterprises, and it must guide and oversee nationwide efforts in attracting foreign investment and other business opportunities, as well as the establishment and trade performance of foreign-invested enterprises in China.

With knowledge of the functions and responsibilities of these departments, one can easily find a way to organize and start operating in Chinese markets. Also in operation are other divisions that comprehensively guide and coordinate the specific work of state-level economic and technological development zones, while being responsible for China's foreign economic cooperation efforts. These divisions' responsibilities include formulating and implementing policies and regulations on foreign economic cooperation; guiding and monitoring the regulation of overseas contract projects, labor cooperation, and designing and consulting businesses; working out administrative measures and specific policies guiding China's overseas investment; approving Chinese companies' investments in and setting up of overseas establishments (excluding financial companies) while supervising their operation; being in charge of China's efforts to provide aid to foreign countries and regions.

From the listed mandates, one is still able to see the strong influence of government interference in the economic sphere and cannot help worrying about potential manipulations by the enactment of rules and regulations for untold purposes.[29] This latter concern is implicit in the continuing argument about whether China truly honors its commitment to perfect its legal and regulatory system to abide by WTO rules.

Before I conclude, some of the innovations of the Chinese trade policy decision-making process are worth mentioning. A short review may provide more confidence in China's further efforts to adapt its legal rules and regulations to WTO rules and to integrate itself more deeply into the global community.

Before China entered the WTO, the third session of the Ninth NPC passed the Legislation Law, enacted on July 1, 2000, to regulate legislative activities and improve the legislative system in order to establish and perfect the legal system with Chinese characteristics while ensuring and developing a socialist democracy and rule of the country by law. This law requires that hearings among relevant institutions, organizations, and citizens be held before any administrative rule is enacted. After China's accession to the WTO, the State Council constructed the Rulemaking Process Ordinance, enacted on January 1, 2002, to ensure the quality of rules and regulations following the Legislation Law. This ordinance stipulates that when relevant institutions, organizations, or civilians have significant disputes over a drafted rule, that draft rule must be made public so that opinions may be gathered from all walks of life. The party drafting the rule can also carry out the hearings.

A second innovation is the working mechanism of four-body interaction, which was originally initiated by the Ministry of Commerce to deal with the increasing numbers of trade disputes. Its key concepts have been developed and tested in the daily activities of fair-trade import and export. The four bodies comprise the central government (the Ministry of Commerce), the local government departments (local foreign trade bureaus and related administrative departments), the intermediate organizations (the professional or industrial associations and professional service institutions), and the enterprises. The Ministry of Commerce is responsible for leading the overall operations of each specific task, decisions on trade policy, negotiations with foreign parties, and settlements to lift the trade barriers. The local government departments function as a bridge between the central government and the local enterprises and intermediate institutions, and they are responsible for transferring information from top to bottom and vice versa, directing and coordinating, and work training. The industrial associations supply industry information to local enterprises, work as spokesmen for the industries' public interests, and organize enterprises within industries. The enterprises are the main body of trading activity and active participants in trading policy–related public affairs.

A third approach is the publishing of regulations and other legal documents. The Chinese government regularly publishes journals with information on the foreign trade system in China, such as *Yearbook of Foreign Trade and Economics, Ministry of Commerce Public Bulletin,* and *China Foreign Economic Cooperation Gazette,* which are all published by the

Ministry of Commerce, as well as the *China Statistics Yearbook* published by the State Statistics Bureau and *China Customs Statistics* compiled and published by the China General Administration of Customs. All Chinese laws, State Council regulations, and ministry ordinances related to foreign trade can be found in unrestricted publications. The information regarding foreign trade rules and regulations can also be found at the official website of the Ministry of Commerce, www.mofcom.gov.cn. The information regarding foreign currency and exchange can be retrieved from the State Administration of Foreign Exchange bulletin and its official website, www.safe.gov.cn. One can find all the bilateral trade agreements between China and its trading partners in the People's Republic of China Treaty Series. Other official journals that publish trade-related information are *People's National Congress (PNC) Standing Committee Communiqué, PRC State Council Bulletin, Laws and Regulations of the PRC, China Foreign Economic Cooperation Gazette, Bulletin of the People's Bank of China,* and the *Ministry of Finance Bulletin.*

One is able, on the basis of my analysis, to distinguish an overall picture of how China has adapted itself to the requirements of the WTO. Most of these efforts have been made through governments at central, regional, and provincial levels. Legislation has been made under strong government guidance and direction. One truly hopes that businesses and other sorts of institutions and organizations are able to play an increasing role in trade dispute settlements and other market-oriented activities, with decreasing government interference.

The year 2011 was the tenth anniversary of China's accession to the WTO. Pascal Lamy, secretary general of the WTO, gave China's performances an A+ in this ten-year period.[30] John H. Jackson, who is the so-called father of GATT/WTO and a law professor at Georgetown University, said that China has become more and more professional in dealing with legal cases within the WTO framework.[31] According to Timothy P. Stratford, the former assistant U.S. trade representative, "China is able to settle disputes responsibly within the WTO frameworks. Even when China loses a case, it can still adhere to the WTO resolution. At the same time, China has learned how to raise complaints against other members through WTO mechanisms."[32]

By 2010 China had become the second strongest economic entity in the world and the largest trade partner of major emerging markets, the second-largest trade partner of the European Union, third of the United

States, and fourth of the Association of Southeast Asian Nations. Behind such attractive trade successes is strong support derived from the improvement and refinement of the Chinese legal systems. During these ten years China actively amended its legal rules and legislations to fulfill the promise of WTO accession and to turn WTO rules into its domestic laws. After December 11, 2001, China became involved in thirty WTO suits relating to twenty-one disputes. Li Chenggang, the director of the Department of Rules and Regulations of the Ministry of Commerce, explained that the ministry has established two departments to deal with the WTO legal cases and has recommended to the WTO seventeen experts to raise issues and concerns about emerging markets and developing countries.[33]

China amended the fourth term in its Copyright Law and the third condition of the twenty-seventh term in its Customs Intellectual Property Protection Rules regarding the execution of intellectual property protection cases. It amended the Printing Administration Rules and the Rules on Video Products in order to be in compliance with the resolutions made by the WTO authorities.[34] These amendments reflect the fact that China respects international rules and regulations and tries its best to support WTO rules and the authority of the WTO dispute-settlement mechanism.

## Notes

1. Long Yongtu, *China's Joining the WTO: China and ASEAN* (International Forum, December 14, 2005).

2. Shen Zongling, "On the Theory of Legal Globalization," *People's Daily*, December 11, 1999.

3. John Carey, Adrienne Carter, and Assif Shameen, "Food vs. Fuel," *Business-Week*, February 5, 2007.

4. Helen Deresky, *International Management: Managing across Borders and Cultures*, 6th ed. (Upper Saddle River, N.J.: Prentice-Hall, 2007).

5. Nicholas R. Lardy, *Integrating China into the Global Economy* (Washington D.C.: Brookings Institution Press, 2002).

6. "Introduction of the WTO," *People's Daily*, November 6, 1999.

7. Pascal Lamy, "About the WTO—A Statement by the Director-General," www.wto.org/english/thewto_e/whatis_e/wto_dg_stat_e.htm.

8. Cao Jianming, *The WTO and an Analysis of Chinese Systematic Problems* (Beijing: People's Legal Press, 2001).

9. Wang Houshuang, *How Far Is a Trade War from China?* (Beijing: Economy Daily Press, 2002).

10. Sino-Foreign Joint Venture Law Implementing Regulations, 1983, www.fairylaw.com/Article/zysd/200802/20080226132258.html; Foreign Enterprise Law Implementing Rules, 1990, www.law-lib.com/law/law_view.asp?id=15261.

11. Guo Daohui, *Contemporary Chinese Legislation* (Beijing: China Democratic and Legal Press, 1998).

12. Li Guohai, "The Legal Philosophic Foundation of Modern Economic Law," *Falü shangye yanjiu* (Legal and Commercial Studies) 6 (1999): 66–74.

13. Ministry of Foreign Trade and Economics, *WTO* (Beijing: China Foreign Trade and Economics Publishing House, 1999).

14. WTO Secretariat, *Trade for the Future* (Beijing: Legal Publishing House, 1999).

15. Wu Haimin, *Power Contest* (Hubei: Yangtze River Press, 2009).

16. Zhang Hanlin and Li Jiguang, The *Road to Rejuvenation: The WTO and China's Economic Future* (Beijing: People's Daily Press, 2002).

17. Charlene Barshefsky, "Testimony on U.S. Trade Policy in China," Senate Committee on Finance, April 13, 1999.

18. Shi Jichun and Deng Feng, *Principles of Economic Law* (Beijing: Law Press, 1998).

19. Huang Jingbo, *WTO Trade Regulations and Their Expansion with Chinese Trade Policy* (Guangzhou: Zhongshan University Press, 2000).

20. Tong Jiadong, *Free Trade, Trade Protection, and Economic Interests* (Beijing: Economic Science Press, 2002).

21. Susan Shirk, *The Political Logic of Economic Reform in China* (Washington, D.C.: Brookings Institution Press, 1993).

22. Hao Xiaohui, "The Risk Control of International Trade Financing," *Financial Theory and Practice* 11 (2001): 31–33.

23. Sang Yucheng, *Political Period of Interest Division* (Shanghai: Xuelin Press, 2002).

24. Shen Minrong, *The WTO and Development of China's Economic Law* (New York: Modern Legal Studies, 2000).

25. Zhang Jianmin, *Analysis of Entry Barriers to the Chinese Service Market* (Beijing: China Financial Economic Press, 1999).

26. See /www.mofcom.gov.cn.

27. Ibid.

28. Ted C. Fishman, *China Inc.: How the Rise of the Next Superpower Challenges America and the World* (New York: Scribner, 2006).

29. Wu Haimin, *Power Contest.*

30. Interview, Xinhua News Agency, December 2011.

31. Ibid.

32. Ibid.

33. Information Bureau of the PRC State Council, *China Trade White Paper,* December 7, 2011.

34. Ibid.

# Further Reading

Cao Siyuan. *WTO and China.* Beijing: Tuanjie Publishing House, 2001.

China Statistics Bureau. *China Statistics Yearbook.* Beijing, 2007.

China Customs Bureau. *China Customs Yearbook,* 2009.

Chinese Ministry of Commerce. *Report of FDI in China.* Beijing, 2006.

Ministry of Foreign Trade and Economics. *China Foreign Trade White Paper.* Beijing: Economic Science Publishing House, 2000.

Walter, Carl E., and Fraser J. T. Howie. *Privatizing China: The Stock Markets and Their Role in Corporate Reform.* New York: Wiley, 2003.

# 7

# The Death Penalty for Economic Crimes in Reformed China

*LiYing Li*

The Sanlu Group, based in Shijiazhuang, the capital city of Hebei Province, near Beijing, had been China's most respected dairy giant for more than a dozen years.[1] When the executives of the Fonterra Group, the world's largest trader of dairy products, went to Beijing to meet with their Chinese joint venture partner in August 2008, Sanlu's tainted milk powder came to light. Test results showed that infant milk powder manufactured and sold by the Sanlu Group contained the industrial chemical melamine, which makes the protein content of milk powder appear to be higher. Consumption of melamine-contaminated milk has been linked to kidney stones and acute kidney failure in infants. Across China, at least six infant deaths and more than 300,000 childhood illnesses related to toxic milk powder were reported.[2]

Government testing soon discovered that the problem was widespread. Inspectors found that 10 percent of liquid milk and other products taken from three additional dairies (Mengniu Dairy Group, Yili Industrial Group, and Bright Dairy) contained up to 8.4 milligrams of melamine per kilogram.[3] Melamine was also found in the products of some twenty other smaller companies around the country, including candy and eggs. Products of international companies (Cadbury, Nestlé, and Unilever) were found to contain traces of melamine, which led to worldwide product recalls.[4]

As investigations and news stories unfolded, dozens of traders, dealers, farmers, and suppliers were arrested, convicted, and eventually sentenced for their roles in the largest food safety scandal in China in recent years. Of these, three received the death sentence. Others received prison sentences ranging from a few years to life. Additionally, the government seized kilograms of suspicious chemicals, including melamine.[5] Zhang Yujun, a cattle farmer, was "convicted of producing and selling a phony protein powder containing melamine, much of it to producers who sold tainted milk to the now-defunct Sanlu Group Co."[6] Zhang, accused of producing and selling about eight hundred tons of the contaminated powder from July 2007 to August 2008, was convicted of endangering public safety by treacherous means and sentenced to death on January 22, 2009.

Geng Jinping, the manager of a milk production center, was convicted of adding melamine to some nine hundred tons of fresh milk. He then sold the milk to the Sanlu Group and other dairy companies.[7] According to *China Daily*, Geng knelt on the courtroom floor and begged the victims' families for forgiveness during the trial.[8] Geng was sentenced to death on January 22, 2009. Both Zhang and Geng appealed their sentences, but both were rejected. Both were executed on November 24, 2009.

Gao Junjie, a dairy producer, was given a death sentence with a two-year reprieve for producing and selling contaminated milk powder. In 2007 and 2008 he and several friends produced more than seventy tons of toxic milk powder. At the time of his arrest, the police found more than six tons of tainted milk powder in his factory.[9] In most cases a death sentence with a two-year reprieve would be commuted to a life sentence, but there is no further information on Gao since he was sentenced in December 2008.[10]

Tian Wenhua, the sixty-six-year-old chairwoman of the Sanlu Group, pleaded guilty to failing to stop production and sale of the tainted milk even after learning that it was contaminated. She was the highest-ranking corporate executive brought to trial in 2009. She was sentenced to life in prison on January 22, 2009, and also fined 20 million yuan, or about $3 million.[11] The victims' families, who believed Tian's sentence too light, demanded her execution.[12]

Three other former executives at the Sanlu Group were sentenced to prison terms ranging from five to fifteen years.[13] Wang Yuliang and Hang Zhiqi, both deputy general managers of the Sanlu Group, were given fifteen- and eight-year prison terms, respectively. Wu Jusheng, a manager of the Sanlu Group, was given five years.[14]

This chapter first discusses the history of the death penalty in China and then explores capital punishment for economic crimes in the post-1978 reform period. Debates regarding the death penalty and the role of public opinion are also examined. Finally, it focuses on the recent case of Zheng Xiaoyu, as well as the latest developments on assigning the death penalty for economic crimes.

## DEATH PENALTY LEGISLATION SINCE 1949

In 1949 the Chinese Communist Party (CCP) took control of the country and established the People's Republic of China (PRC). Although Mao's government repealed much legislation during the Republican era, it was not until 1979 that any substantive or procedural criminal codes were instituted. In other words, from 1949 to 1979 there were no formal criminal laws, which made the criminal justice system the weakest link in the PRC legal system.[15] During this period, however, the PRC, using the former Soviet Union's socialist legal system as a model, developed its definitions of crimes and punishments. The socialist system ostensibly represented the will of the people.[16] For example, people's tribunals were convened, and the public always participated in the legal proceedings. The death penalty was used extensively and swiftly to maintain social order and pursue justice. Executions were carried out on a massive scale, especially during political campaigns, such as those against counterrevolutionaries and corruption during the 1950s. *China Quarterly* estimates that in 1950 alone 2 million people were executed as part of the Campaign to Suppress Counterrevolutionaries.[17]

One unique feature of China's capital punishment is the death sentence with a two-year reprieve. In 1951, at the height of the Campaign to Suppress Counterrevolutionaries (1950–1952), Mao was the first to suggest that the death penalty should be used only for those who had "blood on their hands." Other criminals who committed capital crimes, however, should be given a death sentence with a two-year reprieve and be subjected to reform through forced labor.[18] The purpose of Mao's policy was to limit the growing number of people executed for political reasons. According to Mao, only 10 to 20 percent of death sentences should be carried out immediately, whereas 80 to 90 percent should be stayed for two years.[19] But in reality, 75 percent of all death sentences were carried out immediately, and only 25 percent were granted the two-year reprieve.[20] The majority of the latter, however, ended up having their sentences commuted to life in prison after the two years had been served. In 1954 the two-year reprieve policy was introduced in the *Project of the Guiding Principles of Criminal Law*. In

1979 a modified form of the policy was formally written into the criminal codes.[21]

The National People's Congress (NPC) promulgated the first Criminal Law in 1979, and the drive to establish an effective criminal justice system began. The Criminal Law was subsequently amended seven times, including the substantial revision of 1997. Under the Criminal Law of 1979, there were only twenty-eight capital offenses. Fifteen of these were counterrevolutionary crimes, and the other thirteen were ordinary crimes, including eight against public safety, three against personal and democratic rights, and two against property.[22] Other than embezzlement, there were few nonviolent economic capital offenses under the Criminal Law of 1979.

The year 1982 marked the beginning of capital punishment for nonviolent economic offenses in the modern economic reform era. During the following two decades, the laws became more punitive and the number of capital offenses increased every year. The Decision of the NPC Standing Committee Regarding the Severe Punishment of Criminals Who Seriously Sabotage the Economy (Decision 1982) was adopted at the twenty-second meeting of the Standing Committee of the Fifth NPC. Decision 1982 introduced the concept of nonviolent economic crimes into the Criminal Law, adding seventeen different economic crimes punishable by death.[23] In 1982 the NPC Standing Committee, the top Chinese legislative body, passed two additional supplementary decisions: the Decision concerning the Punishment of the Crime of Smuggling and the Decision concerning the Punishment of the Crimes of Embezzlement and Bribery. These decisions made the crimes of smuggling and bribery capital offenses.[24]

One punitive regulation or decision seemed to pave the way for another. By 1993 there were nearly seventy capital offenses. In fact, from 1981 to 1993 three new capital offenses on average were added to the statute each year. In 1995 serious tax fraud and insurance fraud were added to the list of capital offenses, bringing the total to seventy-four.[25] The bloodiest execution record of the 1980s and 1990s occurred in 1996. Henry Chu estimates that close to four thousand executions were carried out, an average of eleven per day.[26] In 2001 another amendment to the Criminal Law (last amended in 1997) included terrorism as a capital crime; it allowed anyone who funded or carried out terrorism or who belonged to a terrorist organization to be charged with a capital offense.[27] In 2003 the Supreme People's Court (SPC) issued a judicial interpretation applying the death sentence to people with Severe Acute Respiratory Syndrome

(SARS) who had failed to follow public health orders or quarantine. Later that same year, another SPC judicial interpretation applied the death penalty to those who illegally produce, trade, or store a certain amount of toxic chemicals.[28]

The leading legislative principle during this period was the criminal justice system's leniency. With crimes on the rise during the 1980s, Deng Xiaoping, China's de facto leader during that decade, demanded stricter penalties for criminals. Deng believed that crimes such as human trafficking and organizing secret societies had to be dealt with harshly, and that the death penalty was indispensable to the criminal justice system.[29] The party's hard-line approach led to the increasingly broadened definition of capital crimes and made the Criminal Law more punitive.[30] Some local courts established "tribunals for economic crimes" to hear these cases.[31] The SPC reviewed only a small percentage of all capital death penalty cases, whereas lower courts handled the majority of the cases. More often than not, lower courts operated without any oversight and failed to properly review all death penalty cases put before them.[32] As a result, the number of death sentences more than tripled during the 1980s and 1990s.[33]

In February 2011 the NPC Standing Committee passed the eighth amendment to the Criminal Law. The newly revised Criminal Law dropped capital punishment for thirteen economic crimes,[34] reducing the former sixty-eight capital offenses by about one-fifth, to fifty-five.[35] The new Criminal Law signifies a leap forward in China's legal reforms and an effort by China to move closer to international norms.[36] It is the first time China has reduced the number of capital crimes since the implementation of the Criminal Law of 1979. The new law also prohibits the execution of any offenders over the age of seventy-five at the time of their trial—although exceptions will be made in crimes involving "exceptional cruelty." (Previously, only pregnant women and those under the age of eighteen were exempt from the death penalty.)

The Criminal Law of 1997 included three times as many capital offenses as the 1980 Criminal Law. There are nine categories consisting of sixty-eight capital offenses. Of these the majority are nonviolent economic crimes. "Crimes Undermining the Socialist Market Economic Order" (Category III) and "Crimes of Graft and Bribery" (Category VIII) are both categories of economic crimes. Fifteen offenses in Category III and two offenses in Category VIII are punishable by death.[37]

## Nonviolent Economic Capital Offenses
## under the 1997 Criminal Law

Capital punishment for nonviolent economic offenses has long cast China in the legal limelight, both domestically and internationally. China, however, is not the only country in the world that imposes the death penalty on nonviolent economic offenders. Today more than thirty countries make drug trafficking and the sale of drugs capital crimes. For example, the possession of relatively small amounts of illegal drugs carries a mandatory death sentence in Iran, Singapore, Malaysia, and the Philippines. About twenty other countries impose the death sentence on economic crimes such as bribery and corruption of public officials as well as embezzlement of public funds.[38]

China's Criminal Law of 1997 carries the death penalty for these nonviolent economic crimes as well as for currency speculation and the theft of large sums of money from public institutions.[39]

According to Ying Zhang, however, understanding the prosecution of bribery cases in China is more complex than reading the written Criminal Law.[40] The antibribery laws under the Criminal Law do not define bribery. It is unclear whether bribery includes cash, property, or other kinds of cash equivalents, such as stocks. The laws also do not specify exactly what amount constitutes a bribe. Despite these ambiguities, the government imposes severe sanctions, including the death penalty, on "bribe-takers." In recent years some high-ranking public officials were executed for extorting bribes in exchange for favors, government contracts, and so on.

Other nonviolent economic crimes punishable by death under the Criminal Law of 1979 include tax and value-added-tax fraud, counterfeiting, embezzlement, and credit card fraud. According to the *People's Daily,* from 1994 to 2003, 194 people were sentenced to death for value-added-tax fraud; 70 of these had already been executed as of 2004.[41] The Criminal Law of 2011 reclassifies tax fraud as a noncapital offense.

In 2002 the Langfang Metropolitan Intermediate People's Court near Beijing announced the death sentences imposed on the four leaders of a gang of farmers who allegedly damaged electrical equipment in 1998 and 1999. The four accused were reported to have stolen thirty-eight electrical transformers and some eight kilometers of cable as well as 2,195 kilowatts of electricity—worth about 340,000 yuan ($41,000).[42] Even under the new Criminal Law, this is still a death penalty case.

According to Amnesty International's 2002 report on the death penalty, a large number of executions in China involve drug-related crimes. Many such sentences are carried out on or around June 26, the United Nations' International Day against Drug Abuse and Illicit Drug Trafficking.[43]

## RECENT DEBATES ON THE DEATH PENALTY FOR NONVIOLENT ECONOMIC CRIMES

One of the hottest issues currently being debated inside China is capital punishment for nonviolent economic crimes. The newly revised Criminal Law of 2011 is part of the continued effort by the government to bring its penal codes up to the international standard. As recently as August 2010, however, the Chinese government still upheld the use of capital punishment for serious nonviolent economic crimes. Nevertheless, responding to widespread concerns about wrongful executions in recent years,[44] the government started a series of death penalty reforms in order to balance leniency and severity.[45]

The most significant reform, before the new Criminal Law reduced the number of capital offenses, was the decision to have the SPC take back from local higher courts the authority to review all death penalty cases, starting in January 2007.[46] In 2008 the SPC reported that about 15 percent of death sentence verdicts by lower courts were problematic; it overturned 10 percent of all death sentences submitted by the lower courts.[47] In particular, the SPC revoked the death penalty for cases involving crimes of passion, especially if the defendant in question expressed remorse and pledged to compensate the victim's family.[48] As a result, in 2006 China reported the lowest number of people executed annually in nearly a decade. The downward trend continued in 2007, which saw another 10 percent reduction in death sentences compared to 2006.[49] The number of executions in 2008, however, increased markedly over that in 2007.

Another post-2006 death penalty reform is the requirement of open courts for second-instance courts in all death penalty (immediate execution) cases. The SPC established a regulation banning the admission of evidence, including confessions, obtained through torture in criminal trials.[50] The Second Five-Year Reform Plan of the People's Courts (2006–2010) implemented a policy to compel witnesses to testify in trials. Even so, at present not even one in ten key witnesses ever testifies at various levels of the courts.[51] In one bold move, Chi Qiang, president of the Beijing Supreme People's Court, announced that eighteen offenders had their death sentences commuted in 2008 as a result of civil mediation. Compensation settlements of up to 5 million yuan have been paid by the accused to the victims' families.[52] Then, in 2009, the SPC issued new directives urging lower courts to resort to civil mediation in capital cases.

## OPPOSING VIEWS ON THE DEATH PENALTY

Chinese legal and academic scholars who view the execution of nonviolent economic criminals as inhumane have sought reform for years. Chinese public sentiment, however, remains highly in favor of using the death penalty. Chinese legal scholars, such as Liu Renwen from the Legal Study Department of the Chinese Academy of Social Sciences, argued that the consensus among legal scholars and academics is that 67.5 of the 68 capital crimes under the Criminal Law of 1997 should be reclassified; they claimed that premeditated murder should be the only capital crime.[53] Zhao Bingzhi and Wan Yunfeng argued that even though the Criminal Law specifies that the death penalty should be applicable only to crimes involving "a particularly enormous amount of money" or "of a particularly severe nature," the arbitrariness with which capital punishment is applied remains a serious problem.[54]

Others pointed out that sentencing disparities exist, depending on the politics du jour. There are no safeguards in the criminal justice system to provide the accused with the due process provisions of the law and the constitution. This lack of due process, particularly in capital cases, is atrocious. According to LiYing Li and Yue Ma, the Criminal Law and the criminal justice system offer inadequate protection against self-incrimination and double jeopardy, rely on forced confessions or unlawfully collected evidence, and provide the accused with inadequate legal representation. Unlawful and politically motivated police detention is common. Those in police custody are often tortured and sometimes die.[55]

On January 8, 2001, in Jingyang County, Shanxi Province, an eighteen-year-old girl named Ma Dandan was taken by the police to the police station. Ma was accused of prostitution and tortured and assaulted for more than twenty hours at the police station. She was forced to sign a confession. After her release, two medical examinations proved her virginity and cleared her name. The police did not admit any wrongdoing, however, and even the local courts were reluctant to compensate Ma sufficiently for the violation of her rights. Ma eventually took her case to the media. In the end, Ma was awarded over 75,000 yuan by the court.[56]

Furthermore, no meaningful appeals process exists. One gang of bank robbers was executed in May 2001, only fifteen minutes after they were sentenced to death.[57] An example of a well-known wrongful execution involved Nie Shubin, who was sentenced to death for the rape and murder of a young woman in 1995. Ten years after Nie's execution, another man confessed to the crime. Nie's name has never been cleared. His family is still pressuring the government to exonerate him.[58]

Public support for the death penalty remains strong in spite of the controversies surrounding wrongful executions in recent years. Although reliable data are hard to come by, recent small online opinion polls show that the public strongly opposes abolishing the death penalty, especially for corrupt public officials and CEOs who commit economic crimes. For example, Yu Bing conducted an online poll and reported that about 76 percent of the public supported capital punishment,[59] and in recent years as many as 95 percent remained in favor of the death penalty for nonviolent economic crimes.[60] A 2005 study also found that nearly 72 percent of Chinese university students favored the death penalty.[61] Wang Xiaolu, the deputy director of China's National Economic Research Institute, conducted a survey in 2009 of more than four thousand urban households in sixty-four cities and nineteen provinces. The survey data suggested that corruption is pervasive at every level of Chinese society and that the public's anticorruption sentiments are high.[62] Bin Liang and his colleagues also studied pro–death penalty attitudes in China in recent years and found strong ongoing support for capital punishment among Chinese college students, both at home and abroad. Even when life imprisonment was given as an alternative, the students in the sample overwhelmingly chose capital punishment.[63]

Nevertheless, a survey conducted in 2009 challenged the widespread public support for the death penalty in China. The results show that the majority of adults (58 percent) surveyed support the death penalty. When asked about applying the death penalty for specific crimes, however, opinions differed greatly. The survey results further illustrated how little the Chinese public knows of the many egregious practices associated with death penalty cases.[64]

Reasons behind this strong public support include tradition, disgust toward corruption among officials and CEOs, and distrust of the criminal justice system. As for tradition, He Weifang, a law professor at Peking University and an opponent of the death penalty, points out that throughout history the Chinese public has clamored for public executions—the crueler, the better.[65] Regarding corruption, when several media outlets such as *People's Daily*[66] and *Wantchina Times*[67] reported that some incarcerated criminals received VIP treatment while in prison, the public was outraged. One public official in Chengdu, Ma Jianguo, was sentenced to fifteen years for corruption. While in prison, he bribed the prison officials for special treatment, such as not having to wear the prison uniform, staying overnight at home, and entertaining friends at restaurants. As a result of the public outcry over the discovery of these privileges, Ma was sentenced to five additional years and the prison warden was given a fifteen-year sentence for accepting bribes.[68]

## RELIANCE ON PUBLIC OPINION

Early in the history of the PRC, Mao suggested that the existence of the death penalty should be based partially on public opinion. His idea was adopted as the defining principle of the PRC's crime control policies in 1954.[69] After more than sixty years, public opinion still plays a role in the application of the death penalty; the government often needs public political support.[70] Many high-profile corruption cases have involved government officials, and the Chinese public shows no tolerance toward corruption. Surveys and public opinion polls have consistently shown that the public considers rampant corruption by high-ranking government officials or business CEOs to be one of the crimes most deserving of the death penalty.[71]

The execution of a former deputy provincial governor of Jiangxi Province on March 8, 2000, is a case in point. At the time Hu Changqing was the highest-ranking government official in fifty years of PRC history to be put to death in a major graft case.[72] He was convicted of accepting more than $650,000 in bribes between 1995 and 1999. In return, he approved construction projects, bank loans, and business licenses. He also paid more than $10,000 in bribes. On the day when Hu was taken to the execution ground, people lined the city streets as a motorcade of a dozen police cars went by.[73] Hu's downfall was featured in the official press and on the major evening newscasts.[74]

## FOR ZHENG, HEAD OF CHINA'S FOOD AND DRUG ADMINISTRATION, TOO LATE?

On July 10, 2007, China executed the former head of its State Food and Drug Administration, Zheng Xiaoyu. Zheng was the first ministerial-level official to be put to death since 2000 and only the fourth in the last thirty years.[75] Even for China, Zheng's execution came as a surprise and remains highly controversial to this day.[76] Zheng Xiaoyu was convicted of accepting bribes worth over $800,000 in exchange for approving fake medicine, including antibiotics. According to state media reports, between 1997 and 2006 the State Food and Drug Administration approved six drugs that turned out to be fake. Some of the pharmaceutical companies behind these drugs used falsified documents when seeking approval. During Zheng's term, at least one antibiotic caused the death of no fewer than ten people.[77] In another notorious case, at least thirteen infants died of malnutrition in 2004 after being fed fake milk powder.[78] The court on May 26, 2007, handed down the unusually harsh death sentence, which was widely expected to be reduced on appeal.[79] Zheng appealed his death sentence on the grounds that it was too severe and that he had confessed to his crimes.

Since Zheng's sentencing in May 2007, however, contaminated Chinese products have become an international concern. In April 2007 the U.S. government blamed poisoned pet food imported from China for the fatal poisoning of several dogs and cats.[80] In the same year, authorities in North America blocked many other imported Chinese goods, including toxic seafood, juice made with unsafe color additives, and toys with high levels of lead.[81] Early in May 2007 Chinese counterfeit toothpaste, exported to the United States, Australia, Panama, and the Dominican Republic, was found to contain dangerous levels of harmful chemicals.[82] In 2006 dozens of people in Panama died after taking Chinese medicine containing toxic chemicals.[83]

In the end, the SPC upheld Zheng's death sentence. The disgraced head of the food and drug agency was executed less than two months after being sentenced. Within hours of the announcement of Zheng's execution, bloggers inundated China's Internet with responses. One anonymous poster on Sina.com wrote, "Our country will have no peace unless corrupt officials are executed. We should execute more."[84] Another commented, simply, "Good job!"

## A New Direction?

One thing we now know for sure: Zheng Xiaoyu would not have been saved even under the new Criminal Law of 2011. The new law does not limit the death penalty for corruption cases. Nevertheless, many scholars and China watchers welcome the new Criminal Law, but they harbor doubts about any immediate effect it may have on executions. For example, Stephen Minas maintains that the Criminal Law does not "break the instrumental link between overarching state policy and death penalty application. . . . Capital punishment remains an instrument of state policy."[85]

Another noteworthy criticism is the symbolic significance of the new Criminal Law. Major corruption and other economic crimes remain death penalty offenses. Nevertheless, the elimination of thirteen capital offenses would amount to a 1 or 2 percent reduction in China's total number of executions, a significant reduction given the number of executions carried out in China.[86]

Major concerns about the death penalty in China still remain. According to an article in *Dialogue,* major issues include the large number of executions carried out in China, the lack of transparency in the Chinese criminal justice system, and the excessive use of the death penalty for many nonviolent economic offenses. Additionally, there is a lack of consistency in determining death sentence cases, and the lack of due process undermines the protection by the criminal justice system of the accused.[87] Although the new Criminal Law reduces the number of capital offenses, and the SPC's oversight of all death penalty cases increases the consistency in death sentence verdicts, many other issues remain.

These concerns remind us that death penalty reforms in China will happen only incrementally. The new Criminal Law is nevertheless a welcome move and, most important, has generated increased public interest in the discussion about Chinese capital punishment reform.

## Notes

1. Austin Ramzy, "China's Tainted Milk Scandal of 2008," *Time,* September 26, 2008, www.time.com/time/world/article/0%2C8599%2C1844750%2C00.html (accessed November 1, 2010).

2. "China Discovers More Tainted Milk," MSN News, July 9, 2010, http://news.uk.msn.com/world/articles.aspx?cp-documentid=154082230 (accessed December 10, 2010); John Vause, "Death Sentences in China Tainted Milk Case," *CNN,* Janu-

ary 23, 2009, http://edition.cnn.com/2009/WORLD/asiapcf/01/22/china.tainted.milk/ (accessed November 8, 2010).

3. "China Tainted Milk Scandal Widens," *BBC News,* September 19, 2008, http://news.bbc.co.uk/2/hi/asia-pacific/7624498.stm (accessed November 1, 2010); James Orr and agencies, "China's Contaminated Milk Crisis Grows as Tests Show Top Dairy Firms Affected," *Guardian,* September 19, 2008, www.guardian.co.uk/world/2008/sep/19/china (accessed November 5, 2010).

4. Paul Mooney, "The Story behind China's Tainted Milk Scandal," *U.S. News & World Report,* October 9, 2008, http://politics.usnews.com/news/world/articles/2008/10/09/the-story-behind-chinas-tainted-milk-scandal.html?PageNr=3 (accessed November 5, 2010).

5. "More Arrests in China Milk Scandal," *National,* September 18, 2008, www.thenational.ae/news/worldwide/asia-pacific/more-arrests-in-china-milk-scandal (accessed November 5, 2010); David Barboza, "Death Sentences Given in Chinese Milk Scandal," *New York Times,* February 2, 2009, www.nytimes.com/2009/01/22/world/asia/22iht-milk.3.19601372.html?_r=1 (accessed November 5, 2010).

6. Associated Press, "China Executes Zhang Yujun, Geng Jinping for Roles in Deadly Tainted Milk Powder Scandal," *New York Daily News,* November 24, 2009, http://articles.nydailynews.com/2009-11-24/news/17938143_1_zhang-yujun-geng-jinping-sanlu (accessed June 25, 2012).

7. Xu Donghuan, "The Death Penalty: No Room for Error," *Global Times,* February 11, 2010, www.bullogger.com/blogs/heweifang/archives/352770.aspx (accessed November 4, 2010).

8. Ibid.

9. "Sanlu naifen xilie'an Gao Junjie Xue Jianzhong dengren shoushen" (Gao Junjie and Xue Jinzhong Are on Trial for the Sanlu Toxic Milk Scandal), *YNET,* December 29, 2008, http://bjyouth.ynet.com/article.jsp?oid=47380305&pageno=1 (accessed November 8, 2010).

10. Barboza, "Death Sentences Given in Chinese Milk Scandal."

11. Mark McDonald, "Death Sentences in China Milk Case," *New York Times,* January 22, 2009, www.iht.com/articles/2009/01/22/news/23MILK.php (accessed November 5, 2010).

12. Associated Press, "China Sentences Two to Death over Milk Scandal," *Taipei Times,* January 23, 2009, www.taipeitimes.com/News/front/archives/2009/01/23/2003434442/2 (accessed November 5, 2010).

13. Barboza, "Death Sentences Given in Chinese Milk Scandal."

14. Isaac Davison, "Two Sentenced to Death over Tainted Milk Scandal," *New Zealand Herald,* January 23, 2009, www.nzherald.co.nz/world/news/article.cfm?c_id=2&objectid=10553177 (accessed January 22, 2010).

15. Jerome A. Cohen, "Law in Political Transitions: Lessons from East Asia and the Road Ahead for China," Council on Foreign Relations, July 26, 2005, www.cfr.org/publication/8458/law_in_political_transitions.html (accessed November 1, 2010).

16. Luo Wei, *The Civil Procedure Law and Court Rules of the People's Republic of China* (Buffalo, N.Y.: W. S. Hein, 2006).

17. Laogai Research Foundation, "Death Penalty & Organ Harvesting," n.d., http://laogai.org/our_work/death-penalty-organ-harvesting (accessed December 7, 2010); Li Changyu, "Mao's 'Killing Quotas'" *China Rights Forum*, no. 4 (September 6, 2005); Yang Kuisong, "Reconsidering the Campaign to Suppress Counterrevolutionaries," *China Quarterly* 193 (March 2008): 102–121.

18. Mao Zedong, *Mao Zedong xuanji* (Selected Works of Mao Zedong) (Beijing: People's Press, 1977).

19. *Zhongguo gongchandang xinwenwang* (Chinese Communist Party News Network), "Shishuiwei zhonghua renmin gongheguo famingle 'sihuan'xingming?" (Who Created the Term of Death Penalty with Two-Year Reprieve in China?), January 27, 2010, http://news.ifeng.com/history/zhongguoxiadaishi/201001/0127_7179_1527232.shtml (accessed October 29, 2010).

20. Zhao Zuojun, *Sixing xianzhi lun* (Theory of the Limitation of the Death Sentence) (Wuhan: Wuhan University Press, 2001).

21. Ning Zhang, "The Debate over the Death Penalty in Today's China," *China Perspective* 62 (November–December 2005), www.cefc.com.hk/pccpa.php?aid=2026#_ftnref19 (accessed November 6, 2010).

22. Xingliang Chen, "Destiny of the Death Penalty in China in the Contemporary Era," *Frontiers of Law in China* 1, no. 1 (2006): 53–71, www.springerlink.com/content/1134711334610082/fulltext.pdf; and Harold Tanner, *Strike Hard! Anti-Crime Campaigns and Chinese Criminal Justice, 1979–1985* (Ithaca: East Asia Program, Cornell University, 1999), 104.

23. Hong Lu and Lening Zhang, "Death Penalty in China: The Law and the Practice," *Journal of Criminal Justice* 33, no. 4 (2005): 367–376.

24. Keith Forster, "The 1982 Campaign against Economic Crime in China," *Australian Journal of Chinese Affairs,* no. 14 (1985): 1–19.

25. Amnesty International, "The Death Penalty in China: Breaking Records, Breaking Rules" January 8, 1997, www.asylumlaw.org/docs/china/ai_china_death-penalty97.pdf (accessed July 27, 2012); Henry Chu, "China Keeping Its Executioners Busy," *San Francisco Chronicle,* August 1, 2000, www.commondreams.org/headlines/080100–03.htm (accessed November 4, 2010).

26. Chu, "China Keeping Its Executioners Busy."

27. Amnesty International, "People's Republic of China: Executed 'According to Law'?—The Death Penalty in China," March 22, 2004,www.amnesty.ca/china/news/view.php?load=arcview&article=1372&c=China+Reports (accessed November 1, 2010).

28. Ibid.

29. Deng Xiaoping, *Deng Xiaoping xuanji* (Selected Works of Deng Xiaoping), vol. 3 (Beijing: The People's Press, 1993); Jim Abrams, "Executions in China Exceed 10,000 in Firm Crackdown against Crime," *Los Angeles Times,* November

8, 1987, http://articles.latimes.com/1987-11-08/news/mn-21352_1_economic-crimes (accessed November 6, 2010).

30. Chu, "China Keeping Its Executioners Busy."

31. Bingzhi Zhao and Yunfeng Wan, "On Limiting and Abolishing the Death Penalty for Economic Crimes in China," *Chinese Sociology and Anthropology* 41, no. 4 (Summer 2009): 14–40.

32. John M. Glionna, "China Shows Caution on Executions," *Los Angeles Times,* January 8, 2008, http://articles.latimes.com/2008/jan/06/world/fg-chinadeath6 (accessed December 7, 2010).

33. Amnesty International, "The Death Penalty in China."

34. Bao Daozu, "13 Economic Crimes May Lose Capital Punishment," *China Daily,* August 24, 2010, www.chinadaily.com.cn/china/2010-08/24/content_ 11191612.htm (accessed October 31, 2010).

35. Dwyer Arce, "China Not Considering Eliminating Death Penalty for Corruption," *Jurist,* September 29, 2010, http://jurist.org/paperchase/2010/09/ china-not-considering-eliminating-death-penalty-for-corruption.php (accessed December 7, 2010); Bao, "13 Economic Crimes May Lose Capital Punishment."

36. Clifford Coonan, "China Poised to Abolish Death Penalty for Economic Crimes," *Irish Times,* August 8, 2010, www.irishtimes.com/newspaper/ world/2010/0824/1224277442920.html (accessed November 7, 2010).

37. European Initiative for Democracy and Human Rights, "The Death Penalty in China: A Baseline Document," 2003, www.ecba.org/extdocserv/DP_Baseline .pdf (accessed July 22, 2012).

38. "Capital Punishment," in *Encyclopedia Britannica,* 2009 ed., www.britannica .com/EBchecked/topic/93902/capital-punishment (accessed July 22, 2012).

39. *The Criminal Law of the People's Republic of China 1997,* www.china.org.cn/ english/government/207319.htm (accessed December 11, 2010).

40. Ying Zhang, "Complying with Chinese Anti-Bribery Law," *California Lawyer Magazine* (January 2004), www.uschinacounsel.com/files/Chinese%20 Anti-Bribery%20Law%20pdf.pdf (accessed July 22, 2012).

41. "174 ren yindaomai xukai zengzhishui fapiao beipan sixing" (174 Were Sentenced to Death for Fraud Involving Selling and Using Value-Added-Tax Forms), *People's Daily,* August 10, 2004, www.hnsc.com.cn/news/2004/08/10/11413.html (accessed December 11, 2010).

42. Amnesty International, "People's Republic of China: The Death Penalty in 2000," September 2002, www.amnesty.org/en/library/asset/ASA17/032/2002/en/ 5c04855e-d80c-11dd-9df8-936c90684588/asa170322002en.html (accessed November 7, 2010).

43. Ibid.

44. "Death Penalty Review Right to Be Exercised," Xinhua News Agency, December 16, 2006, www.china.org.cn/english/China/192705.htm (accessed November 6, 2010).

45. Susan Trevaskes, "The Death Penalty in China Today: Kill Fewer, Kill Cautiously," *Asian Survey* 48, no. 3 (2008): 393–413.

46. Xinhua News Agency, "Death Penalty Review Right to Be Exercised."

47. Andrew Jacobs, "China Pledges Fewer Death Sentences," *New York Times*, July 29, 2009, www.nytimes.com/2009/07/30/world/asia/30china.html?_r=1 (accessed December 6, 2010).

48. Ibid.

49. Death Penalty Information Center, *The Death Penalty Report in 2000: Year-End Report* (2000).

50. Xinhua News Agency, "China's Highest Court Publishes Rule Banning Torture Confessions," June 24, 2010, http://news.xinhuanet.com/english2010/china/2010-06/25/c_13368460.htm (accessed July 24, 2012).

51. Amnesty International, "Human Rights in People's Republic of China," 2009, www.amnesty.org/en/region/china/report-2009 (accessed July 22, 2012).

52. Human Rights in China, "China's Death Penalty Reforms: An HRIC Issues Brief" (2007), http://hrichina.org/sites/default/files/oldsite/PDFs/CRF.2.2007/CRF-2007-2_Penalty.pdf (accessed June 25, 2012).

53. Xu, "The Death Penalty: No Room for Error." Liu Renwen, statement made during an interview with reporters, March 28, 2008. Liu is a member of the Chinese Academy of Social Sciences.

54. Zhao and Wan, "On Limiting and Abolishing the Death Penalty for Economic Crimes in China."

55. LiYing Li and Yue Ma, "Adjudication and Legal Reforms in Contemporary China," *Journal of Contemporary Criminal Justice* 26, no. 1 (2010): 36–52.

56. Qiang Fang, "The Case of the Virgin Prostitute: Chinese Media and Chinese Legal Reform," *Stanford Journal of East Asian Affairs* 2, no. 1 (Spring 2002): 26–40.

57. John Gittings, "Guilty—and You Have 15 Minutes to Live," *Guardian*, May 21, 2001, www.guardian.co.uk/world/2001/may/22/china.johngittings (accessed November 2, 2010).

58. Bill Schiller, "In China, a Quiet Push against Executions," *Toronto Star*, March 29, 2009, www.thestar.com/article/610076 (accessed November 1, 2010).

59. Yu Bing, "Sixing cunfei: Zhuanjia, pingmin heyiduili" (Death Penalty: Why the Division between Legal Scholars and Public Opinion?), program broadcast on CCTV International Channel, November 29, 2003, www.cctv.com/news/china/20031129/100110.shtml (accessed November 1, 2010).

60. Liu, statement made during an interview with reporters.

61. Chen Xingliang, *The Purpose of Rule of Law* (Beijing: Law Press, 2003), 218–221; Stephen Minas, "'Kill Fewer, Kill Carefully': An Analysis of the 2006 to 2007 Death Penalty Reforms in China," *UCLA Pacific Basin Law Journal* 27, no. 1 (Fall 2009): 36.

62. Mu Tou and Li Jia, "China's Economy Goes Gray: Undisclosed Income and Corruption Rise," *Epoch Times*, October 20, 2010, www.theepochtimes.com/n2/content/view/44538/ (accessed December 10, 2010).

63. Bin Liang, Hong Lu, Terance D. Miethe, and Lening Zhang, "Sources of Variation in Pro-Death Penalty Attitudes in China," *British Journal of Criminology* 46 (2006): 119–130.

64. Dietrich Oberwittler and Shenghui Qi, "Public Opinion on the Death Penalty in China: Results from a General Population Survey Conducted in Three Provinces in 2007/08," Max Planck Institute for Foreign and International Criminal Law (2009).

65. Jacobs, "China Pledges Fewer Death Sentences."

66. "Chendu taiguan Ma Jianguo anyue geiyujing fagongzi fuxing youru dujia" (Convicted Corrupt Official Ma Jianguo Paid Monthly Salary to Prison Guards in Exchange for Privileges behind Bars), *People's Daily*, September 11, 2006, www.people.com.cn/GB/58278/70110/70114/4800147.html (accessed December 10, 2010).

67. "Behind Upscale Bars: Corrupt Chinese Officials Sent to Luxury Jails," *Wantchina Times*, October 17, 2011, www.wantchinatimes.com/news-subclass-cnt.aspx?id=20111017000023&cid=1303 (accessed July 26, 2012).

68. "Tanguan xinghui fuxing rudujiajiaxing wunian" (Corrupt Official Received Additional Five Years of Sentence for Bribery), *Guangzhou Daily*, December 1, 2006, http://news.sohu.com/20061201/n246726924.shtml (accessed December 10, 2010).

69. Zhang, "The Debate over the Death Penalty in Today's China."

70. A good example of the public opinion that is instrumental in court rulings on the death penalty is the case of Yao Jiaxin. Yao was a student at the Xi'an Musical Institute, Shaanxi. Yao struck a woman with his car on October 20, 2010. Instead of taking the woman, who was still alive, to a hospital, Yao brutally stabbed her to death. Although Yao's mother accompanied her son to the local police, where he confessed his crime, public opinion insisted that Yao be executed for his inhumane murder. Apparently under heavy pressure from the public, the high court finally decided to sentence Yao to death. Shuze Chen, "Chinese People Say "Yao" to Death Penalty," USC Annenberg China Media, April 4, 2011, http://ascportfolios.org/chinaandmedia/2011/04/04/chinese-people-say-%E2%80%9Cyao%E2%80%9D-to-death-penalty/ (accessed July 24, 2012).

71. Jeffrey Hays, "Corruption in China," last updated April 2012, http://factsanddetails.com/china.php?itemid=304&catid=8&subcatid=49 (accessed June 25, 2012).

72. Anthony Kuhn, "Former Chinese Official Executed in Bribery Case," *Los Angeles Times*, March 9, 2000, http://articles.latimes.com/2000/mar/09/news/mn-6958 (accessed July 26, 2012).

73. Ibid.

74. Elisabeth Rosenthal, "China Lays Down Law with Bribery Execution: Highest Official Ever Put to Death for Corruption," *New York Times*, March 9, 2000; "Rise and Fall of Hu Changqing," *People's Daily*, April 14, 2000, http://english

.people.com.cn/english/200004/14/eng20000414_38924.html (accessed July 11, 2012).

75. Joseph Kahn, "China Quick to Execute Drug Official," *New York Times,* July 11, 2007, www.nytimes.com/2007/07/11/business/worldbusiness/11execute .html?pagewanted=1&_r=1 (accessed July 26, 2012).

76. Lindsay Beck, "China Ex–Food and Drug Safety Chief Sentenced to Death," Reuters, May 29, 2007, www.reuters.com/article/idUSPEK4362920070529 (accessed November 4, 2010).

77. Mark Magnier, "Chinese Applaud Execution of Former Drug Safety Chief," *Los Angeles Times,* July 11, 2007, http://articles.latimes.com/2007/jul/11/world/ fg-execute11 (accessed November 5, 2010).

78. Beck, "China Ex–Food and Drug Safety Chief Sentenced to Death"; Zhong Wu, "Killing a Big Chicken to Scare the Monkeys," *Asia Times,* June 6, 2007, www .atimes.com/atimes/China/IF06Ad03.html (accessed November 1, 2010).

79. Beck, "China Ex–Food and Drug Safety Chief Sentenced to Death."

80. Jonathan Watts, "China's Food and Drug Agency Chief Sentenced to Death," *Guardian,* May 29, 2007, www.guardian.co.uk/world/2007/may/30/china .topstories3 (accessed November 2, 2010).

81. Magnier, "Chinese Applaud Execution of Former Drug Safety Chief."

82. Watts, "China's Food and Drug Agency Chief Sentenced to Death"; Magnier, "Chinese Applaud Execution of Former Drug Safety Chief."

83. Magnier, "Chinese Applaud Execution of Former Drug Safety Chief."

84. Ibid.

85. Minas, "Kill Fewer, Kill Carefully."

86. Jessica Jiang, "Will China Ease Up on Executions?" *China Daily,* July 24, 2010, www.chinadaily.com.cn/china/2010-07/24/content_11044407.htm (accessed July 22, 2012).

87. "Reducing Death Penalty Crimes in China More Symbol Than Substance," *Dialogue* no. 41 (Fall 2010), www.duihua.org/work/publications/nl/dialogue/nl_ txt/nl41/nl41_cover.htm (accessed July 22, 2012).

# 8

# China's Policies toward Illegal Drugs and Prostitution in the New Era

## Struggle within the Global Context

### Bin Liang and Liqun Cao

Both drug abuse and prostitution have existed in China for thousands of years, being tolerated and regulated as a form of subculture for most of China's history. Both, however, were eliminated for thirty years after the founding of the People's Republic of China (PRC), and both have reemerged since the 1980s. The study of China's control of drugs and prostitution over the past two hundred years is both important and enlightening because it provides not only keys to an understanding of China's social evolution, but also a mirror of convulsive and relentless change in China.[1]

Drug abuse, especially the abuse of imported opium, had escalated into an acute problem in the nineteenth century. Drug control efforts by the Qing government became a focal point of contention between the complacent Qing government and profit-thirsty foreign powers. The breakout of the Opium Wars in the 1840s and 1850s threw Qing's narcotics regulations into chaos. In the late nineteenth century and the early twentieth century, China struggled badly with drug problems, becoming the largest opium importer, consumer, and producer in the world. Consequently, the image of the "sick man of Asia" emerged in the Western media.

The conquering of China by the Chinese Communist Party (CCP) in

1949 dramatically changed the course of both drug use and prostitution. Along with other problems (e.g., gambling), both were viewed as social vices that belonged only to the "old" China; therefore, they were eradicated as a result of a totalitarian system established by the CCP in the new society. This new political system not only assumed control of criminal and deviant behavior, but also, through various social control mechanisms such as constant criticism and self-criticism, managed to gain control of deviant thoughts in the 1950s, 1960s, and 1970s. When the government began shifting its attention from thought control to national economic construction in the 1980s, drug abuse and prostitution resurfaced and quickly spread nationwide, despite the government's crackdowns. Encountering such a strong comeback, the Chinese government has attempted more severe legal penalties to control the situation and is unwilling to change its rhetoric.

In this chapter we first briefly review the history of both drug use and prostitution, paying special attention to their diverse forms and practices in Chinese history. What stands out in our review is the sharp contrast between a mix of diverse practical approaches (e.g., acceptance, tolerance, decriminalization, legalization, and prohibition) taken by the pre-Communist governments and the strict prohibition approach by the Communist government. Second, we discuss the reemergence of both drug abuse and prostitution starting in the 1980s. Then we focus on the draconian approach of the Chinese government and highlight both increasing legislation and the effect of campaign-style policing. Next we examine China's fight against both drug use and prostitution in the global context and see how the Chinese government strategically selected its international stance and approach to build on its official domestic language but ignored other different or dissenting voices. Finally, we discuss a few alternative policies of drug control and prostitution management.

## A Brief History of Drugs, Prostitution, and Their Regulation

China has a rich history of narcotics (especially opium) use and regulations.[2] Historical accounts indicate that opium did not originate in China but was brought into China by Arab traders during the Tang dynasty around 600 CE.[3] Opium was initially used for medicinal purposes and was found effective in controlling bodily fluids and preserving vital energy.[4] A major transformation of opium from *yao* (medicine) to *chun yao* (aphrodisiac) occurred during the Ming dynasty (1368–1644), when opium became "the art of alchemists, sex and court ladies."[5]

Eating or drinking a raw form of opium was less lethal and addictive than inhaling the smokable form of opium, which was introduced in China during the 1500s.[6] In 1589 opium was first listed as a taxable commodity, and opium imports remained legal throughout the Tang, Song, Yuan, Ming, and early Qing dynasties. In 1729 Emperor Yongzheng of the Qing dynasty imposed the first royal opium edict, which banned the sale and distribution of opium, but not the personal use and import of opium.[7] In 1813 the Qing dynasty issued its first decree to outlaw opium consumption, which was followed by a more comprehensive antidrug law in 1839. The breakout of the Opium Wars in the 1840s and 1850s ultimately led to the failure of Qing's narcotics regulations and the fall of the Qing dynasty. Qing's narcotics policies, nevertheless, were not strictly punitive and prohibitive. Rather, the Qing government, given its domestic turbulence, its position and role in the global system, and intervention by foreign powers, struggled between prohibition, decriminalization, and legalization.[8]

After the collapse of the Qing dynasty, China was controlled by warlords and then by the Nationalist government (Guomindang, GMD, or Kuomintang, KMT) from the 1910s to the 1940s. By 1924–1925 the International Anti-Opium Association estimated that China produced at least 15,000 tons of opium annually, which was the equivalent of 88 percent of global production.[9] Despite the fact that the Nationalists' criminal laws (1928 and 1935) made drug use a crime, subject to five years of incarceration and one thousand yuan in fines,[10] the Nationalists did not effectively change the pattern of drug use in China during the 1930s and the 1940s owing to political and military conflicts among various warlords and between China and Japan. During this period political and military leaders all resorted to the control of the opium trade as a means to solve political and financial difficulties, and farmers continued cultivating opium for profit.[11]

The CCP has had long-standing antidrug policies since its establishment in the 1920s. During the late 1920s and early 1930s, opium poppy cultivation was declared illegal in the Communist-controlled regions, though there was evidence of such cultivation by the Communists.[12] By the time the CCP took power in 1949, China was confronted with a staggering problem of drug trafficking and drug use; there were an estimated 20 million drug addicts, 300,000 drug traffickers and manufacturers, and 1 million hectares of poppy cultivation nationwide.[13] The new government launched several rounds of nationwide anti-opium campaigns immediately after the founding of the People's Republic of China.[14] These campaigns mobilized the general public to uncover drug users and conducted mass education about narcotics' harmful effects on the individual and society. In addition, the establishment of neighborhood committees and their ability to penetrate every corner of society to provide surveillance and education significantly improved the effectiveness of the antidrug campaigns. Hundreds of thousands of drug offenders were uncovered, and tens of thousands were convicted and punished. As a result, the CCP largely eradicated drug problems nationwide, and in the next two decades China remained a "drug-free" nation.

The history of prostitution is as long as the written history of China.[15] Historical tales from the Shang dynasty (1523–1028 BCE) suggest that royalty employed singing troupes, entertainers who probably also served as prostitutes. Until the establishment of the Republic of China in 1911, however, prostitution was never condemned by statutes in China. Instead, it was permitted, regulated, and taxed from the era of Guan Zhong (725–645 BCE)—one of the great Chinese philosophers and statesmen who lived more than one hundred years before Confucius (551–479 BCE). Guan was the first statesman in Chinese history to propose a practical way of regulating prostitution through taxation. Brothel keepers were licensed and taxes collected.

In a long period of agricultural society in China that followed, women did not have much chance to receive an education. For women from poor families, prostitution represented a chance to receive an education. Most courtesans were trained and raised as singers, dancers, and occasionally writers. Indeed, some of them became famous poets. Their primary role was as companions for wealthy literati and merchants, and they reserved the right to say no to clients.[16] During the golden eras of Chinese literary history (Tang and Song dynasties), almost every great poet or politician mentioned his visits to prostitutes without any shame. It is not an exaggeration to claim that prostitutes played a role in stimulating some of the best poems in Chinese history.[17]

Scholars' and politicians' attitudes toward prostitutes changed in the late Song dynasty (twelfth and thirteenth centuries). The new version of Neo-Confucianism (traditional Chinese: li-xue) of Zhu Xi (1130–1200) was highly moralistic. It officially reified the hypocritical practice by making elite men's visits to prostitutes a secret activity and by promoting elite women's chastity. The state advocated elevating the patriarchal morality of its subjects, both through exemplary behavior and through the policing of family, social organizations, and cultural activities. Even so, prostitution in its usually recognized forms was not a concern for any dynasty. The rules of etiquette and Confucian ethics during the Ming and Qing dynasties prohibited its public expression in the form of written works. Surprisingly (or not), Confucius's and Buddha's condemnations coexisted with an attitude of acceptance.

The policy of the Republican regime (1911–1949) toward prostitution lacked clarity.[18] The regime had been wavering in the dilemma between occupying a moral high ground by banning prostitution and showing democratic concern for protecting the weak and oppressed groups in society. It was during this period that the term *public health* was used as one of the additional arguments against prostitution. The regime's revolutionary zeal gradually gave way to a regulatory enthusiasm. Despite abolitionist inclinations, the central government, preoccupied by constant wars, did not adopt any harsh means to carry out its policy of controlling prostitution and of suppressing all traffic related to this activity.

Within a few years of the CCP's taking power, prostitution was eliminated entirely. Mao chose to classify prostitution, along with gambling and drug use, as an "ugly social phenomenon" of the "old" China. The propaganda machine during this period viewed the complex phenomenon solely in terms of exploitation of women. Mao even regarded the masses' libidos as a major threat to the Communist Party's authority.[19] Not only did he close all brothels in China, but he also made sexuality one of Chinese society's greatest taboos.[20] This period, however, should be regarded as abnormal, and a double standard continued to exist under Mao's rule.[21] For example, although Mao closed all mass entertainments related to prostitution, he and his comrades continued to have weekly dance parties with selected young and beautiful girls in the Forbidden City in Beijing until his so-called Great Proletarian Cultural Revolution began in 1966.[22]

## REEMERGING DRUG AND PROSTITUTION PROBLEMS IN THE NEW ERA

Both drug and prostitution problems reemerged in the 1980s, once China commenced its economic reforms and adopted an open-door policy. Drug problems quickly spread from the southwest region of China to other parts of the country. Official reports showed that the number of registered drug addicts increased from 148,000 in 1991 to 937,000 by 2007.[23] Unofficial estimates put the number even higher, at millions of drug addicts.[24]

The difference in the new era is that heroin has replaced opium as the primary choice of Chinese drug users. This became evident from the increasing amounts of heroin seized annually. In 1983, for example, the Chinese government seized only 23 grams of heroin, and from 1983 to 1985 the total amount seized was less than 5,000 grams. The total, however, reached 1,600 kilograms (1.6 million grams) in 1990 alone,[25] and further increased to 6,900 kilograms by the end of 2005.[26] Other types of narcotic drugs such as opium, methamphetamine, and marijuana also became quite common in China.[27]

Available studies suggested that the majority of drug users are young males,[28] poorly educated,[29] and either unemployed or self-employed.[30] Studies also showed that drug users tend to smoke, drink alcohol, be sexually active, and have a criminal history.[31] It was also reported that ethnic minorities were disproportionately involved in more drug-related offenses than any other traditional offenses.[32]

Along with this worsening trend, female drug users also increased in the post-reform era of China. There were very few female drug users before the mid-1980s, but the figure escalated quickly in the 1990s.[33] The number of registered female drug users reached 118,000 in 1999, further climbed to 138,000 in 2000, and was estimated to represent about 16 percent of all drug users nationwide in both 2002 and 2003.[34] Some regional studies (e.g., one on Guangzhou in Guangdong province and one on Wuhan in Hunan province) showed even higher percentages.[35] In Zhejiang province there were 2,510 registered female drug users in 2001 (6.63 percent of all drug users there). This number increased to 6,365 (16.73 percent of the total) in 2002, 7,790 (18.8 percent) in 2003, and 9,374 (19.57 percent) in 2004.[36] A study of juvenile female drug addicts showed a similarly increasing trend over the years, though no specific statistics were reported.[37]

The few available studies on female drug dependents consistently show that these women tend to be young (usually under twenty-five years old), be unemployed, live in urban areas (medium or small cities), be unmarried, and be undereducated.[38] Compared with male drug users, women require less time and smaller quantities of drugs to become addicts.[39] Most female drug offenders commit crimes such as prostitution to support their habits, and they tend to experience an extremely high risk of reuse even after intensive treatment; over 90 percent of them reportedly return to drug use.[40]

In addition to its connections to crime and disorder, drug use is related to escalating HIV and AIDS problems in China.[41] The first HIV case was diagnosed in 1985; the official number of infected people in China reached 22,517 in 2000, 40,560 in 2002, and 840,000 in 2003 (and over 80,000 AIDS patients), before it was reassessed and lowered to 650,000 by the end of 2005.[42] Intravenous drug use reportedly accounted for between 60 and 70 percent of these cases,[43] and by 2005 AIDS had become the third largest killer (after tuberculosis and rabies) among all contagious diseases in China.[44]

In a similar fashion, prostitution resurfaced as a social problem after China instituted its open-door policy in 1978. The estimated number of sex workers ranges from 4 million to as many as 10 million.[45] The use of female sex workers by Chinese men from all social classes and all walks of life is extensive.[46] In addition to anxiety about this spiritual "slide," concerns about public health were the driving force behind the study of prostitution in China. One report revealed that almost half (48.8 percent) of all arrested prostitutes in China had one or more sexually transmitted diseases (STD); this compares to the global rates of 8.3 percent in Taiwan to 51.2 percent in central Africa.[47] Another report from the city of Kunming in Yunnan province indicated that 84 percent of female sex workers had at least one STD and 8 percent had both HIV and HSV-2 (genital herpes).[48] Results of STD surveys among prostitutes in Guangxi and Yunnan provinces showed HIV prevalence as 11 percent and 5 percent, respectively.[49]

Prostitutes now are easily found in all major cities and towns, even though prostitution remains illegal in China.[50] Prostitution has grown into an industry that involves a great number of people and produces a certain economic outcome. Prostitutes in China, like their counterparts in the United States, generally lack collective consciousness and occupational control. Like their "sisters" several generations ago,[51] they prefer to work in entertainment establishments (e.g., karaoke, nightclubs, dance halls, discos, and bars) or personal service sectors (e.g., hair salons, massage parlors, saunas, and hotels).[52]

## AGAINST DRUGS AND PROSTITUTION: INCREASING LEGISLATION AND CRACKDOWNS

Facing these reemerging drug and prostitution problems, the Chinese government relied on stricter legislation (see Table 8.1) and its old methods—national campaigns and harsh punishment—to fight the relapse into the

**Table 8.1.** Key legislation against drug abuse and prostitution

| Year | Legislation against drugs | Year | Legislation against prostitution |
|---|---|---|---|
| 1979 | Criminal Law of the PRC, article 171 | 1987 | Security Administration Punishment Regulations |
| 1990 | Decision on Drug Control | 1991 | Decision on Strictly Forbidding the Selling and Buying of Sex; Decision on the Severe Punishment of Criminals Who Abduct and Traffic in or Kidnap Women and Children |
| 1997 | Criminal Law of the PRC, revised, articles 347–355 | 1992 | Law on Protecting the Rights and Interests of Women |
| 2005 | Regulations on Administration of Precursor Chemicals; Regulations on Administration of Narcotics Drugs and Psychotropic Substances | 1997 | Criminal Law of the PRC, revised, articles 358–362 |
| 2008 | Antidrug law of the PRC | 1999 | Regulations concerning the Management of Public Places of Entertainment, articles 132–138 |

old problem. The 1979 Criminal Law of the People's Republic of China was the first national legislation that criminalized the offense of manufacturing, selling, and transporting narcotics. Drug offenders were subject to up to five years of incarceration or custody and fines; and habitual offenders involved with a large amount of narcotics could face even tougher sentences (chapter 1, article 171). In December 1990 the Standing Committee of the National People's Congress (NPC) adopted the Decision on Drug Control, the first key legislation on drug control in the new era. In practical terms, the Decision defined regulated drugs, expanded the scope of narcotic offenses, stipulated (harsh) punishment, implemented forced detoxification of habitual drug addicts, and detailed the application of the law. Noticeably, the death penalty was made applicable to crimes that involve a large amount of drugs (e.g., more than one thousand grams of opium or fifty grams of heroin) or other aggravating factors (e.g., being a ringleader, use of a weapon or violence in smuggling, and transnational crimes).

In 1997 and 2002 the Criminal Law was revised. It expanded drug offenses stipulated in the 1990 law and added new drug-related offenses such as illegal trading, transporting, carrying, and possessing opium poppies or other narcotic plants (articles 347–355). The revised law reaffirmed the death penalty as the potential maximum penalty and demanded that serious drug offenders engaged in smuggling, selling, transporting, and manufacturing would be held criminally liable regardless of the amount of narcotic drugs involved, signaling a much more punitive policy toward narcotics offenses.

In 2005 the State Council issued both Regulations on Administration of Narcotic Drugs and Psychotropic Substances (decree no. 442) and Regulations on Administration of Precursor Chemicals (decree no. 445). Both regulations aimed at facilitating the government's war on drugs through tightened controls over psychotropic substances and precursor chemicals in numerous avenues such as manufacture, experimentation, use, purchase, management, transportation, and imports and exports. In addition, these regulations specified the responsibilities of various entities and procedures for supervision and inspection of psychotropic substances and precursor chemicals (such as methamphetamine), and their legal liabilities if not in conformity with the regulations.

More recently, in December 2007, the Standing Committee of the NPC adopted the PRC's first comprehensive Antidrug Law (*jindu fa*). The new law, which took effect on June 1, 2008, included seven chapters on general provisions, antidrug education, narcotics control and regulation, treatment and rehabilitation, international cooperation in drug control, legal liabilities, and supplementary provisions. Opium, heroin, marijuana, methamphetamine hydrochloride (commonly known as "ice"), morphine, and cocaine were banned by the new law, and it set strict rules on the clinical use of pharmaceuticals and other chemicals and medicines that could be used to make illegal narcotics. The new law allows drug addicts to recover in their communities within three years, and further specifies the conditions under which drug addicts can be confined to rehabilitation centers. The new law makes it clear that it is imperative for the Chinese government to crack down on drug-related crimes in order to protect public health and maintain social order in the twenty-first century. At the same time, it calls for all-around antidrug education and international cooperation.

Along with stricter legislation, the Chinese government increased official crackdowns and campaigns on drug offenses and punished offenders, especially traffickers, severely. For instance, the number of drug cases uncovered by the police was 10,946 in 1991, but it quickly increased to 88,579 by 1996; it gained momentum near the end of the 1990s and reached 112,947 by 2002, before dropping significantly after 2004. The third round of the government's "severe strike" campaign, started in 2001, had begun to come to an end by 2004, and this could be one reason for the drop in numbers.[53] Unlike the fluctuating number of drug cases, the number of drug arrests made by the police grew rapidly and continually from 185 arrests in 1988 to 58,000 in 2005 to 112,400 in 2011.[54]

In the punitive legal climate that had developed, drug offenders and drug traffickers increasingly received harsh punishments, and mass executions as well as death and life sentences were utilized in antidrug campaigns. In the late 1990s, for example, over 20 percent of all those involved in drug trafficking cases were sentenced to death or life imprisonment, whereas 68 percent were given a fixed prison sentence of more than five years. The latter far exceeded the average 30 percent of long-term (over five years) sentences in all cases annually in China.[55] In the first five months of 2005, courts at all levels sentenced 53,205 drug offenders, and 22,371 of them (42 percent) received harsh, long-term incarceration, well exceeding the average 24.3 percent in all other cases.[56] Similarly, 55,671 drug offenders were sentenced nationwide from January 2006 to May 2007, and 21,223 (38 percent) received long-term incarceration.[57] In the first four months of 2008, courts at all levels tried 10,883 drug cases and sentenced 13,435 offenders, 4,625 (or 34.4 percent) of whom received over five years of incarceration, life imprisonment, or death sentences.

In addition to severe punishment, drug offenses are among a few other crimes (e.g., murder and robbery) that have received swift dispositions in the "severe strike" campaigns. For example, a nationwide mass campaign initiated in 1989 targeted the "six evils," of which drug use was one.[58] As a result, efforts from public security organs stepped up: in 1987 public security organs nationwide cleared 56 drug-related cases and seized 137 kilos of opium and 43 kilos of heroin; the numbers increased to 268 cases, 239 kilos of opium, and 166 kilos of heroin in 1988; and to 547 cases, 269 kilos of opium, and 488 kilos of heroin in 1989.[59] The number of drug trafficking cases further skyrocketed from 547 in 1989 to 3,670 in 1990, an increase directly due to the pressure of the campaign.[60] In such campaigns, sentencing rallies and mass executions of drug offenders were quite common, particularly on such special occasions as China's National Antidrugs Day (June 16) and the United Nations' International Day against Drug Abuse and Illicit Drug Trafficking (June 26). In 1996, for example, at least 260 drug offenders were executed to commemorate the Antidrugs Day.[61] It is very difficult to gauge the total number of drug death sentences and executions because information on China's death penalty practice is viewed as a state secret. Despite the Chinese government's efforts in recent years to tighten its death penalty practices (such as the retrieval of the final review and approval right by the Supreme People's Court from the lower courts in 2007) and to reduce the number of death sentences and executions,[62] the Supreme People's Court (SPC) has consistently announced its get-tough policy against drug offenses and its willingness to impose the death penalty whenever appropriate.[63]

Official attitudes toward prostitutes have changed over time. During Mao's era prostitutes were viewed as worthy of sympathy and capable of being saved as victims of circumstances. Now prostitutes are viewed again as those who are morally despicable, lazy, greedy, and deserving of punishment.[64] This attitude is shared in Taiwan and in many other traditional societies in the world.

Officially, prostitution is illegal in China.[65] Prostitution is banned because—in official language—it "seriously corrupts people's minds, poisons the social atmosphere, and endangers social stability. It also [stimulates] other types of criminal offenses and seriously damages the construction of socialist spiritual civilization in China."[66] Indeed, the resurfacing of prostitution as an industry has been accompanied by the revival of organized crime, government corruption, and sexually transmitted diseases.

Until the 1980s prostitution was not viewed as a major concern. Both the Criminal Law and Criminal Procedure Law of 1979 made no explicit reference to the activities of prostitutes and their clients. The control of prostitution was left to the Ministry of Public Safety and was based on administrative measures and other local regulations. The Ministry of Public Safety, for example, published the Security Administration Punishment Regulations in 1987 and made it an offense to "sell sex" (*maiyin*) and to "have illicit relations with a prostitute" (*piaosu an'chang*) (article 30).

Responding to increasing requests, the NPC passed both the Decision on Strictly Forbidding the Selling and Buying of Sex and the Decision on the Severe Punishment of Criminals Who Abduct and Traffic in or Kidnap Women and Children in 1991. A year later the NPC also adopted the Law on Protecting the Rights and Interests of Women, which defines prostitution as a social practice that abrogates the inherent rights of women to personhood (articles 36–37).

In the 1997 revised Criminal Law, the death penalty was made available, for the first time, in exceptional cases involving serious aggravating factors such as organizing prostitution, forcing underage (younger than fourteen years old) girls into prostitution, repeating offences, committing rape, and causing serious bodily injury (article 358). The activities of first-party participants (both prostitutes and their clients) continue to be regulated by administrative measures, with the exception of those who sell or buy sex in the full knowledge that they are infected with an STD (article 360), and of those who have sex with a minor under fourteen years old. Since 2003 male homosexual prostitution has also been prosecuted under the law. In addition, the 1997 Criminal Law codified provisions to regulate high-risk public places, especially places of leisure and entertainment, for prostitution (articles 361–362). The 1999 Regulations concerning the Management of Public Places of Entertainment adopted by the State Council lent further support for governmental regulations in such places.

The actual enforcement of prostitution laws turns out to be rather selective. Enforcement is generally directed at commercial sex workers with the fewest resources, who work at the bottom of the commercial sex industry's hierarchy. Periodic crackdowns since the 1980s have produced short-term effects on the number and prevalence of those sex workers' activities. But prostitutes would reemerge after a particular campaign because prostitution was intertwined with local economies.[67] As scholars have noted, the punitive and selective enforcement strategy against prostitution in China since its return to normalcy in the 1980s has not been working.[68] Even those who support continued criminalization of prostitution and advocate drastic measures against prostitution agree that the current policy has met unprecedented difficulties.[69] Under the current increased social stratification, the contrast between the nouveaux riches and the poor is indeed shocking. The desire for money—and for quick and easy money—is widespread.[70] Penal policy based on moral panic[71] or on moral crusade[72] is likely to fail. Like campaign-style policing in general, antiprostitution campaigns have been presented as the draconian yet ineffective display of law and order. These campaigns have no real hold on the campaign-fatigued Chinese public.

## Fighting Drug Use and Prostitution in the Global Context: A Selective Method

China's drug control history has always been a key component of global narcotics movements.[73] It is worth mentioning that China's successful anti-drug campaigns in the 1950s were achieved by dissociating China from the global system and Western influences. It is not surprising that drug problems resurfaced in China after China initiated its economic reform and reopened its door in the 1980s.

In the new era China has realized that it can no longer fight drug problems alone, as it did decades ago. Instead, in addition to its domestic efforts, China has sought help from international organizations and reembraced the global drug prohibition system. In the mid-1980s China had already begun to send delegations to attend international drug control meetings held by such key organizations as the United Nations, the International Criminal Police Organization, and the World Health Organization. In 1985 China acceded to both the United Nations Single Convention on Narcotic Drugs of 1961 and the United Nations Vienna Convention on Psychotropic Substances of 1971. In 1988 China actively participated in the draft and enactment of the United Nations Convention against Illicit Traffic in Narcotic Drugs and Psychotropic Substances, and it acceded to that convention the following year, becoming one of the very first member countries.

Since the 1990s China has begun to exert a leading role in working with regional associations and neighboring nations. As early as 1989 China had already held an Asian Region Antidrug Seminar in Beijing. In May 1991 the National Narcotics Control Commission of China hosted the first meeting of senior officials of China, Thailand, Myanmar, and the United Nations International Drug Control Program in Beijing to discuss proposals on multilateral cooperation against drug abuse in the subregion. Since 2000 China has actively participated in the meetings of Heads of National Drug Law Enforcement Agencies for Asia and the Pacific. In 2000 and 2005 China and the Association of Southeast Asian Nations (ASEAN) approved and reaffirmed the ASEAN and China Cooperative Operations in Response to Dangerous Drugs to seek opportunities to expand cooperation. In working with neighboring nations, China also transitioned from being an "assistance recipient" in the 1990s to being an "assistance provider" in the new century, particularly for narcotics-stricken nations in the area of the Golden Triangle, such as Burma and Laos. By the end of 2004 the Chinese government had reportedly already spent more than 500 million yuan ($63 million) for this purpose.[74]

One dominant feature of China's global drug control collaboration is its selective approach; that is, China's international orientation is predetermined by its domestic agenda. The Chinese government turns to various components to buttress its domestic fight against narcotics, including emphasizing China's drug history, preaching about antidrug heroes such as Lin Zexu, boasting about the Communist government's feat of eliminating drugs in the 1950s, and calling on the needs of "socialist civilization" in the new era. As a result, the government's official language has become the people's will through media propaganda, and there is little room allowed for different voices. For instance, a longitudinal study of all drug stories in the *People's Daily* (the Party's newspaper) from 1946 to 2009 showed very little divergence in the official language.[75] On the subject of drug rehabilitation, for example, despite increasing attention to the need for rehabilitation, drug users have been viewed primarily as offenders. Only in 2004 did a few *People's Daily* stories discuss drug addicts as "patients" who need medical treatment.[76] These stories suggested that such an understanding is a "new vision," and it requires "reconsideration and readjustment of China's detoxification model." Such a voice, however, turned out to be too weak and too little, and it was quickly overwhelmed by the dominant punitive language. Internationally, when the idea of narcotics legalization was brought up at the thirty-sixth meeting of the United Nations Commission on Narcotic Drugs in 1993, China adamantly opposed it and called it "a step backward."[77] Such a radical, different voice would not be tolerated in China, a stance that is consistent with its domestic drug control efforts. What is lacking in the official language is a serious discussion of public opinion about and tolerance of drug use and of public support for treatment.

Public attitudes toward prostitution are complex.[78] They are the product of historical, religious, cultural, political, social, and economic influences that can be evaluated only in relation to the larger cultural milieus. The gathering of comparative data is especially difficult for two reasons.[79] First, data from different political regimes are difficult to compare. In an authoritarian society, individual opinions about politically sensitive topics are hard to get, and, even those regarding politically less sensitive but morally loaded issues (such as drug abuse and prostitution) are likely to be inaccurate because respondents are afraid of government persecution or are unwilling to express their true feelings. Similarly, in a society with a strong religious consensus, expressed opinions on moral issues may be less reflective of true sentiment. Second, opinions obtained in a nation with a collectivist orientation should be viewed differently from those gathered in a society with an individualistic orientation.[80] *Collectivism* refers "to the tendency to be more concerned about the consequences of one's behavior for in-group members and to be more willing to sacrifice personal interests for the attainment of collective interests."[81] To different degrees, most Eastern and Muslim societies tend to belong to such a collectivistic tradition. In contrast, most Western European and North American nations are considered societies with more of an individualist orientation[82] or expressive culture.[83]

With these two caveats in mind, Liqun Cao and Steven Stack compared worldwide public opinion on prostitution.[84] Their data show that there is a high level of consensus among Chinese in their attitudes toward prostitution, and this high level parallels the level of consensus in Vietnam and many other autocratic or Muslim nations. In contrast, there is much less consensus in the attitudes toward prostitution in democratic and non-Muslim societies, such as Spain and the United States. Despite having become more liberal and cosmopolitan, the public in China, under an authoritarian regime, has changed little in its self-expressions, especially on sensitive topics constantly monitored by the government. Chinese society remains troubled by a host of economic and political insecurities and operates, unlike a fully developed civil society, under a mechanistic solidarity. Attitudes toward prostitution in China reflect that solidarity.

Cao and Stack concluded that public opinion and penal policy toward prostitution are central in defining societal type.[85] In autocratic and Muslim countries, prostitutes are morally condemned and publicly scorned, and they live on the bottom rung of society without any protection from government. This is true in today's China as well. In contrast, in more democratic and secular societies, such as the Netherlands and the Scandinavian nations, prostitutes as a marginal group are morally condemned, but the penal code has become vaguer in prosecuting them; their rights as human beings, to various degrees, are recognized and protected, and they are sometimes able to organize collective actions to advance their own interests.[86] These conditions are clearly missing in China.

### Conclusion: Draconian Approach versus Management: What Lessons to Learn?

In this study we focus on drug abuse and prostitution and the attempts of the Chinese government to control them. To our knowledge this is the first time these issues have been examined together. As discussed above, the CCP's inflexible, draconian criminalization approach toward both stands out in sharp contrast to more tolerant, practical approaches adopted by previous regimes of China as well as by present-day Western European governments. Seemingly the biggest challenge comes from the government's dogmatic ideology. From the very moment when the PRC was founded, drug use and prostitution were labeled social vices that would not be tolerated. Drug addicts and prostitutes were viewed as victims of the so-called feudal society and were forcibly "saved" by socialist China. When politics was in command from the 1950s to 1970s, social vices were completely suppressed, and few would dare try the forbidden fruit for fear of being reported and prosecuted as enemies of the state.

China's economic reform and reintegration into the global system beginning in the 1980s have relegated politics to a secondary position and brought the economy to the forefront. Economic reform has made significant changes to Chinese society, and its effects go well beyond the economic sphere. One byproduct is the transformation from Mao's totalitarian system to Deng's authoritarian regime. Along with a new economic ethos (e.g., being rich is glorious), greater freedom of population movement, increased economic and social inequality, and changing family and personal values (including sexuality), we find that illegal drug use and commercial sex in China have both reemerged and become widespread. Although there seems to be a consensus in public opinion, illegal drug and prostitution markets could not exist without hundreds of otherwise law-abiding men's and women's willing participation.

Facing the new challenge, the Chinese government finds it difficult to drop its official ideological language and change its course. Indeed, it has harked back to its old methods—tough crackdowns and mass education—in the hope that it can contain their spread. Without Mao's style of total thought control, without his readiness for massive persecution and class struggle as the central concern, these methods lost their magic. And drugs and prostitution continue to multiply and broaden their extent. In the meantime, the HIV epidemic, in which both commercial sex and illegal drugs play a role, has posed another challenge to China. The government has added public health rhetoric to its arsenal against both drug use and prostitution. Internationally, the Chinese government has been reaching out to the global community, but only with its own goals in mind; it will not allow any dissenting voice (either internal or external) to meddle with its set agenda (particularly with regard to drug control).

When we compare drug use to prostitution, it is not surprising to see an even tougher approach toward the former, both in lawmaking and law enforcement. Though official propaganda targets both, drug offenses bear the more direct brunt of official punishment, whereas prostitution often faces more selective law enforcement locally owing to its being a profitable business. Nevertheless, both are still consistently condemned by the Chinese government in its official language, and there is no sign of change in the near future.

Our review here suggests, if anything, that the CCP's draconian approach toward drug use and prostitution needs rethinking. As the former Chinese president Jiang Zemin said, China must further emancipate the mind and keep pace with the times (*jiefang sixiang, yushi jujin*). China must realize that both drug use and prostitution are part of a normal society.[87] As the United States' experiences in criminalizing both drug use and prostitution have shown,[88] a repressive policy through the criminal law in a normal society is an ineffective custodian of moral norms. Such enforcement interventions only put police officers in an impossible position. Moreover, as can be seen in the United States, drug use and prostitution have never been eliminated; they have only been relocated, and prostitutes have been exposed to more health risks, more violence, and more loss of life.[89]

In regulating such behavior, Mao's strategy of complete suppression with a goal of elimination is impossible to duplicate under the current situation. The complexity of both phenomena needs a more sensible policy to minimize their harmful effects and provide medical treatment to those who need it. The current draconian approach has not worked well and may well have negative effects. For example, valuable information on needle sharing and lack of condom use, both of which lead to the spread of HIV, cannot be obtained if the government continues to criminalize these activities. In contrast, regulation instead of criminalization may alleviate, if not eliminate, many concerns over drug abuse, drug trafficking, human trafficking, child prostitution, and forced prostitution.[90] It may also help health-related education reach prostitutes and drug users. A management-oriented policy is, inter alia, more attainable and more humane. It is also consistent with both ancient Chinese wisdom and the contemporary goal of building a harmonious society in which individual differences and human foibles are tolerated. Durkheim's theory of social change and Inglehart's theory of cultural change both predict that economic development tends to promote individual freedom.[91] Specifically, cultural attitudes toward deviant behavior, including drug use and prostitution, shift toward greater tolerance. Such a lesson may turn out to be important as China continues in its economic progress.

## NOTES

1. Liqun Cao and Steven Stack, "Societal Type and Attitude toward Prostitution: Where Does China Belong?" (paper presented at the sixteenth annual conference of the Association of Chinese Professors of Social Sciences in the U.S., Harvard University, Cambridge, Mass., November 5–7, 2010).

2. Timothy Brook and Bob T. Wakabayashi, eds., *Opium Regimes: China, Britain, and Japan, 1839–1952* (Berkeley: University of California Press, 2000); Frank Dikotter, Lars Laamann, and Zhou Xun, "Narcotic Culture: A Social History of Drug Consumption in China," *British Journal of Criminology* 42, no. 2 (2002): 317–336; Edward R. Slack, *Opium, State, and Society: China's Narco-Economy and the Guomindang, 1924–1937* (Honolulu: University of Hawai'i Press, 2001); William O. Walker, *Opium and Foreign Policy* (Chapel Hill: University of North Carolina Press, 1991); Yongming Zhou, *Anti-Drug Crusades in Twentieth-Century China: Nationalism, History, and State Building* (Lanham, Md.: Rowman & Littlefield, 1999); Su Zhiliang and Zhao Changqing, *Treaties of War on Drugs* (Beijing: China Democracy and Law Publishing House, 1998); Jiang Qiuming and Zhu Qingbao, *Zhongguo jindu lichen* (China's Anti-Narcotics History and Progress) (Tianjin: Tianjin Education Press, 1996); Qi Lei and Hu Jinye, *Zhongguo jin du Shi* (A History of China's Narcotics Control) (Lanzhou: Gansu People's Press, 2004); Su Zhiliang, *Zhongguo dupin shi* (Chinese Narcotics History) (Shanghai: Shanghai People's Press, 1997); Yangwen Zheng, *The Social Life of Opium in China* (Cambridge: Cambridge University Press, 2005); Hong Lu, Terance Miethe, and Bin Liang, *China's Drug Practices and Policies: Regulating Controlled Substances in a Global Context* (London: Ashgate, 2009).

3. Su and Zhao, *Treaties of War on Drugs,* 111–112.

4. Dikotter, Laamann, and Zhou, "Narcotic Culture"; and Zheng, *The Social Life of Opium in China,* 11–13.

5. Zheng, *The Social Life of Opium in China,* 12–13.

6. Martin Booth, *Opium: A History* (New York: St. Martin's Press, 1998).

7. Zhao Bingzhi and Zhigang Yu, *Dupin fanzui* (Drug-Related Crimes) (Beijing: People's Public Security Press of China, 1998), 10; Brook and Wakabayashi, *Opium Regimes,* 6.

8. Lu, Miethe, and Liang, *China's Drug Practices and Policies.*

9. Slack, *Opium, State, and Society,* 6.

10. Zhao and Yu, *Dupin fanzui,* 14–16.

11. Slack, *Opium, State, and Society;* Frederic Wakeman Jr., *Policing Shanghai: 1927–1937* (Berkeley: University of California Press, 1995).

12. Yongming Zhou, *China's Anti-Drug Campaign in the Reform Era* (Singa-

pore: Singapore University Press, 2000); Zhou, *Anti-Drug Crusades in Twentieth-Century China;* Wakeman, *Policing Shanghai.*

13. Zhao and Yu, *Dupin fanzui,* 27; He Xiaodong and Min Fang, *Zhongguo jindu da shijiao* (An Overview of China's Anti-Narcotics) (Beijing: Beijing University Press, 1998); Alan Dupont, "Transnational Crimes, Drugs and Security in East Asia," *Asian Survey* 39, no. 3 (1999): 433–455.

14. Zhou, *Anti-Drug Crusades in Twentieth-Century China;* Zhou, *China's Anti-Drug Campaign in the Reform Era.*

15. Fang F. Ruan, *Sex in China: Studies in Sexology in Chinese Culture* (New York: Plenum Press, 1991); Susyan Jou, Charles Hou, and Liqun Cao, "Civil Society and Attitudes toward Prostitution in the World" (paper presented at the International Symposium of Civil Society, University of Macao, 2009).

16. Sue Gronewold, *Beautiful Merchandise: Prostitution in China 1860–1936* (New York: Haworth Press, 1982). Ruan, *Sex in China;* Shan Guangding, *Prostitutes in China: Past and Present* (in Chinese) (Beijing: Law Press, 1995).

17. Ruan, *Sex in China,* 1991.

18. Christian Henriot, *Prostitution and Sexuality in Shanghai: A Social History, 1849–1949* (New York: Cambridge University Press, 1997).

19. George Wehrfritz, "Unbuttoning a Nation," *Newsweek International Edition,* May 15, 1996, 38–40.

20. Emily Honig, "Socialist Sex: The Cultural Revolution Revisited," *Modern China* 29 (2003): 143–175; Fang Fu Ruan and Vern L. Bullough, "Sex Repression in Contemporary China," in *Building a World Community: Humanism in the Twenty-first Century,* ed. Paul Kurtz (Buffalo, N.Y.: Prometheus Books, 1989), 198–201; Everett Yuehong Zhang, "Rethinking Sexual Repression in Maoist China: Ideology, Structure and the Ownership of the Body," *Body and Society* 11 (2005): 1–25.

21. Liqun Cao, "Returning to Normality: Anomie and Crime in China," *International Journal of Offender Therapy and Comparative Criminology* 51 (2007): 40–51.

22. Li Zhisui, *The Private Life of Chairman Mao: The Memoirs of Mao's Personal Physician* (New York: Random House, 1994).

23. Lu, Miethe, and Liang, *China's Drug Practices and Policies,* 102–103. The Chinese Ministry of the Public Security keeps records of the number of registered drug addicts with its operations of compulsory drug treatment centers, Rehabilitation-through-Labor centers, and rehabilitation medical centers.

24. Drug Enforcement Administration (DEA), *Drug Intelligence Brief: China,* DEA-03081 (February 2004), www.hsdl.org/?view&did=446537 (accessed August 7, 2012); Joshua Kurlantzick, "China's Drug Problem and Looming HIV Epidemic," *World Policy Journal* 19, no. 2 (2002): 70–75.

25. Zhao and Yu, *Dupin fanzui,* 32.

26. Lu, Miethe, and Liang, *China's Drug Practices and Policies,* 103.

27. DEA, *Drug Intelligence Brief: China;* DEA, *Drug Trafficking in the People's Republic of China and Hong Kong* (Washington, D.C.: Drug Enforcement Adminis-

tration, Strategic Intelligence Section, Europe, Asia, Africa Unit, 1996); Xiaoming Li, Yong Zhou, and Bonita Stanton, "Illicit Drug Initiation among Institutionalized Drug Users in China," *Addiction* 97, no. 5 (2002): 575–582; He and Fang, *Zhongguo jindu da shijiao;* Information Office of the State Council of the People's Republic of China (IOSC), "Narcotics Control in China" (June 2000), http://news.xinhuanet. com/zhengfu/2002–11/18/content_633171.htm (accessed June 27, 2012).

28. DEA, *Drug Intelligence Brief: China;* DEA, *Drug Trafficking in the People's Republic of China and Hong Kong;* Dupont, "Transnational Crimes, Drugs and Security in East Asia"; Kurlantzick, "China's Drug Problem and Looming HIV Epidemic"; Clyde B. McCoy, Shenghan Lai, Lisa R. Metsch, Xue-ren Wang, Cong Li, Ming Yang, and Yulong Li, "No Pain, No Gain: Establishing the Kunming Drug Rehabilitation Center," *Journal of Drug Issues* 27, no. 1 (1997): 73–85; Wu Zunyou, Jiapeng Zhang, Roger Detels, Song Duan, Hehe Cheng, Zhirong Li, Lelong Dong, Sufen Huang, Manhong Jia, and Xiuqiong Bi, "Risk Factors for Initiation of Drug Use among Young Males in Southwest China," *Addiction* 91, no. 11 (1996): 1975–1985.

29. DEA, *Drug Intelligence Brief: China;* DEA, *Drug Trafficking in the People's Republic of China and Hong Kong;* McCoy et al., "No Pain, No Gain"; Li, Zhou, and Stanton, "Illicit Drug Initiation among Institutionalized Drug Users in China."

30. DEA, *Drug Intelligence Brief: China;* DEA, *Drug Trafficking in the People's Republic of China and Hong Kong;* McCoy et al., "No Pain, No Gain"; Zhao and Yu, *Dupin fanzui.*

31. Wu et al., "Risk Factors for Initiation of Drug Use among Young Males in Southwest China"; Li, Zhou, and Stanton, "Illicit Drug Initiation among Institutionalized Drug Users in China"; Zhao and Yu, *Dupin fanzui;* DEA, *Drug Trafficking in the People's Republic of China and Hong Kong.*

32. DEA, *Drug Intelligence Brief: China;* DEA, *Drug Trafficking in the People's Republic of China and Hong Kong;* Robert C. Bonner, "The New Heroin Corridor—Drug Trafficking in China," in *China at the Crossroads,* ed. Donald Altschiller (New York: H. W. Wilson, 1994), 229–236.

33. Yao Jianlong, "A Study of Female Drug Use," *Qingshaonian fanzui wenti* (Issue of Youth Crimes) 6 (2001): 47–51.

34. Gui Wen, "A Study of Female Drug Offenses," *Faxue shiyong* (Application of Law) 7 (2005): 40–43.

35. Ibid.; Yao, "A Study of Female Drug Use."

36. Wang Y. and Shi R., "Investigation of Female Drug Use in Zhejiang," *Zhejiang gongshang daxue xuebao* (Journal of Zhejiang Industrial and Commercial University) 5 (2005): 51–55; Wang Ye and Qing Zhou, "A Study of Female Drug Use in Zhejiang Province," *Gong'an xueka-zhejiang gong'an gaodeng zhuanke xuexiao xiaobao* (Journal of Public Security–Zhejiang Police College) 2 (2005): 88–90.

37. Hao Weimao, "A Study of Reasons of Increasing Female Juvenile Drug Use," *Qingshaonian fanzui yanjiu* (Study of Youth Crimes) 4 (1998): 7–8.

38. Gui, "A Study of Female Drug Offenses"; Ji Longhua, "A Study of Female

Drug Offenses in Yunnan Border Areas," *Faxue zazhi* (Law Magazine) 3 (1998): 25, 36; Ji Longhua, Wang Yuli, and Tao Pang, "A Study of Female Drug Offenses in Yunnan Border Areas," *Yunnan faxue* (Yunnan Law) 4 (1997): 87–89; Li Xiongying and Ling Yang, "Female Drug Users' Social Attitude and Its Changes," *Sheke zongheng* (Social Science Forum) 19, no. 2 (2004): 35–36; Ruan Huifeng, "A Case Study of the Female Drug-Related Crime," *Yunnan minzu daxue xuebao* (Journal of Yunnan Nationalities University) 24, no. 1 (2007): 49–53; Wang and Shi, "Investigation of Female Drug Use in Zhejiang"; Wang and Zhou, "A Study of Female Drug Use in Zhejiang Province"; Yao, "A Study of Female Drug Use."

39. Yao, "A Study of Female Drug Use."

40. Huang Shuhua, "Characteristics of Female Drug Use and Selling and Their Harmful Effects," *Fanzui yanjiu* (Criminal Studies) 4, no. 6 (2000): 46–48; Wang and Shi, "Investigation of Female Drug Use in Zhejiang"; Wang and Zhou, "A Study of Female Drug Use in Zhejiang Province"; Yao, "A Study of Female Drug Use."

41. McCoy et al., "No Pain, No Gain"; Bonner, "The New Heroin Corridor"; Kurlantzick, "China's Drug Problem and Looming HIV Epidemic."

42. Lu, Miethe, and Liang, *China's Drug Practices and Policies*, 108; Amnesty International, *Annual Report on China, 2004*. For the number for 2005, see Ministry of Health of the PRC, *2005 Update on HIV/AIDS Epidemic and Response in China* (January 2006), http://data.unaids.org/publications/External-Documents/rp_2005chinaestimation_25jan06_en.pdf (accessed July 18, 2012).

43. Lu, Miethe, and Liang, *China's Drug Practices and Policies*, 108; Zhou, *Anti-Drug Crusades in Twentieth-Century China*.

44. Lu, Miethe, and Liang, *China's Drug Practices and Policies*, 108.

45. Yan Hong, Xiaoming Li, Xiaoyi Fang, and Ran Zhao, "Correlates of Suicidal Ideation and Attempt among Female Sex Workers in China," *Health Care for Women International* 28, no. 5 (2007): 490–505; Liqun Cao and Steven Stack, "Exploring *Terra Incognita*: Family Values and Prostitution Acceptance in China" *Journal of Criminal Justice* 38, no. 4 (2010): 531–537.

46. Yinying Huang, Gail E. Henderson, Suiming Pan, and Myron S. Cohen, "HIV/AIDS Risk among Brothel-Based Female Sex Workers in China: Assessing the Terms, Content, and Knowledge of Sex Work," *Sexually Transmitted Diseases* 31 (2004): 695–700.

47. Vincent E. Gil, Marco S. Wang, Allen F. Anderson, Guo M. Lin, and Zhongjian O. Wu, "Prostitutes, Prostitution and STD/HIV Transmission in Mainland China," *Social Science and Medicine* 42, no. 1 (1996): 141–152.

48. Xiang-sheng Chen, Yeu-ping Yin, Guo-jun Liang, Xiang-dong Gong, Huasheng Li, Gilles Poumerol, Nguyen Thuy, Mei-qin Shi, and Yan-Hua Yu, "Sexually Transmitted Infections among Female Sex Workers in Yunnan, China," *AIDS Patient Care and STDs* 19, no. 12 (2005): 853–860.

49. Huang et al., "HIV/AIDS Risk among Brothel-Based Female Sex Workers in China."

50. Allen F. Anderson and Vincent E. Gil, "Prostitution and Public Policy in

the People's Republic of China," *International Criminal Justice Review* 4 (1994): 23–36; Cao and Stack, "Exploring *Terra Incognita*"; Hong et al., "Correlates of Suicidal Ideation and Attempt among Female Sex Workers in China"; Elaine Jeffreys, *China, Sex and Prostitution* (New York: Routledge Curzon, 2004); Ouyang Tao, "Prostitution Offenses in Contemporary China," *Chinese Sociology and Anthropology: A Journal of Translations* 30 (1997): 45–56; Shan, *Prostitutes in China*.

51. Gronewold, *Beautiful Merchandise*.

52. Hong et al., "Correlates of Suicidal Ideation and Attempt among Female Sex Workers in China"; Huang et al., "HIV/AIDS Risk among Brothel-Based Female Sex Workers in China."

53. Bin Liang, "Severe Strike Campaign in Transitional China," *Journal of Criminal Justice* 33, no. 4 (2005): 387–399.

54. Lu, Miethe, and Liang, *China's Drug Practices and Policies*, chap. 4. For 2011 data, see http://society.people.com.cn/GB/223276/203009/241842/index.html (accessed July 18, 2012).

55. He and Min, *Zhongguo jindu da shijiao*, 141; Yao Zhihun and Le Xue, eds., *Jindu da shijiao: Zhongguo jindu lishi gaikuang* (The Vision of Narcotics Control: A Brief History of China's Narcotics Control) (Beijing: Chinese People's Public Security University Press, 2004), 297.

56. Lu, Miethe, and Liang, *China's Drug Practices and Policies*, 114.

57. Ibid.

58. Bin Liang, "Severe Strike Campaign in Transitional China"; Li Ning, Liu Yuan, and Cao Xiaowu, *Guomen weishi: Zhongguo jidu jishi* (Guards at the Border: China's Anti-Narcotics Report) (Taiyuan, Shanxi: Beiyue Literature and Art Press, 1992); Zhou, *China's Anti-Drug Campaign in the Reform Era*; Zhou, *Anti-Drug Crusades in Twentieth-Century China*.

59. Li, Liu, and Cao, *Guards at the Border*, 1992.

60. Richard Baum, "Political Stability in Post-Deng China: Problems and Prospects," *Asian Survey* 32, no. 6 (1992): 491–505.

61. Slack, *Opium, State, and Society*, 155.

62. Bin Liang, *The Changing Chinese Legal System, 1978–Present: Centralization of Power and Rationalization of the Legal System* (New York: Routledge, 2008), 139.

63. Lu, Miethe, and Liang, *China's Drug Practices and Policies*, 115.

64. Jou et al., "Civil Society and Attitudes toward Prostitution in the World."

65. Anderson and Gil, "Prostitution and Public Policy in the People's Republic of China"; Hong et al., "Correlates of Suicidal Ideation and Attempt among Female Sex Workers in China"; Huang et al., "HIV/AIDS Risk among Brothel-Based Female Sex Workers in China"; Jeffreys, *China, Sex and Prostitution*; Ouyang, "Prostitution Offenses in Contemporary China."

66. Ouyang, "Prostitution Offenses in Contemporary China."

67. Cao and Stack, "Exploring *Terra Incognita.*"

68. Vincent E. Gil and Allen F. Anderson, "State-Sanctioned Aggression and

the Control of Prostitution in the People's Republic of China: A Review," *Aggression and Violent Behavior* 3 (1998): 129–142; Cao and Stack, "Exploring *Terra Incognita.*"

69. Shan, *Prostitutes in China.*

70. Cao, "Returning to Normality."

71. Borge Bakken, "Moral Panics, Crime Rates and Harsh Punishment in China," *Australian and New Zealand Journal of Criminology* 37 (2004): 67–89.

72. Ronald Weitzer, "The Social Construction of Sex Trafficking Ideology and Institutionalization of a Moral Crusade," *Politics and Society* 35 (2007): 447–475.

73. Lu, Miethe, and Liang, *China's Drug Practices and Policies,* chap. 6.

74. Niklas Swanström and Yin He, *China's War on Narcotics: Two Perspectives* (Washington, D.C.: Central Asia–Caucasus Institute & Silk Road Studies Program, 2006).

75. Bin Liang and Hong Lu, "Drug Issues and Problems in the Eyes of the Government on Behalf of the People: A Longitudinal and Content Analysis of All Drug-Related Reports in the *People's Daily,* 1948–2009" (paper presented at the Annual Conference of the Association of Chinese Professors of Social Sciences in the U.S., Harvard University, Cambridge, Mass., November 5–7, 2010).

76. Ibid.

77. Ibid.

78. Cao and Stack, "Exploring *Terra Incognita.*"

79. Liqun Cao and Velmer Burton Jr., "Spanning the Continents: Assessing the Turkish Public Confidence in the Police," *Policing: An International Journal of Police Strategies and Management* 29, no. 3 (2006): 451–463; Cao and Stack, "Exploring *Terra Incognita.*"

80. Gunter Bierbrauer, "Toward an Understanding of Legal Culture: Variations in Individualism and Collectivism between Kurds, Lebanese, and Germans," *Law & Society Review* 28 (1994): 243–264.

81. Kwok Leung, "Some Determinants of Reactions to Procedural Model for Conflict Resolution: A Cross-National Study," *Journal of Personality and Social Psychology* 53 (1987): 898–908.

82. Bierbrauer, "Toward an Understanding of Legal Culture"; Leung, "Some Determinants of Reactions to Procedural Model for Conflict Resolution."

83. Ronald Inglehart, *Culture Shift in Advanced Industrial Society* (Princeton: Princeton University Press, 1990).

84. Cao and Stack, "Societal Type and Attitude toward Prostitution."

85. Ibid.

86. Steven Stack, Amy Adamczyk, and Liqun Cao, "Survivalism and Public Opinion on Criminality: A Cross-National Analysis of Prostitution," *Social Forces* 88, no. 4 (2010): 1703–1726.

87. Cao, "Returning to Normality."

88. Robert F. Meier and Gilbert Geis, *Victimless Crime? Prostitution, Drugs, Homosexuality, Abortion* (Los Angeles: Roxbury, 1997).

89. Cao and Stack, "Exploring *Terra Incognita*"; K. Shannon, M. Rusch, J. Shoveller, D. Alexson, K. Gibson, and M. W. Tyndall, "Mapping Violence and Policing as an Environmental-Structural Barrier to Health Service and Syringe Availability among Substance-Using Women in Street-Level Sex Work," *International Journal of Drug Policy* 19 (2008): 140–147.

90. Cao and Stack, "Exploring *Terra Incognita*."

91. Emile Durkheim, *The Division of Labor in Society* (1893; repr., New York: Free Press, 1947); Inglehart, *Culture Shift in Advanced Industrial Society.*

Part Three

# Civil Liberties
# and Human Rights

# 9

# Legal Institution Building for the Rule of Law and Human Rights

## Yuchao Zhu

The human rights issue in China continues to be contentious. The issue can be examined in a context of, among other things, the reconstruction of China's legal system since the 1980s, and although the overall direction of legal reform has tended toward "the rule of law,"[1] if, or to what extent, China has built itself a "rule of law" society is still very debatable.[2] The Chinese government acknowledges serious problems of *youfa buyi* (having laws but not practicing them accordingly) and *zhifa buyan* (inadequate law enforcement).[3] Critics either claim that they do not trust China's legal system at all[4] or accuse the Chinese government of "abusing the rights according to the law."[5] But still, examination of its legal reform and law regimes has significant implications for the discussion of China's human rights.[6] This is largely because documentary law is most "explicit, codified, relatively stable, and resistant to the whim of individual leaders,"[7] and it can fundamentally decide the legal parameters for the relationship between citizens and the state, as well as between rights and power. All the relevant institutional or noninstitutional actors have to live within these legal parameters.

This chapter first describes and identifies the progress and deficiencies of China's legal reform relating to human rights protection, particularly through a brief examination of China's constitution, its criminal law, and its administrative law. Second, it appraises legal reform and its attribution to the rule of law and human rights in China. Third, it discusses the changing societal environment and political conditions that may influence or even determine legal institution building as an entrenched legal order for China's human rights.

## Legal Reform in Different Law Regimes

Since the early 1980s China has conducted fundamental legal reform through which the overall law regime has been reconstructed from the constitution as well as from criminal, civil, economic, and administrative law.[8]

As the essential law for a state, the constitution was the first law to be rewritten. Before 1982, the People's Republic of China (PRC) had three constitutions. The 1954 constitution followed the model of the Soviet Union's constitution and was comprehensive, but it contained some serious defects. The 1975 constitution and the 1978 constitution are highly problematic, and their constitutional value is minimal, mainly because of the negative influence of the Cultural Revolution. The current 1982 constitution, with its central theme of restoring the spirit of the 1954 constitution while stipulating a wide range of rights and freedoms, is designed mainly to serve China's most imperative goal: modernization.[9] There have been four important constitutional amendments since 1982. Overall, the 1988, 1993, 1999, and 2004 amendments confirm as constitutional the ideas and results of China's market-oriented economic reforms. These amendments have redefined the individual economic rights that can strengthen the legal stand for rights protection in general. The 1999 amendment added a significant article (5) regarding *yifazhiguo* (ruling the country in accordance with the law). The 2004 amendment is particularly committed to the principle of protection of public and private property, the rule of law, human rights, and constitutionalism.[10]

On the other hand, there is no provision to guarantee political and civil rights, and there exist very few restrictions on the state's arbitrary power. No real political structural change has been made as far as the constitution is concerned.[11] Thus, the current constitution, including its amendments, has some intrinsic deficiencies. For example, the scale of human rights protection is still limited. Although the constitution makes a general commitment to the protection of political, economic, cultural, and civil rights,[12] if we compare its provisions with what has been included in the international human rights regime, especially in the three international human rights treaties that China has already signed,[13] we find that a number of fundamental rights are still missing. These include workers' right to strike and to organize independent unions, and freedom of movement, thought, belief, opinion, and expression. In fact, some of these rights and freedoms appeared in former constitutions.[14] For instance, freedom of movement was written into the 1954 constitution, but with the establishment of the *hukou* system (residential registration system) in 1958, this right was subsequently removed. The *hukou* system discriminates against rural people and creates harsh segregation and inequality between rural and urban residents.[15]

There are in the constitution no provisions that provide remedies for citizens whose constitutional rights and freedoms are impaired or legal sanctions for violators.[16] Though the constitution makes a commitment to the general protection of rights and freedoms, it is also supplemented by restrictive provisions.[17] Obviously, the concept of rights in the constitution has strong imprints from China's legal tradition. For example, article 33 of the constitution proclaims that "every citizen is entitled to the rights and at the same time must perform the duties prescribed by the constitution and the law." It indicates that "the unity of rights and duties is a basic principle of China's legal system."[18] The constitution stresses citizens' obligations, not their rights, and even hints that the entitlement to rights depends on the fulfillment of obligations.[19] This adheres to China's legal tradition, under which such rights are not derived from the "inherent dignity" of being human or from "natural rights," but are granted from the political authority as "legal rights," or as "discretionary entitlements."[20] Logically, because rights are granted by authorities, they can be withdrawn as well.[21] Finally, because China is a country with written laws, the adoption of a constitution should be an important indication that "a significant change has taken place in the government or in society and that it is conceived to be long-lasting."[22] Thus, the constitution should be authoritative as well as stable, and it should contain a rigid amendment procedure. But such a function and status of the Chinese constitution have not yet been established. In the last fifty years, China has promulgated four constitutions and one constitutional "Common Program" and a number of amendments. Such elastic treatment toward the constitution demonstrates that it has often been utilized instrumentally and that the amendments have been made pragmatically. In essence, both the letter and spirit of the Chinese constitution remain extremely instrumentalist.[23] This has largely contributed to a shallow basis of constitutionalism and to citizens' low expectations of the constitution.

In China's legal system, criminal laws have always enjoyed a preeminent status. This is because, according to China's legal tradition, the purpose of a law is to maintain order through threat of punishment. From 1949 to 1979 the legal protection of rights by the criminal justice system was basically absent. Since the Criminal Law (CL) and the Criminal Procedure Law (CPL) were promulgated in 1979,[24] and especially after the 1996 CPL amendment and the 1997 CL amendment, protective mechanisms have been inserted into the criminal justice process. Particularly noteworthy is the formal confirmation of three basic principles in conformity with international legal standards, namely, "conviction and penalty according to law," "equality of everyone before the law," and "severity of penalty commensurate with the offender's crime and due criminal liabilities."[25] The new CPL not only formalizes and standardizes the criminal procedure but also identifies the judicial body's power of competence and the citizen's defense rights. Article 12 recognizes, though only implicitly, the "presumed innocent" principle in distinctive wording: "No one should be convicted guilty before the people's court passes a ruling according to law." Another publicized move in criminal justice was to replace the highly politicized crime of "counterrevolution" with a more common crime of "jeopardy of state security." Of course, though the title of this crime was changed, there are still several types of crimes that carry similarly serious weight and are always treated harshly.[26]

Some procedural justice elements have been introduced in an obvious attempt to conform to international standards. According to some studies, China's criminal justice system is moving away from the "inquisitorial" system toward a mix of "inquisitorial and adversarial" systems.[27] But criminal justice based on these two approaches still has inadequate appreciation of due process and procedural justice, and it contains very few remedial provisions specifying measurable legal consequences.[28] In this sense China still focuses more on substantive justice rather than procedural justice.[29] Defendants' rights have been enhanced and become an indispensable part of the criminal justice process, but there are still critical restrictions on defense lawyers when practicing these rights. For example, defense lawyers' participation in the criminal justice process, including their access to case information, is very much restricted when compared with the access available to prosecutors and police.[30] In terms of the temporary coercive measures to detain people before they are formally charged, both legal codes and practice lack protection rights and judicial recourse measures.[31] This is why in 2004 China's criminal justice regime made serious efforts to curb the number of cases of unlawful lengthy detention of suspects.[32] Also, while judicial independence is essential for fair and impartial adjudication of cases, this principle is largely compromised by the structures of China's court system, in which final decisions are made by the Chinese Communist Party (CCP), which dominates court adjudication committees, rather than the presiding court judges.[33] Because of the Party's interference in the adjudication process, some politically motivated or influenced trials continue to occur. In two of 2004's high-profile "economic crime" cases—Shanghai's Zhou Zhengyi and Guangzhou's *Nanfang dushibao* (Southern Metropolis Daily)—the disparate rulings, a light sentence and an unreasonably severe sentence, clearly reflected political interference in the trials.[34]

With respect to the most serious criminal justice punishment—the death sentence—the relevant provisions have increased.[35] The 1997 CL increased the number of "absolute" cases involving the death penalty and further decentralized the judicial procedure of death sentencing appeal.[36] Both these measures have increased the possibility of a death sentence. Though the attempt to expand the scale of the death sentence reflects the government's concerns about growing crime in China, this is certainly inconsistent with the worldwide trend to reduce or to eliminate the death sentence.[37] Finally, in spite of the fact that China has signed two key international human rights treaties, such principles as judicial independence, the right to remain silent as a protection against self-incrimination, and prohibition of double jeopardy, still do not truly exist in China.[38]

In short, the new CL and CPL have become relatively comprehensive, and in many aspects have become more adherent to international standards, as they have included more measures to protect rights, as well as some procedural justice elements.[39] On the other hand, the government's serious overemphasis of penalties reflects China's legal tradition, in which punishment is the core purpose of law, and punishment of crime is more important than protection of rights.[40] This also reflects the traditional view that the state's authority to maintain social order from which all people will benefit should always be preserved. These two laws clearly represent the government's intention to maintain political stability and social order. Guided by legal instrumentalism, they have perpetuated the tradition that the nation's collective interests transcend individual rights. Nevertheless,

China's criminal process has begun to move away from the old predominant "criminal control model" toward the "due process model."[41]

The most important aims of lawmaking in China's legal tradition are to control society and to regulate social behavior, not to define and protect individual rights. This idea is best illustrated in China's administrative laws. Before China began its current reforms, the state controlled the actions of society mainly through three mechanisms in which legal elements were largely minimal; first, the administrative management of such areas as the working unit (*danwei*) and the residential registration system (*hukou*); second, the governing CCP's political control through its organizational networks, which penetrate into almost every locality; and third, establishment of the official ideologies through propaganda and their unification functions.[42] All three mechanisms, however, have been seriously weakened since economic reforms began. As the fast-growing market economy has become increasingly diversified and localized, the state has found it necessary to decentralize and diminish its control. The administrative sources of government's power have been greatly reduced, which makes its totalitarian control over society unsustainable. Thus, there seems to be a reciprocal process in which the state retreats from its domination, and this is accompanied by the expansion of a pluralistic society. This happened first in nonpolitical areas, such as popular culture and social life, and has spread to other areas. One evident consequence is an improvement in people's economic, social, and cultural freedoms. In this process, a large part of government's administrative powers has been either transferred to local governments or replaced by other forms of control mechanisms. One new control mechanism is the administrative law regime.[43]

In the last twenty years, according to the constitution's article 89, the State Council, as the central administrative body, has been granted legislative competence and jurisdiction to enact administrative laws. Up until now, administrative laws and regulations have accounted for more than 60 percent of all laws and regulations in China.[44] The State Council alone has issued more than eight hundred administration rules and regulations. Among the five thousand local laws and regulations, those administrative ones have accounted for more than half. On the positive side, the entire administrative system has been rebuilt according to new rules, regulations, and laws; therefore it has become more regulative, transparent, and accountable. For instance, the Administrative Litigation Law, the Administrative Punishment Law, and the State Compensation Law have begun to provide citizens with judicial recourse when their rights are violated by the government's actions.[45] These new laws signal a significant judicial practice: people can sue the government for its wrongdoing, even though at the beginning this might have been merely symbolic. But at least it establishes the notion of judicial review of administrative acts and sets forth a starting point for further use of current law to check government power.[46] For example, the most recently enacted administrative law, the Administrative Permission Law, sets a legal restriction and judicial review mechanism on the government's administrative power to grant licenses and permissions. This new law is intended to restrain "rent-seeking" behavior by the government, a departure from China's long tradition of centralized power accountable to no one. These administrative laws have increasingly played a critical role "in curbing and rectifying unjust treatment of citizens by government officials" and in providing crucial judicial recourse to citizens.[47]

There are, however, some obvious flaws in the administrative law regime. For example, the regime's priority is to strengthen the government's governing capacity rather than to monitor and check its power. The main aim is to promote compliance by administrative agencies with substantive law rather than to establish procedural safeguards for persons subject to administrative decision making.[48] Thus, administrative laws are often made first in favor of responsible government agencies, rather than ordinary citizens. From content to procedure, administrative laws have inadequately taken into account public opinion or citizens' rights and instead are concerned primarily with improving effective management. Moreover, in administrative lawmaking, the lack of openness and transparency reflects the lack of procedural justice and the restriction of a citizen's right to information. Because of this, many practical rules and regulations that should protect rights turn out to restrict rights.[49] All these problems make it difficult to protect citizens' rights sufficiently against government misconduct.[50] In sum, these laws have not become reliable legal instruments that will enable ordinary citizens to defend themselves against government infringement of their rights.

Within the administrative law regime there have been two widely criticized measures in terms of violation of basic human rights—*laojiao* (Reeducation through Labor, or RTL) and *shourong qiansong* (the Custody and Repatriation Law, or C&R), which was abolished in 2003.[51] These are both lawlike coercive administrative measures.[52] The first legal source of RTL was the State Council's Decision on the Question of RTL in 1957. In 1979 the State Council decreed supplementary regulations regarding RTL, and in a 1980 document it combined forced-labor education and detention-investigation into the single practice of RTL. Then the Ministry of Public Security issued detailed instructions on how to enforce RTL, and the government, through various administrative regulations and judicial interpretations, provided formal rules, expanding RTL to cover a wide range of offenders, from minor "counterrevolutionary" and "anti-Party, antisocialist elements" to "drug dealers, prostitutes, people who sabotage railway transportation, and members of regressive sects." In total, there have been more than twenty relevant laws and regulations governing RTL enacted.[53]

As for the C&R, the first relevant legal document, the State Council's Decision on the Measures to Detain and Repatriate People Who Illegally Stay in Cities, was published in 1982, after which the Ministries of Civil Affairs and Public Security gave specific instructions on its implementation. The original purpose of the measure was not punishment but recourse. The State Council in 1991, however, greatly expanded the coverage of this regulation and particularly included those rural migrants living and working in cities without *sanzheng* (three certificates: a personal identification card, a temporary residential card, and a work permit). Many local authorities then created bylaws to regulate custody and repatriation activities, and especially to impose fines on detainees to enrich themselves. In the process of enforcement, a wide range of abuses occurred. The most highly publicized case happened in April 2003, when a newly graduated college student, Sun Zhigang, was beaten to death by security guards and inmates in Guangzhou's C&R facility, simply because he was not carrying his temporary residential card and quarreled with the police. This outrageous crime caused outcry, anger, and condemnation across China. Many news reports and legal commentaries expressed their severe criticism, targeting particularly the C&R and demanding a constitutional review and invalidation of it. After tremendous public criticism and pressure, the State Council, under the newly appointed premier Wen Jiabao, made a prompt decision to abolish the C&R in June 2003.[54]

There are severe problems regarding these two coercive measures within the administration law regime.[55] For example, the responsible administrative agencies that practice these measures often act arbitrarily, without necessary judicial authority or supervision, and they are widely criticized as loose cannons. Though RTL and C&R are not criminal justice measures, but merely administrative measures, in many ways the punishments meted out are just as severe as the punishments given to "normal" criminals. The cases are not managed according to criminal justice procedures, however; rather, they are managed exclusively by administrators at various levels of government. In reality, these are coercive measures intended to deprive persons of their freedom without due process, even though this freedom is clearly guaranteed in China's constitution. In short, the common problem of these two administrative measures is arbitrariness; they lack accountability, grant the responsible administrators excessive power, and provide no supervision of those administrators, and infringement of personal liberties is often the result.

Many legal scholars have pointed out that these two coercive administrative measures are legally invalid. According to China's Legislation Law and the Administrative Punishment Law, any coercive measures involving limitation or deprivation of personal liberty must be authorized by either the NPC or the NPC Standing Committee. Such coercive measures, however, are excluded from the list of authorized lawmaking for administrative bodies by the legislative institutions. In other words, these two coercive measures should not be decided by administrative bodies. They must be decided by the relevant authorities in legislative institutions. According to the Administrative Litigation Law, it is clear that administrative punishment measures should not include measures that deprive personal liberty. Thus, these two measures should be declared invalid because they are an inconsistent enactment of law.

Though its capacity to control has been considerably weakened, in areas where the government is most concerned, the government, rather than retreating, has actually strengthened its power by introducing administrative laws. This seems to reflect a certain ambivalence. That is, on the one hand, the government must accept the fact of diversified social interests and the pluralistic nature of society; on the other hand, the state is very reluctant to give up its control of areas it deems crucial for maintaining its power. The justification for this self-contradictory position is that the government must retain its strong capacity to promote economic growth and to preserve much-needed political stability and social order. Because of this strong conviction, the first reaction by the government to any potential challenge is to strengthen its control and management capacity, mainly using convenient administrative mechanisms. For instance, to meet challenges from the increasingly powerful Internet, the government has made a set of regulations, using primarily administrative means, to manage and to control news reports and communications through the Internet. If people read them carefully, they will find that most articles in the regulations are restrictions and administrative punishment measures, and they neither provide management's responsibilities nor indicate any administrative remedies for violations of people's relevant rights.[56]

There is no doubt that the state's control over society has been reduced in many key areas. For example, China's *hukou* segregation system is a violation of people's freedom of movement, right to employment, and right to education, and it is clearly against the equality principle in China's constitution. Because of the development of the market economy, millions of migrant workers have moved from rural areas to China's coastal urban centers looking for jobs. That has fundamentally restructured China's labor market and presented an acute challenge to *hukou* segregation. The government has to gradually relax its control and allow some rural people to migrate to cities.[57] Some NPC deputies propose a constitutional amendment to reinstate the "mobility right."[58]

In all, the positive aspect of the law regime I have examined is that "the shift away from policy-making by Party edict to increasing the 'rule of law' means the Party-State's rules for social behavior are clearer and more predictable and may even herald the beginning of a contractual state-society relationship."[59] As Murray Scot Tanner notes, "Economic structural reform has eroded the underpinnings of CCP economic control over low levels of governments and society, [and] the institutional transformation of lawmaking politics is leading to a more far-reaching, potentially liberalizing change."[60] Though the state's control over society is still intrusive, the new legal regime has begun to provide more rights protection, and this, along with the gradual decline of the state's power, is leading to a greater awareness of rights in society. It is thus evident that two of the main branches of China's substantive law, criminal and administrative, now conform more to international legal practices.

## A Preliminary Assessment of the Legal Reform

Since the 1980s, because of an increasingly supportive environment for legal reform in Chinese society as a whole, people's awareness and consciousness of their rights, the idea of using legal means to protect those rights, and jurisprudence studies of rights have all made significant progress. This progress has had a very consequential effect on China's law regimes and the state. Two interesting but somewhat contradictory trends can be observed: separation of law and the state, and "bringing the state back in" to reinforce a new rule of law.[61] The former trend is to restrain the state's power and the latter is to press the state to use its power to pursue justice.[62] Both trends appear to serve the purpose of promoting rights vis-à-vis the state, albeit from different perspectives.

In terms of economic development, reduction of poverty, and expansion of citizens' economic, social, and cultural freedoms, China's improvements during the last twenty years or more have been impressive. Because the government has made economic development its highest policy priority, economic lawmaking has become the major component of China's new legislative activities. As the government tends to make sure new laws do not harm the state's authority and social stability, and especially do not weaken its capacity to promote economic growth, human rights protection has been subordinated to the government's economic agenda. Beyond remarkable economic growth, however, a widening income gap and rising inequality, as well as corruption in Chinese society, have become very serious. Thus, economic laws have to be supplemented with rights protection measures for social justice purposes. Since the mid-1990s more protective laws have been legislated, particularly concerning the protection of specially targeted groups such as women, minors, the handicapped, and elders. As Ronald Keith and Lin Zhiqiu observe, "The new generation of rights legislation offered moral and legally derived assurances of state remedy against the vicissitudes of the changing market place."[63] In the area of civil and political rights, however, the lack of protective measures remains conspicuous. One reason is that the advancement of those rights might be attained as a result of institutional restrictions on the state's power, which government is unwilling to relinquish. Though government believes that the state is the critical instrument for the promotion of rights, it is reluctant to acknowledge that the state could equally be a violator of rights.

Nevertheless, China's legal reform is moving toward establishing a comprehensive legal system. Regarding the establishment of the foundation for human rights protection, both achievements and deficiencies are evident. Also, individual discretion rather than the practice of rule of law is still the most common phenomenon in the area of human rights improvement. The outcome of abolition of the C&R in 2003 is a good example of this phenomenon.[64] Although having received many proposals from China's legal scholars demanding that the NPC initiate a constitutional review of the C&R, the State Council instead pursued a convenient administrative self-review mechanism and abolished this notorious law rather than allowing the NPC, as the highest legislative body, to play a constitutional review role. In many legal scholars' opinions, the NPC's "no action" in this case missed an excellent opportunity to start adjudication of the constitution in China, which is what the process of legal reform really needs.[65]

The general criteria for assessing a legal system are the following: proper procedure; transparency; public, readily accessible law; and citizens' awareness of law. Using these criteria, Randall Peerenboom's research revealed many problems, such as excessively generalized and vague laws, omissions, undefined terms, inconsistencies, and lack of practical experience. Thus, he believes, certain measures must be taken, including steady change, improving consistency, fair application of laws, due process, conformity of laws, and normative acceptability of law.[66]

Nevertheless, the root cause of the rights protection problem is still within China's legal system. First, the constitution should provide sufficient rights protections, but so far it has failed to do so. There is no special human rights charter in the constitution, and with respect to the existing rights protection articles, there has been no adjudication of the constitution. Also, the constitution must have the highest authoritative legal status and be absolutely respected. But because of the domination of legal instrumentalism, the constitution and its pragmatic amendments have failed to achieve such status. Though pressed by many legal scholars, China has not yet decided to establish a constitutional court and an adjudication mechanism to curb unconstitutional activities.

Second, the constitution only presents a list of citizens' rights and freedoms, but adequate practical mechanisms are needed to truly realize them. For example, though the constitution guarantees citizens' freedom of speech, expression, and association, those freedoms are not precisely defined and concretely protected, and some of them have been eliminated by legislation. Though the constitution guarantees freedom of association, the Trade Union Law does not permit workers to organize independent trade unions other than to join the All China Federation of Trade Unions (ACFTU). In fact, China entered a reservation in its ratification of the International Covenant on Economic, Social and Cultural Rights (ICESCR) on the issue of allowing independent trade unions. China's Social Organization Management Regulation (chapter 13, article 2) actually eliminates citizens' right to join a political party other than the Communist

Party and eight so-called democratic parties. There are no laws guaranteeing freedom of the press and no laws ensuring political participation and organization, so the related rights in these areas have not materialized. Moreover, many practical laws and regulations have control and management rather than protective functions.

Third, legislative practice has certain serious defects; for example, there has been a lack of clear procedural standards and legislative competence. The whole legislative system has had various issues of unclear boundaries of authority, allowing action without a clear basis of authority, and competing and conflicting norms.[67] Even the Legislation Law itself has some unconstitutional elements. Because the NPC grants legislative power to the administrative bodies, the administrative law regime is seen as accumulating too much legislative power.[68] Moreover, effective judicial review mechanisms are not really established, and even when there are reviews, many of them are internal reviews with no supervision and no accountability; therefore, these mechanisms have difficulties functioning properly. China's legislative authority has no actual authority to invalidate substantive laws or regulations if they are inconsistent or contrary to the constitution. The example of the abolition of the C&R demonstrated this problem.

All these problems are caused mainly by the dominant legislative ideas in China, namely, instrumentalism, elite determinism, experimentalism, and an economic-centered approach.[69] These ideas have in various ways determined the conduct of lawmaking, resulting in a multitude of complications; in some cases they may promote rights, but in other cases they may perpetuate the obstruction of rights.

Moreover, one very important characteristic of China's legal reform is an "adaptation" effort to conform to international standards.[70] For example, the Administration Litigation Law, the State Compensation Law, public inquiry practice, and the three key principles in the CL and the CPL were all introduced because of this conscious effort.[71] As Daniel Chow's study finds, in China's legal system the aspect most consistent with modern international practice is "the enactment of new or revised codes of procedure for criminal, civil and administrative cases, along with codes for non-litigation methods of dispute settlement through mediation and arbitration."[72] Particularly in China's drive to enter the World Trade Organization (WTO), many existing laws and regulations have been sorted out, rewritten, amended, or abolished in order to meet the WTO legal standard. This is an emulating activity of institution building, but the major driving force is the market economy and the need for international economic integration. The adaptation effort is best exemplified in the area of the economic and civil law regime.[73] One popular slogan, *jiegui* (connecting rail), illustrates this conscious attempt that puts pressure on the government to make a structural change to meet the requirement of the WTO and other international institutions, including the international human rights community. The implications of this adaptation effort are extremely significant: it has not only changed laws but also altered "the ideas of laws." For example, the old idea of "absolute state sovereignty" is gradually being replaced by the view of "relative state sovereignty," and the statist idea is being replaced by the more cosmopolitan view of lawmaking.[74] Also, under international legal standards, human rights are part of the customary international laws.[75] This poses a keen challenge to China because the Chinese government has difficulty justifying lawmaking activity that only partially or selectively conforms with international law. Beijing has begun to realize that if its policies and laws are not in conformity with all the international standards, its economic reform and opening-up policies are not sustainable.[76] This acknowledgment in turn helps increase awareness of rights and promotes the rule of law in society. Its influence has spread from the economic legal order to the human rights area.

In brief, this is an emerging legal system with Chinese characteristics. The progress and deficiencies are self-evident. In this system the tradition that duties are more important than rights, and punishment is more important than protection, remains strong. The government's control over society through administrative law mechanisms remains potent, although it is constantly being challenged. The adaptation of international legal standards has become a trend, but more attempts have been made in economic lawmaking than in other areas. The two principles of constitutionalism, the protection of rights and the restriction of government's arbitrary power, are still weak.

How does this legal order reveal the situation of human rights in China? The Chinese government's declared human rights principles have some key premises. The government emphasizes the right of subsistence and the right of development; it emphasizes state sovereignty and rejects human rights intervention; it stresses the collective interest over individual interest; it addresses the unity between rights and duties between state interest and individual interest; and it claims economic and social rights are just as important as civil and political rights.[77] From what I have observed, present legal reform mostly reflects these principles, and the improvements and deficiencies are equally evident.

These characteristics have been influenced by China's legal and political transition. Zhang Jinfan simplifies China's modern legal system transition and rebuilding since the late Qing dynasty in the following expression: from divine emperor to constitutional monarchy and finally to republicanism; from the rule of man to the rule of law; from the duty-centered approach to the rights-centered approach; from integrated judicial administration to separation of judicial from administration and finally to judicial independence; from criminal law as a core to a multisection-law integrated legal system. This fundamental transition occurred after 1979. However, China still has a long way to go to accomplish the final goal—rule of law, human rights, and constitutionalism.[78]

## Institution Building toward Rights Protection Based on the Rule of Law

In recent years many Chinese scholars have begun to argue that in order to further promote human rights in China, its legal system must be completely rebuilt. Starting with the constitution, necessary monitoring, supervising, and judicial review mechanisms need to be established to restrict the state's arbitrary power. Scholars propose that only in so doing will a genuine rule-of-law society be established and human rights be fully protected.[79]

Surely, a successful lawmaking scheme does not necessarily bring the realization of the rule of law to the society as a whole. The authoritative status of laws depends largely on society's acceptance of the letter and spirit of the legal documents and their consistency with the dominant values and mores in society. The promising prospect is that the current protection of rights from the existing legal order has already heightened people's consciousness of rights, and Chinese society has begun to press the state in this regard. In recent years, at least four types of human rights promotion and protection activities have surfaced: (1) dissent groups, including political dissidents, environmentalists, and public health advocacy groups such as *Aizhi* (to battle AIDs); (2) news media groups, including some civil society–type liberal news media; (3) citizens' open-petition activities, including a collective call for removal of some corrupt local officials and some ad hoc protests; and (4) collectively or individually signed open letters to domestic and foreign news media on imperative issues, such as Dr. Jiang Yanyong's 2003 letter to expose the Severe Acquired Respiratory Syndrome (SARS) crisis in Beijing and his 2004 letter to demand a change in the official verdict of the June 4, 1989, tragedy in Tiananmen Square.[80] Having to face these kinds of human rights–oriented social movements, which forcefully represent the emergence of "rights and interests fundamentalism,"[81] the state can no longer authoritatively "guide" social values and mores but instead must be more responsive, influenced, or even formulated by them. Therefore, rights-centered legal ideas and practices are becoming part of everyone's consciousness and social reality.

Yet the idea of instrumental function of law is still deeply rooted in China's legal tradition, under which political authority and moral norms must take primacy over the legal protection of individuals. The continuing discussion and debate about *fazhi,* especially in the last few years, clearly reflect the battle over this instrumentalist legal tradition.[82] From 1996 on, *fazhi* as "the rule of law" has been recognized as the guiding principle of legal reform.[83] It is realized that for the state, "in its instrumental form, law facilitates domination, but does not legitimate it."[84] In fact, as long as the instrumentalist view is still dominant, the real legal legitimation of political power and the legal system is difficult to attain. Here, according to Edward Epstein, "legal legitimation means the exercise of political power justified on the basis of legal authority created with relatively autonomous legal institutions by the ideological functional law."[85] Thus, more demands for legal legitimation have been made.

The most important problem now is that what the Chinese state is doing to deal with demands has seemingly created a bottleneck, as the state itself is unable to continue to legitimize its authority through traditional ways. Any further breakthrough will require a systematic change. Basically, there are two complementary tasks. One is a complete rebuilding of the legal system, within which, in order to resolve the legitimacy issue, a fundamental political change such as democratization must be accomplished. The other task is to depart from the Chinese legal tradition, especially in establishing a rights-centered legal system. Obviously, from what one can observe, it is difficult to imagine either one of the tasks being accomplished smoothly in the near future. In terms of general obstacles, the "path-dependent" nature of reforms determines the difficulties in building a new legal order. According to Peerenboom, "Tradition and culture, corruption, regionalism, the absence of a vigorous civil society, and China's unfinished economic transition are among the most important factors shaping, and in some cases limiting, legal reforms."[86]

On the basis of the analysis above, I suggest that China's current legal system should be strengthened, particularly in the area of rule of law and rights protection, making it a real institutional entity with independent legal and political status.[87] This institution should contain some crucial elements, not only of the legal regime but also of the agents or institutional players who are responsible and capable of building such a new legal order. This is why the growth of China's lawmaking organs, especially the rise of the NPC as the legislative body, often has had powerful, unintended institutional implications.[88] In fact, the pressure for change has come less from the laws themselves than from the growth of the institutional structures that have been built to draft, interpret, and implement the laws.[89] Other key agents include legal scholars and the jurisprudence community, which have become extremely assertive in pressing for change.

How is this suggested institution building a viable option? It is true that legal regime building in China has been directed mainly at economic reform, and rights protection has been only a secondary goal. For the government, the idea of rule of law is mostly about better governing rather than checking itself. But it is worth contemplating newly emerged favorable conditions that could make such legal institution building succeed.

From the societal perspective, the development of a rights-oriented, open, and pluralistic society justifies the effort to fulfill various rights protection demands. Therefore, society as a whole begins to accept "rights and interests fundamentalism."[90] Particularly noticeable is that several important rights-related events since 2003 have set a much more favorable environment for further legal reform to promote human rights protection: the 2004 constitutional amendment; the outbreak of SARS, which not only revealed China's public health crisis but also pressed the government to be more transparent and responsible; Sun Zhigang's death and the subsequent abolition of the C&R; China's entering the WTO and its repercussions; and the various grassroots protests, including peasants' spontaneous protest over an unfair and unbearable tax, migrant labor's protest over unpaid salaries, and local residents' protests over relocation compensation scandals. Against this social background, *renquan* (human rights) and *weiquan* (human rights protection) have increasingly become the key words for social justice and fairness, denoting a potentially broader and more powerful human rights movement.[91]

From the perspective of legal professionals and scholars, more independent, competent, and conscientious jurists have actively participated in the legal reform and social justice effort. For example, two important unofficial conferences to discuss constitutional amendments were held in Beijing (June 5, 2003) and Qingdao (June 19–20, 2003) before the NPC Special Session on the constitutional amendment was held. Many of China's top political scientists, economists, and legal scholars attended those conferences and made their proposals for constitutional amendments to the public. Some well-known legal scholars were also invited by the CCP and NPC Constitutional Amendment Committee to contribute their opinions. Some constitutional specialists, such as Cao Siyuan, presented a comprehensive view of constitutional amendments. Obviously, China's jurisprudence community has established its status with authoritative opinions and has begun to be involved actively in high-level lawmaking and legal reform affairs. Because of this dynamic legal reform environment, we can expect a more autonomous legal system that should greatly promote the ideal of rule of law and therefore a relatively independent legal order.[92]

The government recognizes, because of the decentralization of power and state-promoted, top-down structural changes, the growing importance of various institutions for rule making and administration.[93] Gradually, the state has begun to recognize that, as Tanner observes, "in order to lure low-cost, voluntary mass compliance with its policies, it must increasingly submit to being voluntarily bound by its own legal rules and must consult a broader array of social interests in making those rules."[94] Within China's official legal community and legislative bodies, more autonomous functions are strongly demanded,[95] and institutional assertiveness (of those such as the NPC and the jurisprudence community) becomes very compelling.[96] What is emerging is the ideological power of law, which explains voluntary submission to the law as well as other institutions of social control.[97] Of course, regarding the two major aspects of the concept of an autonomous legal order, law as a restraint to government power and law as formal and procedural justice, China is still far from the establishment of order and balance.[98] Even among the ruling elite, concerns about the "legitimacy deficit" are growing.[99] As the old practice of arbitrary, unpredictable, and highly secretive policy making now carries with it enormous costs, many individual leaders have begun to express their desire for more predictable and procedural politics; therefore, they have become less opposed to such institution building.[100] Among the high-ranking Party leaders, the view that the Party should operate within the limits of the constitution has been increasingly recognized. In practice, many of the Party's traditional mechanisms for internal administration have been shown to be inconsistent with the constitution and have caused problems. For example, the debate on the constitutionality of *shuanggui* as the Party's disciplinary measure continues within the Party and the jurisprudence community.[101]

Nevertheless, it seems that all the major forces that could influence the process and result in rebuilding the legal system have an impulse in that direction, albeit to different extents. In other words, the legal reform that will contribute to the formation of the legal regime's independent status is increasingly supported by China's changing and increasingly favorable political, economic, and social environments.

Moreover, an institutionalist perspective can fortify the chance of success under China's conditions, in which state-sanctioned legal reform is always constrained by the government according to its perceived interests and priorities. During institutional change, if an institution becomes salient, the original intention the state had in creating it may gradually lose its meaning, and the new institutional entity can thereby develop its own intrinsic coherence and power. When the legal institution reaches a relatively independent status, the legal foundation for rights protection will be accepted by the society as a whole. By then the government's preference, if it is not consistent with rights-centered ideas, will be rejected by society. Only then can the legal regime provide real human rights protection. As Pitman Potter observes, "The operation of law is subject to evolution and challenge by reference to external standards: once a principle of law is enunciated it becomes part of the public domain and open to uses that the regime may not be able to control."[102]

There are examples of how a shift in the socioeconomic or political context can cause certain previously latent institutions to become salient. In the process, the meanings and functions of institutions are shaped by features of the socioeconomic and political context in which they are embedded; but at the same time they also constrain and shape political strategies and behavior. Sven Steinmo and his colleagues note: "People fight about both institutions and policy outcomes. Battles over institutions are important precisely because broad policy paths can follow from institutional choice."[103] In return, institutional choice can shape people's ideas, attitudes, and preferences.[104] Obviously, the interplay between institution building and the changing socioeconomic context is critical. In China, because of the increasingly favorable socioeconomic and political conditions, it is likely that the new legal regime will be based on human rights principles and treat individuals as rights-bearing entities. Laws that formulate the legal order therefore would serve "an education function" to deliberately set out "new benchmarks for behavior appropriate to the values of society and social justice."[105] Tanner asserts that "the emergence of the legislative system may be pushing China toward an 'inadvertent' transformation."[106] This would have important international implications. As Mahmood Monshipouri and Claude E. Welch claim, "The most effective way to protect human rights in a transnational political context is to facilitate the creation of a culture of law—that is, strengthening local and national mechanisms of legal accountability."[107]

In practical terms, the constitution must provide more comprehensive and systematic elements of the rule of law for rights protection. This is because if there is no enforcement machinery consisting of remedial rules, specific legal sanctions, and established procedures, the rights guaranteed by the constitution will still be difficult to be realized.[108] Also, the highest legal status of the constitution should be confirmed institutionally by, for example, setting up an effective constitutional court. For criminal justice, a more balanced and consistent approach should be taken, and a protective function should be incorporated into punishment functions. And though a qualified respect of the state's capacity to promote economic growth and social development should be maintained, the legal recognition of diversified social interests, decentralization and transparency of administrative power, and comprehensive protection of rights should become the central ideas of the administrative laws.

Moreover, it should be noted that many problems of rights protection could be resolved within the current legal system, such as RTL and mobility rights. People should not lose sight of, or become too cynical about, the prospect for China's human rights simply because the Chinese legal tradition does not provide "natural rights" or the constitution and laws have a wide range of unbalanced rights protections. In fact, decent protection of human rights might not necessarily require a radical approach to legislation and lawmaking. A prudent or even conservative treatment of the current legal system may be a better, more practical way of promoting human rights in China. One reason is that we have to acknowledge that ending abuses of human rights in China and creating effective protections for rights require various interventions, since rights violations are often complex and not perpetrated solely by the state. In other words, many human rights abuses in today's China are, as Ann Kent asserts, "the result of discrepancies between domestic laws, some of which have been amended in progressive ways, and their practical implementation, not the result of ignorance of international law and criminal procedures in civil and common law."[109] Therefore, achieving the aim of promoting human rights also depends on the long-term process of heightening awareness of human rights among the general population and the development of a domestic human rights movement that will benefit from the continued building of the current legal regime.[110] Most agree that it is impossible to have a comprehensive and institutionalized legal order with a high degree of authority when the law is neither "autonomous" nor "supreme" but is used only as an instrument of the Party's rule.[111] The bottom line, however, is that institution building could promote change of the state political structure. In the short run, it is likely, as Tanner remarks, that "such a state would still be authoritarian and imposed by the Party-state on society rather than contractual. But it would also be far more predictable, procedurally less arbitrary, and would involve greatly increased consultation both with the Party elite and between the Party-state and society."[112]

## CONCLUSION

Generally speaking, China's traditional view of human rights is that rights are not derived from human nature but are granted by the state, are united with duties, and are contingent on society's level of development and historical and cultural traditions. These views are different from conventional views in the West. Just as the original sources of rights, the nature of rights, and main sources of rights abuse are seen differently, so too is the way to promote and protect rights. How the state's responsibility is defined and how the infringement of rights is judged also differ. For one thing, international human rights organizations usually treat the state as the major source of rights violations, but China often regards the state as the foremost instrument in the promotion of rights. Both views have some validity, and throughout modern history in this area, the state indeed has been schizophrenic.

A proper perspective can provide a better overview of human rights in China. It is hoped that the description of China's legal reform in this chapter can help us reach a better understanding of China's legal system for human rights. Growing awareness and consciousness about rights in Chinese society, frank criticism, bold proposals made by legal professionals and scholars, journalists, and legislators, and the development of legal institutions will begin to supply a fertile soil for the spread of "the spirit of rights" in China, and its definition of human rights in the future will still have its own characteristics. From an institutionalist perspective, a primary goal might be, according to Yuanyuan Shen, to "build a legitimate order, a legal system with a high degree of predictability, and an enforcement machine sufficient to offset official arbitrariness without sacrificing attention to social welfare and equalities."[113] To establish this, Ronald Keith and Lin Zhiqiu, argue, "rights would be comprehensively enjoyed on the basis of appropriate principles of justice."[114] It is my belief that continued legal institution building will assist in fulfilling that principle.

## NOTES

1. On China's view of "the rule of law," particularly see Ronald C. Keith, *China's Struggle for the Rule of Law* (New York: St. Martin's Press, 1994); Randall Peerenboom, *China's Long March toward Rule of Law* (Cambridge: Cambridge University Press, 2002); Yuanyuan Shen, "Conceptions and Receptions of Legality," in *The Limits of the Rule of Law in China,* ed. Karen G. Turner, James V. Feinerman, and R. Kent Guy (Seattle: University of Washington Press, 2000), 20–44.

2. For example, Peerenboom claims that China's legal reform is most likely to build a "thin" rule of law society. Peerenboom, *China's Long March toward Rule of Law,* 6. Also see Shen, "Conceptions and Receptions of Legality," 24; Keith, *China's Struggle for the Rule of Law,* 7–8; Ronald C. Keith and Zhiqiu Lin, *Law and Justice in China's New Marketplace* (New York: Palgrave, 2001), 27–29.

3. See Zhu Rongji, "Report to the National People's Congress," March 5, 2002, http://www.hprc.org.cn/wxzl/wxysl/lczf/dishiyijie_2/200908/t20090818_27744 html (accessed July 17, 2012); some Western scholars also emphasize that the central problem is the gap between the law as written and the law as implemented in practice. See Daniel C. K. Chow, *The Legal System of the People's Republic of China* (St. Paul: Thomson West, 2003), 61–66.

4. Stanley Lubman claims that China does not have a real legal system because China continues to lack a unifying concept of law as a result of instrumentalist approaches to law and the fundamental reluctance of the Party to tolerate any significant diminution of its authority. Stanley B. Lubman, *Bird in a Cage: Legal Reform in China after Mao* (Stanford: Stanford University Press, 1999), 3, 317.

5. "Abusing Rights according to the Law," *China Rights Forum* (Winter 1999–2000), www.hrichina.org/what-we-do/research-and-publications/publication-list (accessed July 17, 2012).

6. Keith finds that "the Chinese human rights debate is entwined with the ongoing internal discussion of the rule of law. The domestic issue of the conceptualization and materialization of human rights has been centrally located within the contradiction of the rule of law and rule of man." Keith, *China's Struggle for the Rule of Law*, 54; Peerenboom, *China's Long March toward Rule of Law*, 515.

7. Murray Scot Tanner, *The Politics of Lawmaking in Post-Mao China: Institutions, Processes and Democratic Prospects* (New York: Oxford University Press, 1999), 25.

8. Regarding China's legal system and legal reform, see particularly Chow, *The Legal System of the People's Republic of China*, and Peerenboom, *China's Long March toward Rule of Law*.

9. According to a well-known Chinese legal scholar, Yu Haocheng, all four Chinese constitutions are modeled on the Soviet Union's constitution. Yu points out seven major problems in this model: (1) no separation between the Communist Party and the government, which leads to "rule of the Party," not "rule of law"; (2) proletarian dictatorship; (3) a Marxist-Leninist view of law and rights, whereby rights are not natural but granted by the state; (4) no principle of separation of powers—rather, the concentration of power; (5) provision of a list of rights and freedoms without concrete articles to uphold those rights and freedoms; (6) no independent judiciary; and (7) no judicial review mechanism. See Yu Haocheng, "Zhongguo xianzheng gaige de qianjing" (The Prospect of China's Constitutional Reform), *Modern China Studies*, no. 1 (1997): 107–117.

10. Meng Yan, "Experts: Laws Must Specify Rights," www.chinadaily.com.cn/english/doc/2004-03/31/content_319310.htm (accessed June 29, 2012).

11. It is worth noting that the exact wording regarding rights in this constitution is specifically *gongmin quanli* (citizens' rights), not the general term *renquan* (human rights). Keith claims that this noticeably different usage implies a lack of formal constitutional reference to human rights. But this attitude might be consistent with China's once-dominant ideology about law, which stresses the class nature of society and claims that any abstract concept of "human rights" is misleading. The class view of law has been basically abandoned. See Keith, *China's Struggle for the Rule of Law*, 66; Lubman, *Bird in a Cage*, 42; Ji Weidong, "Zhongguo xianzheng gaige de tujing yu caichanquan wenti" (The Path of China's Constitutional Reform and the Right to Property), *Modern China Studies*, no. 3 (1999): 26–31.

12. Chow, *The Legal System of the People's Republic of China*, 69.

13. The three international human rights treaties are the Universal Declaration of Human Rights (UDHR), the International Covenant on Civil and Political Rights (ICCPR), and the International Covenant on Economic, Social and Cultural Rights (ICESCR).

14. For example, the 1982 constitution removed the right to strike. The reason given was that workers are the masters of the state and their interests are identical with the state's, so a strike is not in the interests of both workers and the state. See

Zhang Youyu, "Guanyu xiugai xianfa de jige wenti" (A Few Questions about the Constitutional Amendment), in *Xianfa lunwenji* (Collection of Discussions on the Constitution) (Beijing: Mass Press, 1982), 14. In China's Trade Union Law, which was promulgated on October 27, 2001, the right to strike is absent.

15. See Yu Depeng, "Nongmin fudan wenti de shehui he falü fenxi" (A Social and Legal Analysis of Peasants' Burdens and Other Problems), *Twenty-first Century* (Hong Kong), no. 2 (2001): 132–134. Moreover, the 1958 *Hukou* regulation proclaimed by the National People's Congress (NPC) Standing Committee attached some constraints that deepened inequality in the areas of education, employment, social security, and even political rights. For example, in China's current Electoral Law, article 16, the quota of the NPC deputies is determined in a ratio of one deputy from rural areas for every four deputies from urban areas. Thus, rural people's right to select their deputies in the national legislative body is worth only one quarter of urban people's. It is clearly a violation of the right to political equality, which is confirmed in the constitution.

16. Shen, "Conceptions and Receptions of Legality," 33.

17. For example, on the one hand the constitution guarantees the freedom of religion, but on the other hand it demands in the preamble that people behave under "the guidance of Marxism-Leninism and Mao Zedong Thought," and in the General Principle it demands that people receive "dialectical and historical materialism education" (article 24). The constitution says that all power belongs to the people (article 2), but the preamble actually deprives citizens of their rights to choose different social systems and governing parties by virtue of the four cardinal principles (upholding Marxism-Leninism-Mao Zedong Thought, upholding the leadership of the Chinese Communist Party, upholding the people's democratic dictatorship, and upholding the leading role of socialism). And it claims in the General Principles that "disruption of the socialist system by any organization or individual is prohibited" (article 1). The Chinese legal scholar Du Gangjian frankly states that the so-called four cardinal principles in the preamble to the constitution might be a reasonable requirement for the members of a political party, but treating these principles as the guideline for all the citizens is against the international human rights standard, to say the least. See Du Gangjian, "Yirenquan zhunze zhiguo yu xinguojia zhexue" (Rule the Country according to Human Rights Principles and New National Philosophy) www.china001.com/show_hdr.php?xname=PPDDMV0&dname=EAU3V31&xpos=5 (accessed July 17, 2012); Chow, *The Legal System of the People's Republic of China,* 69.

18. State Council Information Office, *White Papers of the Chinese Government* (Beijing: Foreign Language Press, 1991).

19. Keith, *China's Struggle for the Rule of Law,* 69.

20. As I mentioned previously, not all legal scholars in China agree with this official view. For example, Li Buyun uses Western liberal democratic concepts to define human rights; see ibid., 55. Also see Wang Jiafu, Liu Hainian, and Li Lin,

eds., *Renquan yu ershiyi shiji* (Human Rights and the Twenty-first Century) (Beijing: Chinese Legal System Press, 2000), 50–55.

21. Andrew J. Nathan, *Chinese Democracy* (New York: A. A. Knopf, 1985), 113; Chow, *The Legal System of the People's Republic of China,* 107.

22. William C. Jones, "The Constitution of the People's Republic of China," *Washington University Law Quarterly* 63 (1985): 712.

23. Regarding instrumentalism in China's legal tradition, see Edward J. Epstein, "Law and Legitimation in Post-Mao China," in *Domestic Law Reforms in Post-Mao China,* ed. Pitman B. Potter (Armonk, N.Y.: M. E. Sharpe, 1994), 22–24; also Chen Duanhong, "Lifa de minzhu hefaxing yu lifazhishang: Zhongguo lifa piping" (The Democratic Legitimacy of Legislation and Lawmaking and the Legislation Frenzy: A Critique of China's Legislation and Lawmaking), *Zhongwai faxue* (Chinese and Foreign Jurisprudence), no. 6 (1998): 59–69.

24. For an analysis of these two laws and their progress and deficiencies, see particularly Donald C. Clarke and James V. Feinerman, "Antagonistic Contradictions: Criminal Law and Human Rights in China," in *China's Legal Reforms,* ed. Stanley B. Lubman (New York: Oxford University Press, 1996), 135–154; Keith and Lin, *Law and Justice in China's New Marketplace,* chap. 5; Lubman, *Bird in a Cage,* 160–172; also see Human Rights in China (HRIC), "Empty Promises: Human Rights Protections and China's Criminal Procedure Law in Practice," March 2001, www.hrichina.org/crf/article/4565 (accessed July 17, 2012).

25. It should be noted that these three principles are not really new to China's legal system. They were already included in the New Criminal Law of the Qing Dynasty in the early twentieth century, and in the Criminal Law of the Republic of China. Between 1949 and the 1990s, the three principles were absent. See Yuan Weishi, "Xingfa de bianqian yu ershishiji zhongguo wenhua de ruogan wenti" (The Evolution of the Criminal Law and a Few Questions about Chinese Culture in the Twentieth Century) (1998), www.confucius2000.com/poetry/xfbqy20wh.htm (accessed July 17, 2012).

26. For example, "subversion" and the lesser crime of "stealing state secrets" are also serious charges. But the concept of "state secrets" is very elastic. In the last decade, a few "spy" charges, such as those against Song Yongyi, Li Shaomin, Xu Zerong, and Gao Zhan, showed that there was no clear and consistent definition of what constitutes "state secrets." See, e.g., www.hrichina.org/sites/default/files/oldsite/PDFs/Reports/HRIC-HRW_Gao-Yu-1995.pdf or www.cnd.org/HXWZ/ZK00/zk206-2.hz8.html (accessed July 17, 2012).

27. According to these studies, the inquisitorial system focuses on maintaining social order and punishing criminals, and the adversarial system stresses protection of social equality, individual rights, and the control of state power. See Peter Liu and Yingyi Situ, "Mixing Inquisitorial and Adversarial Models: Changes in Criminal Procedure in a Changing China," in *Crime and Social Control in a Changing China,* ed. Jianhong Liu, Lening Zhang, and Steven F. Messner (Westport, Conn.: Greenwood Press, 2001), 144–145.

28. Shen, "Conceptions and Receptions of Legality," 32–33; according to Clarke and Feinerman, "Antagonistic Contradictions," "the CL is as much a political text as a legal one." So "its drafters were concerned with providing a legal basis for state action, not with worries about due process, and it was designed to be used by judicial and public security cadres with a low education level" (138–139).

29. Clarke and Feinerman, "Antagonistic Contradictions," 138. In China more and more advocacy of procedural justice was heard in the first decade of this century; one example is Liu Jinyou, "Jianlun chengxu bi shiti geng zhongyao" (On Procedure Being More Important Than Substance), *Fazhiribao* (Legal Daily), February 18, 2002.

30. The CPL's article 37 indicates that a defense lawyer's investigating, collecting evidence, and interviewing a witness must be agreed on by the court and People's Procurators; compare that with article 45, which grants the state's law enforcement institutes the freedom to do the same thing. Access is clearly unbalanced. See Chen Guangzhong, "Lianheguo gongmin quanli yu zhengzhi quanli guoji gongyue yu zhongguo xingshi susong" (ICCPR and China's Criminal Law and Criminal Procedure Law) (1999), www.hflib.gov.cn/law/law/falvfagui2/cxf/lwj/1075.htm (accessed July 17, 2012).

31. For example, during the time of their temporary detention, detainees have no legal means to pursue justice through the courts, and there is no legal consequence for law officials who ignore or abuse the law regarding pretrial detention. Though relevant laws have begun to grant defendants the right to sue the legal enforcement authority for compensation afterward, the State Compensation Law has set a very low standard. One example is a wrongfully charged death sentence defendant who received only about 70,000 yuan (about $10,000) for his four years' imprisonment. The news reports about this case instigated a hot debate and led to strong demands for changing the State Compensation Act. See http://news.sina.com.cn/s/l/2006-11-29/082311650073.shtml (accessed July 17, 2012).

32. Particularly in political dissidents' cases, detentions of unlawful length are very common. The case of Wang Bingzhang and Yang Jianli is but one instance; see, for example, the reports in http://articles.cnn.com/keyword/wang-bingzhang (accessed June 29, 2012).

33. See Margaret Y. K. Woo, "Law and Discretion in Contemporary Chinese Courts," in *The Limits of the Rule of Law in China*, ed. Karen G. Turner, James V. Feinerman, and R. Kent Guy (Seattle: University of Washington Press, 2000), 163–195. In some cases, adjudication committees even make decisions before the trial; Chow, *The Legal System of the People's Republic of China*, 214; Lubman, *Bird in a Cage*, 166–167.

34. In the final verdicts of these two cases, Zhou Zhengyi, who had personal connections to Shanghai's local Party officials, received a very light sentence, but the editor in chief of *Nanfang dushibao*, which was the first media outlet to openly report on the SARS epidemic and on the Sun Zhigang case, thus offending local Party officials, received an unreasonably heavy sentence. In both cases, local Party committees' involvement and interference largely decided the final sentencing.

Many legal scholars openly expressed their criticism of these two court verdicts, and others linked this to political persecution and corrupt officials' revenge. See Du Guang, "Sifa fubai yu minzhu geming" (Corruption in Adjudication and a Democratic Revolution) (July 7, 2004), www.epochtimes.com/b5/4/7/7/n589742. htm (accessed July 17, 2012).

35. The number of crimes for which one can be convicted and sentenced to death increased from twenty-eight to sixty-eight in the 1997 CL. Some economic crimes can be punished by death, which is unusual in modern criminal law. But the government sees this move as necessary to combat the increase in economic crimes and corruption in China.

36. Before 2006, in some cases the final appeal of the death sentence was granted to the Provincial Supreme People's Court (e.g., in the case of Yunnan), rather than the National Supreme People's Court's retaining this power. But in 2006 the National Supreme People's Court took back this power; see, e.g., "Zuigao fayuan tongyi xingshi sixing fuhequan" (Supreme Court Now Unilaterally Retains Its Decision-Making Power in Reviewing Capital Sentencing), June 22, 2012, http://www.66law.cn/laws/58364.aspx (accessed July 17, 2012).

37. Within China's legal circles a debate continues about the death sentence, and there is strong criticism about the expansion and continuation of the death sentence. See, e.g., Zhang Peihong, "Tantan sixing de jiazhi he xianzhi" (Talk on the Functions and Restraints of Capital Sentencing) (2001), www.chinamonitor .org/view/discussion/sxjzxz.htm (accessed July 17, 2012).

38. Wang Peizhong "Shilun woguo xianxing xingshi susong zhidu yu lian-heguo gongmin quanli ji zhengzhi quanli guoji mengyue deng de chaju" (A Brief Discussion of the Difference between Our Existing Criminal Procedure Law and the United Nations ICCPR) (2001), www.zlcool.com/lw/2/8/1b54e 626f3745253e0732dce38d60a0a.html (accessed July 17, 2012). Regarding the detailed comparison between China's legal order and the Universal Declaration of Human Rights, see Liu Dasheng, "Lun guoji renquan xianzhang de yingdui" (On How to Conform to the Universal Declaration of Human Rights) (September 2002), http://fjthk.now.cn:7751/article.chinalawinfo.com/Article_Detail.asp? ArticleID=22581&Type=mod (accessed July 17, 2012).

39. Mireille Delmas-Marty, "Present-Day China and the Rule of Law: Progress and Resistance," *Chinese Journal of International Law* 2, no. 1 (Spring 2003): 11–28.

40. For instance, in the CL the rights protection articles are in section 4, not corresponding to the constitution's section 2, "The Fundamental Rights and Duties of Citizens." See Zhao Bingzhi and Xie Wangyuan, "Xingfa gaige yu renquan baozhang" (Reform of the Criminal Law and Human Rights Protection) (February 12, 2001), www.law-lib.com/lw/lw_view.asp?no=467 (accessed July 17, 2012).

41. Keith and Lin, *Law and Justice in China's New Marketplace,* 200.

42. Gu Peidong, "Zhongguo fazhi jiangshe ruogan wenti sanlun" (On Some Questions of China's Legal System Building), *Zhongguo yanjiu* (China Studies), no. 5 (1996): 14.

43. See particularly Jiang Mingan, "Cong renzhi zouxiang fazhi zhongguo xing-zhengfa shinian de huigu yu zhanwang" (From "Rule of Man" to "Rule of Law": Review and Prospects for China's Administrative Laws in Ten Years) (1997) www .lunwennet.com/thesis/2003/7943.html (accessed July 17, 2012).

44. The general view is that there is a big chasm between the normal channel of lawmaking through the legislative body—the NPC—and administrative law-making, which is supposed merely to supplement the former. This is why many Chinese legal scholars are critical of this emerging "two-track legislation and law-making" behavior. See, e.g., Chen Duanhong, "The Democratic Legitimacy of Leg-islation and Lawmaking," 62–65.

45. On administrative law reform, see, e.g., Jiang Mingan, "From 'Rule of man' to 'rule of law'"; also see Potter, *Domestic Law Reforms in Post-Mao China*; Edward L. Rubin, "Administrative Law and the Complexity of Culture, " in *Legis-lative Drafting for Market Reform*, ed. Ann Seidman, Robert B. Seidman, and Jan-ice Payne (New York: St. Martin's Press, 1997): 88–108; and Pei Minxin, "Citizens v. Mandarins: Administrative Litigation in China," *China Quarterly* 153 (1997): 832–862.

46. Potter, *Domestic Law Reforms in Post-Mao China*, 290.

47. Pei, "Citizens v. Mandarins," 859.

48. Potter, *Domestic Law Reforms in Post-Mao China*, 288.

49. For example, most local authorities have made regulations to implement people's rights to protest, demonstrate, and rally in public; however, these regula-tions are usually written through restrictive measures that in fact deprive citizens of those rights; see Chen Dunhong, "The Democratic Legitimacy of Legislation and Lawmaking," 68.

50. For example, twelve years after the Administrative Litigation Law was first issued, of a total of 700,000 cases, more than two-thirds were never completed; the cases of plaintiff withdrawal were as high as 57 percent; and the winning cases ruled by the court represented no more than 20 percent. See Ying Songnian, "Xiugai xingzheng susongfa shizai bixing" (Further Amendment of the Adminis-trative Litigating Law Is Inevitable) (2002), www.legalinfo.gov.cn/zt/2004-06/10/content_105873.htm (accessed July 17, 2012).

51. In a direct translation, *shourong qiansong* means "collection and repatri-ation." But because in practice the "collection" of targeted people is carried out through detention and custody, the more accurate expression is "custody."

52. Lubman calls this practice "nonjudicial sanction," as a part of the "criminal process." Lubman, *Bird in a Cage*, 169.

53. For a detailed analysis of the RTL system in domestic discussions, see, e.g., Liu Renwen, "Laodong jiaoyang zhidu jiqi gaige" (The RTL System and Its Reform) (January 5, 2001), www.law-lib.com/lw/lw_view.asp?no=260 (accessed July 17, 2012).

54. For example, five well-known scholars, He Weifang, Shen Kui, Sheng Hong, Xiao Han, and He Haibo, sent a formal proposal to the National People's Congress

to demand that it conduct a special investigation and a constitutional review of the C&R; they argued that the C&R was unconstitutional. See "Wuwei faxuejia tiqing renda qidong tebie chengxu diaocha sunzhigang an" (Five Legal Scholars Demand National People's Congress to Launch a Special Procedure to Review the Sun Zhigang Case), *Zhongguo qingnianbao* (China Youth Daily), May 28, 2003, www.china. com.cn/chinese/2003/May/337024.htm (accessed July 17, 2012). On June 18, 2003, the decision was made to abolish the C&R and replace it with a new regulation to provide help to homeless people; see "Chinese State Council to Abolish the C&R," June 18, 2003, http://news.boxun.com/news/gb/china/2003/06/200306182247. shtml (accessed July 17, 2012). I will revisit this issue later.

55. According to the HRIC Report, "Reeducation through Labor (RTL): A Summary of Regulatory Issues and Concerns," some of the abuses associated with RTL are: (1) no judicial process is involved; (2) it is vague and arbitrary in scope; (3) punishments are severe; (4) local regulations have been expanded; (5) conditions of RTL facilities are abusive. See http://hrichina.org/content/4691 (accessed June 30, 2012).

56. Song Hualin, "Hulianwang xinxi zhengfu guanzhi zhidu de chubu yanjiu" (A Preliminary Study of Government's Control over Internet Information) (August 7, 2009), www.law1954.com/article/sort08/info-32911.html (accessed July 17, 2012); Ren Bumei, "Zhongguo hulianwang lifa pipan" (Critique on China's Internet Laws) (October 10–18, 2002), http://blog.boxun.com/hero/renbm/52_1. shtml (accessed July 17, 2012).

57. At the end of 2001 Guangdong became the first province to announce the elimination of the *hukou* differentiation, and then other provinces followed suit. The current residential registration policy provides that a legally owned, permanent residence and stable employment or income are the basic qualifications for registration. See http://gd.news.sina.com.cn/focus/hjgg/index.html (accessed July 17, 2012).

58. For example, Guangdong's NPC deputy, Chen Lini, made this proposal at the 2002 National People's Congress Annual Meeting, "Guangdong renda daibiao: Huan gongmin ziyou qianxi quan" (NPC Deputy: giving mobility right back to citizens), March 7, 2001, www.china.com.cn/chinese/2002/Mar/115719.htm (accessed July 17, 2012).

59. Tanner, *The Politics of Lawmaking in Post-Mao China*, 8.

60. Ibid., 39.

61. Keith and Lin, *Law and Justice in China's New Marketplace*, 5.

62. According to Monshipouri and Welch, for example, to fulfill the international standard of human rights, political action by the state is definitely required. "Without the effective cooperation of legitimate and relatively strong governments, legal mechanisms are weak." Mahmood Monshipouri and Claude E. Welch, "The Search for International Human Rights and Justice: Coming to Terms with the New Global Realities," *Human Rights Quarterly* 23, no. 2 (2001): 376.

63. Keith and Lin, *Law and Justice in China's New Marketplace*, 13. It is also

noteworthy that the government began to openly use the term *ruoshi qunti* (vulnerable social groups) to refer to those social sectors that are in disadvantaged positions because of economic reform and committed itself to help them through government-sponsored support programs. See Zhu Rongji, "Report to the National People's Congress," Xinhua News Agency, March 5, 2002, www.hprc.org.cn/wxzl/wxysl/lczf/dishiyijie_2/200908/t20090818_27744.html (accessed July 17, 2012).

64. For the full story of the process of the abolition of the C&R, see Zhao Ling, "Feizhi shourong qiansong banfa de juece licheng" (The Process of Abolishing the C&R), *Nanfang zhoume* (Southern Weekend), June 28, 2003, http://bbs.cnhan.com/simple/?t4503.html (accessed July 17, 2012).

65. Chen Xiaoping, "Zhongguo renda cuoshi qidong weixian zhidu lingji" (The Chinese NPC Lost a Chance to Start Adjudication Laws' Constitutionality), June 23, 2003, http://club1.kdnet.net/dispbbs.asp?page=1&boardid=52&id=583599 (accessed July 17, 2012); Gu Su, "Guanyu weixian shencha de ruogan lilun yu shijian wenti" (Some Questions on Judiciary Review of Constitutionality), December 12, 2003, www.china-review.com/sao.asp?id=2303 (accessed July 17, 2012).

66. Peerenboom, *China's Long March toward Rule of Law*, 316.

67. Chow, *The Legal System of the People's Republic of China*, 185–190.

68. For example, in the Legislation Law, division 8 somewhat confuses the legislative power and competence of the NPC, which is the highest legislative body, with that of its Standing Committee, which is a regular organ of NPC. The law provides that some of the NPC's originally exclusive legislative power be shared with the NPC Standing Committee, which thereby reduces the NPC's legislative power. See Zhou Aqiu, "Woguo lifa liangxing weixian xianyi xianxiang qianxi" (A Brief Analysis of China's Positive Unconstitutional Legislative Behavior), *Renda Yanjiu* (People's Congress Research), no. 10 (2000): 24–25. Of course, regarding administrative lawmaking power, there are continuing debates about the importance and justification of administrative laws and regulations. See Jiang, "From 'Rule of Man' to 'Rule of Law.'"

69. Chen, "The Democratic Legitimacy of Legislation and Lawmaking," 59–60.

70. I use the word *adaptation* rather than *convergence* to describe this behavior. The main reason is that convergence connotes two sides converging their ideas, rules, and standards. But in China's legislative activities this may not be the case. See Keith and Lin, *Law and Justice in China's New Marketplace*, 234–235.

71. Shen Zongling, "Dangdai zhongguo jiejian waiguo falu de shilie" (Contemporary China's Legal Imitation of Foreign Legal Practice), *Zhongguo faxie* (China Legal Science), nos. 5–6 (1997).

72. Chow, *The Legal System of the People's Republic of China*, 308.

73. Peerenboom, *China's Long March toward Rule of Law*, 158; Clarke and Feinerman "Antagonistic Contradictions," 91.

74. Shi Wenlong, "Rushi yu woguo faluguan de biange" (Entering the WTO and Changing Lawmaking Ideas) *Yunnan daxue xuebao* (Yunnan University Journal), no. 5 (2004): 1–4.

75. The issue of universal jurisdiction on human rights is beyond the scope of this paper, but it is very important to contemplate the effects of "internationalization of human rights," of which China's adaptation effort is a typical example. Monshipouri and Welch, "The Search for International Human Rights and Justice," 386–387.

76. Peerenboom, *China's Long March toward Rule of Law*, 20.

77. State Council Information Office, *White Paper* (1995), www.scio.gov.cn/zfbps/ndhf/1995/200905/t307995.htm (accessed July 17, 2012).

78. Zhang Jinfan, *Zhongguo falü de chuantong yu jindai chuanxing* (China's Legal Traditions and Modern Transformation) (Beijing: Law Press, 1997), esp. sec. 2.

79. The best attempt is reflected in Xia Yong, ed., *Zouxiang quanli de shidai: Zhongguo gongmin quanli fazhan yanjiu* (Toward an Age of "Rights": Research on the Development of China's Citizens' Rights) (Beijing: China University of Political Science and Law Press, 1995). In this book the authors argue that in China the main elements obstructing citizens' rights development are four: (1) the longtime state socialist ideology emphasizes collective interests over individual rights; (2) state power is totalitarian and is regarded as the sole representative of justice; (3) the strong demand for social order and stability in the face of chaotic modern conditions strengthens the state's authoritative power at the expense of individual rights and freedoms; and (4) social justice is pursued not through legal means but through political means, and therefore it is difficult for laws and legal practice to become part of people's social life. It is worth noting that Xiao Yong, the director of the Institute of Legal Studies in the Chinese Academy of Social Sciences, has become an adviser to the current Chinese president, Hu Jintao.

80. Yang Yinbo, "Nian zhongguo zhishi qunti de weiquan kangzheng" (Chinese Intellectual Community's Rights Protection Struggle in 2004), April 14, 2004, www.epochtimes.com/gb/4/4/14/n509613.htm (accessed July 17, 2012).

81. Epstein, "Law and Legitimation in Post-Mao China," 31.

82. Peerenboom, *China's Long March toward Rule of Law*, 558.

83. It is worth noting that in Chinese *fazhi* has two different meanings (with the same pronunciation but different characters); one is "rule by law," the other is "rule of law." The former is very instrumentalist and was widely used as the guideline for China's legal reform. It was after 1996 that the CCP leaders and state policy documents began to use *fazhi* (rule of law) to refer to the guiding principle of the building of China's legal system. Since then, the hot debate about "rule of law" and "rule by law" among legal professionals and scholars has reached a consensus that confirms the principle of rule of law. On the debate about these two *fazhi* concepts in Chinese sources, see Yu Xuede, "Fazhi haishi fazhi, zhimin haishi zhiquan: Guanyu yifazhiguo wenti taolun guandian zongshu" ("Rule by Law" or "Rule of Law," "Controlling People" or "Controlling Power": Overview of the Discussion about the Question of "Rule of Law") *Faxueyanjiu* (Jurisprudence Studies), no. 3 (1996); also see Li Buyun, "Yifazhiguo: jianshe shehuizhuyi fazhi guojia" (The Rule

of Law: To Build a Socialist Rule-of-Law Country), *Zhongguo renda xinwen* (NPC News), July 4, 2001; among English sources, see Shen, "Conceptions and Receptions of Legality," 24; Keith and Lin, *Law and Justice in China's New Marketplace,* 27–29.

84. Epstein, "Law and Legitimation in Post-Mao China," 20.

85. Ibid., 9–21; according to Epstein, the ideological function of law means that "law is becoming an ideology which secures submission to power exercised according to law with little or no resort to coercion."

86. Peerenboom, *China's Long March toward Rule of Law,* 17–18.

87. In fact, this argument is borrowed largely from "historical institutionalism": "By focusing on institutions that are the product of political conflict and choice but which at the same time constrain and shape political strategies and behaviors, historical institutionalism provides a framework for directly confronting the central question of choice and constraint in understanding political life." See Kathleen Thelen and Sven Steinmo, "Historical Institutionalism in Comparative Politics," in *Structuring Politics: Historical Institutionalism in Comparative Analysis,* ed. Sven Steinmo, Kathleen Thelen, and Frank Longstreth (New York: Cambridge University Press, 1992), 28.

88. Tanner, *The Politics of Lawmaking in Post-Mao China,* 9.

89. Ibid., 37.

90. Peerenboom, *China's Long March toward Rule of Law,* 517.

91. See, e.g., Gu Su, "Some Questions on Judiciary Review of Constitutionality"; Qiu Feng, "Xinminquan yundong: Shuxie zhongguoren de quanli" (New Human Rights Movement: Claiming Chinese People's Rights), January 5, 2004, www .gongfa.com/qiufengzhongguorenquanli.htm (accessed July 17, 2012).

92. For example, according to Keith and Lin, China's "jurisprudence has increasingly endorsed a number of important and familiar principles such as the protection of human rights, the supremacy of law, judicial independence, equality before the law and the rationalization of contemporary legal culture." Keith and Lin, *Law and Justice in China's New Marketplace,* 16.

93. As some have observed, "The institutional evolution of the lawmaking system is creating pressure for significant further decentralization of power and is opening up windows for new public 'constituencies' to get involved in policymaking." Tanner, *The Politics of Lawmaking in Post-Mao China,* 11.

94. Ibid., 9.

95. For example, Li Buyun proposed ten basic principles for legal development. According to him, those principles must have a tripartite foundation: the market economy, democratic polity, and a rational culture. See Keith and Lin, *Law and Justice in China's New Marketplace,* 36.

96. For example, the four successive Standing Committee chairmen of China's NPC, Peng Zhen, Wan Li, Qiao Shi, and Li Peng, though their political and ideological stances are different, have all shown their assertiveness on the new role of the NPC and its organizational development. Tanner, *The Politics of Lawmaking in Post-Mao China,* 238.

97. Epstein, "Law and Legitimation in Post-Mao China," 9.

98. Shen, "Conceptions and Receptions of Legality," 28.

99. Peerenboom, *China's Long March toward Rule of Law*, 523.

100. Tanner, *The Politics of Lawmaking in Post-Mao China*, 36–39.

101. *Shuanggui* literally means that "at a certain place and at a certain time, the target person will be required to be subjected to interrogation" from the party disciplinary committee regarding his or her suspected wrongdoing, usually an economic criminal offence. The problem with this measure is that this type of detention or confinement is not conducted by the criminal justice authority, but by an agent of a political party. This measure is, legally speaking, a violation of the target person's personal liberty, and it therefore should be declared unconstitutional. Because public opinion overwhelmingly favors tough measures to crack down on corruption, however, legal challenges of *shuanggui* are rare.

102. Potter, *Domestic Law Reforms in Post-Mao China*, 326.

103. Steinmo et al., *Structuring Politics*, 20–22.

104. Ibid., 27.

105. Keith and Lin, *Law and Justice in China's New Marketplace*, 13.

106. Tanner, *The Politics of Lawmaking in Post-Mao China*, 11.

107. Monshipouri and Welch, "The Search for International Human Rights and Justice," 400.

108. Shen, "Conceptions and Receptions of Legality," 33.

109. Ann Kent, "Form over Substance: The Australia-China Bilateral Human Rights Dialogues," *China Rights Forum* (Fall 1999): 30–46.

110. "I Protest: Citizens' Movements," *China Rights Forum* (Fall 1998), www.hrichina.org/what-we-do/research-and-publications/publication-list (accessed July 17, 2012).

111. Shen, "Conceptions and Receptions of Legality," 30.

112. Tanner, *The Politics of Lawmaking in Post-Mao China*, 36; Peerenboom, *China's Long March toward Rule of Law*, 513.

113. Shen, "Conceptions and Receptions of Legality," 38.

114. Keith and Lin, *Law and Justice in China's New Marketplace*, 15.

## Further Reading

Baker, Philip. "Human Rights, Europe and the People's Republic of China." *China Quarterly* 169 (2002): 45–63.

Bauer, Joanne R., and Daniel A. Bell, eds. *The East Asian Challenge for Human Rights*. New York: Cambridge University Press, 1999.

Bell, Daniel A. *East Meets West: Human Rights and Democracy in East Asia*. Princeton: Princeton University Press, 2000.

Davis, Michael C., ed. *Human Rights and Chinese Values: Legal, Philosophical and Political Perspectives*. New York: Oxford University Press, 1995.

Edwards, R. Randle, Louis Henkin, and Andrew J. Nathan. *Human Rights in Contemporary China*. New York: Columbia University Press, 1986.

Han, Li. "Paoxi zhongguo lifa guocheng de feizhengshixing" (An Analysis of the Unformalization in China's Legislation and Lawmaking). *Modern China Studies*, no. 2 (2002).

Keller, Perry, ed. *Chinese Law and Legal Theory*. Aldershot, U.K.: Ashgate, 2001.

Kent, A. E. *China, the United Nations and Human Rights: The Limits of Compliance*. Philadelphia: University of Pennsylvania Press, 1999.

Peerenboom, Randall. "Ruling the Country in Accordance with Law." *Cultural Dynamics* 11, no. 3 (1999): 315–351.

Potter, Pitman. "Riding the Tiger: Legitimacy and Legal Culture in Post-Mao China." *China Quarterly* 138 (1994): 325–358.

Potter, Pitman, and Li Jiangyong. "Regulating Labour Relations in China: The Challenge of Adapting to the Socialist Market Economy." *Cahiers de Droit* 37, no. 3 (1996): 753–775.

Santoro, Michael A. *Profits and Principles: Global Capitalism and Human Rights in China*. Ithaca: Cornell University Press, 2000.

Shih, Chih-yu. *Collective Democracy: Political and Legal Reform in China*. Hong Kong: Chinese University Press, 1999.

Wang Chengguang and Zhang Xianchu, eds. *Introduction to Chinese Law*. Hong Kong: Sweet & Maxwell Asia, 1997.

Weatherly, Robert. *The Discourse of Human Rights in China: Historical and Ideological Perspectives*. New York: Palgrave, 1999.

# 10

# Sound Is Better Than Silence

## Reporters, Freedom Writers, and Cyber Guerrillas

### Xiaobing Li

Because of the revolution from paper communication to digital technology, few areas of research in contemporary China pose more difficulties than the study of the mass media. According to official statistics, by the end of 2003 more than 30 million computers in the country were connected to the Internet, and the number of households that logged on reached 79.5 million, the second highest in the world. By the end of 2009 there were 384 million "netizens" in China.[1] By 2003 the number of Chinese households with telephones increased to 263.3 million, and mobile phone users increased by 62.7 million, to 268.7 million. With 532 million telephone users, or forty-two for every one hundred individuals, China is among the top countries in terms of the pace and scale of communications development.[2] In 2005 the *Super Girl* contest, a television program broadcast on satellite out of Hunan province along the same format as *American Idol*, counted votes from millions of cellular phone users to determine the winner. According to the PRC Ministry of Industry and Information Technology (MIIT), by April 2012 the number of cell phone users had reached a record high of 1.03 billion.[3] These tremendous changes in communications technology, and particularly the transition from printed media to more rapid, digital formats, are challenging the authority of official Chinese political and social institutions. The government has little tolerance for criticism or calls for greater transparency and accountability. When some reporters, activists, and political dissidents, such as Liu Xiaobo and Chen

Guangcheng, expressed their concerns and posted their criticism online, they faced prosecution, jail time, or deportation.

Nevertheless, the digital revolution has had a strong and positive effect in the public arena and on civil society. As the Chinese people become better informed and connected, the effect of the digital transformation on the evolution of democratic and civil rights, as well as the influence it will have on the flexibility of government policy in the context of this major social and political transition, is uncertain. In the past the Chinese Communist Party (CCP) used the media as an instrument to articulate and build support for its policies. In recent years, however, the Party Center has adjusted its approach while maintaining its control of the mass media and public opinion. This chapter examines government policies concerning this topic. The stories of Chinese journalists and foreign reporters in the country provide unique insights into those who have shaped the struggle for the freedom of information and freedom of the press during the first decade of the twenty-first century and beyond. Furthermore, it places individuals participating in the struggle for personal rights in the context of international events and greater Chinese society.[4]

## Public Information and Official Regulations

In the 1950s through 1970s, the Party Center began using domestic media outlets as a mouthpiece for its propaganda machine, both to mobilize the masses and to manage the impressions given to the citizens of its own country and to the outside world. During the economic reform and liberalization movements of the 1980s, the government began adopting more flexible policies toward the media, emphasizing rights guaranteed by the constitution. According to article 35 of the 1982 constitution, "Citizens of the People's Republic of China enjoy freedom of speech, of the press, of assembly, of association, of procession, and of demonstration."[5] Later the government established the spokesperson system at all levels. China's spokesperson system started with the Ministry of Foreign Affairs in 1983, opening an important information channel, only for diplomatic and other important political occasions. In 1999 the provincial government of Guangdong in south China began experimenting with the spokesperson system in fifteen provincial departments. According to official records, Shanghai designated twenty-four spokespeople for departments of the municipal government in April 2002 and assigned two spokespeople for city officials in June 2003.[6] After the outbreak of Severe Acute Respiratory Syndrome (SARS) in the fall of 2002, the Chinese government tried to improve its image by upgrading its spokesperson system. In early 2003, for example, Beijing began a training program for spokespeople. By September the training program involved one hundred spokespeople from sixty-six central government ministries and departments. At the beginning of 2006 the Ministry of Justice announced that various levels of the country's courts would also establish the spokesperson system. Additionally, the public information system was improved, and, according to the government, citizens' freedom of information and of the press, as prescribed by law, was further protected.

The authorities state that they have made new efforts to increase transparency of administrative affairs, enabling citizens to enjoy more access to information and participation in public life. The National People's Congress (NPC) and its Standing Committee have become more engaged in shaping major policies and exercising the legislative power of the state. The NPC has also begun to pay attention to petitions from ordinary people. In 2003, for example, the NPC Standing Committee received 31,000 visits to its Beijing offices and handled more than 57,000 letters from all over the country. In the meantime, the Chinese People's Political Consultative Conference (CPPCC) has also actively participated in policy debates and social surveys in order to play a better supervisory role in the government. In 2003 the CPPCC National Committee investigated specific issues, such as rural poverty, resulting in 37 investigative reports and 114 proposals within specialized fields. Other parties under the CPPCC submitted 84 proposals and passed on 1,674 reports of public opinion through the CPPCC.[7]

Although the public's access to information has improved, the Party Center continues to exercise strict control over the media, effectively keeping the bulk of China's press as components of a vast national propaganda system. With some minor variations, the government maintains control of news outlets in several different ways. The first of these is government regulation. Even though article 35 of the constitution guarantees freedom of the press, article 51 makes clear that this liberty cannot infringe on the "interests of the state."[8] A series of national agencies such as the Propaganda Department of the CCP Central Committee, the Ministry of Public Security, the General Administration for Press and Publications (GAPP) of the State Council, and the Ministry of Information Industry establish regulations and rules that prohibit any material that "harms the honor or the interests of the nation," "spreads rumors," or "harms the credibility of a government agency."[9]

These vague guidelines and amorphous legislative acts are an impediment to the media's freedom. Aside from establishing rules for the publication of books, GAPP regulates more than nine thousand weekly and monthly magazines and journals throughout the country. It issues regulations on a regular basis in an attempt to control news, public opinion, and editorials. Each magazine or journal must follow strict directions from the relevant government departments or risk losing its publishing license. The Propaganda Department of the CCP Central Committee also plays an important role in controlling publications and domestic media. In August 2008, for example, the Chinese government allowed foreign and domestic journalists to interview citizens and report events during the Beijing Olympic games. The Party's Central Propaganda Department, however, set up numerous rules for Chinese reporters during the games. According to the department's directives, the domestic media were barred from reporting on Tibetan and Uyghur movements, news from foreign websites, and problems in the Olympic security system, among other topics.

Local governments at the provincial, county, and city levels also have set up their own guidelines for the restriction of media activities. For example, in December 2001 the Dunhuang City government in Gansu province issued its Opinion on Strengthening the Supervision of Correspondents' Offices in Dunhuang and Journalists Conducting Interviews in Dunhuang. The city government's Opinion specifically stipulates: "Critical reports that involve the leadership of this municipality and cadres ranked assistant section chief and above must be submitted to the local propaganda department (of the Party's committee) for approval, and must also be transmitted to the persons concerned and the relevant leaders."[10] According to the report by an international human rights organization, in August 2002 the Public Security Bureau of Lanzhou City in northwestern Gansu province sent an official letter to all news media in the city naming sixteen journalists who had published "inaccurate" reports concerning law enforcement personnel breaking the law. The journalists on this "blacklist were banned from future interviews and investigations with police and public security officers."[11]

The second measure of state control is government ownership of all media, in whole or in part. This concentrated control protects the Party authorities and political supervision, and it ensures that media companies

are run by handpicked executives and staff. All the reporters, editors, producers, and administrators are employed by either central or local governments, and they are closely monitored. Market reforms, however, have
forced Chinese media providers to consider the income provided by advertisements, subscribers, and viewership. The bureaucracy of the Chinese
media has begun to submit to these economic pressures and to embrace
commercialization and business strategies. The government has shifted its
control mechanisms to include elaborate censorship and licensing procedures. More and more, journalists can enjoy relatively broad discretion in
their ability to report on topics such as sports, entertainment, consumer
lifestyle, and local news without extensive political implications.

The third measure of state control is government censorship of sensitive stories, from the bottom up, focusing on the news reporting system. Reporters must know the line between what is permitted and what is
forbidden. They are expected to practice self-censorship, since their jobs
are on the line, and their editors use the same rules to approve or with-
hold a news report. Editors can reject an article or may reassign a reporter
with the use of overt intimidation, and their producers and directors act
as further instruments of control. If a reporter or editor is perceived to
have crossed the line, his or her employer can kill the product and relocate,
demote, or even fire individuals responsible as punishment. On important
issues, upper management must report to Party officials and the CEOs of
their outlets for final approval. These latter two groups receive the Party's instructions, reporting guidelines, and official news releases on a daily
basis from the central government's agencies, including the CCP Central
Committee's Propaganda Department, the official Xinhua (New China)
News Agency, and local organizations such as city and provincial Party
committees. When a newspaper or television station has made a mistake
by releasing a piece that differed from the official Party line, the CEOs have
either lost their jobs or faced criminal charges.

The fourth measure is the government's control of access to information. Many sources of records, such as courthouses, police stations, and
city and provincial government offices, remain closed to reporters. The
government controls all information concerning the Tibetan areas, as well
as access to the region, which makes it difficult to accurately determine the
scope and condition of civil liberties. In many cases, reporters must gain
permission before beginning interviews or investigations. It is even more
difficult for foreign reporters to apply for these types of access. Before and

during the 2008 Olympic games in Beijing, the Chinese government issued temporary regulations, in effect from January 1, 2007, to October 17, 2008, giving foreign correspondents permission to interview anyone who consented. Bao Tong, a well-known dissident who has been under house arrest at his Beijing home since the 1989 student-led prodemocracy movement in Tiananmen Square, said he was very pleased with these new rules.

This temporary reprieve from censorship did not, however, extend to Chinese journalists or foreign correspondents' assistants, researchers, or sources. The government and pro-Party media continue to crack down on "unofficial news," or what is officially called "fake news" and "illegal news coverage." Some Chinese journalists and writers continue to be harassed, detained, and intimidated by police officers or local thugs if they fail to follow official regulations. Bao Tong and other dissidents also questioned the durability of the new interview policy beyond the Olympic games and warned that nothing could be taken for granted. Bao said, "We should be vigilant, because there are still plenty of evil forces in China that would love to rip apart press freedom."[12] During an interview in February 2008, he cited the case of a reporter from the *China Trade Journal* who was beaten to death after trying to get to the truth regarding a mining disaster in central Shanxi province. In its "Reports on Human Rights Practices for 2011: China," the U.S. State Department pointed out that "the Committee to Protect Journalists (CPJ) December Prison Census reported that of 27 known journalists imprisoned in the country, 10 were Tibetan and six were Uighur. The CPJ documented one new imprisonment case during the year [2011]."[13]

## "Good News" and "Bad Reporters"

State control of the news is successful because the government manages all media outlets; its powers include production, hiring of journalists, and restriction of access to information. Media outlets received regular guidance from the Central Propaganda Department of the CCP. The Party department lists topics that should not be covered, including politically sensitive topics or negative images of the government. For example, after the Sichuan earthquake on May 12, 2008, the department's don't-report list included demonstrations by parents whose children had died in the earthquake when their schools collapsed. Moreover, the government continued to monitor, harass, detain, arrest, and imprison journalists, writers, editors, and their families if there was a violation of official reporting guidelines.

Many Chinese journalists resign themselves to playing the role of Party mouthpieces or seek to exploit their social influence for personal gain. Those with a sense of social responsibility must balance their reports by reinforcing a positive image of the state and deemphasizing the object of their reports, such as corruption, by stating that it occurs strictly at lower levels, or that accidents resulting in the loss of life resulted purely from the individual actions of a minority of officials. On the one hand, these self-protective approaches at least guarantee the journalists' personal safety, job security, and professional careers. On the other, however, because people watch, read, and listen exclusively to official reports, it is easy for the government to cover up major issues such as mining disasters, mass poisonings, and labor uprisings.

The Severe Acute Respiratory Syndrome (SARS) outbreak in southern China in 2002–2003 is a major example of the government's controlling access to information. In its primary viral form, this epidemic disease has a 70 percent mortality rate. It began in southern Guangdong province in November 2002, and, despite taking some measures to control it, government officials did not inform the World Health Organization (WHO) of the outbreak until February 2003. During those critical months the government restricted media coverage and did not allow reporters to interview concerned families and medical personnel. The Chinese authorities attempted to preserve public confidence and to assure foreign investors, as well as tourists, that everything was business as usual.

In early April Chinese health officials insisted that the epidemic was under "effective control." In Beijing they reported only thirty-seven cases and continued to delay reporting or to give false figures. In May Chinese censors blocked the airing of an American-based CNN program criticizing Beijing's handling of the SARS epidemic. This lack of openness resulted in delayed efforts to control the disease, and the censorship process predated the worst of the outbreak. By July 31 there were 5,328 cases in the country and 349 fatalities. In the interim, the disease spread from China and rapidly infected individuals in approximately thirty-seven countries around the world. Following this rapid spread of the disease, the government acknowledged it had underreported the number of SARS cases, and, as a result, both the mayor of Beijing and the health minister were fired, but only after the outbreak had killed more than seven hundred people in nine countries.

Frequent cover-ups and a general lack of openness on the part of the government indicate that Chinese authorities do not yet fully respect freedom of the press. Throughout 2005 and 2006 critical media reports on corruption in the appropriation of land and environmental damage were followed by intensified crackdowns on journalists, including several incidents resulting in the dismissal of chief editors, the closure of popular newspapers, and violent attacks on journalists attempting to cover sensitive stories. The government-instituted control of such information is a crucial barrier to the formation of an independent civil society. Attacks on the independence of the press have a ripple effect on society, and crackdowns on this sector discourage others, such as grassroots activists, petitioners, and dissatisfied workers, from speaking out.

Chinese journalists continue to risk severe repercussions if they report on and publish controversial views to the domestic population or even forward them to overseas audiences. In the spring of 2001 hundreds of residents of Shangzhou, Shaanxi province, were found to be infected with AIDS, a rate of 4 percent, far exceeding that of some African countries. The provincial government issued orders that no further random checks (testing) be conducted on tens of thousands of potential victims. Several journalists for *Shaanxi ribao* (Shaanxi Daily) provided the public with a true picture of the AIDS situation, reporting that the spread of the virus was caused by the selling of blood in Henan province. Later these journalists were investigated and prosecuted for "violating the State Secrets Law concerning unauthorized publication of information on serious epidemics."

In 2005 Chinese authorities had thirty-two journalists in prisons, more than any other country. In 2007 twenty-nine were imprisoned. For the ninth consecutive year, China was one of the leading nations in the incarceration of journalists. According to the CPJ, some of those prosecuted have served lengthy sentences. Two of those, Chen Renjie and Lin Youping, have been jailed since 1983 for publishing a pamphlet entitled *Ziyou bao* (Freedom Report), and the reporter Chen Biling has been executed.[14] The Freedom House, an international rights organization, reported the case of Shi Tao, a similar criminal prosecution and punishment by the government against an individual writer. In 2004 Shi Tao, an editor with the *Dangdai shangbao* (Contemporary Business News) in Changsha, central Hunan province, was arrested for "leaking state secrets." His actual offense was divulging the Propaganda Department's instructions to his paper. In April 2005 Shi received a ten-year prison sentence from the Changsha Intermediate People's Court. In February 2006 the top editors of *Bingdian* (Freezing Point), a popular weekly magazine, were removed after an article appeared that criticized China's textbooks.[15] The Human Rights Watch group also closely followed details of the death of Lan Chengzhang, a reporter with *China Trade News* who was murdered in January 2007 while investigating an illegal coal mine in Datong, Shanxi province. In mid-August of the same year, five journalists, including a reporter from the Party mouthpiece *Renmin ribao* (People's Daily), interviewed witnesses to the Fenghuang bridge collapse in Hunan province, in which sixty-four people were killed. During these interviews, a group of unidentified thugs interrupted the proceedings and began kicking and punching the journalists. When the police arrived on the scene, they arrested the journalists—but not the assailants. Law enforcement, criminal prosecution, and punishments have been employed by the government against domestic journalists, writers, and their controversial writings.[16]

Many magazines and journals face the threat of closure from government departments if they expose official corruption or political problems. To survive, some of them feel it necessary to change the tone of or to give up on what they intended to publish. *Baixing* (Ordinary People, or Commoners) became a popular monthly when it ran hard-hitting exposés of governmental corruption and the abuse of power among local officials in the countryside. In August 2006, for example, it printed "Ground-Level Investigation into Evictions and Demolitions in Jiangyin City," an article on how Jiangyin municipal officials had taken land from local rural families and evicted them, imprisoning their representatives in manacles. In late 2006, the editor in chief, Huang Liangtang, came under pressure from various government agencies, and by early 2007 he and nearly all his team, from deputy editors and reporters to circulation and advertising staff, had to leave the magazine. In May 2007 *Baixing* had an extreme makeover in which it changed from a cutting-edge magazine into a cultural and lifestyle digest of previously published materials. The magazine no longer employs its own in-house staff writers or publishes original articles. The government, including GAPP and the Ministry of Agriculture, in this case effectively neutralized the popular periodical. Another successful magazine, *Sanlian shenghuo zhoukan* (Sanlian Life Weekly), suffered a similar fate following the publication of articles on politically sensitive topics, including the western Sichuan earthquake (also known as the Wenchuan earthquake). Following this incident, the magazine was ordered, on threat of closure, to stay away from these topics. This order came from the

Propaganda Department of the Party's Central Committee, which tightly controls China's media. Miao Wei, executive editor of *Sanlian shenghuo zhoukan*, confirmed in April 2007 that he had been demoted in connection with the publication of the articles.

The Chinese government limits the access of foreign reporters and journalists to information. Beijing continues to jam Radio Free Asia (RFA), the British Broadcasting Corporation (BBC), and the Voice of America (VOA). As they broadcast to China in the Chinese, Tibetan, and Uyghur languages, the potential audience includes activists, ordinary citizens, and even government officials. Some of these institutions' reporters, researchers, and assistants are not allowed to conduct interviews or visit sites, and the taking of pictures is prohibited. In September 2004 Zhao Yan, a researcher for the *New York Times,* was detained for "providing state secrets to foreigners." Zhao, who had revealed the retirement of Jiang Zemin before the official announcements, was subsequently charged with fraud and sentenced to three years' imprisonment in a trial closed to the public. In March 2007 residents of Yongzhou, Hunan province, went to the streets in protest of a large increase in public bus fares. A few of the protesters turned violent and set some buses on fire. When BBC reporters went to the scene, they were stopped by armed police. Chinese officials can be punished for unauthorized contact with foreign journalists, and according to Reporters without Borders, Li Fuguo, a municipal official in Fuyang, eastern Anhui province, was arrested in August 2007 after he spoke with a journalist about an illegal requisition of farmland.[17] In March 2008 Li was reported to have died in prison. The police claim that Li took his own life.

In September 2007 British TV Channel Four's reporters Andrew Carter and Aidan Hartley interviewed and filmed visitors appealing to the central government for assistance. Beijing's police arrested the journalists and destroyed their films. During interrogations, the police demanded the reporters sign a confession that they had violated Chinese law. The Foreign Correspondents' Club of China (FCCC) reported in September 2008 that local authorities continued infringing on the freedom of foreign journalists to travel and conduct interviews after the central government issued the temporary regulations that gave foreign correspondents permission to interview anyone who consented. During 2008, however, harassment of foreign journalists rose sharply.

From January 24 to 26, 2008, a German television crew traveled to eastern Shandong province to interview Yuan Weijing, whose husband is the imprisoned human rights activist Chen Guangcheng. When German reporters entered her neighborhood, a group of thugs began attacking the crew by throwing rocks and pushing them away from Yuan's house. Between July 25 and August 23, the FCCC reported thirty cases of "reporting interference" before and during the Olympic games. On July 22 several Beijing residents were injured when a huge crowd attempted to purchase Olympic tickets and police lost control of the crowd. When a group of Hong Kong reporters tried to cover the events by taking pictures and interviewing people at the scene, they were manhandled by Beijing police. On August 4, four days before the opening ceremony of the Beijing Olympic games, a bomb exploded and killed eight members of the People's Armed Police in Kashgar, Xinjiang. When two Japanese journalists arrived in Kashgar and tried to cover the aftermath of the deadly attack, they were arrested by local police. The Japanese journalists were detained for days and were beaten several times by Xinjiang police. On August 13 a journalist from Independent Television News attempted to cover a Tibet-related protest near the Olympic village. Beijing police pushed him away and detained him.[18] The FCCC also complained that foreign correspondents were still unable to visit Tibet without official permits, which rarely were granted,[19] and in November thugs beat a Belgian television crew attempting to cover the HIV/AIDS epidemic in Henan province.

According to the FCCC, between January 1 and December 2, 2008, there were 178 incidents of harassment of foreign journalists conducting interviews, compared to 160 cases for all of 2007. More recently, representatives from World Press Freedom met with Chinese officials and asked to visit jailed reporters. Even though the Chinese officials agreed to the request, no visit has been arranged. In their annual report on world media freedom, American-based Freedom House ranked China on the same level as Iran, 181st; only Communist countries and dictatorships, such as Cuba, North Korea, and Myanmar (Burma), are lower on the list. World Press Freedom ranked China 163rd in its annual report on global freedom of the press. The U.S. State Department reported in 2012: "According to the FCCC, one of five foreign respondents surveyed experienced visa threats or visa delays. Some reporters were explicitly told that issuance of their visa was related to the content of their reporting. Among the correspondents surveyed, 70 percent experienced interference or harassment during the year [2011]; 40 percent said their sources were harassed, detained, or called in for questioning for interacting with foreign journalists; and 33 percent said their Chinese assistants encountered pressure from officials or experienced harassment."[20]

## INTERNET POLICING AND NEW BATTLES

In China the Internet has become popular for communication, education, and business operations. According to official statistics, the country had a total of 103 million users by June 30, 2005, and a particularly high percentage of those were youths between the ages of eighteen and twenty-four. The number had grown to an estimated 144 million users at the end of 2006. According to research completed by Tsinghua University (China's equivalent of MIT), the country had one hundred million bloggers in 2007. The China Internet Network Information Center reported that the number of Internet users increased to 298 million in 2008. By the end of 2009, there were about 220 million bloggers in China.[21] Among Internet users, 91 percent had broadband access. While encouraging Internet use for business and educational purposes, the government has kept tight controls on its use for political discussion. The authorities fear that critics could organize the netizens into an effective source of opposition and disseminate their views to China's fast-growing population of cybersurfers. The Party Center has strengthened its control of the Internet by setting up new regulations and establishing a new central governmental agency. At a Politburo meeting in January 2007, President Hu said that the Internet was related to the country's safety and security and was a source of sensitive information. As a result, the State Council established the Bureau of the Internet in the State Council's Media Department, while a mirror organization, the Bureau of Internet Propaganda, was formed in the office of External Propaganda in the CCP Central Committee.

Government censorship and surveillance have increased in cyberspace in response to the Internet's growing popularity and its use as a medium for activism throughout China. More than a dozen regulations relating to the Internet have been implemented by the Party Central Committee's Department of Propaganda, the Ministry of Public Security, the Ministry of Information Industry, the Ministry of Culture, and relevant departments of the ministries at various levels. In May 2007, for example, China's Internet authorities issued the Regulations for the Management of Internet Publishing. These new guidelines brought online magazines, or webzines, under the same controls as print publications. Webzines must now obtain prior agreement from GAPP before seeking approval to set up a telecommunications business from the Ministry of Information Industry. In September 2007 the Ministry of Information Industry issued a new set of rules aimed at curbing the spread of interactive Internet sites such as bulletin boards, chat rooms, blogs, and discussion forums. According to these guidelines, all providers offering these services had to reapply for a license in order to operate, and, if denied, were to be closed down. Tens of thousands of police monitor the Internet around the clock, and the government is heavily invested in a network infrastructure that boosts efficiency, aiding in the monitoring of web content. By August 2005, the government had already spent at least $800 million on state-of-the-art equipment in an attempt to control its citizens online.

Foreigners call China's elaborate system of censorship the "Great Firewall of China." This well-developed network is in fact aided by extensive corporate- and private-sector interests, including some of the world's major international technological and Internet-based companies, such as Google, Yahoo, and Microsoft. In the spring of 2005 Yahoo-China merged with the Chinese-owned Alibaba. After this $1 billion merger, Yahoo, as an international partner and 40 percent stakeholder, had to follow Beijing on issues of censorship and devolve all related decisions to local management teams. American and other foreign information-technology companies' contributions to official censorship raise serious issues concerning socially responsible corporate practices and policies. In September 2005 the former U.S. president Bill Clinton gave a keynote address at the fifth China Internet Summit in the booming and tech-savvy city of Hangzhou, in which he lauded the ability of the Internet to make information available to anyone in that country. His speech, however, did not mention the control the Chinese government has in place over the medium or whether American companies should protect the rights, property, personal safety, and interests of their Chinese customers.[22]

New advances in technology have greatly enabled the government, through several different measures, to tighten its grip on cyberspace. The first is instant control over the content of online information exchanges. Officials have developed lists of sensitive key words, or "bad words," that are used to facilitate censorship. Major search engines, service providers, and technology companies like U.S.–based Yahoo, Cisco, and Microsoft have been cooperating with the Chinese government to restrict information that includes words such as "1989 Tiananmen Incident," the outlawed

Falun Gong "evil cult," "separatist" elements in Tibet and Xinjiang, "Taiwan independence," and "democracy." Whenever these words occur in search results, or whatever content the government does not like that originates in China, servers block the content. According to a recent report by the Harvard University–backed Open Net Initiative, China's Internet-filtering capabilities are the most sophisticated of their kind in the world, involving multiple levels of technical control. The government also censors pornography and online religious materials. This instant "bad word" system of control is expected to increase self-censorship by netizens who realize the problem and will then stop writing about these sensitive topics. Officials continue to censor, ban, and sanction reporting and writing about labor, health, environmental crises, and industrial accidents.

A second measure used to control Internet communication is enhanced identification procedures, including online registration, identifying users by their real names, and password verification. These measures are performed by public security departments, police, or Internet service providers acting on behalf of the authorities. Chinese bloggers who use their own domain names are required to register, a process that requires the relinquishing of the name and address of all site administrators, who are in turn responsible for moderating site content. Thus, organizers must scrutinize speech themselves for fear of getting into trouble. Residents in Shenzhen, Guangdong province, for example, are required to have their real identities verified by IM Company of Tencent in Shenzhen if they wish to use instant messaging software to engage in group discussions. Through this procedure, a person's actual identity is connected with the opinion expressed online. This provides authorities with more control in cyberspace and greater surveillance capabilities regarding public opinion. Because of the loss of privacy, however, many users are not comfortable with real-name registration.

The third measure the government uses to exercise control over the Internet is to have its own bloggers and commentators. The Propaganda Department and public security departments have trained a network of online commentators to manipulate the public opinions expressed in Internet forums and message groups. They are either employees of the government or paid by the departments as part-time workers. They hide their real identities to communicate government ideas or fabricate false public opinion through multiple levels, such as web pages, web logs, online discussion forums, university bulletin board systems, and e-mail messages. Even though the government has these multiple control mechanisms, it can always shut down websites or individual blogs if officials think it necessary.

After Liu Xiaobo coauthored the Charter '08 and posted it online, calling for increased political freedoms and human rights in China, he was arrested and sentenced in 2009 to eleven years' imprisonment for the "crime of inciting subversion of state power." In October 2010 Liu was awarded the Nobel Peace Prize for his "long and non-violent struggle for fundamental human rights in China."[23] The Nobel Committee is still waiting for him to collect his medal, pick up his prize money, and give his Nobel lecture, but Liu remains in jail.

## ONLINE GUERRILLAS AND CYBER WARFARE

The government can shut down websites with "unauthorized" content that includes everything from news of natural disasters to reports on corruption scandals that might embarrass the Party Center. From July to August 2007 authorities closed several dozen websites, including "Briefing China's Development" and "Forum for Contemporary Poems" because of "violations of government regulations." Under such pressure, foreign Internet servers have also had to stop service to their Chinese customers who registered and paid for access but were also on the government list of "bad websites." For example, Godaddy.com had to shut down several Chinese websites after the American-based Internet server received an official notice from the Chinese government. In August 2007 Shanghai Internet police shut down the online journal *Minjiang* (Min River). The authorities also blocked the overseas edition, hosted on a non-Chinese server. The same year, the Chinese government shut down a site dedicated to those with the hepatitis B virus (HBV), which had been running for six years without any interference. China now has 120 million known carriers of the disease, and this site had been a strong force in fighting social discrimination against those infected. The HBV forums had provided a slender lifeline to those affected by the virus who were experiencing severe mental difficulties as a result of their diagnosis.

In 2007 officials reported that the government shut down more than 62,600 illegal websites as part of a nationwide crackdown on "illegal and pornographic" publications. Many websites included images of cartoon police officers that warn users to stay away from forbidden content. Between April and November 2008, Xinhua News Agency reported that authorities closed 14,000 illegal websites and deleted more than 490,000 items of "harmful" content from the Internet.[24] Government filters also block access to sites from abroad that are run by dissidents, human rights groups, and some news organizations.

Writers, bloggers, and journalists risk punishments that range from immediate dismissal from their positions to prosecution and lengthy jail terms for various offenses, such as sending news via e-mail to those outside the country or posting articles critical of the political system. Authorities enforce official regulations and punish those who violate them, especially political dissidents. In May 2004 Du Daobin, a former government official in Hubei province, was arrested and tried behind closed doors without access to legal representation. He was charged with inciting subversion of the state's power after he posted several essays critical of the Chinese government. By the time of his arrest, officials had detained more than thirty individuals as part of a crackdown on online dissent. In April 2005 Shi Tao, the editor arrested for divulging the Propaganda Department's instructions to his paper, was sentenced to ten years' imprisonment for sending an e-mail to an overseas rights group detailing the activities of the same CCP Central Committee organization. Reportedly, Yahoo provided evidence that contributed to Shi's arrest and conviction for activities that did not threaten China's national security. The company's representative in Hong Kong, however, stated that the company must comply with the laws of the country in which it operates.[25]

An online author, Li Hong (the pen name of Zhang Jianhong), was one of those punished for expressing their political opinions on the Internet. Li Hong created a website, "Aegean Sea," that published news, articles, and comments. Some of his discussions were critical of government policies, and he became considered an online political dissident. Before the end of 2006 Li Hong was arrested, and in March 2007 he was sentenced to six years' imprisonment under the charge of "inciting subversion of the government." In May 2007 he began serving his term at Changhu Prison in Huzhou, Zhejiang. In the summer he became very sick, and his family asked for a medical parole, which was denied. Upon his death at the end of 2010, dissidents and human rights activists were prevented from attending his funeral.[26]

On May 13, 2008, Qi Chonghuai, a journalist in eastern Shandong province, was convicted of "extortion and blackmail" and sentenced to four years in prison. Qi was arrested in June 2007 after he and a friend published an article on the Xinhua website alleging official corruption in the Tengzhou CCP Committee. Just before his release in June 2011, he was retried and sentenced to eight additional years. His coauthor, the photographer Ma Shiping, remains in jail in 2012. On May 13, 2008, He Yanjie, who was working as Qi's research assistant, was sentenced to two years in prison and released in 2009.[27]

In November 2008 authorities in the eastern province of Jiangsu arrested a prominent blogger, Guo Quan. Guo was a founding member of the prodemocracy Chinese New People's Party at the end of 2007. He called for the creation of a Chinese Netizen Party to combat online censorship, and he had been posting open letters on his blog calling for democratic reforms. He had also set up a network to help victims of the devastating May 12 earthquake in the southwestern province of Sichuan. On May 18, 2008, he was arrested and held for ten days by the Nanjing police; after his release he was fired from his teaching position at Nanjing University, one of the key universities in China.

Sometimes online users were punished merely because they made local government leaders unhappy. In June 2007, for example, an Internet user put some photos online that showed the luxurious offices of a newly completed city government building. The municipal officials in Tengzhou, Shandong province, were upset and worried that the photos might incite criticism of the city government, and they sent metropolitan police to arrest the Internet user. In November 2007 police in Shanghai raided the home of a blogger and confiscated his computer and equipment after he posted a detailed account of the closure of his magazine earlier that year.

The government's measures, however, are not universally effective. An increasing number of Chinese rights activists are also taking their battle for freedom of expression to the Internet. The activists engage in guerrilla-style tactics of posting dissenting opinions and critiques on bulletin boards, chat rooms, and YouTube. They set up quick-moving websites and link them together. These numerous "hacktivists" seek out or create ways to circumvent government controls. Because of developments such as this, many are stating that the battle for the rights of the Chinese people is now online. Surveillance programs established by the Chinese police are not always capable of completely suppressing online political debates and dissenting opinions. Internet police cannot monitor all online traffic as well as numerous Internet cafés. Wu Wei, a web activist, set up a site in June 2001, but it was quickly shut down, whereupon Wu and two students started a new website, "Democracy and Freedom Forum," on a free bulletin-board space. By 2006 the forum had been closed forty-eight times, and each time Wu and his friends found a new space for it, where it could last anywhere from a few hours to several months. Wu is one of a growing number of similar activists known as "mice." During their cat-and-mouse games Wu and his colleagues have been harassed by officials but so far have managed to stay one step ahead of the authorities. Not all mice are as lucky, and Liu Di, a student Internet activist known as the Stainless Steel Mouse, was arrested in 2002 and jailed for two years. In 2008 China's Internet authorities issued new guidelines for the use of the web that remain largely unchanged in their level of censorship.

Many rights groups are demanding better protection of netizens, especially in the area of freedom of speech and the press. Chinese activists fear that a long, hard road may be ahead before individuals are able to truly express their views and achieve civil liberties online. Many prominent Chinese academics and journalists have spoken out against restrictive rules and believe the government should open up more channels in which civic groups and the mass media may engage freely in public discourse with the Party and state, especially on important issues such as the environment, corruption, and welfare. Moreover, they believe the government should invite representatives of civic groups to testify before congresses or publicize their opinions through the media. Officials should fully respect and protect freedom of the press and the rights of journalists, welcoming rather than fearing the public expression of contentious and diverse views.

## NOTES

This chapter appeared in slightly different form in Xiaobing Li, *Civil Liberties in China* (Santa Barbara, Calif.: ABC-CLIO, 2010).

1. PRC State Department, "Progress in China's Human Rights in 2009" (September 26, 2010), http://www.news.xinhuanet.com/english2010/china/2010-09/26/c_13529921_2.htm.

2. See "China's Progress in Human Rights: 2003," www.china.org.cn/english/2004/Mar/91638.htm.

3. "China's Mobile Phone Users Hit 1.03 Billion," Xinhua News Agency, May 23, 2012, http://capitalfm.co.ke/news/2012/05/Chinas-mobile-phone-users-hit-1-03-b/.

4. Some of the background material is from Xiaobing Li, *Civil Liberties in China* (Santa Barbara, Calif.: ABC-CLIO, 2010).

5. Standing Committee of the National People's Congress, *The Constitution of the People's Republic of China* (Beijing: People's Publishing House, 2004), 37.

6. "China to Reinforce Government Spokesperson System," www.china.org.cn/English/.

7. Information Office of the PRC State Council, comp., "Progress in China's Human Rights Cause in 2003," in Information Office of the PRC State Council, comp., *White Papers of the Chinese Government* (Beijing: Foreign Languages Press, 2005), 4:408.

8. Standing Committee of the NPC, *The Constitution of the People's Republic of China*, 165.

9. Phelim Kine, "A Gold Medal in Media Censorship," in *China's Great Leap: The Beijing Games and Olympian Human Rights Challenges,* ed. Minky Worden (New York: Seven Stories Press, 2008), 117–118.

10. *Zhongguo qingnianbao* (China Youth Daily), January 14, 2002.

11. See www.hrichina.org/fs/.

12. "Former Top Chinese Aide in Warning over Press Freedom," www.rfa.org/englilsh/china/.

13. Bureau of Democracy, Human Rights and Labor, U.S. State Department, "Country Reports on Human Rights Practices for 2011: China (includes Tibet, Hong Kong, and Macau)," www.state.gov/j/drl/rls/hrrpt/humanrightsreport/index.htm#wrapper.

14. U.S. Congressional Executive Commission on China (CECC), "Political Prisoner Database," in *2006 Annual Report,* www.cecc.gov/pages/annualRpt/annualRpt06/PoliticalPrisonerDatabase.php.

15. For more details of the Shi Tao case, see www.freedomhouse.org.

16. See china.hrw.org/press/review/.

17. "US 2008 Human Rights Report: China," *Journal of Turkish Weekly,* February 26, 2009, www.turkishweekly.net/news/65500/us-2008-human-rights-report-china.htmlThis.

18. Ibid.

19. U.S. Department of State, "2008 Human Rights Report: China (includes Tibet, Hong Kong, and Macau)," www.state.gov/g/drl/rls/hrrpt/2008/eap/119037.htm.

20. Bureau of Democracy, Human Rights and Democracy, U.S. State Department, "Country Reports for 2011: China."

21. PRC State Department, "Progress in China's Human Rights in 2009."

22. Before the summit, two overseas rights groups called on President Clinton's office to bring up the jailing of Shi Tao. His speech, however, failed to mention the case of the Chinese journalist. Clinton later told reporters that he "had a bad cold," and was unaware of Shi's case. He would have mentioned it, had he known. The details are available from "China's Internet Controls Raise Tough Questions," *Radio Free Asia,* September 14, 2005, www.rfa.org/english/china/china_internet-20050914.html.

23. Michael Bristow, "One Year On: Nobel Winner Liu Xiaobo Still in Jail," *BBC News,* October 6, 2011, www.bbc.co.uk/news/world-asia-pacific-15195263.

24. The statistics are available in "US 2008 Human Rights Report: China."

25. Patrick Moore, "China: Controlling the Internet," *Radio Free Europe,* September 16, 2005, www.rferl.org/content/article/1061453.html.

26. Xin Fei, "Chinese Freelance Writer Sentenced to Six Years Imprisonment," *Epoch Times,* March 23, 2007, www.theepochtimes.com/news/7-3-23/53205.htm; "Renowned Dissident Writer Li Hong Dies, Chinese Authorities Prevent Funeral," January 5, 2011, http://chinaview.wordpress.com/2011/01/05/renowned-dissident-writer-li-hong-dies-chinese-authorities-prevent-funeral/.

27. For more details, see Andrew Jacobs, "China Jails Journalist Who Reported on Corruption," *New York Times,* July 29, 2011, www.nytimes.com/2011/07/30/world/asia/30china.html; "2012: Journalists Imprisoned," n.d., http://en.rsf.org/press-freedom-barometer-journalists-imprisoned.html?annee=2012; "He Yanjie," n.d., www.pen.org/viewmedia.php/prmMID/2394/prmID/172.

# Acknowledgments

The completion of this volume on such an important subject from a multidisciplinary perspective required not only close cooperation among participating individuals, but strong support from two academic organizations: the Association of Chinese Professors of Social Sciences (ACPSS) in the United States and the United Societies of China Studies (USCS). Some of the chapters that appear in this volume are drawn from several ACPSS and USCS conferences, including the international conference titled "China: Challenges of Complex Realities in an Era of Globalization and Digitization" at Cornell University in 2008; the fifteenth ACPSS annual conference, "China Facing World Financial Crisis and Other Challenges," at Ohio State University in 2009; and the international conference "Engaging China: Sino-American Relations, Sustainable Development, and Beyond," at Harvard University in 2010. We are deeply grateful for the ACPSS and USCS organizational support of this publication.

We wish to thank our colleagues and collaborators both in China and in the United States. We are grateful to Yang Kuisong, Zhang Pengfei, and Chinese scholars at the Chinese Academy of Social Sciences (CASS), China Society for Strategy and Management (CSSM), Peking University, East China Normal University, and Southwest University of Political Science and Law for their help and advice on our research in China. Special thanks to Professor Yonglin Jiang of Bryn Mawr College in Pennsylvania, who proofread some of the chapters. Five anonymous readers for the University Press of Kentucky (UPK) offered valuable criticism and provided important suggestions. We also appreciate Professor Shiping Hua's scholarly leadership of the Asia in the New Millennium series at UPK.

Many people at the University of Central Oklahoma (UCO) have contributed to this book and deserve recognition. We would like to thank Provost William (Bill) J. Radke, Vice Provost Patricia A. LaGrow, and Dean of the College of Liberal Arts Gary Steward. They have been very supportive of the project over the past several years. The Research, Creative, and Scholarly Activities (RCSA) Grant Program sponsored by the Office of Research and Grants at UCO provided funding for our student assistants. The Editing Program sponsored by Professor Laura Dumin, director of

Technical Writing in the Department of English at UCO, edited the entire manuscript. Among the editors are Lauren Brandeberry, Matthew Lloyd Cherry, Sheri Gaches, NhuQuynh Luu Nguyen, Kathryn Rose Reichert, Beverly Ann Rorem, and Alexandra Renee Temblador. Several UCO graduate and undergraduate students contributed to the book, including Jia Chen, Michael Molina, and Kevin Yang. Sharon Kelting provided secretarial assistance.

Our appreciation also extends to the University of Minnesota in the Twin Cities and the University of Minnesota at Duluth for generous grants and awards. Jing Duan, GIS coordinator and associate planner at the West Central Wisconsin Regional Commission, helped with several useful maps and images. Fang Dongning, a student at Shanghai Nan Yang Model High School, helped collect important data and documents for chapter 1.

We wish to thank Stephen M. Wrinn, executive director of UPK, and Allison Webster, executive assistant to the director of UPK, for their excellent editorial guidance. Any remaining errors of facts, language usage, and interpretation are our own.

# Contributors

**LIQUN CAO** is professor of sociology and criminology at the University of Ontario Institute of Technology, Canada. He has held previous positions at Eastern Michigan University, Salem State College, and Miami University in the United States. His research interests include comparative sociology, criminological theory, gun ownership, confidence in the police, police integrity, public attitudes toward prostitution, and race and ethnicity in criminal justice. His research essays have appeared in many top national and international journals, including *Criminology, Journal of Criminal Justice, Justice Quarterly, Policing,* and *Social Forces.* He is the author of *Major Criminological Theories: Concepts and Measurement* (2004). His coauthored paper "Crime Volume and Law and Order Culture" (2007) won the 2008 Academy of Criminal Justice Sciences' Donal MacNamara Award. Cao is bilingual and has published two books in Chinese. He was a visiting scholar at Max Planck Institute for Foreign and International Criminal Law in Germany (2000) and a Fulbright Senior Specialist in Lithuania (2004). He served as the president of the Association of Chinese Criminology and Criminal Justice in the United States (2010–12). He is an honorary member of the Albanian Institute of Sociology.

**QIANG FANG** is an assistant professor of East Asian history at the University of Minnesota–Duluth. His book project, *Chinese Complaint Systems: Natural Resistance,* currently is forthcoming in 2013. He has published numerous articles in major journals, including *Modern Chinese Studies, Collected Papers of History Studies, Journal of Asian Studies, Journal of Asian History, Stanford Journal of International Law, Education about Asia,* and *Stanford Journal of East Asian Affairs.*

**JIELI LI** received his doctoral degree in sociology from the University of California at Riverside. He is currently an associate professor in the Department of Sociology and Anthropology at Ohio University. His research and teaching revolve around social change and development, historical and comparative sociology, sociological theory, and conflict resolution. His research articles have appeared in such major scholarly journals as *Sociological Theory*, *International Journal of the Sociology of Law*, *Sociological Perspectives*, *Sociological Focus*, *International Journal of Public Administration*, and *Michigan Sociological Review*. In addition, he currently serves as council chair of the United Society of China Studies (USCS), president of the Association of Chinese Professors of Social Sciences (ACPSS) in the United States, and council member at large for the North Central Sociological Association (NCSA).

**LIYING LI** is a professor and chair of the Department of Criminal Justice and Criminology at Metropolitan State College of Denver. She received her Ph.D. in Sociology from the University of Utah, Salt Lake City. She received her M.S. in demography from the University of California at Berkeley. Her research interests include criminological theories, sex offenders, serial killers, human trafficking, and comparative criminal justice and criminology. She is the author or coauthor of numerous articles and book chapters. Li has been a board member of the Denver Community Corrections Board for the last few years.

**XIAOBING LI** is professor and chair of the Department of History and Geography and director of the Western Pacific Institute at the University of Central Oklahoma. He is the executive editor of the *Journal of American Review of China Studies*. His recent books include *China at War: An Encyclopedia* (2012), *Civil Liberties in China* (2010), *Voices from the Vietnam War* (2010), *New Historiography in the Contemporary West* (coedited, 2008), *A History of the Modern Chinese Army* (2007), *Voices from the Korean War* (coauthored, 2004), *Taiwan in the Twenty-first Century* (coedited, 2003), *Chinese Immigrants in the United States* (coauthored, 2003), *Mao's Generals Remember Korea* (coedited, 2001), and *Social Transition in China* (coedited, 2000).

**XIAOXIAO LI** is a faculty member in China Studies at the University of Oklahoma. Before he began his college teaching career, he worked as general manager of Asian projects for Smith Cogeneration Management, Inc., from 2001 to 2008; deputy manager of Xinjiang Carpet and Arts and Crafts Import-Export Corporation (China) from 1996 to 1999; and general manager of Joint Venture Lejia Carpet Corporation Ltd. (China) from 1994 to

1997. Among his major business achievements was the construction of a 550-megawatt gas turbine Power plant in China between 2001 and 2007.

**BIN LIANG** is an associate professor of sociology at Oklahoma State University at Tulsa. He received both a Ph.D. and a J.D. in 2003. He is the author of two books, *The Changing Chinese Legal System, 1978–Present: Centralization of Power and Rationalization of the Legal System* (2008) and *China's Drug Practices and Policies: Regulating Controlled Substances in a Global Context* (coauthored, 2009). Another coedited book (in Chinese), titled *Jurisprudence,* is forthcoming. His current research interests include globalization and its effect on the Chinese legal system, crime and deviance in China, and comparative studies in criminology and criminal justice. His works have appeared in a number of peer-reviewed journals in the United States and other nations. He has recently served as a board member and an officer of the Association of Chinese Criminology and Criminal Justice in the United States (2010–2012).

**YUNQIU ZHANG** is an associate professor at North Carolina A&T State University. He obtained his Ph.D. in history from the University of Toronto. He once worked as an editor of *Historical Research* and *Social Sciences in China* in the Chinese Academy of Social Sciences. He has published on Chinese labor issues (trade unions and labor legislation), local state entrepreneurship, Chinese historiography, and urbanization.

**YUCHAO ZHU** received his Ph.D. in political science from Queen's University, Canada, in 1996. He taught at the Royal Military College of Canada, Queen's University, and the University of British Columbia (Kelowna campus) before he moved to the University of Regina in 1999, where he is currently professor of political science. His research interests include China's legal reform, ethnic issues, and Canada-China relations.

# Index

ASIA IN THE NEW MILLENNIUM

SERIES EDITOR: Shiping Hua, University of Louisville

Asia in the New Millennium is a series of books offering new interpretations of an important geopolitical region. The series examines the challenges and opportunities of Asia from the perspectives of politics, economics, and cultural-historical traditions, highlighting the impact of Asian developments on the world. Of particular interest are books on the history and prospect of the democratization process in Asia. The series also includes policy-oriented works that can be used as teaching materials at the undergraduate and graduate levels. Innovative manuscript proposals at any stage are welcome.

ADVISORY BOARD

William Callahan, University of Manchester, Southeast Asia, Thailand
Lowell Dittmer, University of California at Berkeley, East Asia and South Asia
Robert Hathaway, Woodrow Wilson International Center for Scholars, South Asia, India, and Pakistan
Mike Mochizuki, George Washington University, East Asia, Japan, and Korea
Peter Moody, University of Notre Dame, China and Japan
Brantly Womack, University of Virginia, China and Vietnam
Charles Ziegler, University of Louisville, Central Asia and Russia Far East

BOOKS IN THE SERIES

*The Future of China-Russia Relations*
Edited by James Bellacqua

*Contemporary Chinese Political Thought: Debates and Perspectives*
Edited by Fred Dallmayr and Zhao Tingyang

*The Mind of Empire: China's History and Modern Foreign Relations*
Christopher A. Ford

*State Violence in East Asia*
Edited by N. Ganesan and Sung Chull Kim

*Korean Democracy in Transition: A Rational Blueprint for Developing Societies*
HeeMin Kim

*Modern Chinese Legal Reform: New Perspectives*
Edited by Xiaobing Li and Qiang Fang

*Inside China's Grand Strategy: The Perspective from the People's Republic*
Ye Zicheng, edited and translated by Steven I. Levine and Guoli Liu

*Challenges to Chinese Foreign Policy: Diplomacy, Globalization, and the Next World
    Power*
Edited by Yufan Hao, C. X. George Wei, and Lowell Dittmer

www.ingramcontent.com/pod-product-compliance
Lightning Source LLC
Chambersburg PA
CBHW030257100426
42812CB00002B/472

*9 7 8 0 8 1 3 1 4 1 2 0 6 *